Christian Spirituality
for Seekers

Christian Spirituality for Seekers

Reflections on the Spiritual Exercises of Ignatius Loyola

ROGER HAIGHT, S.J.

ORBIS BOOKS

Maryknoll, New York 10545

Founded in 1970, Orbis Books endeavors to publish works that enlighten the mind, nourish the spirit, and challenge the conscience. The publishing arm of the Maryknoll Fathers and Brothers, Orbis seeks to explore the global dimensions of the Christian faith and mission, to invite dialogue with diverse cultures and religious traditions, and to serve the cause of reconciliation and peace. The books published reflect the views of their authors and do not represent the official position of the Maryknoll Society. To learn more about Maryknoll and Orbis Books, please visit our website at www.maryknollsociety.org.

Published by Orbis Books, Box 302, Maryknoll, NY 10545-0302.

Library of Congress Cataloging-in-Publication Data

Haight, Roger.
    A Christian spirituality for seekers : reflections on the Spiritual exercises of Ignatius Loyola / Roger Haight.
        p. cm.
    Includes index.
    ISBN 978-1-57075-987-1 (pbk.); ISBN 978-1-60833-222-9 (ebook)
    1. Ignatius, of Loyola, Saint, 1491-1556. Exercitia spiritualia. 2. Spirituality—Catholic Church. 3. Spiritual exercises. I. Title.
    BX2179.L8H25 2012
    248.3—dc23
                                                            2012008736

*To my colleagues and friends at
Union Theological Seminary*

Contents

PART I

Ignatius and the Spiritual Exercises

PART II

Reflections to Accompany
the Spiritual Exercises

Preface

Some years ago at Union Theological Seminary in New York City I was asked to participate in a resource team that attended to the spiritual formation of the community, particularly the students. As part of that program I offered the Spiritual Exercises of Ignatius Loyola (1491-1556) to thirty-five students over a period of eight weeks in the spring of 2007. These Exercises consist of a series of meditations and contemplations on the stories of Jesus found in the gospels. The program is highly versatile and can extend over a couple of days or for a month, and in some formats over a longer period of time. Distinct considerations and patterns of prayer structure the process and reflect its Ignatian character. I offered the same practicum in following years to smaller but not less enthusiastic groups. In the most recent iteration I spent five weeks introducing the Exercises and five weeks directing them. I began by adapting the Exercises for Union students.

Union is a distinctive place. It describes itself as a liberal Protestant interdenominational seminary that has a strong ethos of social engagement and is centrist in doctrinal and theological issues. Its pluralistic student body represents many traditions; it includes Unitarians, Roman Catholics, Christians affiliated with no particular denomination or church, and people who belong to other religions or no religion at all. In my experience, the Spiritual Exercises can be engaged and appreciated by people of varied spiritual backgrounds and identities.

I am certain that the Spiritual Exercises have been offered to people outside the Catholic Church innumerable times in every set of circumstances that can be reasonably imagined. Jerome Nadal himself at the time of Ignatius saw the possibility of presenting the Exercises to Lutherans.[1] If one considers the multiple missionary frontiers in which Jesuits and others have been engaged over the centuries, one can begin to calculate the many different ways Ignatius's Exercises have been pressed into service to communicate a Christian spirituality. The distinct intent of this project is not to draw people into the Christian church but simply to make Jesus available to spiritualities of various kinds.

---

1. Jerome Nadal, *Epistolae et Monumenta P. Hieronymi Nadal* (Monumenta Historica Societatis Jesu, 90A Rome: Monumenta Historica Soc. Jesu, 1964), Par. 228, p. 100.

In this work I interpret the Spiritual Exercises for a broad audience, not excluding Catholics but more pointedly addressing Protestants and also people outside Christianity, perhaps members of other religions, perhaps with no religious affiliation, who are looking for spiritual depth. Hence the title of this work, *Christian Spirituality for Seekers*. Chapter 4 provides a more formal but still broad definition of a seeker as well as a description of spirituality as it pertains to the Exercises. In general, the term "seekers" refers to people who may or may not have a comprehensive framework for understanding human existence but are looking for deeper meaning in their lives. Insofar as such lives are free, reflective, and consistent, they are spiritual.

In our religiously pluralistic nation, many religions rub shoulders with one another in cities, towns and rural areas. In our interreligious world, which assumes an increasingly secular climate, people feel the need to move beyond religious tolerance and reach for a much more welcoming attitude toward other religious faiths. Interreligious contact has become personal and familial. In such a situation it is much more natural, and precisely not extraordinary, to be able to offer the Spiritual Exercises to anyone who requests them on the basis of the purely spiritual benefit of their content.

Interpreting the Spiritual Exercises for people of another religious culture or no religious culture at all resembles entering into an interreligious dialogue or a broader conversation between diverse parties. If one wants to communicate with others, one has to speak a language the others understand. But changing a language or idiom always entails a shift in the meaning of the subject matter. And we have little control over how our words are interpreted. In the end, no "pure" communication is ever possible because reception always colors meaning. Communication relies on symbols, and meaning shifts subtly with the differences in appropriating these symbols.

Such reflections employ relatively obvious principles that are presupposed by those engaged in the many forms of dialogue or intercultural communication. Accommodating the listener entails adjusting basic principles, employing different strategies, and testing new language geared at faithful communication. Everyone who has administered the Exercises understands this. Whatever one's theology might be, if others are not aware of it, one should not proceed as if it were an established presupposition and expect a successful communication of ideas. One has to begin from spiritual experiences that are either shared or available to general recognition. When these ideas are applied to communicating the Spiritual Exercises, they shift emphases and connotations. First principles and foundations vanish and become spiritual questions that may open up new possibilities for the spiritual seeker. Standard tropes may provoke seminal questions. For example, if Christian teaching assumes a latent sense of sin and guilt, how should a director of the Exercises address a person who does not experience guilt? Should a minister incite a sense of guilt in another so that he or she can then point to the offer of forgiveness to relieve it? Christians by definition understand Jesus Christ in a way that distinguishes him from all others. But how should Jesus of Nazareth be presented to the seeker who approaches him for the first time? These questions penetrate to the core of Christian faith. But if the goal of giving the Spiritual Exercises is not to create Christian faith where it does not already exist, should that faith and a particular theology get in the way of a more open presentation of the Spiritual Exercises?

These questions show how deeply various connotations attached to insider–outsider language influence the way the Exercises are presented and received. Accommodating an audience of seekers, those who precisely lack many of the presuppositions on which the Spiritual Exercises are built, forces the person presenting them to shift the aspect of any given consideration to a more accessible point of view. One has to appeal to that dimension of Christian faith language that is analogous to experiences present within other religions and human existence generally. The presenter must stress possibilities and options that are imaginable from multiple perspectives, and set out spiritual standards that have roots in our common human experience.

All of these things happened in the preparation and reception of the Spiritual Exercises at Union. No common appropriation occurred. There was no typical response. All absorbed the story of Jesus in ways that merged with the trajectories of their own lives up to that point. This, of course, is what always happens, but at the same time these distinctive audiences generated some surprising results. Each seeker imposes a distinctive point of view on the unfolding of the Exercises, thereby expanding the scope of the practice. The open character of the spiritual language leaves behind the official religious perspectives of the churches and forces attention to the data of human subjectivity that are experienced in an almost sensible way. The appeal to the sphere of common human experience has to be authentic. When it is, it gives the consideration of the spirituality involved a striking relevance.

Another distinctive result of a religiously neutral but spiritually charged perspective lies in the way it opens up new dimensions of the story of Jesus. The focus of the imagination becomes fixed on Jesus' humanity. The imagination of the writers in constructing the vignettes that make up the story of Jesus licenses the imagination of seekers considering them to reconstruct the details of events and to enter into them as realistically as possible. Concrete events and historical possibilities take on a new importance for the retrieval of Jesus into meaningfulness for life today. The spirituality taught by Jesus takes on a new plausibility precisely by the historical realism that a probing and then a visionary imagination can supply.

These first commitments to authentic common experience and imaginative immersion into gospel vignettes enable another larger reorientation. Entering into the concrete spirituality of Jesus of Nazareth, who is the foundation of Christianity, gives a person a fresh entrée to the Christian metanarrative of salvation history, independent of doctrinal confinement. In the narrative underlying the New Testament, which is especially clear in the two-volume work of Luke, the story of Jesus' ministry is carried forward by the disciples. Their Easter experience that Jesus was raised from death generated the Jesus movement that eventually became a church and initiated the interpretation of Jesus as the Christ. The Spiritual Exercises in their way re-present that history and hold out the possibility that each seeker may relate to that historical movement from a distinct position. The focus on the story of Jesus allows the approaching seeker to imagine the possibilities that Jesus opened to those who encountered him prior to the development of Christian theological interpretation.

Scarcely distinct from these results, and perhaps as a summary of them, interpreting the Spiritual Exercises for seekers mediates a new perspective on Christianity as a religion. Organized religion is a social reality: it consists of a community that is institutionalized with a leadership structure, and it assembles around doctrines and rituals of worship. To learn about Christianity one studies its doctrines and practices.

The Spiritual Exercises, when they are engaged by seekers, provide a very different view of the Christian churches. The historical basis of Christianity reappears as the spirituality of Jesus, what he said and did in his ministry, and the effects this had on his followers. The substance of Christianity then lies in the many appropriations of emulating Jesus, the praxis it entails, the social loyalties it recommends, and the commitments it generates. Christianity before anything else consists of a corporate spirituality from which everything else is derivative. This begs the question of the fuller meaning of spirituality, but that is the subject matter of the whole book.

I have had a lot of help in this project and I want to acknowledge it. First and foremost I am grateful to Union Theological Seminary, its administration and staff, and its faculty and students, all of whom have had a role to play in this project. I would never have taken up this research and practice without Union's invitation to do so. Like

Calvin's theology in Geneva, this spirituality would not have come out the way it has in any other place. I'm grateful to the groups of students who did the Exercises as a spiritual practicum and hope that they received their rewards. I want to thank two Union students, Jenn Lindsay and Brianne Jacobs, who each gave me a good part of a summer in research on the secondary literature surrounding the Spiritual Exercises. Still others have read a first draft of the book or other segments of it and have given me feedback that was extremely important. Jenn Lindsay did some copyediting for me. Randy Sachs, S.J., of Boston College's School of Theology and Ministry, read the first draft of the book and offered several seminal suggestions. Jeannine Hill Fletcher of Fordham University's Theology Department entered into an extensive dialogue with the text and proffered invaluable advice. Brian O. McDermott, S.J., who teaches theology at Loyola University in Baltimore and is expert in the Exercises, also read the work. Otto Hentz, S.J., of Georgetown University's Theology Department, meticulously studied the manuscript and offered pointed amendments to the text. I also want to thank Rev. Fran Thiessen, Pastor of The Presbyterian Church in Norwood, New Jersey, who worked with me in the ministration of the Exercises at Union by providing spiritual direction. And, finally, I am deeply indebted to Patrick Amer, of Hilton Head, South Carolina, who gave the final draft of this work close and keen attention and gave me sound, insightful recommendations that greatly clarified the text. I am most grateful to them all.

Introduction

The title of this work, *Christian Spirituality for Seekers*, is straightforward. But each operative term points to such a variety of examples, all of which bear many interpretations and valuations, that the exactness of the phrase communicates little of the actual content. The best way to introduce this book, then, will be to describe its audience and subject matter. Who are the envisioned seekers? What does the term "spirituality" mean? What brand of Christianity will be represented? A crisp discussion of each of these questions will give the lay of the land. Each topic suffuses the whole work and will receive more focused attention along the way.

A key term in the title is "seekers," the primary but not the exclusive audience of this work. Seekers are those who are looking for something, and this implies that they do not yet possess what they are searching for. The search is primarily interior; the quest envisages personally fulfilling and motivating experiences that envelop human existence with meaning and value.

Part of the fruitfulness of the term "seeker" lies in its deliberate vagueness, and this work exploits its ambiguities. On the one hand, self-styled seekers by definition confess to a desire for something they lack. They want to organize their self-understanding and abilities in ways that make sense of their actual commitments and actions. Seekers are frequently located outside the sphere of organized religion. Transcendental religious thinkers contend that seekers actually possess some rudimentary knowledge of such a "space" or they would not be seekers at all. At an intuitive level, seekers know what they are looking for, and they will recognize it when it is found. But this does not necessarily entail a religious conversion or lead to a commitment within a specific framework of meaning.

On the other hand, seekers today also exist within religions that profess to supply the answers to their ultimate questions. The explosion of knowledge in the second half of the twentieth century and the globalization that has made the whole world our neighbors have set up new conditions for the meaningfulness of basic Christian doctrines. But Christian language has neither sufficiently accommodated to the new situation nor responded to the questions it raises. More and more, the responses to ultimate questions of meaning no longer ring true, or the language describing the vision no longer communicates it.

Writing from the perspective of the Western Christian churches in a period of decline, one cannot fault the message for the fact that many are abandoning it; one has to suspect the quality of the messengers. This work attempts to listen more carefully to the seekers in order to rediscover the spiritual meaning of the Christian message. The method involved here does not consist of a correlation of concepts from the past to the conditions of understanding in the present time. It does not attempt to employ new language to preserve old meaning. It rather attends to the questions of seekers and tries to find where and how the contents of a religious tradition respond to the demands of contemporary spirituality.

The subject matter of this book and what it offers seekers is called "spirituality." The term has no single consistent usage. If one assigned it a comprehensive and inclusive definition, it would be so broad that it communicated little. So many people use the term to refer to specific areas of their lives, from the occult to psychological self-help to mystical experience, that one cannot suppose a common sphere of meaning. Within Christianity, spirituality tends to be related to the religious sphere. Up to this time, Catholics would be more comfortable with the term than Protestants. The churches of the Reformation use terms like the Christian life or piety and worship for what Roman Catholics and Orthodox refer to as spirituality. For example, Calvin has a short treatise on the Christian life in his *Institutes* that corresponds exactly with what a traditional Catholic would understand as spirituality.[1]

The idea of spirituality becomes more complicated when it reaches beyond the sphere of organized religion and the church. Sociologists associate the beginnings of a distinction between the spiritual and the religious in America with the 1960s when "boomers" began to contrast spirituality and the conventional religion of churchgoers, as in the phrase "spiritual but not religious."[2] This distinction deserves attention. Religion or the religious sphere designates behavior in a public social arena. Religion refers to the organization of spirituality, the life of the churches, the actual assemblies of belief and worship. Spirituality refers to the interior life of a person, with its overtones of experience, personal meaningfulness, and motivation. Optimally, those who are religious find spiritual depth in their religious practice, and people display their spirituality publicly in action. But the point is that the spiritual can no longer be exclusively tied to the religious; people can experience a deep spirituality independently of religious belonging.

---

1. John Calvin, *Calvin: Institutes of the Christian Religion*, ed. John T. McNeill (Philadelphia: Westminster, 1960), Book III, Chapters 6-10.

2. Robert D. Putnam and David E. Campbell, *American Grace: How Religion Divides and Unites Us* (New York: Simon & Schuster, 2010), 97.

This does not mean that spiritual experience has become privatized and individualistic; a searching spirituality may in fact carry deep social commitment, just as social religious belonging can generate an individualistic spirituality. In this book, the term "spirituality" refers to the relation of a person or group toward what they consider absolute, and the term "religious" usually refers to the public social manifestations of those values.

The interplay between the spheres of religion and spirituality communicates aspects of the goal of this book. The contemporary distinction between the two highlights a problem that needs to be addressed by those who stand on the side of religion in a growing divide between religious people and those who are "spiritual but not religious." If it is true that religion contains resources for the spiritual life that are not being perceived by a younger generation and a growing body of people beyond it, then it is incumbent upon those who are religious to communicate better their spiritual riches. One way to reach genuine seekers of spiritual meaning is to enter their perspective and respond to their questions with answers that are not constrained by formal religion.

This book's concept of spirituality refers to the sphere of human existence in which persons are reflectively conscious of themselves. It relates to primal urges such as a desire for life and to fundamental questions about the meaning of being. On this elemental level it makes sense to say that everyone has some kind of spirituality. Spirituality refers to the fundamental organization of people's lives, to the center of gravity that supplies coherence to the sum total of their behaviors. All people have a spirituality insofar as their lives bear a certain consistency. This way of viewing human lives shows how spirituality can be operative whether or not a given individual recognizes it in these terms. This treatment of the term gives spirituality a substantial place in human life, retrieves it from the occult and the esoteric, and provides a common reference point for many different conceptions and languages about "the spiritual." In short, this book accepts the contemporary usage of the word "spirituality," a meaning that is neither Protestant nor Catholic nor Orthodox but secular, and invites Christianity to address it.

This book presupposes two qualities of the concept of spirituality: its scope and its narrative structure. Because spirituality defines a person's way of being, considering it easily leads to fundamental questions of human purpose. Spirituality has an implicit transcendent dimension because it engages ultimate questions. Reflecting on the pattern of one's own ordinary activities and values entails a broad consideration of the whole of one's life, a focus that transcends the minutiae of daily experience. Although spirituality may or may not have an explicitly religious dimension, it introduces people into realms of transcendence and ultimacy.

The other aspect of spirituality that plays a major role in this book is its narrative quality. Because spirituality has been defined as the logic or pattern that organizes a human life, its character is explicitly narrative. In other words, a person's spirituality both reflects and describes the story of his or her life. The way people live their lives constitutes their spiritualities. In turn, spirituality defines people's lives because people construct their selves in the sum total of their actions by the way they pattern their behavior. It is commonplace today to introduce persons through their story because the story of each person, depending on how deeply it is told, can encapsulate a person's identity. Spirituality thus refers less to a permanent state of being than to a quality of being that is enacted, in motion, and influenced by constant interchange with the world.

As the title indicates, the spirituality discussed in this book is Christian. Christian spirituality represents a wide swath of human experience and knowledge. The *Dictionnaire de Spiritualité*, in seventeen volumes published between 1932 and 1995 by the French Jesuits, shows the breadth and diversity of Christian spirituality.[3] The sheer multiplicity and significant differences in the many styles of Christian spirituality require further specification of the kind of spirituality represented in this book.

The Christian spirituality represented here falls under the heading of "following Christ." This genre of Christian spirituality, *imitatio Christi*, could be considered fundamental to Christianity: Christianity continues the movement of those who initially followed Jesus. Such a following of Jesus Christ, however, has taken many significantly different forms over the centuries. In the fifteenth century, Thomas à Kempis, a monk, adopted the phrase as the title of his famous book, *The Imitation of Christ*. Although his ascetic spirituality tended to define *imitatio Christi* as a retreat from the world, in fact the concept of imitation also describes the logic of many Christian spiritualities of social activism, because the very nature of Christian commitment bears reference to the ministry of Jesus of Nazareth. This broad genre of Christian spirituality corresponds neatly with the narrative character of spirituality.

The Christian spirituality represented in this book is characteristically Ignatian, named after the spiritual master Ignatius of Loyola.

---

3. *Dictionnaire de Spiritualité: Ascétique et Mystique, Doctrine et Histoire*, ed. Marcel Viller et al. (Paris: G. Beauchesne et ses fils, 1932-1995).

Chapter 1 introduces Ignatius, whose ideas direct the content of this book. During his thirties, after an experience of conversion from conventional Christianity and royal service to a life dedicated to following Jesus, Ignatius formulated his itinerary in a manual, *The Spiritual Exercises*, that enabled him to share his experiences with others.[4] Among other sources, Ignatius had read à Kempis's *Imitatio Christi*, but he translated its piety into an activist and socially engaged spirituality and a decidedly more militant following of Jesus. In the Exercises he guided people who sought spiritual direction imaginatively to enter into the stories of Jesus in the New Testament as ways of identifying with him and drawing inspiration for their own lives. The Christian narrative spirituality offered here appropriates the Spiritual Exercises of Ignatius. It shares their engaged activism as distinct from a quiet and withdrawing spirituality.

This active and engaged Ignatian spirituality is also narrative. This is illustrated through a distinction between two characteristics of the Christian story. These can be named in various ways: the small story and the big story, the historical narrative and the metanarrative, the story of Jesus and the supranatural Christian story behind the story. The first has four versions in the collected vignettes about Jesus' ministry in the gospels; the second grew out of the faith commitment to Jesus and developed over centuries into a sacred story of the universe. These narrative levels have been intertwined for centuries. They grew together from the beginning; and because they each bestow meaning upon the other, they cannot really be separated. But they can be distinguished, and the distinction helps to clarify how a person can relate to them and how they have bearing on Christian life. For example, it is difficult to interpret Jesus of Nazareth apart from the Christian story because the Christian story of faith already influences the gospel narratives; and yet, Jesus of Nazareth lived prior to the interpretations of him within a grand metanarrative or a sacred story of the universe. Whether we can know more or less about Jesus prior to Christian faith's interpretation of him, the facticity of his ministry enhances his relevance. Academics have argued for centuries about how, how much, and with what kind of historical accuracy we can know about Jesus. But after the arguments have been completed, all agree that the real person, Jesus of Nazareth, represents the source and the basis of the Christian story.

---

4. Ignatius of Loyola, *The Spiritual Exercises*, in *Ignatius of Loyola: The Spiritual Exercises and Selected Works*, ed. George E. Ganss (Mahwah, NJ: Paulist Press, 1991). This edition and translation contains an authoritative introduction and set of notes. When the book of the Exercises is being referred to, the name will be italicized. When the content of the text is being referred to, the name Spiritual Exercises will not be italicized and will frequently be simply referred to as the Exercises.

The Christian spirituality proffered in this book appeals primarily to Jesus of Nazareth and secondarily to the Christian religion. The relationship between the stories about Jesus and the larger sacred story drawn from them is neither absolute nor exclusive, and the Spiritual Exercises of Ignatius Loyola capitalize on the fact that the vignettes of Jesus' ministry are broadly accessible. One can read in the Exercises the whole Christian story from creation through sin and redemption to the church and the end of time; but the narrower focus of the Exercises is on the gospel stories of the ministry of Jesus. In these exercises the seeker is asked to relate to Jesus as leader and teacher. This inward focus cultivated by the Spiritual Exercises allows entry for seekers who are not Christian. The possibility of an experience of Christian spirituality for even non-Christian seekers lies precisely in the humanity of Jesus and his ability to be approached and understood by any other human being.

That seekers come to the Exercises from different cultures, Christian and others, and bring a variety of approaches to the Christian story may seem to complicate what should be simple. After all, a whole body of Christians seems satisfied with just asking, "What would Jesus do?" and deriving answers from the pages of the gospels. But this book envisions a set of readers who will not be satisfied with that strategy. It tries to be accountable to the spiritual conditions and backgrounds of readers who are not steeped in Christian doctrine, who are schooled in either secular culture or the academy. More specifically, this book speaks to the demands of three different groups of readers: people who are interested in the spirituality of Ignatius Loyola; people who are not Christian but are looking for sources that will address, at a fundamental level and with a critical edge, a source of enlightenment on the meaning of human life; and people whose Christian faith has been eroded by post-modern culture. Each of these groups deserves comment.

Since the sixteenth century, the Spiritual Exercises of Ignatius Loyola have emerged as a classical locus for Christian spirituality in the West. The book is at the source of a school of spirituality that has appealed to Christians in all sorts of different contexts. Ignatian spirituality is enhanced by historical research into Ignatius's authorship, the meaning of Ignatius's primary texts and their supporting literature, the history of their influence in different historical contexts, and how the Exercises can be adapted for effective presentation across different cultures and among various constituencies. The Spiritual Exercises come in many translations and have received extensive attention from scholarly and popular writers. Thus, an interpretation of the Exercises for seekers must respect the experience and questions of the audience as well as the historic meaning of the texts being interpreted.

The first part of this work draws the reader into the world of these Spiritual Exercises so that their logic, which interprets the logic of Christian spirituality itself, can function as the overt point of entry into the story of Jesus.

Using the Spiritual Exercises of Ignatius to interpret the story of Jesus for seekers serves to interpret the Exercises themselves. This book, therefore, also envisions among its readers both scholars and ministers who know and use the Spiritual Exercises. Employing the Exercises to introduce Jesus of Nazareth to seekers shows the versatility and range of Ignatius's program. One of his fundamental principles was that the Exercises could and should always be adapted, in terms of language and style, to the situation of the people who engage them. Nothing should prevent the outreach of the ministry of Jesus to all people. But the Exercises are not meant to convert seekers; they are presented here as nothing other than the story of Jesus for those who would engage it. Like Jesus, the Exercises can be appreciated at some level by any person who is genuinely seeking deeper spiritual meaning in life. It may be hoped that an unconventional audience will throw new light on the potentialities of this classic source of spirituality.

A wholly different set of readers are seekers who are not Christians but know that the Christian tradition has provided meaning for countless people over the past two millennia. These may be Westerners who have had no exposure to the churches, or they may be members of other religious traditions seeking to expand their spiritual experience. For these seekers Jesus is a spiritual teacher and guide, and the source of a massive spiritual tradition; therefore he must possess some spiritual authority. The Christian Bible contains the New Testament, whose gospels present the collected stories about Jesus: his teachings, his ministry, and the stories he told about the rule of God and how it impacts human life. Anyone can pick up the Bible and read the stories of Jesus. But the Spiritual Exercises direct seekers to be newly receptive to these stories; they provide methods of approaching the texts and appropriating their meaning in a most intimate and personal way. The Spiritual Exercises were not written for people standing outside the circle of Christian faith; such a practice would have been uncommon in Ignatius's time. But that very reflection highlights the new and different world of the twenty-first century. Today, Hindus, Buddhists, and Muslims living as neighbors in a large urban setting and approaching Jesus is as plausible as a Christian entering a Buddhist temple or a Hindu ashram.

But the thoroughly secular person in a Western urban culture who has never been exposed to religious sensibilities has a very different way of relating to Christian spirituality than do members of other religious traditions. The religiously alienated may feel indifference or even hostility to formal religious questions, even though it is hard to escape questions of human destiny and the urge to respond to them, at least implicitly. Nevertheless, at any given time a desire for integral meaning may stimulate people to investigate or deepen their spirituality, understood as responsibility for one's life in the light of ultimacy. It is not easy to convey the ultimacy represented either by Jesus or Christianity in nontheistic language. One has to presuppose that a seeker who turns in this direction is prepared to hear God language. But I have made an effort in this book not to presuppose that everyone knows what the word "God" means. It approaches God language through various human experiences that potentially uncover areas in which transcendent meaning arises. Reverence for the ineffability of God and for a pregnant silence that approaches agnosticism or unknowing remains an integral part of the Christian spiritual tradition.

The last large group of readers addressed by this book consists in the growing number of Christians who are dropping out of their churches and perhaps feeling alienated from the Christian message itself. The number of people who fell into this category in Europe across the span of two or three centuries made it plausible some time ago to predict the demise of Christianity. This movement continues, and it has some analogous resonances in North America even though sociologists do not expect that North America will follow the European withdrawal from religion.[5] One way of addressing religious decline is to be rigorously accountable to contemporary conditions when undertaking theological reinterpretation of Christian doctrine. But this is a work of spirituality and not theology. Spirituality that engages social and cultural data can address the problem of meaning from a different perspective than that of doctrine and theology. Focusing on the Jesus story rather than the larger doctrinal story leads to a genuine, personalized spiritual response, one that both precedes and undergirds the interpretive metaphysical story. Much of Jesus' ministry intentionally challenged the theological suppositions of his audience and with abrupt images confronted the imaginations of his hearers with new possibilities. The Exercises raise these stories of Jesus up against the vacuum left by theological language that no longer seems credible and the embarrassing public postures of the churches. In this way they can revitalize spirituality and provide a springboard for renewal.

The book is divided into two parts. Part I discusses the Spiritual Exercises of Ignatius Loyola. Part II presents forty-two reflections on

---

5. Putnam and Campbell, *American Grace*, 76.

topics that together provide the subject matter for the seeker undertaking these Exercises.

It is not possible to present Christian spirituality as if it were an integrated whole, and it would not be responsible to create a perspective on it entirely out of one's own imagination. Hence the turn to the Spiritual Exercises. Representing Christian spirituality through the lens of Ignatius Loyola's Exercises combines the classic and the modern within a living tradition. This task requires introduction, explanation, and a straightforward account of how it is being interpreted to meet a distinctive current situation. These are found in the first part of this book.

Part I unfolds in four chapters. The first introduces Ignatius Loyola and recounts his composition of the Spiritual Exercises, showing how they flowed out of his experiences and how intimately connected they are to his biography. This background not only clarifies the Exercises but releases readers from the need to appropriate them literally. The second chapter describes the Spiritual Exercises and the sources and language that Ignatius employed to compose them in their first rudimentary form. The third chapter is an analytical examination of the logic of the Exercises. It considers ways of grasping conceptually what they intend and how they work. It looks for an understanding of what happens existentially for people as they undergo the prayerful processes of meditation and contemplation. Chapter 4 gives a theoretical account of interpreting the Exercises or adapting them to an audience of seekers. For many the Spiritual Exercises enjoy the status of a "sacred text," a designation that requires an account of the method of interpretation. This first part then closes with some practical considerations of prayer and spirituality as they are described by the Exercises and then applied in the reflections that make up Part II.

Part II consists of a set of reflections on subjects that are either directly drawn from the Spiritual Exercises or suggested by them. They are arranged in four sets; Ignatius called them "Weeks," because doing the Exercises in their full form was meant to take about a month. The structure of the Four Weeks can be imagined according to a pattern of introductory material (Week One) that is followed by three chronological installments of the ministry of Jesus: his public ministry of doing good and preaching the rule of God (Week Two), his being seized, arrested, tortured, and brutally executed (Week Three), and finally the stories of his appearances after his death indicating his resurrection (Week Four). It is crucial to keep in mind the fact that the essence of Ignatius's Spiritual Exercises consists of meditations on the gospel stories of Jesus; this spirituality is so deeply rooted in the gospels that it has to be called evangelical.[6] Its particular Ignatian accent, imparted by key meditations interspersed along the way, steer the line of interpretation and the energy of the seeker toward an active, engaged spiritual life.

A glance at the Table of Contents of Part II will show that a number of topics have been added at the beginning and the end of Ignatius's Exercises. During the First Week, where Ignatius proposed meditations on the purpose of human existence, sin, and forgiveness, this book offers a fuller range of topics concerning human existence in order to pull the language out of the late Middle Ages and into a twenty-first-century conceptual framework. During the Fourth Week, while Ignatius restricted his attention to the gospel stories of Jesus' post-resurrection appearances, this book includes stories of the incipient Jesus movement from the Acts of the Apostles. This device implicitly extends Jesus' story to the present time by explicitly linking it to the story of his followers today.

Because this book has been designed and written to address the different constituencies described earlier, it may be helpful to suggest some different approaches to reading it. People who have religious identities other than Christian or no religion at all may be curious about the resources of Christian spirituality. Alienated Christians, the hundreds of thousands who yearly are drifting away from the mainline Protestant churches and the European-American Catholic Church, may have serious questions left unsatisfied by available answers. And specialists in the Spiritual Exercises may wonder how they can be accommodated to an audience of seekers.[7]

Relative to all of these groups, it should be noted that the reflections of Part II are not meant to be presented in this form to retreatants. These literary reflections are fairly dense in character. They grew out of imaginative immersion in the subject matter represented by the chosen texts and are not meant to substitute for that immersion. They have an analytical character that does not automatically lead the reader back to imaginative engagement with actual history or to prayer. They are deliberately called reflections. Yet they could easily be adopted as a program of spiritual reading for those engaged with the Exercises that would run in parallel with contemplation and prayer.

---

6. This use of the term "evangelical" reflects its root sense of being drawn from the gospels and not the common meaning it has in North American Christianity, which refers to a fear of a critical historical reading of the Bible and is associated with Fundamentalism and Pentecostalism.

7. For those giving the Spiritual Exercises, these reflections fall within the early tradition of the "directories," which contained supplementary material that expanded and commented on the Exercises in order to assist in their presentation.

These three examples do not exhaust the possibilities but suggest that this book can be approached in many different ways. They highlight how different points of view on Christian spirituality entail different ways of engaging the text.

For example, this book may be read as an introduction to Christian spirituality. To be sure, the text represents a certain kind of Christian spirituality and does not devalue myriad other traditions. It engages Christian spirituality deeply, methodically, with actual content, presented in a way that attends to contemporary social and cultural factors. This work can accompany and comment upon the text of Ignatius's manual. It appeals mainly to people with a university education, where the academy's hostility to religion sometimes extends to spirituality. The issues this work addresses may not be felt by everyone. On one side, many interested in spirituality do not participate in the intellectual culture of our time; on the other, too little has been written that directly appeals to people who do.

This book may be read as an introduction to Christianity, not as it is usually presented as a set of beliefs, but as a way of life. Here the story of Jesus, the first-century Jewish prophet, healer, and teacher, takes center stage, and the reader is invited to enter into his audience before the beliefs about him were developed and the larger Christian story encompassed him. This larger framework cannot be fully set aside, but this approach allows one to see the distinction between imagining Jesus as he was and how later interpretation co-opted his ministry. It allows a person to be caught up in Jesus' vision as he presented it before his followers formalized it into Christianity.[8]

This book can be read as a text that explicitly undertakes an extended and open-ended dialogue with the reader. In place of didactic assertions, the reflections emerge out of the imagination's engagement with a subject matter or a scene from the stories of Jesus. As Part I will show, Ignatius allowed space for the human imagination to roam and, from God's side, for the Spirit to direct it. Many of the questions asked by seekers do not have neat answers, and so the dialogue may continue beyond the text.

This book can be read as an interpretation of the Spiritual Exercises of Ignatius Loyola. As such it takes its place among many others. But the seekers who are envisioned here do not take anything for granted and ask questions that bring a freshness to the subject matter and newly showcase the versatility of this classic work of spirituality.

---

8. The idea is captured by the title of the popular book of Albert Nolan: *Jesus before Christianity* (Maryknoll, NY: Orbis Books, 1978).

PART I

Ignatius and the Spiritual Exercises

At the age of thirty Ignatius of Loyola underwent a conversion experience that completely changed his life. His record of this deep spiritual experience is preserved, not in the form of a journal, but in a form that he hoped might benefit others. These reflections turned into what is now a book or a manual called *The Spiritual Exercises of Ignatius Loyola*. A correlation between the content of the Exercises and Ignatius's life, including his character and identity, can be found on the surface and at various levels beneath it. Yet as he captured his reflections with the intention of sharing them with others, Ignatius described his narrative experience objectively and created a distance between himself and the text, so that the journey he traversed might be available to others in different times and circumstances.

Part I of this presentation of Ignatius's Spiritual Exercises introduces the text. The first chapter tells the story of Ignatius's conversion experience because it has a direct bearing on the content of the Exercises and the spirituality enshrined in it. The second chapter tries to describe what is contained in the book, *The Spiritual Exercises*. It would be most helpful if one had a copy of it in hand, but that is not strictly necessary. The third chapter attempts to characterize the overall logic and structure of the Exercises. This cannot really be done definitively since the text can be viewed from many different perspectives. But this chapter discloses the suppositions of this book. The fourth chapter takes a step in the same direction by explaining the methodological premises of this effort at interpretation. It discusses the conception of spirituality behind this proposal and how it relates to Jesus. Finally, it responds to the difficult question of how the Exercises may be given to seekers who may not be Christian and how they can benefit from undertaking them.

CHAPTER ONE

Ignatius and the Spiritual Exercises

A good path into the Spiritual Exercises of Ignatius Loyola is to describe the way they reflect the life of their author. This biographical accent does not imply that their meaning and relevance are limited to being a product of Ignatius's experience; rather, an account of how these Exercises grew out of his experience dramatizes the possibilities to which they give rise. The history of their influence, which is long and wondrously adaptable, making them a spiritual classic, discredits such a reduction. To put it simply, after his conversion Ignatius sought to record and offer to others the fruits of his extended experience, and he gradually composed a set of practices gravitating around the gospel stories of Jesus that could be shared. This automatically deprivatized them. But at the same time, the text of the Exercises cannot be completely understood if it is sundered from Ignatius's story.

This first chapter, then, has clear goals. It responds to the first elementary question of where these Spiritual Exercises come from. More specifically it shows the close connection, indeed the parallelism, between these Exercises and the narrative of their author. This symbiotic relationship means as well that several aspects of the personality of Ignatius Loyola were injected into his Spiritual Exercises that have little to do with eternal truths but everything to do with dimensions of his personality and character. The narrative that inspired these Exercises, and the historical and biographical dimensions of the text, reveal the universal relevance of the Exercises to our twenty-first century stories.

Ignatius Prior to His Conversion

Ignatius Loyola was born around the year 1491 as Iñigo, in the family home of Loyola in Azpeitia in the Basque region of the north of Spain and the province of Guipúzcoa. He was the last, or at least the last boy, of thirteen children, eight boys and five girls.[1] The family

---

1. Candido de Dalmases, *Ignatius of Loyola, Founder of the Jesuits: His Life and Work* (St. Louis: Institute of Jesuit Sources, 1985), 12-13. This work will be cited in the text

was well off. Documents of the sixteenth century show that "the lord of Loyola was the possessor of a considerable patrimony," which included the church of Azpeitia and its possessions (CD, 21). "In the political field, the Loyolas were always loyal servants of the crown of Castile," and the crown showed "recognition to the lords of Loyola for their services and loyalty" (CD, 17-18). Thus Ignatius grew up in a tradition of service to royal authority. He was "conscious and proud of belonging to an important family of Guipúzcoa that had distinguished itself in the service of the kings of Castile" (CD, 27). Oriented toward achievement, he identified with a family accustomed "to signalize themselves" in royal service. Ignatius used the phrase "to distinguish oneself" in both secular and religious contexts; it is an important phrase in the Exercises.

Dalmases believes that Ignatius spoke Basque as a youth at home. A tutor provided his early education in reading, writing, and the catechism. Juan de Polanco, an associate of Ignatius's in his later life, describes his education: "Iñigo's education was more in keeping with the spirit of the world than of God; for from his early years, without entering into other training in letters beyond that of reading and writing, he began to follow the court as a page" (cited by CD, 32).

Ignatius's life at court evolved out of his family's loyalty to the crown. A bond of friendship united the family of Ignatius with Juan Velázquez de Cuéllar, the Royal Treasurer of Castile residing in Arévalo. He extended to the Loyolas the opportunity for one of the sons to continue his training in his household. Sometime around the death of Ignatius's father in 1507 when Ignatius was sixteen, or perhaps earlier, Ignatius took up residence at Arévalo. "His would be the life of a courtier in the service of high officials, who would set him on a career of public administration, political intricacies, and eventually the profession of arms" (CD, 29). Ignatius remained in the service of Juan Velázquez for at least ten years until the latter's death in 1517.

Ignatius adopted the lifestyle of a courtier. Pedro Ribadeneira, another of Ignatius's associates in his later years and his first biographer, describes Ignatius at Arévalo as "a lively and trim young man,

---

as CD and the page number. Most of the data of this short account is drawn from Ignatius's autobiography: Ignatius Loyola, *The Autobiography*, in George E. Ganss, ed., *Ignatius of Loyola: The Spiritual Exercises and Selected Works* (Mahwah, NJ: Paulist Press, 1991). The *Autobiography* is written in the third person; he frequently calls himself "the pilgrim." This work is cited in the text as AB by paragraph number. William W. Meissner provides an account of Ignatius's upbringing and development up to Pamplona in 1521 in *The Psychology of a Saint: Ignatius of Loyola* (New Haven and London: Yale University Press, 1992), 3-43.

very fond of court dress and good living" (cited by CD, 32). In his *Auto-biography* Ignatius writes of himself that "up to the age of twenty-six he was a man given to the vanities of the world; and what he enjoyed most was warlike sport, with a great and foolish desire to win fame" (AB, 1).[2] The idea of "winning fame" suggests a person of ambition, and this trait works its way into the Exercises.

At court Ignatius developed a noble demeanor and a courtly bearing. He became used to dealing with the great people of the realm and "acquired the traits of that fine distinction and courtesy, which in his [later] years at Rome brought him the reputation of being 'the most courteous and polite of men'" (CD, 33). Polanco expands upon Ignatius's description of his life at court: "Up to this time [of his conversion], although very much attached to the faith, he did not live in keeping with his belief or guard himself from sins; he was particularly careless about gambling, affairs with women, brawls, and the use of arms . . ." (CD, 33).

When Juan Velázquez died in 1517, Ignatius gained employment as a gentleman of Antonio Manrique de Lara, the Duke of Nájera, who had recently become the Viceroy of Navarre. Ignatius was not a soldier but an assistant who carried out orders and executed requests and missions. He was a fixer, and this included participating in military campaigns. Dalmases describes him during these four years in a way that included experience of fighting: "His aim, above all, was to secure for himself a brilliant future in the world; and in the society of his day he could not attain this without the use and experience of arms" (CD, 37). He was participating in a military battle when this style of life came to an abrupt end.

In May of 1521 a large French force attacked the city of Pamplona during an absence of the viceroy and when defensive troops were insufficient. On May 18 Ignatius arrived in the company of his brother from Loyola with a small force from Guipúzcoa. Ignatius's brother, realizing the situation was hopeless, retreated with his band of men. Ignatius stayed, and after the surrender of the city, he initiated a defense of the city's fortress. As tradition would have it, Ignatius was gravely wounded on May 20. "A cannon ball of a culverin or falconet passed between the young soldier's legs, shattering the right one and damaging the other." With Ignatius down, the resistance ended. Ignatius was initially tended to by the French and then carried back to the family home in Loyola by his countrymen in a litter (CD, 39-41).

---

2. If Ignatius is referring to himself prior to his conversion in 1521-1522, given his postulated date of birth in 1491, he relays his age incorrectly. He may be referring to the year of the death of Juan Velázquez in 1517.

Ignatius's Conversion Experience:
The First Phase of an Extended Experience

Conversion experiences are of great interest to anyone interested in a great figure, because they often contain or reveal an inner logic that then influences the person's whole subsequent life. This hypothesis has some merit in the case of Ignatius Loyola. Ignatius arrived back at his home in Loyola in June of 1521 and would leave home at the end of February of 1522 a changed man.[3] Most of what we know about that initial experience comes from his own witness many years later in his *Autobiography*.

When he arrived back at Loyola the doctors and surgeons who were consulted decided "that his leg ought to be broken again and the bones reset" (AB, 2) because they were out of place and the leg could not heal properly. That painful process left him close to death. But he rallied. Once out of danger, however, he faced a new problem. As Ignatius tells it, when his bones had finally knit together,

> one bone below the knee was left riding on another, which made the leg shorter. The bone protruded so much that it was an ugly business. He could not bear such a thing because he was set on a worldly career and thought that this would deform him; he asked the surgeons if it [the protrusion] could be cut away. They said that it could indeed be cut away, but that the pain would be greater than all that he had suffered, because it was already healed and it would take a while to cut it. And yet he chose on his own to make himself a martyr, though his elder brother was shocked and said that he himself would not dare suffer such pain; but the wounded man bore it with his wonted endurance. (AB, 4)

His leg was saved but he would thereafter walk with a decided limp.

This story, which Ignatius singled out as important enough to recall, sharply demonstrates the degree of his vanity and the strength of his will. When he set his mind to a goal, he followed through.

After this last of his surgeries Ignatius convalesced for months. His house lacked the popular literature he wanted to read, and he was left with two large religious works. The first was the *Flos Sanctorum*, a well-known thirteenth-century collection of brief biographies of the

---

3. Meissner's analysis of what went on during both phases of his conversion, at Loyola and then at Manresa, drawn from the testimony of the *Autobiography* and the basic meditations of the Exercises, shows clearly the continuities and discontinuities between the converted Ignatius and his former self. *Psychology of a Saint*, 44-108.

saints by the Dominican Jacobus de Voragine and also known as *The Golden Legend*. The Spanish edition of 1511 contains a prologue that "spoke of the saints as the 'knights of God' who did resplendent deeds in the service of the 'eternal prince, Christ Jesus,' whose 'ever victorious banner' those knights were following."[4] The second work was the *Life of Christ* by Ludolph of Saxony (1300-1377), translated into Spanish early in the century. A work of one thousand pages in four volumes, it was not a continuous narrative about Jesus but a collection of meditations on the phases and stories of Jesus' life compiled from extensive patristic and later sources.[5] It contained a lengthy introduction that included a description of how to meditate on the scenes of Jesus' life. In this and other respects Ludolph provided a principal inspiration for Ignatius's Spiritual Exercises.

Ignatius tells us that as "he read [these works] over many times, he became rather fond of what he found written there. But, interrupting his reading, he sometimes stopped to think about the things he had read and at other times about the things of the world that he used to think of before" (AB, 6). These are the ostensible tensions of his internal debate and conversion. On the one hand Ignatius dreamed of what he might do in Christ's service; on the other hand he mused over "the feat of arms he would perform" in the service of a certain lady (AB, 6). On the one hand, Ignatius emulated the saints. "What if I should do what St. Francis did, and what St. Dominic did? . . . St. Dominic did this, therefore I have to do it; St. Francis did this, therefore I have to do it" (AB, 7). And on the other hand, he thought of the worldly exploits he wished to perform.

While the opposing and alternating attractions were themselves quite clear, his emotions about each scenario were complex. Ignatius attended to them. He found that the delights of worldly adventure left a residue of emptiness and dissatisfaction, but the dreams of a penitential life in the pattern of the saints consoled him, and "after putting them aside he remained satisfied and joyful. Little by little he came to recognize the difference between the spirits that were stirring, one from the devil, the other from God" (AB, 8).[6] Gradually he

---

4. "General Introduction," *Ignatius of Loyola*, ed. George E. Ganss, 16. "These ideas undoubtedly made a strong impression on Ignatius. They contain a fundamental idea which was to dominate the rest of his life: to give an outstanding service to Christ, following the banner of this King who has the saints as his knights. Desire to be an outstanding knight of Christ replaced his thoughts of chivalrous service to ladies." Ibid.

5. Mary Immaculate Bodenstedt, *The Vita Christi of Ludolphus the Carthusian* (Washington, DC: Catholic University of America Press, 1944), 94-95.

6. The person taking Ignatius's dictation at this point added this comment: "This was his first reflection on the things of God; and later, when he composed the Exercises, this was his starting point in clarifying the matter of diversity of spirits" (AB, 8).

recognized that he had to choose between good and evil, to do God's will or Satan's, and he found his decision made.

In the course of this process he began to write down his thoughts. "As he very much liked those books, the idea came to him to note down briefly some of the more essential things from the life of Christ and the saints" (AB, 11). Ignatius generated three hundred pages of notes, including all the words of Jesus he could find in Ludolph. These notes provided him with a written record of this first set of experiences and a basis for his further reflection during the next phase of his conversion experience.

By the end of his stay at Loyola the decision that would propel the rest of his life was firmly in place, though its shape in his life was still evolving. His new commitment contained several elements. He would dedicate himself to God after the pattern of the saints. Essentially this meant shifting his allegiance from an earthly leader or king to the divine leader Jesus Christ. This entailed redirecting many of the qualities that defined his person toward a new transcendent goal; less positively, "he began to think more earnestly about his past life and about the great need he had to do penance for it" (AB, 9). At one point he speaks of a "loathing for his whole past life and especially for the things of the flesh" (AB, 10). Ignatius translated his new penitential spirit into extreme measures of self-discipline. Dalmases says that "he measured sanctity by the severity of corporal austerities" (CD, 45). He admitted later that he did not know any other way. He also decided to make a pilgrimage to Jerusalem. He described this as "the one thing that he wanted to do" (AB, 9). After that other things would begin to fall into place.

Ignatius recuperated for almost nine months at home from the leg injury that, with its treatment, almost cost him his life. By the time he left Loyola for Montserrat in late February of 1522, he was in one sense an utterly different person. In another sense he had applied his characteristic iron will and determination to a new life mission.

The Vigil at Montserrat. Ignatius probably arrived some time in mid-March at the Benedictine Abbey of Montserrat, in northeastern Spain in the mountains west of Barcelona, where the statue of the Black Madonna was displayed. There he sealed his new commitment in a medieval ritual of his own design. Histories of Ignatius associate this ritual moment chronologically with what immediately followed it, an extended sojourn in the nearby town of Manresa. But it can also be understood as integrally associated with Ignatius's experiences at Loyola. This vigil brought closure to Ignatius's conversion experience at his home; he sealed his dedication with a solemn feudal transaction.

Following tradition, Ignatius laid down the arms and livery of nobility, and he assumed the pilgrim's attire in the presence of the Madonna as a representative of the divine sphere. Dalmases calls it an "investiture ceremony," in which Ignatius clothed himself "with the arms of his new spiritual warfare, in the fashion of young knights who entered upon the service of earthly warfare. This investiture ceremony was always preceded by a night vigil, during which the would-be knight stood watch over his arms" (CD, 5).

So it was with Ignatius. He purchased a pilgrim's cloak made of sackcloth, designed to be uncomfortable. Then he performed a sacramental rite of purification, a confession of the sinful behavior of his whole life. He took three days to review his life, and he wrote out his self-accusations before presenting them to the priest for absolution (CD, 53). He was then ready for his self-dedication. This is how Ignatius recalls his actions: "Thus he decided to keep a vigil of arms one whole night . . . before the altar of Our Lady of Montserrat" (AB, 17). "On the eve of the feast of Our Lady in March, at night, in the year 1522, he went as secretly as he could to a beggar and, stripping off all his garments, he gave them to the beggar. He dressed himself in his chosen attire and went to kneel before the altar of Our Lady. At times this way and at other times standing, with his pilgrim's staff in his hand, he spend the whole night" (AB, 18). He left Montserrat the next morning, bound for Barcelona to sail for Italy and then on to Jerusalem.

First Formulas of the Spiritual Exercises: The Second Phase of the Experience

Ignatius left Montserrat the next day dressed as a pilgrim on his way to Jerusalem. He chose a less public route through the town of Manresa, where he wanted to stay "in a hospice a few days and also to note some things in his book; this he carried around very carefully, and he was greatly consoled by it" (AB, 18). As it turned out, he stayed in Manresa for eleven months leading an ascetic and prayerful life. The period was pivotal for the development of his Spiritual Exercises. Given the importance of these Exercises in his own life and the future effectiveness of the religious order he would found, he gives relatively little information about how they began to fall into place during this period. However, he does tell us that during his time there he went through three distinguishable phases that can be reconstructed through the testimonies of his associates during the last years of his life.

The first phase of life in Manresa was relatively calm and joyous.

He assisted at Mass in the morning and at Vespers and Compline in the evening, and he begged alms each day. He fasted during the week, and ceased caring for his hair and nails. During this first period he "remained always in nearly the same interior state of very steady joy, without having any knowledge of interior things of the spirit" (AB, 20). Some estimate that this period lasted through April and May.[7]

The second period was one of spiritual distress. Ignatius began seeing things, and the whole period of Manresa is noted for his intellectual illuminations and "visions." It began gradually with a vision of a bright serpent that appeared to him for several days in broad daylight. This vision gave him considerable pleasure, and when it disappeared he was displeased. Around the same time he started to be attacked by radical doubts about his conversion, but he managed to suppress them through sheer will. He then experienced severe alternations between peaceful joy in his religious practices and feelings of emptiness, what he called "sadness and desolation" (AB, 21). This was followed by "scruples," feelings associated with the sacrament of confession signifying that sins not confessed, or not confessed properly, are not forgiven. This penetrating sense of guilt that implicitly doubts whether God has or even can forgive a person can absolutely immobilize human agency. Ignatius in this period was undergoing something analogous to Luther's experience of inescapable guilt: although he had carefully bared his soul over days and in writing, "still at times it seemed to him that he had not confessed certain things. This caused him much distress, because although he had confessed them all, he was not satisfied" (AB, 22). He tried everything: severe practices of penance, confession, consultations with a priest, fasting, long hours of prayer. But in none of these practices "did he find any cure for his scruples, and it was many months that they were tormenting him" (AB, 23). This period may have extended through June and July.

How did it end? Ignatius looked upon this whole stay at Manresa as a kind of schooling during which "God treated him . . . just as a schoolmaster treats a child whom he is teaching" (AB, 27). Everything comes from God's grace. The cure of his scruples came in an almost abrupt way. Ignatius realized that these scruples were not positive; their effects were negative and getting in the way of his spiritual development. "He thus decided with great lucidity not to confess anything from the past anymore; and so from that day forward he remained free of those scruples and held it for certain that Our Lord had mercifully deigned to deliver him" (AB, 25).

The third period of Ignatius's stay at Manresa was much more con-

---

7. Ganss, *Ignatius of Loyola*, 27.

structive, and aspects of it would come to define his future life and persona. During this time Ignatius had what are usually referred to as his mystical experiences. The term "mystical" raises all sorts of questions about what exactly went on: what was the character of these experiences, where did they come from, and what is the best way to approach or talk about them? These issues cannot be decided apart from a whole range of presuppositions, premises for a discussion, and a method of approach. Ignatius viewed these experiences religiously as impelled by God as Spirit at work within him. At the same time they cannot be conceived apart from natural psychological mechanisms.

The other major development during these months relates to Ignatius's Spiritual Exercises. Unfortunately he does not describe how he actually sat down and began his work on them. When explicitly asked by the scribe of his *Autobiography* how he wrote them he replied "that he had not composed the Exercises all at once, but that when he noticed some things in his soul and found them useful, he thought they might also be useful to others, and so he put them in writing . . ." (AB, 99). Many commentators draw close lines of influence between the mystical experiences and the writing of the Exercises. On the one hand, the two areas of experiences were deeply related; on the other hand, it would be excessive to consider the Exercises as divinely dictated. In the end, one can reconstruct in a broad way that Ignatius began to formulate his Spiritual Exercises during this period and did so on the basis of his sources and ordinary religious experience, insofar as religious experience is ordinary.

Given these parameters, what should be said about the mystical experiences? Ignatius singled out five intense religious experiences he had at Manresa. They occurred in very different situations. All of them included an expansion of his understanding, an illumination in the sense of a penetrating and comprehensive appreciation of an aspect of transcendent reality, accompanied by an image or imaginative symbol. One time, for example, on the steps of a monastery while he was praying "his understanding began to be elevated so that he saw the Most Holy Trinity in the form of three musical keys" (AB, 28). Presumably the three created a harmonious single note. He did not keep this to himself; in fact, he could not stop talking about it. "Once, the manner in which God had created the world was presented to his understanding with great spiritual joy. He seemed to see something white, from which some rays were coming, and God made light from this" (AB, 29). One time during Mass "he saw clearly with his understanding . . . how Jesus Christ our Lord was there in that Most Holy Sacrament" (AB, 29). He had frequent interior appreciations of the humanity of Jesus in the form of a white body (AB, 29). His most important illumination came one day along the banks of the river that ran through the town. It was a clarifying expansion of his understanding that transformed his whole life, what one might today call a "mind-blowing" experience that exceeded all the knowledge and learning of his whole life together.[8]

These so-called mystical experiences of Ignatius have been discussed at length. Ganss associates their subject matter with things he had been reading or thinking about. They engaged "much the same topics which had loomed large in Ignatius's prayerful, reflective reading of Ludolph at Loyola, and in much the same order."[9] The degree with which one estimates God's being "directly" involved in these experiences will depend on one's conception of human existence and its relation to an ultimate. At the very least, Ignatius's mysticism testifies to his intense religious concentration, and it is remarkable how eager and ready he was to share his experiences with others and talk about their subject matter.

Polanco says that, after the great illumination by the river, "Ignatius began to make those Exercises now contained in his book, and then to put them into writing for the instruction of others."[10] The next chapter will discuss this text, but something should be said here regarding Ignatius's authorship.

A most intriguing question relative to Ignatius's launch into the design and composition of the Spiritual Exercises is how one with such a rudimentary education and courtier's background could have composed a religious classic. Undoubtedly his illuminations brought focus and enthusiasm; but what was there to synthesize? Ganss gives a measured response to this question: Ignatius brought to Manresa his "experiences and reflections on them during his convalescence at Loyola, along with similar experiences in his first four months at Manresa. Also present was what he had learned from his readings at Loyola, especially in Jacobus' lives of the saints and Ludolph's life of Christ."[11] He possessed at Manresa a copy of the *Imitation of Christ* by Thomas à Kempis, which he cherished. He had access to the *Short Compendium of Spiritual Exercises* representing the thought of Abbot

---

8. Ignatius described this experience as follows: while seated facing the river below "the eyes of his understanding began to be opened; not that he saw any vision, but he understood and learnt many things, both spiritual matters and matters of faith and scholarship, and this with so great an enlightenment that everything seemed new to him" (AB, 30).

9. Ganss, *Ignatius of Loyola*, 30.

10. Cited in ibid., 32. The term "make," if carefully chosen, suggests that Ignatius experimented with certain patterns of prayer.

11. Ibid.

García de Cisneros of Montserrat.[12] He had also learned much about assessing his interior movements and feelings. We will find later that these sources provided a good deal of material that Ignatius appropriated for his own ends as he developed the Exercises.

The intention that Ignatius brought to his creative process also sheds light on the purpose of the Spiritual Exercises and the way they were composed. Ignatius recorded his experiences because "he thought they might also be useful to others." Dalmases draws out a twofold significance of this observation: Ignatius "himself was the first exercitant. The Exercises which he wrote were the fruit of his personal experiences at Manresa. He put them in writing to help others, communicating to them the ideas and sentiments which had transformed him" (CD, 66). This means, first of all, that the Exercises have a narrative genesis. Ignatius internalized his Loyola-Manresa experiences and preserved them in his notes. He then began to experiment with prayerful Exercises that incorporated what he had learned, and recorded his experiences in the forms and language he had acquired. This contemplative process related the Spiritual Exercises quite closely to his own experience, reflecting the first thirty years of his life and the condensed period of Loyola and Manresa with its antecedents and consequences. In the second place, the mechanism of codifying and writing down his experiences in narrative form enabled him to objectify them. He presented these experiences as Exercises in a relatively structured and objective pattern designed to represent what others might pass through. The originality of the Exercises did not come from synthesizing extensive study but from intense actual encounter, structured by fundamental categories designed by Ignatius.

By February of 1523 Ignatius knew that he would have to leave Manresa if he were to embark for Italy and Venice to catch a boat for Jerusalem. Most commentators agree that he departed with sketches of the essential components of the Spiritual Exercises and a firm grasp on their fundamental logic.

Pilgrim, Student, Organizer, and Administrator

Ignatius developed and refined the Spiritual Exercises considerably as he began using his pages in spiritual conversations with others. But

---

12. Garcia de Cisneros had written a *Book of Exercises of the Spiritual Life* before he died in 1510. After his death the Benedictines at Montserrat gathered his thought into a shorter more accessible form in the *Compendium*. Javier Melloni is convinced that through his Benedictine spiritual director, Dom Jean Canon, Ignatius had a copy of this work in hand during his days at Manresa. Javier Melloni, *The Exercises of St. Ignatius Loyola in the Western Tradition* (Leominster Herefordshaire, UK: Gracewing, 2000), 9.

we have no record of the stages of this development. In the following schematic overview of how Ignatius's career unfolded, one has to imagine how his continual engagement of people in spiritual matters stimulated more precision in his core presentations.

Pilgrimage to Jerusalem (1523-1524). Ignatius left Manresa on or near February 18, 1523, for Barcelona. There he would spend some time raising money and begging passage for Rome to secure the papal permission needed for a pilgrimage to Jerusalem. He then went overland to Venice and set sail on July 14 to arrive finally at Jerusalem on September 4. Ignatius spent about a month in Palestine filling his imagination with scenes from the places where Jesus had lived and taught. He wanted to remain there, but it was politically impossible, and he was ordered to return by religious authorities under threat of excommunication. He left Jerusalem on September 23 and sailed from Jaffa in early October. His ship made it back to Venice by mid January, and Ignatius threaded his way through French and imperial forces to Genoa. There he found passage for Barcelona, where he arrived in February of 1524. During his trip back to Spain Ignatius had to face the question of what he would do upon return. He decided that, if he were to accomplish anything for the kingdom of God, he needed academic learning. He came back from Jerusalem committed to obtaining an education, a quest that would last eleven years.

The University Years: Spain and Paris (1524-1535). Latin was the language of education and scholarship. Ignatius knew no Latin; he had to begin at the beginning. He was thirty-three years old. He spent four years in Spain, principally in Barcelona and Alcalá with a short stay in Salamanca, before deciding that he needed to go to the University of Paris for an uninterrupted university education.

During his time in Barcelona he studied Latin and grammar, preparing himself for the study of philosophy. He also engaged in spiritual direction of others. "It seems that during this time in Barcelona [Ignatius] made his first attempts at giving the Spiritual Exercises to others, and it is probable that through them he attracted as followers those whom he might call his first three companions" (CD, 88-89). Ignatius himself tells us that he gained companions in his way of life in Barcelona (AB, 56).

After about two years of study in Barcelona his teachers told Ignatius that he was ready to study philosophy, and they recommended the university at Alcalá. He was there from March 1526 to June 1527. Ignatius says that "while at Alcalá, he was engaged in giving Spiritual Exercises and teaching Christian doctrine, and this bore fruit for the glory of God" (AB, 57). Dalmases comments, "The fact is, too, that he devoted himself more to his apostolic activities than to his studies" (CD, 94). While he was in Alcalá a fourth follower joined them. At one point Ignatius and his four companions were imprisoned and examined by the Inquisition. Although they were found innocent of heresy, the inquisitors "were closing the door for him to help souls, without giving him any reason except that he had not studied" (AB, 63). In mid-July of 1527 Ignatius moved on to Salamanca. His four companions had preceded him.

He was only in Salamanca twelve days before he was investigated by the Dominican inquisitors there. In the course of the questioning he submitted his Exercises to be examined. This is the earliest written form of the Exercises to which Ignatius makes reference. He writes, "The bachelor Frías came to examine each of them separately, and the pilgrim gave him all his papers, which were the Exercises, to be examined" (AB, 67). Once again he was freed, but he determined that he could not continue his project in Spain but had to go to Paris and leave his four companions in Spain.

Ignatius passed through Barcelona and received support to travel to Paris, where he arrived on February 2, 1528, and began a long program of studies leading to a Bachelor of Arts (1532), License in Arts (1533), and then a Master of Arts degree in philosophy (1534). He also studied theology there from 1533 to 1535, at which time he ended his studies before he had completed the theology necessary for ordination. He would study more theology later in Venice.

Ignatius also generated another group of friends in Paris. Although he had deliberately curtailed his spiritual work in the interest of his studies, he gradually gained colleagues or collaborators. He gave the Spiritual Exercises to several of them. In 1534, on August 15, Ignatius and six companions took vows together to become a group committed to work for the kingdom of God. "They were to live in strict poverty in imitation of Christ, and to devote themselves to the Spiritual welfare of their fellow men and women. As a first step they would make a pilgrimage to Jerusalem . . ." (CD, 37). If that were to fail, as it did, they were to present themselves to the pope and be at his service.

By the spring of 1535 Ignatius was exhausted, and doctors suggested that he needed his native air to restore his health. He thus interrupted his study of theology and left Paris for his home country. By that time the Spiritual Exercises had become refined by his use of them to direct people and through the distinctions contributed by his theological education. They were nearing their final form as a manual. Before Ignatius left Paris a rumor circulated that attacked his orthodoxy; he insisted on an investigation and a formal statement of their soundness. "The book of the Exercises was formally approved by the Inquisitor of Paris, the Dominican Valentin Liévin, in March, 1535" (CD, 124).[13]

Ignatius the Organizer (1535-1540). The new Ignatius was virtually unknown outside of Paris when he left there in the spring of 1535. His few months at home gave him a chance to greet his family and to establish his new persona. In July he moved on, traveling through Spain visiting the families of his Paris companions, then on to Venice via Bologna by the end of 1535. In 1536 he studied more theology in preparation for ordination to priesthood. The seven pilgrims, plus three more Frenchmen who now comprised the original ten companions, came together in Venice in early 1537 in an attempt to sail to Jerusalem. Ignatius was ordained in June of 1537, and in November he transferred his residence to Rome. When it finally proved to be impossible to go to Jerusalem, in 1538 Ignatius and his companions presented themselves to the pope who assigned them certain ministries. The following year they discussed the possibility of forming a religious order, and they submitted a plan, which functioned as a provisional rule, to the pope. It was accepted in 1540, and the Society of Jesus (known today as the Jesuits) was formally constituted. All of these decisions were discussed thoroughly among the companions. Ignatius's organizational leadership seemed to reside more in the force of his person and ideals than in a dictatorial spirit.

Ignatius the Administrator. In the early 1540s Ignatius, elected superior of the new order, collaborated in forming and communicating its Constitution, a rule that remains in effect today. The Spiritual Exercises were first published in book form in 1548. This included all the increments that were incorporated during the Paris years and thereafter. In the late 1540s, the new order began accepting invitations to establish colleges for the instruction of youth, a form of ministry that flourished. Ignatius died on July 31, 1556, leaving behind a greatly expanded group of Jesuits working in Europe, Asia, and Latin America.

Ignatius, courtier, gentleman, soldier, convert, mystic, pilgrim, founder of a religious order and source of a lasting spiritual tradi-

---

13. This is the second time, Salamanca being the first, where we have a reference to the Exercises in a written form. The inquisitor, Ignatius writes, "wanted to see his manuscript of the Exercises. When he saw it he praised it very much and asked the pilgrim to let him have the copy; and he did so. Nevertheless, the pilgrim again insisted that the case be carried through to the sentence. As the inquisitor excused himself, the pilgrim brought a public notary and witness to the inquisitor's house, and obtained a testimonial on this whole affair" (AB, 86).

tion, presents a complex figure. The Spiritual Exercises have an utterly unique origin and design. To conclude it will be helpful to describe some of the personality traits of Ignatius that emerge from his story and leave their mark on the spirituality of the Exercises.

Biographical Dimensions of the Spiritual Exercises

The Spiritual Exercises of Ignatius Loyola are linked quite closely to his biography. Telling his story provides a basic understanding of the author, his creative perspective, and the work they generated. The category of "narrative" emphasizes the historical aspects of the experience of the author. History highlights contingency and chance: did not the Exercises come into existence because of the trajectory of a cannon ball one spring morning in northern Spain? Despite such specific historical contingencies, it will become clear later that to reduce the Exercises to biographical interpretation is to kill their broader meaning and blunt their wider relevance. Part of Ignatius's individuality lay in the common tradition that helped define him, and the Exercises are a classic precisely because of their general applicability and the universal experiences they draw from and elicit. But at this juncture the focus falls on the correlation between the Spiritual Exercises and the character of their author. This correlation shows how some of the aspects of the personality of Ignatius Loyola as seen in his *Autobiography* became qualities of the spirituality reflected in the Exercises.[14] An enumeration of these qualities foreshadows the introduction of the text in the next chapter.

A Teleologically Ordered World. Ignatius lived in a narrow ideological world of kingship and Catholicism. It had strong teleological underpinnings. Sometimes the early Ignatius is depicted as a wild, unruly man to accentuate his personal change following conversion, but his indiscretions occurred within an orderly universe and a neatly structured world inherited from the Aristotelianism implicit in scholastic philosophy and theology. Ignatius lived within this world; he thought in terms of ends and means; he took the steps necessary to achieve goals. He was a man of his times.

A Hierarchical World of Good and Evil. Hierarchy represents another slice of Ignatius's cultural world that shaped his acquired second nature. It

---

14. I accept wholeheartedly Meissner's caution in dealing with the mystery of a human person. He writes of his own psychoanalytic portrait of Ignatius: "Consequently, the picture that emerges from this synthesis may bear some plausible relation to the real person of Ignatius, but the links are uncertain and the result no more than conjectural and probable at best." *The Psychology of a Saint*, 361.

had one of its prime expositors in the influential Pseudo-Dionysius.[15] The universe had tiers or ranks of being that existed in an orderly relation to one another. Feudal society, although really based on sheer power, seemed to reinforce a natural political order. Ignatius was loyal to church and his king, and he lived in a command–obey relationship to authority. He also lived in a medieval Catholicism whose moral dualism divided the world into good and evil. This has firm roots in the Bible. Under the one God the battle goes on between the forces of light and darkness, good and evil, good spirits and bad spirits. Ignatius was well disposed to appropriate Augustine's division of history into the two cities and the two camps of the kingdom of Christ and the kingdom of Satan, of Rome and Babylon. He did not discover but rather recognized the world of good spirits and evil spirits contending for possession of human persons.

An Uncritical Framework of Revelation and Faith. Ignatius's religious world was pre-modern, Catholic, and medieval. He is rightly considered as breaking with the traditions of other religious orders and introducing an early modern body of mobile, engaged religious leaders. But one has to be discriminating in noting his incipient modernity; one should not ignore the contrast between his world and post-Enlightenment sensibilities. He had no sympathy for the Reformers. Nor did he appreciate Erasmus, despite some obvious shared convictions about an action-oriented spirituality of engagement in society,[16] because of his criticism of the church. In his precritical imagination the gospel scenes occurred as they are described, and the doctrines too represented transcendent reality, if not literally, at least in a fairly direct descriptive way. He copied down the words of Jesus; he was concerned about preserving in his imagination the position of the last footprints Jesus left on earth as he ascended. Ignatius operated in a religious world of first naiveté, as this is characterized by Paul Ricoeur, in contrast to a postcritical reappropriation of the content of faith in a second naiveté.[17] For

---

15. Pseudo-Dionysius was a late-fifth- and early-sixth-century theologian, writing in the name of a person who appears in the Acts of the Apostles, who presents a hierarchically ordered universe from top to bottom. He was translated into Latin early in the medieval period and had an enormous influence throughout it and beyond.

16. Erasmus (1466-1536) was the most famous humanist of his age. Among his most popular works was his *The Enchiridion (Handbook of the Christian Soldier)* in which he adapts themes of the *Imitation of Christ*, noted for recommending withdrawal from the world, to militant engagement in society on the basis of the ideals of Jesus Christ. There are strong parallels at certain points between Erasmus and Ignatius but no literary dependence.

17. In Paul Ricoeur's distinction, first naiveté refers to belief in the world represented by spontaneous religious language as if it directly described the transcendent

example, Ignatius's story of how he allowed the direction taken by his mule at a crossroad to decide God's will on whether or not he should attack a Muslim with a knife for insulting the Virgin Mary well illustrates an uncomplicated view of providence (AB, 15).

Conversion. The Exercises closely reflect the trajectory of Ignatius's own conversion and are designed to bring about conversion of life in others. At this point the fruitfulness of a narrative perspective becomes apparent. The before, during, and after of Ignatius's dramatic experiences are mirrored in the structure of his Spiritual Exercises. By definition conversion signifies a radical change in a person's life. On one side is the old self; on the other is the new. The old has to be thoroughly shed and the new schooled in equal proportion. The Exercises offered the persons coming to them a provident, loving God and an orderly universe in which to operate; they instructed these persons on how to rid themselves of their negative pasts and find confidence for a way forward; they gave them a goal to aim for; they provided them a guide and taught them how to approach, identify with, and appropriate the right direction from Jesus Christ; they instructed them on how to manage their inner resistance; they urged them to the highest ideals of which they were capable and more; they showed them how to make life decisions; and they provided the reasons for feeling completely comfortable in their decisions despite the difficulty of the prospect. Ignatius reproduced his conversion story in his Exercises in order to help others do the same thing. At a certain formal level the Exercises propose a spirituality of *imitatio Ignatii*.

Single-Minded and Strong Willed. These qualities of Ignatius are not buried in his subconscious; they are overt. They reinforce each other. Single-mindedness describes his service to the crown and to the Duke of Nájera; it explains why he would not surrender Pamplona without a fight. In his conversion this single-mindedness is transferred to God and to Jesus Christ, who appears as his new leader. One could say that Ignatius was driven, on both sides of his conversion: beforehand, he displayed an absolute loyalty to his secular lord; afterward, his absolute dedication was to the cause of Christ. Unwavering commitment was a constant in his feudal world and in that of his newfound commitment to the Catholic faith. The strength of his will appears constantly in his *Autobiography*. He dismisses external hazards, even

---

order. When that meaning is shattered by criticism, the same language may be appropriated symbolically and, as such, subject to interpretation. Ricoeur calls such appropriation a second, that is, critically reflective, naiveté. Paul Ricoeur, *The Symbolism of Evil* (Boston: Beacon, 1967), 352-54.

mortal dangers, that stand in his way. He faces pain unflinchingly. He cures his spiritual torment with an act of the will, although he recognizes the support of God's assistance. Strong will sometimes entails impetuousness, lack of reflection, and unreasonableness. Yet Ignatius's entire conversion was a "schooling," and he builds rational reflection into the process at every stage.

Orientation to Service. Ignatius was always committed to service; his conversion shifted the object of his commitment. But the self-transcending character of his dedication is arresting. He devoted his freedom to an object outside himself, and his own self-realization came through the gift of self to a high ideal. This was symbolized dramatically at Montserrat, where in his "investiture ceremony" he transformed a chivalrous commitment to service from one object to another. The next chapter discusses the contemplation of Christ the king, wherein service supplies the dynamic power. That consideration from the Exercises reflected Ignatius's new commitment to Jesus that in turn impelled his pilgrimage to where Jesus lived and imbued his life with a mission. The phrase "to help souls" gradually assumed prominence in Ignatius's language as he recounted the Manresa sojourn. This idea defined his dedication to service beyond the individual goal of his own personal sanctification and salvation. The phrase occurs frequently in the *Autobiography* and often functions as a criterion or reason for decisions.

Practical and Action Oriented. These characteristics also marked Ignatius's conversion. Not without reflection, but precisely within a highly reflective framework, the Exercises appeal almost directly to the affections and the will as they call a person to a decision for a new and particular way of life. Ignatius was a doer and a fixer, and after his conversion he adopted a spirituality of action. This involved rational planning, establishing goals and fitting means to an end. This was a constant pattern of his life. For example, he was not sure what he would do after his pilgrimage to Jerusalem. When he "realized that it was not God's will that he remain in Jerusalem, he continually pondered within himself what he ought to do. Eventually he was rather inclined to study for some time so he would be able to help souls, and he decided to go to Barcelona" (AB, 50). Study was the practical requirement to achieve his goals. He made this connection explicit in reporting his experience in Salamanca: "he still felt the same desire that he had to help souls, and for that reason to study first and to gather some others with the same idea . . ." (AB, 71). Ignatius combined the qualities of being rational, pragmatic, and emotional in a remarkable synthesis.

Achievement Oriented. Ignatius was a striver; this quality was central to him. Ignatius sought to distinguish himself. He described his early life in his *Autobiography* as one driven by "a great and foolish desire to win fame" (AB, 1). He wanted to be counted among those who accomplished something with their lives. This quality embraced him on both sides of his conversion and thus finds a noticeable place within his Spiritual Exercises. The Exercises urge persons to strive to do their utmost and then "more." As Hugo Rahner puts it: "The Ignatian ideal of the Spiritual Exercises, therefore, is contained in the four words: *señalarse mas en servicio,* 'to distinguish oneself more in His service.'"[18] The two ideals, then, were "service" and always "more" of it; the basic idea was to distinguish oneself by committed action.

This desire of achievement was translated to the spiritual sphere by a desire to emulate the saints. He asked himself during his convalescence, "'What if I should do what St. Francis did, and what St. Dominic did?'" Dreaming became determination: "St. Dominic did this, therefore I have to do it; St. Francis did this, therefore I have to do it" (AB, 6). His orientation to achievement spilled over into the penitential sphere. His self-imposed external hardships were perhaps a way of atoning for past sin, of proving his hatred of his past. To whom did he have to prove himself? To God? To himself? They were also meant to demonstrate that he was now singly attached to God through Jesus Christ. On the road to Montserrat his ideas about asceticism shifted: "he decided to do great penances, no longer with an eye to satisfying for his sins so much as to please and gratify God" (AB, 14). If one of the saints did something, he would do the same thing in a more intense way. In the beginning he did not dwell on his interior disposition but fixed his attention on great external works "because the saints had done so for the glory of God" (AB, 14). The object to be achieved evolved still further as the glory of God became more closely associated with being of service to others, that is, "helping souls."

A Vivid Imagination. Ignatius had a powerful imagination. He used his imagination to formulate his goals and depict his plans in the future. He was a dreamer, a romantic. He imaginatively created parallels between what was happening to him at any given time and events in the lives of Jesus and the original disciples. While he was recuperating "he imagined what he would do in the service of a certain lady" by way of a "feat of arms" (AB, 6). He deliberately employed his imagination in alternatively imagining worldly exploits and penitential religious

---

18. Hugo Rahner, *The Spirituality of St. Ignatius Loyola: An Account of Its Historical Development* (Westminster, MD: Newman Press, 1953), 12.

extremes and measuring the affective residuals (AB, 7-8; see AB, 75). As we shall see, in the Spiritual Exercises he uses the imagination as a vehicle for enabling contact with God through Jesus. In short, he had a vivid and active imagination, which he employed deliberately and constructively to practical purpose. His imagination was also a major element of his profound religious experiences, or enlightenments. In most cases these new understandings had a certain image that enfolded them or were associated with them. This imaginative sensibility became a significant feature of the spirituality he left behind.

Deference to Legitimate External Authority. Ignatius always showed deference to legitimate authority insofar as it was binding. This was part of his metaphysical universe and the world as he knew it. He did not look kindly on criticism of the church as it was represented by its hierarchical authority. He obeyed it. He was not uncritical of various acts of authority, but he always acted within the system. He did not lack the practical ability to discern authentic and inauthentic uses of authority. One has to be impressed by the mixture of obedience and self-confidence he displayed before the various incidents of inquisitorial authority. When he did not agree with a certain legitimate order or command, he would still obey it. But when questions were unfair, he did not respond. For example, at Salamanca, he sensed a trap, "was somewhat on his guard," and refused to answer a line of questioning (AB, 65-66). One can find an analogous parallelism between Ignatius the military man or the servant of a temporal lord and Ignatius the person operating within a system of ecclesial authority. Deference did not mean subservience.

This biographical account of Ignatius's early life and his conversion experience only hints at the inner resources of this extraordinary person. It describes a historical life in a particular situation, a point of departure for understanding the Spiritual Exercises as a product of their author. The next chapter introduces the world of the text.

CHAPTER TWO

Description of the Spiritual Exercises

Ignatius assembled the Spiritual Exercises over an extended period of time. The final version developed by increment; no single Platonic idea holds them together. Narrative describes their core in several respects. The previous chapter showed how "conversion" lies behind the Exercises. They flow from conversion and are meant to stimulate a decisive change in people's lives. Conversion involves a past, present, and future; it has a beginning, a turning point, and an open-ended new life. Also, the substance of the Exercises consists in Jesus' story. The Exercises thus flow out of a narrative, have a narrative structure, and proffer a narrative experience to those who embark upon them.

This chapter describes the elements and form Ignatius used to construct the Spiritual Exercises. The book is a manual, analogous to those that accompany technological products, a "how-to" for actual performance of prayerful spiritual practices of meditation. But to use a manual a person must know its subject matter and the language it employs. A large body of literature is devoted to explaining Ignatius's manual. Those who have made their way into its conceptual framework frequently forget how unintelligible this book appears to the unprepared who randomly pick it up. It ranks among the most unwieldy of texts. This chapter, then, aims at helping to open the door to this house of meaning. The next chapter will enter it more deeply with an analytical interpretation of the floor plan.

This first approach to the Exercises proceeds in stages. It begins by identifying the essential substance of the Exercises and then characterizes the basic beliefs of Christian faith that shape the metanarrative or metaphysical worldview that encompasses the work. The discussion then turns to the way Ignatius used the materials he had at hand to construct the Exercises. A great deal of work has been done on this historical level, and it illumines what is going on in the text. A glossary of key Ignatian terms will supply another look into this semantic world. Familiarity with this language increases sensitivity to the distinctive Ignatian proposal of how Jesus can be brought to bear on spiritual life. The concluding section offers an appreciation of the genius of the Spiritual Exercises, the elementary move that enables them to address all people.

Meditations on the Life of Jesus

The Spiritual Exercises of Ignatius Loyola essentially consist of meditations on the life and ministry of Jesus as he appears in the gospel
stories. Much more needs to be said, but in the end their core and substance consist in imaginative, thoughtful, and engaged considerations
of the person of Jesus as the gospels represent him.[1] This chapter will
call attention to several other features of the Exercises that have a major
role in influencing how people appropriate these stories of Jesus. Several key considerations that are typically Ignatian shape the encounter with Jesus; they "package" him and influence the perception of
those being led through the gospel stories. It would be misleading to
reduce the Exercises to meditation on the life of Jesus, but the accompanying considerations should not so absorb attention that the central
subject matter and practice become obscured. The greater part of this
introductory chapter in fact deals with the rhetorical superstructure
that organizes the considerations of Jesus of Nazareth. It is important,
then, that this discussion be seen as reinforcing the centrality of Jesus
of Nazareth in the Exercises.

Placing Jesus of Nazareth at the center of the Spiritual Exercises plays
an important role in the way they are interpreted in this work. That
placement revolves around the public character of Jesus, his potentially
universal availability through the gospels, and his accessibility as a
human being. Jesus was not a Christian but a Jew. Yet, as a classic religious figure, he possesses an appeal that continues to reach out across
cultural and religious boundaries. Jesus was of course a theist. But people whose spiritual or religious convictions do not include a personal
God within their beliefs can find in him teachings about human existence in relation to ultimate reality, other persons, society more broadly
conceived, and the world. His teaching can be instructive and moving.
It is true that each portrait of Jesus offered in the gospel stories carries
with it theological interpretation. But the human imagination can also
penetrate the theology to reach a plausible image of the man and his
teaching without too much work.[2]

---

1. Ignatius did not have the New Testament to consult at Loyola or at Manresa.
Only later in the sixteenth century was the whole Bible translated and printed in Spanish. Ignatius drew his stories of Jesus from the text of Ludolf which reproduced the
gospel stories.

2. The project of finding the "real" Jesus behind the stories has been going on since
the nineteenth century and is generally referred to as the quest for the historical Jesus. It
has taken various shapes and each new initiative has its critics. The criticisms are often
dependent upon greater or lesser expectations of what can be accomplished by this
quest. Whether or not one is sympathetic to the methods and goals of this effort, at least
it reinforces not a separability but a distinction between the theological interpretations

The Spiritual Exercises are christocentric, a characterization that indicates the central place that Jesus of Nazareth enjoys as the principal focus of attention from start to finish. But a distinction between two significantly different meanings of that centrality will clarify the strategy adopted in the present interpretation. "Christocentrism" can draw its meaning from a context that is theological and implicitly metaphysical. This meaning builds on the understanding that Jesus is the Jewish Messiah and, by extension in a Christian theological context, expands that initial belief with the affirmation that Jesus is an incarnation of the Word of God and thus the Son of God. This implicitly trinitarian framework[3] turns christocentrism into a comprehensive metaphysical view of God and the Christian story into a sacred narrative that encompasses all of reality. This worldview was part of the furniture of Ignatius's mind and is shared by many Christians who embark upon the Exercises today.

But christocentrism can have another more modest sense that limits the range of its reference to the sphere of history and prescinds from metaphysical and theological considerations. From this perspective the Spiritual Exercises are christocentric because they revolve around Jesus of Nazareth. This does not exclude the fact that Christians understand Jesus to be the Messiah or, its Greek translation, Christ; it simply affirms that Jesus is the center of attention. This more restricted aspect of Jesus of Nazareth fits well with Ignatius's imaginative approach to the gospel stories. Ignatius also attends to the pre-existent Word of God, who by incarnation became Jesus of Nazareth, and Jesus raised from death, but far more attention falls on the historical figure of Jesus in the gospel stories. The reasons why and exactly how Ignatius emphasizes the Jesus of history in his Exercises will be discussed later. But at this preliminary stage in introducing the Exercises certain things should be stipulated. One is that Ignatius builds his Exercises around the stories about the ministry of Jesus of Nazareth. Another is that this focus on the human being Jesus as a public figure in history makes him available to the apperception of all. Finally, this distinction should not be construed exclusively; it does not preclude further theological interpretation.

To the extent that it is possible, then, the interpretation of the Exercises in this book keeps the focus on the human being, Jesus of Nazareth, thus embracing christocentrism in the second sense but not to the exclusion of the first. This strategy opens up the possible influence of the Exercises beyond the Christian community to any human being

---

of Jesus and his actual historical appearance. Jesus' appearance was that of a human being like all other human beings in their concrete humanity.

3. Because in the Christian imagination the Father and the Word of God are distinct and spontaneously joined by the Spirit of God to form a trinity.

who is seeking his or her way in a spiritual life. In Ignatius's language, the motivation is to share these Exercises more widely in helping others. The open character of the Exercises will come up again in the conclusion of this chapter.

The Christian Narrative

The Spiritual Exercises of Ignatius were composed and are situated within a large metaphysical framework that implicitly gives them their rationale and justifies the strategy for human living that they offer. This context is the Christian metanarrative, and relating the Exercises to this implicit but decisive big picture helps to clarify what is going on in them.

The Christian Story. The Christian story, or metanarrative, refers to the story behind empirical history that embraces all human existence, the whole world, and all reality. The story begins with a conception of creation by God, the source of all being, and tells how humanity "fell" into a situation of sin. This introduces the need for salvation from the sin and death that characterize human history. The final emissary and mediator of that salvation is Jesus Christ, revealer of God and authentic human existence. His revelation tells of a new heaven and earth in a final everlasting salvation offered to all. Situating an understanding of the Spiritual Exercises of Ignatius within the context of this sacred story of salvation history drawn from the Bible places them firmly within the heart of the Christian tradition. The spine of the Christian message concerning the economy of God's salvation constitutes the backbone of Ignatius's Exercises and thus provides a framework for interpreting them. "The objective content is God's revealed message of salvation as found in the Scriptures and proposed to the exercitant. Thus the call which he or she perceives corresponds with the very data of God's revelation."[4] Gilles Cusson believed that Ignatius learned this big picture in a formal way from Ludolph at Loyola and Manresa. He recorded the process of being introduced into it so that it could be shared with others. The goal of the Exercises is to provide a set of experiences by which others may find their own place within the narrative of God's economy of creation and salvation.

The Strategy: Imitation of Christ. Cusson reads the Christian story of creation and salvation in the ancient pattern of a coming from and a

---

4. Gilles Cusson, *Biblical Theology and the Spiritual Exercises: A Method toward a Personal Experience of God as Accomplishing within Us His Plan of Salvation* (St. Louis: Institute of Jesuit Sources, 1994; original, 1968), 42. Cited hereafter as BTSE.

return to God. All things come forth from God creator; God is active in all things; all things oriented to their ends are part of God's holistic design. In God's plan the universe that came from God is moving back to God. In this scheme human beings are meant to be conscious participators in this movement, so that they "ought to assume the responsibility for this return of the world to the Father."[5] "To bring order into one's life, then, means to become aware, in the light of the divine truth, of one's creaturehood with all that it implies, and consequently to insert oneself into the magnificent plan of the Creator and Redeemer, into the history of salvation."[6]

The way in which a person enters into this Christian narrative in order responsibly to participate in it consists in "imitating," or following, Jesus Christ. At this point the fundamental building blocks of the Exercises, the meditations on the scenes of the life of Jesus, fall into place. People making the Exercises enter into the Christian story by following Jesus Christ. According to God's plan Jesus Christ is the agent of salvation. He reveals God and becomes the exemplar of human existence. Entering into God's plan for the Christian consists in associating with Jesus Christ and taking up his way of life. All of this was laid out quite clearly by both Ludolph's *Life of Christ* and Thomas à Kempis's *The Imitation of Christ*. They viewed it in largely individual and personal terms, but it also has a larger historical outcome. Identifying with and following Jesus of Nazareth sets up a two-way social traffic of learning and implementing. People in their present situation who are addressed by Jesus learn from him; and through them Jesus' way of life is drawn into distinctive life situations. By such appropriation, the Jesus story constantly achieves new meanings in various Christian communities from the people who internalize it.

The Structure of Four Weeks. Ignatius divided the process of making the Spiritual Exercises into four stages or phases. He decided that making the Exercises integrally should last about a month, and he divided the series of considerations into four sets of roughly seven days. During the first week of the Exercises the persons making them attend to a review of their lives. Ignatius focuses on sin, but the orientation is toward a consideration of God's mercy, forgiveness, and complete acceptance of each person. This correlates neatly with Ignatius's own experience at Loyola and Manresa.

The next three phases, or weeks, are divided along the lines of the story of Jesus in the gospels: they deal successively with the public

---

5. Ibid., 63.
6. Ibid., 92.

ministry of Jesus, then his passion and death, and finally Jesus risen as reflected in the post-resurrection appearance narratives. The more or less month-long series of experiences thus has a fairly straightforward narrative structure. After spending some time preparing oneself the person enters into the three-stage way that Jesus walked as a way of entering into the dramatic story of salvation that Jesus himself demonstrated. As Cusson conceives it, the four weeks of the exercises fit within the template of the divine plan of history and the economy of salvation. Jesus and each person following him enters the pattern of self-appropriation and then self-dedication to service, through death, and into resurrection.[7]

Reading the Story of Jesus in Other Frameworks. Reception of the Spiritual Exercises in a context that transcends Christianity will generate new moral, spiritual, and religious meaning. Different understandings of history, the world, the universe, and ultimate reality will occasion analogous reactions to Jesus; that is, the same Jesus will stimulate different receptions. Jesus of Nazareth is available to all as a spiritual teacher; but not all who approach him share the Christian narrative. A Unitarian, a member of another religious tradition, or a secular seeker will relate to Jesus in a way that differs from the Christian believer. From inside the Christian story Jesus appears as the exemplary cause of salvation, and this means that Jesus has a constitutive role in revealing the personal character of God and a salutary pattern of human existence in relation to God. Someone approaching Jesus from outside the Christian story may recognize him as a spiritual teacher or guide or by another title of respect. This will generate different accents of interpretation and increase Jesus' meaningful relevance.

Ignatius's Sources

The previous chapter raised the question how Ignatius could have begun to write this classic work without a formal education. The answer was that he used what he had available: his written sources, his past and present experiences, including his illuminations at Manresa, his spiritual practices, and his conversations with others. Although he never described in detail the process by which he composed the Exercises, tracking the sources helps to understand the finished product. Historical research into these sources has greatly expanded appreciation of Ignatius's text relative to a historical tradition. But his eclectic use of sources and his reliance on his own experience account for the distinctive character of this spirituality.

---

7. See ibid., 98.

A New Set of Notes. During his period of recuperation Ignatius wrote out all the words of Jesus he could find in Ludolph's *Life of Christ*. Many infer that Ignatius began a new notebook or set of notes at Manresa, less for his own edification and more as notes for considerations that would be useful in dealing with others. He seems to indicate this in his *Autobiography* in response to a question about the genesis of the Exercises. He had a spiritual confessor and director in the Benedictine Dom Jean Chanon, and more generally he engaged in spiritual conversation with people who were at hand with whom he wanted to share his experiences. The intention to make use of his experiences in order to help others represents a distinct new goal for his note-taking. "This would naturally lead him to write notes about his recent experiences, and to refer to items from Jacobus[8] and Ludolph in his copybook. Soon he had another handful of pages. He used it to refresh his own memory for the conversation he was about to have with one or another of his spiritual friends. It was now a means to aid himself in leading them to a sequence of prayerful activities."[9]

Christocentrism. The christocentrism sketched earlier was amply represented in Ludolph's *Life of Christ*. In Ludolph the life of Jesus Christ begins in the Godhead as the second person of the trinity. Ignatius would have immediately recognized the language of the sacred story. Jesus Christ is the basis of human salvation; the call to salvation involves two stages: forgiveness and following Christ. The first involves contrition, penance, leading to accepting forgiveness; the second consists of following Christ, after having been forgiven and regenerated.[10]

Use of the Imagination in Prayer. Ignatius learned his methods of prayer from Ludolph. Ludolph's long introduction to his *Life of Christ* had extensive explanations of different methods of prayer, and Ignatius

---

8. Jacobus de Voragine was the author of *The Golden Legend*, or lives of saints, that Ignatius read at Loyola.

9. George E. Ganss, ed., *Ignatius of Loyola: The Spiritual Exercises and Selected Works* (Mahwah, NJ: Paulist Press, 1991),33.

10. Cusson, BTSE, 11-13. P. H. Watrigant, in *La Genèse des Exercises de Saint Ignace de Loyola* (Amiens: Yvert & Tellier, 1897) did a textual comparison of later editions of the Exercises and Ludolph's *Life of Christ* and found many places where Ignatius borrowed more or less directly from Ludolph. Only in a few instances, however, did these amount to near literal transcriptions. Some of the major parallels are these: the turn to the humanity of Jesus, an "imitation of Christ" spirituality, the use of the imagination in contemplating Jesus' life, responding to God's love more in deeds than in words. He also finds sometimes close dependencies on Ludolph in the content of the contemplations on the life and ministry of Jesus. See pages 79-86 for a long series of correspondences.

made notes on them and used the notes. Most distinctive is the use of the imagination to enter into and participate in the scenes as they were portrayed. This method springs from Franciscan roots and shows a familiarity with Jesus as a human being, one who is approachable and able to be imitated.[11] It reflects a nonliterary culture in which the beliefs of Christian faith were depicted in visual forms in the stone and windows of cathedrals. Imaginatively entering into an event of the gospel story creates a lively actualized consciousness of events and persons that increases their affective impact. This in turn draws a person "to imitate the divine exemplar and make himself again into the divine image that has been effaced through sin."[12] Ludolph's *Life of Christ* offers "a simple way of meditating, which consists in the imaginative exercise of the senses upon some mystery of Our Lord's life to move the heart to pious affections and the will to good resolutions in conformity with Christ's example."[13]

At Loyola during his recuperation Ignatius would have read these words in the prologue of Ludolf's *Life of Christ* under the heading "How to Meditate on the Life of Christ": "If you want to gain the greatest benefit from this exercise, put aside all other concerns and tasks, and with your whole heart strive with diligence, delight, and determination to be present when Jesus speaks and acts. As you read the narrative, imagine you are seeing each event with your own eyes and hearing it with your own ears. . . . Although these accounts describe events that occurred in the past, you must meditate upon them as if they were taking place now: there is no question but that you will savor them with greater pleasure."[14] Ignatius adapted this method as his own, and it became a significant feature of his approach to Jesus.

---

11. Ewert H. Cousins, "Franciscan Roots of Ignatian Meditation," in *Ignatian Spirituality in a Secular Age*, ed. George P. Schner (Waterloo, ON: Wilfrid Laurier University Press, 1984), 51-64.

12. Mary Immaculate Bodenstedt, *The Vita Christi of Ludolphus the Carthusian* (Washington, DC: Catholic University of America Press, 1944), 120.

13. Ibid., 120-21. Remarkably, one can trace the same appeal to Jesus of Nazareth as exemplar of human existence through the medieval, modern, and postmodern periods of research. Despite the changes in the method and content, the conviction that Jesus provides a criterion for criticism and reform appears to be continuous and consistent. See Anthony J. Godzieba, "From 'Vita Christi' to 'Marginal Jew': The Life of Jesus as Criterion of Reform in Pre-Critical and Post-Critical Quests," K U Leuven, Symposium *Sourcing the Quests* (April 30, 2004). Available online at www.kuleuven.be/theometh/peter/papers/godzieba2.pdf

14. "The Prologue of the *Vita Christi*," in *To Always Be Thinking Somehow about Jesus*, trans. Milton Walsh (Studies in the Spirituality of Jesuits 43/1; St. Louis: Jesuit Sources, 2011), 33-34.

The Colloquy. A colloquy is a dialogue, a conversation, perhaps an intimate interchange with another. At the end of his presentation of a scenario in Jesus' life, Ludolph recommends that one turn to God or to Christ and directly address to either one a prayer suggested by the particular scene of the gospel. The affections stimulated by the imaginative participation in the scene carry over to the present time and to one's personal or social needs. Ludolph wrote out the prayers with which one meditating on the life of Jesus addressed God. Interestingly, Ignatius did not, except in a couple of instances. "The prayers in the *Vita* are largely prayers of petition for spiritual help to practice virtue."[15]

Thomas à Kempis. Thomas à Kempis, a monk who was born in the Netherlands in 1380, wrote the immensely popular *Imitation of Christ,* which Ignatius loved and had with him at Manresa. This book represents in classic form the spirituality typical of northern Europe in the fifteenth century. Some of its qualities parallel those found in the Spiritual Exercises. For example, it is resolutely christocentric and marked by an affective devotion to Jesus as he appeared in his earthly ministry. This spirituality involves discipline, meditation, and consistent practice of virtue. "In the morning thou shalt take a good purpose for that day following, and at night thou shalt examine diligently how thou hast behaved thee, in work, in deed, and in thought."[16] À Kempis encourages self-knowledge and awareness of one's obligations. "Where art thou when thou art not present to thyself?" (IC, 2.5). Ignatius did not accept the whole package, by any means, but parts of this straightforward following of Jesus spirituality deeply affected him.

García de Cisneros. Ignatius found another source in the writing of the Benedictine abbot García de Cisneros, and his confessor, Chanon, who could explain Cisneros to him. Through Cisneros, Ignatius would be exposed to some classic schools of spirituality: "the Benedictine tradition with its liturgical ordering of time; the Carthusian tradition, source of the ascending sequence *reading, meditation, prayer,* and *contemplation;* the Franciscan tradition with its devotion to the humanity of Christ; the New Spirituality of the time (*Devotio Moderna*) with its methods of interiorizing prayer; and as a patrimony common to all these, the mystical tradition of the *three ways,* which goes back to Denys the Areopagite."[17] These three ways, often seen as ascending

---

15. Bodenstedt, *Vita Christi,* 128. See also 123.

16. Thomas à Kempis, *The Imitation of Christ,* ed. Edward J. Klein (New York: Harper & Brothers, 1941), Book 1, Chap. 19. Citation in the text by book and chapter.

17. Javier Melloni, *The Exercises of St Ignatius Loyola in the Western Tradition* (Leomin-

stages of progress in the spiritual life, refer to self-discipline (purgative), interior illumination and growth in wisdom (illuminative), and finally a union with God (unitive) that could be described in various ways, including mystical union. Later Ignatius associated the first week of the Exercises with the purgative way and the second week with the illuminative way (SE, 10).

Javier Melloni hypothesizes that, when one compares the Spiritual Exercises with a spirituality that understands human life growing closer to God by stages of self-discipline, spiritual enlightenment, and surrender to union with ultimate reality, Ignatius manifests a striking departure from the pattern. For him union with God is forged by a union of wills mediated by a process of discernment of God's will and a decision to embrace it in action.[18] It would be hard to imagine that Ignatius during the period at Manresa had already formulated this idea in such clear conceptual terms. But it would be plausible to look for embryonic traces of such a formula operating in the early composition.

Two Key Considerations. Most commentators agree that two complementary considerations provide the principal architectural ideas that shape the Exercises; they constitute or are part of the root metaphor that controls the narrative logic of the whole construction. They are called "The Call of the Temporal King" and "The Two Standards." They will be the subjects of a good deal of commentary in future chapters. But it is relevant at this point to raise the question of where they came from, especially since historians believe that in one form or another they were in place when Ignatius left Manresa. Ganss notes that an imitation, or following, of Jesus Christ represents a standard formula for Christian spirituality. But Ignatius, internalizing this through his particular lens, "saw him as the inspiring King sent by his Father on a mission to conquer the world, in order to win all humankind to faith and salvation; and calling for cooperators who would volunteer for this enterprise."[19] He highlighted the combative character of this struggle by insisting on a dualism that drove history, the conflict between good and evil forces. The followers of Christ's banner

---

ster Herefordshire, UK: Gracewing, 2000), 11. The Denys mentioned here is the Pseudo-Dionysius referred to in Chapter 1, n. 15.

18. Ibid., 52-54. "Both knowledge and affectivity are mobilized and worked on from the beginning of the Exercises. Both converge upon the act of election, where knowledge of the will of God is converted into a volitional impulse of the exercitant to commit him- or herself to it. Hence the way to union with the will of God implies simultaneously a progressive unifying of the whole person." Ibid., 54.

19. Ganss, *Ignatius of Loyola*, 32-33.

would "help to win over those who, following the banner of Satan, were caught by his characteristic snares."[20]

Hugo Rahner offers a relatively coherent interpretation of how several factors found in Ignatius's sources and in his previous life experience came together at Manresa and generated these thematically defining ideas. The last chapter indicated how his service to a royal lord and the logic of conversion made the shift of allegiance to Christ the king an appropriate metaphor. His reading about Augustine's division of history into two cities or kingdoms in Jacob de Voragine's lives of the saints must have made perfect sense of the competition between good and evil spirits that Ignatius experienced at Loyola and again at Manresa. The battle between higher forces of good and evil had much more immediate significance in late medieval European culture than it does today. Finally, these illuminating experiences at Loyola and Manresa must have helped a jumble of things fall into place in a somewhat coherent picture and plan: Christ the leader, an intense desire to serve him, in a way conceived in military terms, and with a total dedication to the highest degree, in a dualistic world of competitive forces, that were also operative within, so that they constantly tested a person's resolve.

Juan de Polanco, one of Ignatius's later assistants and his biographer, tells us how the experiences of illumination and understanding synthesized and integrated what he had learned in the course of his experiences from Loyola to Manresa. Here is Polanco's account of the most significant riverside experience and its effects:

> He saw in a marvelous manner into the divine mysteries. This light was extended also to the power of discernment between good and evil spirits, and was so overwhelming that he beheld, so it seemed to him, all human and divine things with wholly new eyes of the spirit. . . . Thereupon he set himself to devise a plan or method for purifying the soul from its sins by contrition and confession, for meditation on the life of Christ and making a right election of a state of life and of all other things, and for progressing in everything which tended to inflame the soul more and more with love of God. In this way he created a little book of very great profit for the salvation of his neighbor.[21]

---

20. Ibid., 33.

21. Polanco, *Life of Ignatius Loyola*, cited by Hugo Rahner, *The Spirituality of St. Ignatius Loyola: An Account of Its Historical Development* (Westminster, MD: Newman Press, 1953), 53.

This testimony of Polanco relative to Manresa also describes rather precisely the core of Ignatius's Spiritual Exercises in their final form.

Rahner adds to this the testimonies of Jerome Nadal, another assistant of Ignatius late in his life, to the effect that this illumination communicated a kernel that sparked everything that came after it. "Above all, the ideal of the King and the Two Standards, with which Iñigo was already familiar even before this date, takes on a wholly new meaning in the whole of this constructive refashioning of the Spiritual Exercises."[22] Rahner specifies this as a shift from a concern for holiness to a concern for service in the church and for helping others. Ignatius moved from a self-centered desire to imitate Christ in an ascetic and self-perfecting way to entering into the cause of Christ in the church and in the world of the day.[23] In the course of his stay at Manresa, his emerging desire to "help souls" or be of help to others becomes formulated as a noble cause or project. The Exercises would become a manual for pursuing that goal and helping others to do so as well.

Discerning Spirits and Making an Election. The ability to discern and judge the character of the movements he experienced first at Loyola and then at Manresa came with practice. In this area Ignatius felt that he was slowly being taught by God. In his *Autobiography* he refers to critical discernment of the spirits as an experience from Loyola that found its way into the Spiritual Exercises. He links this discernment particularly but not exclusively with making life decisions. Ignatius's scribe says, "He told me that he derived the elections in particular from that diversity of spirit and thoughts which he had at Loyola when he was still suffering in the leg" (AB, 99). This linkage shows that at Manresa he already implicitly possessed the titular formula that describes the goal of the Exercises, which in the present-day text reads: "Spiritual Exercises to overcome oneself, and to order one's life, without reaching a decision through some disordered affection" (SE, 21). Disordered affections are effects of negative spirits that have to be discerned and overcome if persons are properly to order their lives.

The correspondences between Ignatius and his sources could be drawn out further. But these broad lines of connection begin to fill out this first description of the Spiritual Exercises: considerations of the scenes of Jesus' ministry, death, and resurrection, within a chris-tocentric biblical worldview of creation and salvation, shaped par-ticularly toward providing a series of practices, which will aid people

---

22. Jerome Nadal, cited by Rahner, *The Spirituality of St. Ignatius Loyola*, 54.
23. Rahner, *The Spirituality of St. Ignatius Loyola*, 54-58.

to order their lives and direct them according to the pattern of life modeled by Jesus.

Ignatian Language

Thus far, Ignatius's Spiritual Exercises have been presented as a series of meditations on the Jesus of the gospels. These lie embedded within the framework of the interpretive Christian story and involve a two-fold christocentrism. Ignatius ordered the considerations of Jesus into four phases: after a preparation the exercitant turns to the life, death, and resurrection of Jesus. The distinctive character of Ignatius's slant on this material resulted from his conversion and the sources he used to formulate his experiences. The best way to introduce how his interpretive framework materialized in the text will be to explain the distinctive meditations he uses to structure his presentations of Jesus. Ignatius inserted into his Exercises six topics for reflective meditation that, like a skeleton in a body, give the meditations on Jesus their particularly Ignatian form. Of equal importance are three topics that do not appear condensed into a single meditation but are themes describing either a whole week of meditations or a specific idea. They should be added to the six because of their importance to the basic logic of the Exercises. A comparison with the Table of Contents, Part II, will show where each of these considerations appears in the whole course of meditations.[24] These topics will be treated more extensively in later chapters and in the reflections.

Principle and Foundation. This consideration lies at the beginning of the series of Exercises and functions according to its name. It states a shared cultural and religious supposition of a stable world. It represents the metaphysical principle that all human beings exist in order to move to their appointed destiny of happiness with God. I have changed its title to "Looking for Principles and a Foundation" because this reflects more accurately the culture of those to whom this interpretation of the Exercises is addressed. Most commentators think that this consideration was in place when Ignatius left Manresa. But its formulation in the final text bears a precision that could only have been gained by reworking it.

---

24. The names of these meditations as they appear in the Table of Contents have been altered but not beyond recognition. They appear in the text here with the names that Ignatius gave them. For example, Ignatius's Principle and Foundation becomes Looking for Principles and a Foundation.

Consideration of Human Sin and God's Mercy. This is not a single distinctive consideration but a topic spread across the whole first week. It appears dramatically in the meditation on sin in the form of a conversation with God in the form of Jesus on the Cross who has died for my sins (SE, 53). But this theme possesses major significance in the logic of the Exercises as a whole. Human beings have failed in their purpose, but are forgiven and empowered to move forward. It has been appropriated in the meditations of the First Week, "Stories of Sin" and "Jesus' Story of Divine Forgiveness."

The Call of the Temporal King. Many commentators identify this consideration as the quintessential Ignatian meditation. It picks up the motive of gratitude for God's forgiveness and shows how people can reshape their lives. It negotiates the transition from the First to the Second Week by comparing Jesus Christ with a temporal sovereign inviting companion knights to join him in a noble cause. The elaborate analogy resonates with Ignatius's life and provides the motivational impetus for the considerations of Jesus that follow. It sets up the contemplations of the ministry of Jesus that define the content of his project. This meditation appears in the Table of Contents with the name "Jesus as Leader: Following Christ."

The Two Standards. This meditation shares the imaginative background of "The Call of the Temporal King" and identifies further the terms of the struggle between Christ and Satan, good and evil. It has a binary simplicity that pushes a person toward considering options. In the Table of Contents this meditation has the title "Two Types of Life."

Three Classes of Persons. This meditation presents a typology of responses to Jesus' leadership in ascending degrees of commitment. It can be inserted anywhere in the stream of considerations of Jesus' ministry. It is designed to question the motivation of the one making the Exercises. These examples of commitment challenge those making the Exercises to become explicitly aware of and assume responsibility for their own degree of dedication. The meditation appears in the Table of Contents as "Three Types of People."

Three Ways of Being Humble. This meditation, analogous to the last one, also offers a typology of three degrees of commitment to stimulate self-examination. The three examples of people proposed in the meditation, all of which are positive, represent increasingly intense commitments to Jesus and his cause. The meditation assumes that a personal relationship with Christ has been established and explores the rationale and the degree of the commitment. The broad audience for this presentation of the Exercises partly explains the new title in the Table of Contents, "Three Ways of Commitment."

The Passion and Death of Jesus. This topic is not a single particular meditation proposed by Ignatius but the subject matter of the Third Week of the Exercises. It presents an essential element of both the Jesus story and the Christian story. The two meditations of the Third Week that most directly engage this topic are entitled "Jesus' Torture and Execution" and "The Significance of Jesus' Death."

The Easter Experience and Resurrection. In the same way, this topic is the subject matter of the Fourth Week and, like the last, essential to the Christian story. The importance of this topic for the Christian vision cannot be overstated: this experience and belief account for the rise of Christianity. The first few meditations of the Fourth Week all raise up aspects of this subtle spiritual experience and belief.

Contemplation to Attain Love. Ignatius presents this consideration as the concluding exercise of the program. The contemplation builds on the doctrine of creation and God's being present to and working within the finite order. Many commentators would agree that the three considerations—Principle and Foundation, Call of the Temporal King, and Contemplation to Attain Love—together contain the uniquely Ignatian formula for understanding the content of the gospel narrative. Or, phrasing the same idea a bit differently, these three meditations define in a radically condensed form the operative lens by which Ignatius interprets the Christian story in his Spiritual Exercises.

These nine themes or topics provide a way of conceiving the essential logic of the Spiritual Exercises. The next chapter will develop that proposition in more detail. At this point the progression of these topics shows how Ignatius converted his spiritual experiences into what developed into the program of the Exercises. While they define the core of the book, *The Spiritual Exercises* also contains elements that play a supporting role.

Other Ignatian Devices and Instructions

The Spiritual Exercises contains instructions on different aspects of spiritual life generally, directions for the comportment of one approaching the Exercises, and guidelines for the director who accompanies a person or group through them. The terms in this section refer to Ignatian ideas and conventions that are part of this spiritual world.

Some terms are more important than others, and still others may not be applicable. But practices and procedures such as the discernment of spirits and ways of approaching a life decision approach the heart of Ignatian spirituality. Each of these elements will be discussed in later chapters in measures appropriate to their importance. The point here is to introduce the language.

Annotations and Additions. The unfamiliar term "Annotations" refers to "Introductory Explanations," a translation that states succinctly exactly what they are. They explain the nature and purpose of the Spiritual Exercises, how they unfold, the dispositions needed to make them, the strategy of a director, and various possible adaptations in their presentation.[25] "Additions" are recommendations of certain practices to keep the attention of the person focused on communion with God. Their full title expresses what they are: "additional directives for making the Exercises better and finding more readily what one desires" (SE, 73).

Prayer. Ignatius has much to say relative to prayer. His conceptions and directives are spread throughout the Exercises. Prayer consists in focusing the mind and affections on God and being intentionally before God either in words or wordless presence. In the course of the Spiritual Exercises Ignatius presents several different *methods of prayer.* A method of prayer holds up a process or procedure of entering into a conscious relationship with God. Vocal prayer usually refers to pronouncing or reading prayers already written. This could be done by an individual in solitude or publicly in a group. By contrast mental prayer goes on in the silence of a person's inner consciousness. In a section at the end of the formal course of the Exercises Ignatius has a section entitled "Three Methods of Prayer." All are forms of mental prayer, but the second and third are ways of using the texts of standard formulas of prayer in quiet, contemplative ways.[26]

As to the first method of prayer, Ignatius gives four examples. The first two are methods of considering one's sins before God that are differentiated by whether one measures oneself by the ten commandments or what are called the "capital sins" or vices that lead to sinful actions, such as pride, covetousness, lust, and others. This form

---

25. Ganss, *Ignatius of Loyola*, 387.

26. "The second method of praying consists in contemplating the meaning of each word of a prayer" (SE, 249). The Lord's Prayer provides a good example. "The third method of praying is to pray according to rhythmic measures." A good example is the "Jesus Prayer," a well-known practice of rhythmically repeating a statement such as: "Jesus Christ, Son of God, have mercy on me."

of prayer is mainly applicable to the first week of the Exercises where one prepares to use them for self-examination, much as Ignatius did at Montserrat and Manresa.

The second and third examples of this first method of mental prayer are quite significant. They are described briefly here and more fully in Chapter 4. The one he calls "Meditation" and the other he calls "Contemplation." These two categories name the principal methods of prayer operative in the Spiritual Exercises.

Meditation may be a generic term, but it is associated in the Exercises with mental prayer. It explicitly calls for the use of memory, intellect, and will to consider a subject matter before God. Within the context of faculty psychology in place at the time, where every conscious act is elicited by a power to perform that kind of act, these refer to the three powers of human consciousness. Memory calls up a subject matter for consideration. For example, persons can recall what they have learned about creation and providence and place it before the mind. Using the intellect, a person can think about, examine, and "ruminate" on it in greater detail. Then a person employs the will in order decisively to react to what has been intellectually and meditatively engaged (SE, 90). This schematic statement does not do justice to the inner depths to which the practice can carry a person or to the possible life-changing insight and experience it can enable.

Contemplation is distinctive in engaging the imagination with reference to sensory images. Ignatius turns to it at the beginning of the second week when the subject matter becomes historical: the stories of Jesus. As we have seen, he learned this technique from Ludolph. This method of mental prayer "consists in attending to the persons, their words, and their actions, largely by use of the imagination. In general, contemplation is viewing or gazing and it stimulates reflections and emotions."[27] Ignatius's instructions are these: "I will see the various persons" (SE, 106); "I will listen to what the persons on the face of the earth are saying" (SE, 107); "I will consider what they are doing" (SE, 108). This imaginative reconstruction leads to reflection, affective response, and willing.

Application of the senses is closely aligned with contemplation, but it may be considered a distinctive method of prayer because it stays more closely tied to detailed imaginative sensory participation. Ignatius appeals to each of the five senses as channels of self-projection

---

27. Ganss, *Ignatius of Loyola*, 402.

into the scenes of the gospels in order to draw profit from the engagement (SE, 122-125).

A *Repetition* designates a retrieval of the fruit from past meditations or contemplations that were moving. Repetition does not mean doing an exercise over again, but recalling significant things that happened subjectively while doing them. The Spiritual Exercises are not about covering ground or completing a course but about staying with considerations that connect a person with what appears as transcendent meaning for his or her life.

Examination of Conscience. An examination of conscience refers to a review of one's life with a special focus on one's failings before God.[28] These sins may be committed by thoughts, words, actions, or omissions in the light of responsibility as measured by the commandments and principal vices, as noted earlier. Ignatius recommends but does not require a *confession*: this refers to a recitation of one's sins before a priest, who mediates God's forgiveness ritually in the sacrament of penance. A *general confession* would cover one's whole life to the best of one's recollection. The system of confession that developed over centuries distinguished between *mortal sins* and *venial sins*. Mortal sins were conscious voluntary actions of such a grave nature that they cut the ties from the human side between the self and God. Venial sins were real sins but of a less drastic nature. Ignatius also proposes *daily examinations of conscience* at morning, noon, and the evening so that a person may assume full responsibility for his or her life and self.

Election. An election refers to what might be called today a "life decision," that is, a decision that sets or fixes the course of the rest of one's life: a permanent commitment. Such life choices were more firmly reinforced by society at the start of the sixteenth century than they are today. The best examples of such options in Ignatius's time were *states of life* that could not be changed, and Ignatius introduces a brief "Introduction to the Consideration on States of Life" in the Exercises (SE, 135). For example, being married or a vowed member of a religious order would be a permanent state of life. Obviously such decisions were large steps. A principal goal of the Exercises is to assist people in making such decisions and, as indicated in the last section, to do so without being influenced by disordered desires. Thus Ignatius

---

28. Ignatius built adaptability into the Exercises. This fixation on sin, especially personal sin, provides a significant area where this adaptation goes on today: many directors place equal or more emphasis on a review of a person's talents and accomplishments.

raises as an ideal condition for making such decisions what he calls *detachment*. Detachment is freedom from dependencies, a state of passionate equilibrium that has freed the self from uncontrolled desires and addictions, and from clinging to things that would compromise a proper response to what is ultimately valuable.

Spirits and the Discernment of Spirits. Spirits and the discernment of spirits have already appeared in Ignatius's lived experience at Loyola and Manresa. He translated his extended experience into some specific conceptions and rules for handling these episodes that make up an important part of the text and the process of the Spiritual Exercises. As noted earlier, the world of Christian Europe was filled with angels and demons. To people of that time, the spirits were real beings who had access to our inner selves. They caused consolation and desolation within the human person. *Consolation* occurs "when some interior motion is caused within the soul through which it comes to be inflamed with love of its Creator and Lord" (SE, 316). *Desolation* is its opposite, "darkness of soul, turmoil within it, an impulsive motion toward low and earthly things, or disquiet from various agitations and temptations" (SE, 317).

In his early wrestling with transcendence Ignatius developed one of the most basic of his principles about these spirits: the spirits are to be judged in terms of their effects and not in terms of their immediate affective quality. The spirit of darkness can appear as a spirit of light. Spirits therefore have to be distinguished by objective considerations of how they interrupt the course of a person's life. Do these impulses of a spirit promote a spirituality consonant with the end for which humans are created and the possibilities of a person's proper response to the "Call of the Temporal King"? Knowing that these were not easy questions, Ignatius elaborated two series of principles that are to help someone work his or her way through spiritual impasses. These are called his *Rules for the Discernment of Spirits,* and he defines them this way: "rules to aid us toward perceiving and then understanding, at least to some extent, the various motions which are caused in the soul: the good motions that they may be received, and the bad that they may be rejected" (SE, 313). Taken together these rules offer perennial insight into ways of gaining self-knowledge and freedom.

Compared to a dictionary, which preserves a culture in abstract schematic form, actual culture unfolds in action, speaking, and prose. So too, Ignatian language begins to live when a people participate in the actual processes described by the manual. This involves working within the recommendations for doing the Exercises, entering into the meditations and contemplations, allowing them to stimulate existential engagement with transcendence, gaining personal self-knowledge and freedom by discerning interior movements, and making some decisions that could be life changing.

The Genius of the Spiritual Exercises

Immersion in the terminology of Ignatius's manual may have communicated an impression of an utterly complex linguistic world that remains impenetrable. Not so. This sixteenth-century book does have terms all its own, but they are hardly different in that regard from any other school of spirituality. This introduction to Ignatius's world of meaning began with the simple formula that, at bottom, the Spiritual Exercises were a series of reflections on the gospel stories of Jesus. The description of that core expanded with its division into weeks following the career of Jesus, and the key formative considerations that he used to shape the whole series of gospel stories. All the attendant devices serve the essential substance: contemplations of the stories about Jesus. As a conclusion to this introduction to the Spiritual Exercises, which has taken the form of a *reductio ad simplicitatem*, a simplification, one more quality can be noted, which ultimately has its grounding in Jesus of Nazareth. As in the story of Jesus, the genius of Ignatius's Exercises lies in their openness to all. I noted this earlier, but it needs explanation.

The Spiritual Exercises revolve around Jesus Christ and have been described as christocentric. They unfold within the Christian metanarrative, which is built on the conviction that Jesus of Nazareth has universal relevance. Ignatius himself had the highest possible Christology; for him Jesus was God. His acceptance of the divinity of Jesus Christ and the terms with which he affirmed it were part of his culture. But the Exercises have a distinctive take on Jesus that makes him approachable by all. This approachability by all is so essential that, if the universal relevance of Jesus were expressed in such a way that it alienated people from him, that formulation would be called into question. The universal relevance of Jesus cannot be understood in a way that excludes or turns people away.

In the Spiritual Exercises Ignatius represents Jesus as one to be followed. This entails a concentrated attention on his earthly existence and his complete participation in the human condition without reservation.[29] Ignatius related to Jesus as a human being without in any

---

29. Some Christians might react to this idea with the conviction drawn from Christian scripture that Jesus was sinless. The meaning of this sinlessness can certainly bear further discussion. But whatever one means by sin, as a defect it does not make one more but less fully human.

way compromising his divine provenance. Thus far he was firmly within the tradition of the following of Christ. But unlike much of that literature, Ignatius did not read in Jesus withdrawal from the world or society. Quite the opposite. Ignatius sought engagement in society, and he read in Jesus the way to do it. Still more strikingly, Ignatius proposed Jesus as a leader, in fact, a militant leader, who engaged the world actively and aggressively. Ignatius envisioned Jesus as an attractive figure with a project of the highest worth, so that persons would relate to him by joining him and aligning themselves with his cause. Ignatius does not generally propose Jesus as one to be worshiped but as one to be followed, although these are not exclusive and no antithesis is intended here. In fact, apart from a possible sacramental confession of sin at the start, the Exercises contain practically no sacramental spirituality in striking contrast with à Kempis's *Imitation of Christ*.[30] The first mark of the openness of the Exercises then lies on their focus on the public character of the person of Jesus and his appeal not to a private spirituality but to a public enterprise.

The second mark of the openness of the Exercises lies in an implied theology of the Spirit and the way the dynamism of the Spirit operates. One way of drawing this to the surface is to move through the dynamics of the discernment of spirits. In his *Autobiography* Ignatius used this language of the discernment of spirits to describe his experience during his time at Loyola. This sphere of experiences proved to be crucial during his long conversion experience. The discernment of spirits represents the most decisive of all his battles, the battle that took place within himself. From that period forward the spirits became symbols for the forces of good and evil. With the term "spirits" Ignatius may have meant real angels and real demons; the symbolism was vivid and the language experiential and realistic. But these spirits could not be directly known. Exactly who and what these spirits were could only be known by discernment: he had to judge which kind of spirit was at work from their effects, and these were affects within him.

In today's Western culture individual spirits appear less real to many, not to all surely, but to those affected by the disenchantment that accompanies secularization. Yet the sphere of the spirit remains meaningful, and spirit language resonates. In Christianity "Spirit" refers primarily to God. God is God, creator, and universally present by virtue of creating, an immanent presence within the world and human beings, so that all the world and every aspect of it subsists in God. This immanence of God, God present and active in finite cre-

---

30. Ignatius, of course, does not exclude sacraments. He even suggests that moving to a secluded place where Mass is available will contribute to the experience (SE, 20).

ation, is called Spirit or God as Spirit, so that the referent of the experience of God "within" is the Spirit of God. Christian language also works in the opposite direction: the experience of authentic spiritual depth bears an implicit reference to God as Spirit. Thus discernment of spirits in modern spirituality comes down to recognizing God as Spirit within a person's life, as distinct from but mixed up with all sorts of "spirits" of the world that draw human beings in directions that alienate the self from the true self and the truly human. The shift that occurred in modern philosophy, from reflection on the external world to reflection on the human subject, presents an open field for discovering the universal possibility of an encounter with God within each person's own being, whether or not individuals can actually name this presence. If God is God, creator of all, then all bear a relationship to God within themselves, a relationship that is real because God as Spirit is the within of all that exists. This deep metaphysics forms an implicit underpinning of Ignatius's Exercises, and it is constantly at work.

This implies that all persons who come to the Spiritual Exercises bear the ultimate subject matter of these Exercises within themselves. Each person carries some relationship to transcendence that can in some degree be experienced within. This modern conception would be hard to establish as such in Ignatius's text, and no clear argument for this construction can be found in Ignatius's explicit consciousness and intention because the premises for it were rare.[31] But Ignatius's language can be interpreted as implicitly leaning in this direction to the degree to which he relied on the Holy Spirit. Commentators consistently emphasize Ignatius's trust in the Spirit in the Exercises. It enabled him to leave behind the didacticism of Ludolph. Ignatius did not dictate the content of the contemplations on Jesus' life or write out the colloquies,[32] but he trusted the Spirit to awaken them in the person making the Exercises. Directors are not to get in the way of God as Spirit. Ignatius's rules relative to the working of the Spirit are flexible in their respect for individual differences among people and the freedom of God's Spirit. This does not add up to a theology of the uni-

---

31. Few in Ignatius's time had an open theology that was able to discern revelation from God, grace, and the Spirit of sanctity in other religions. The brilliant Cardinal Nicolas of Cusa proposed such a view in the mid-fifteenth century in the wake of the fall of Constantinople, but one does not sense that he expressed a common view. See Nicholas of Cusa, *Nicholas of Cusa on Interreligious Harmony: Text, Concordance and Translation of De Pace Fidei*, ed. James E. Beichler and H. Lawrence Bond (Lewiston, NY: Edwin Mellen Press, 1990).

32. Ludolph's presentations of the scenes of Jesus' life were highly elaborated. As for the colloquies, two notable exceptions are found in the words that Ignatius suggests for one's response to the Call of the Temporal King and the Contemplation to Attain Love.

versal effectiveness of the Spirit, but from Ignatius's trust in the Spirit present-day interpretation can conclude that the openness described here carries his thinking forward.[33]

The goal of the Spiritual Exercises is to help persons become conscious of and personally responsible for this relationship to God at work within as Spirit through the mediation of Jesus of Nazareth even when this ultimate reality is known by another name. This mediation in its turn should be understood within the sphere of the openness of human subjects, in their individuality and social situation, and the activity of the Spirit animating them. The genius of the Spiritual Exercises lies in their moving through Jesus to an openness to God as Spirit.

---

33. The theme of the internal Spirit of God and the human ability to "discern" runs so consistently in the Exercises that it could serve as a basis for an Ignatian "method" of theology. See Christoph Theobald, "Une manière ignatienne de faire de la théologie: La théologie comme discernement de la vie authentique," *Nouvelle revue théologique* 119 (1997), 375-96; Eng. trans. in *The Way* 43.4 (October 2004), 146-60, and available online at http://www.theway.org.uk/back/434Theobald.pdf.

CHAPTER THREE

The Logic of the Exercises

The Spiritual Exercises of Ignatius Loyola sprang from his conversion. His composition of the early drafts was part of the process of his appropriation of that religious experience. The previous
chapter introduced some of the language that Ignatius drew from
his sources to record his experience. These initial formulations then
evolved over the next two decades. This chapter analyzes the logic of
the final product.

The meaning of the term "logic" remains somewhat loose. It refers
to a coherent representation of the whole course of meditations. On
the one hand, from various perspectives interpreters have offered
theories about what Ignatius intended the Exercises to accomplish and
what goes on when one makes them in their integral form. On the
other hand, the Exercises assume the particular dynamics of anyone
who undertakes them. Because Ignatius envisioned them as adaptable
to the persons making them and to the movements of the Spirit in each
person's life, one cannot speak of a single logic of the Exercises. The
text is intrinsically variable in its effects.

Exploring the idea of a logic, however, serves the goal of transparency in the interpretation that underlies this book. Several logics
thread through the Exercises and hold them together, and the interpretation given here does not aim to be exclusive or exhaustive. This
chapter represents these Exercises holistically in order to show that
a number of organizing structures can be seen at work within them.

The discussion begins with a description of three comprehensive views of the Exercises. It then follows the principal stages of the
unfolding of the Exercises that were introduced in the last chapter.
The meditations and contemplations have a narrative substructure as
they follow the story of Jesus within the larger Christian story.

A View of the Whole

Many commentators work within a comprehensive theory of the Exercises that recapitulates them and provides a framework that organizes
their many parts. Such theories operate from distinctive points of view,

and they do not have to be considered in exclusive terms. The following three representations of the Exercises from different perspectives all contribute to an analytical description of what they entail.

A "salvation history" view of the Exercises focuses on their content, their specifically Christian provenance, and the narrative that defines them. In this view the Spiritual Exercises provide a concentrated program that mirrors the Christian story and leads the people making them through the stages of the Christian narrative. The Christian story has two dimensions and both are operative. On a most comprehensive metaphysical level it refers to the grand narrative for understanding reality: creation, sin, salvation, church, and the endtime. More particularly, it refers to the scriptural story of Jesus: his ministry, his destiny, and the development of a movement that keeps him alive in history. The Exercises reproduce those New Testament stories of Jesus and through them draw people into the great plan of human history. "To bring order into one's life, then, means to become aware, in the light of the divine truth, of one's creaturehood with all that it implies, and consequently to insert oneself into the magnificent plan of the Creator and Redeemer, into the history of salvation."[1] This description of the exercitant's purpose fits neatly with this first view of the whole. Jesus of Nazareth provides the answer to the anthropological quest for a coherent meaning of history.

A second holistic interpretation, the "anthropological" view, comes from a theological anthropology with deep roots in Augustine's appropriation of Neo-Platonism that in effect contains a Christian philosophy of religion. Human existence dynamically interacts with the world through knowledge, desire, and action. The ceaseless quest for the true and the good is driven by a basic instinctual desire to know, will, possess, and *be* absolutely. These dynamisms become actualized in and through human freedom that passes into decision and action. Human freedom on this understanding refers to the ontological condition of a person, the basic ground of self-consciousness and self-actualization. This human transcendence of matter and determinism can also be called "spirit." Human existence actualizes itself by its personal and communitarian self-disposition. On this premise, the Spiritual Exercises most fundamentally provide a program for decision making, for a taking possession of the self and directing it toward the highest imaginable goal, in order that, in the end, persons unite themselves with what they perceive to be absolute value.[2]

---

1. Cusson, BTSE, 92.

2. Some examples of this understanding are Gaston Fessard, *La Dialectique des Exercices Spirituels de Saint Ignace de Loyola* (Paris: Aubier, 1956); Edouard Pousset, *Life in Faith and Freedom: An Essay Presenting Gaston Fessard's Analysis of the Dialectic of the Spiri-*

A third description of the Exercises, the "social/historical" view, comes out of the perspective of the persons who make them, and it works within the framework of the first two. It does not regard the Exercises as a system but describes what people do when they make the Exercises. This view stems from a perspective that is conscious of the contingency of history. The Spiritual Exercises appear as a program in which persons correlate their stories with the stories of Jesus of Nazareth in a dialogue of mutual exchange that enhances life before ultimate reality. The mutually critical fusion of narratives opens up new possibilities for freedom. The key to this understanding of the Exercises lies in their narrative character and how that gets translated into the lives of those who make them. The Exercises are a school of life before the ultimate.[3]

These three abstract interpretations of the Exercises work together. Humanistically, the Exercises present a program aimed at the highest possible actualization of freedom, which occurs within the framework of the Christian story, by a process of existentially entering into the stories of Jesus of Nazareth. The following sections show more directly how these logics play out by describing the meditations that serve as markers and turning points in the course. In each case the reader can consult the indicated Reflection in Part II.

Principle and Foundation[4]

The consideration Principle and Foundation stands at the beginning of Ignatius's Spiritual Exercises. As the title suggests, it governs the whole program, and theories of the Exercises reflect that. In the words

---

tual Exercises of St. Ignatius (St. Louis: Institute of Jesuit Sources, 1980); James L. Connor, ed., *The Dynamism of Desire: Bernard Lonergan and the Spiritual Exercises of Saint Ignatius* (St. Louis: Institute of Jesuit Sources, 2006), 37-50; John English, *Spiritual Freedom: From an Experience of the Ignatian Exercises to the Art of Spiritual Direction* (Guelph, ON: Loyola House, 1982), 45-55.

3. This view draws inspiration from the hermeneutical theories of Hans-Georg Gadamer and Paul Ricoeur and adapts them to narratives. Works that are representative of this move are Hans-Georg Gadamer, *Truth and Method* (New York: Seabury, 1975); Paul Ricoeur, "Appropriation," in *Hermeneutics and the Human Sciences*, ed. J. B. Thompson (Cambridge: University Press, 1981), 182-93; idem, "Toward a Narrative Theology: Its Necessity, Its Resources, Its Difficulties," in *Figuring the Sacred: Religion, Narrative, and Imagination* (Minneapolis: Fortress, 1995), 236-48; Stephen Crites, "The Narrative Quality of Experience," *Journal of the American Academy of Religions* 39 (1971), 291-311.

4. The text of the consideration Principle and Foundation is found in Part II, Reflection 1 (II.1). The meditations are referred to here by the names Ignatius gave them. In Part II the reflections on them have titles that better represent the interpretation that is proffered.

of Luis de la Palma, a commentator, "It is called a *principle* because in it are contained all the conclusions which are later explained and specifically expounded; and it is called a *foundation* because it is the support of the whole edifice of the spiritual life."[5] The Principle and Foundation stipulates the goal of human existence, the means to attain this goal, the method of purifying one's freedom for authentic self-disposition, and the norm for making right choices.[6] Because it is so basic, each of the perspectives seen in the three interpretations of the Exercises illumines a distinct facet or possibility within this consideration.

Looking at the Principle and Foundation in terms of the objective content of the vision contained in Ignatius's text reveals it to be a succinct statement of the divine plan of creation and salvation history. The consideration announces all at once the strategy of the Exercises: to enable a person to fit his or her life into the pattern of creation and salvation. From beginning to end, throughout the contemplations of the narratives of Jesus' ministry, the Principle and Foundation is never superseded: it describes what is going on all the time. People are to order their lives by assuming their part in the creator's plan of the universe, first by identifying with Jesus, and then by ordering their own lives accordingly. The Principle and Foundation contains the double-sided structure of the Exercises themselves, namely, God's project and the appropriation of it by human beings: "the expanse of the divine plan with its attractive goal in which we are involved, and God's invitation to us to take our own part in it."[7]

From the perspective of the anthropological point of view, Ignatius's Principle and Foundation addresses the meaning and purpose of human existence. The text should be read in close connection with the intent of the Exercises to address these issues. The Exercises aim at helping persons take possession of themselves, rid themselves of addictions, and make the free decisions that will determine their future (SE, 21). The Principle and Foundation restates the basic disposition one should bring to them: complete openness to the desires of God (SE, 5). The idea of the purpose of the Exercises clarifies the program as a process that leads to a decisive commitment reorienting a person's whole life. All the elements of the Exercises are marshaled toward breaking the attachment to things that constrict human freedom, allowing reflection on values and feeling for ideals to attract freedom in a new direction, and then finally taking hold of the self in a decision that

---

5. Cited by George E. Ganss, ed., *Ignatius of Loyola: The Spiritual Exercises and Selected Works* (Mahwah, NJ: Paulist Press, 1991), 393 n. 18.

6. Ibid.

7. Gilles Cusson, *The Spiritual Exercises Made in Everyday Life: A Method and a Biblical Interpretation* (St. Louis: Institute of Jesuit Sources, 1989), 32. Cited hereafter as SEMEL.

changes, reorients, or rededicates a person's trajectory. The many factors involved in the Exercises all converge on a climactic self-disposition in a life decision. A decision like this does not leave the principles
behind: "the Foundation is never superseded. It remains a basic point
of reference throughout the Exercises—and throughout life."[8]

Approaching the Principle and Foundation from the perspective of
a seeker who identifies with a postmodern culture suggests a social/
historical interpretation of it. An evolutionary context and a radical
historical consciousness challenge the purposefulness and stability that suffuse Ignatius's text. Genuine seekers often presuppose
relativity and plurality and seek meaning within and not apart from
this situation. "Ignatian spirituality speaks to postmoderns because
it is based on a personal, imaginative exploration of the gospel, and
it invites people to choose freely to deepen their intimacy with God
through a deepened understanding of who they themselves are."[9]
This approach will reorient the seeker from an attempt to internalize an objective vision and favor a more personal engagement with
Jesus of Nazareth. Three qualities of the seeker will thus transpose
the Principle and Foundation into another register: objective teachings
become imaginative constructs that invite new possibilities of meaning; the closure suggested by the discovery and election of a single
path mapping one's destiny cedes to a fundamental openness and
receptivity stemming from a dialogue with Jesus; and constant desire
for self-transcendence in the face of challenging ideals remains a guiding principle.[10]

All three perspectives on Ignatius's Principle and Foundation shed
light on the logic of the Exercises and how they move the people who
make them.

Sin and Grace

The heading Sin and Grace is not the name of a specific consideration in Ignatius's Spiritual Exercises but one of the dominant themes
of the First Week. During this week Ignatius proposes five discrete
meditations: on (a) the three prototypical sins of the angels, the first
humans, and a typical damned soul, (b) a review of the retreatant's

---

8. Michael Ivens, *Understanding the Spiritual Exercises. Text and Commentary: A
Handbook for Retreat Directors* (Herefordshire, UK: Gracewing, 1998), 26. This so-called
"anthropological" interpretation of the Principle and Foundation borrows from the
analysis of Ivens. See ibid., 22-23. Cited hereafter as USE.

9. Tim Muldoon, "Postmodern Spirituality and the Ignatian *Fundamentum*," *The
Way* 44.1 (January 2005), 96.

10. These three attitudes are drawn from Muldoon, "Postmodern Spirituality,"
96-100.

personal sins, (c) a repetition of these two, (d) another résumé of the third, and (e) a final meditation on the hell that is earned by sin. We've seen the biographical roots of these considerations at Manresa. They correspond with an emphasis on sin in traditional piety. Theological tradition has put together considerations of creation, sin, and grace to form the subject matter called Christian theological anthropology, a synopsis of the human condition culled from the basic Christian story. On the basis of the Principle and Foundation, which implies a theology of creation, one could consider the whole First Week of Ignatius's Spiritual Exercises as dedicated to anthropology. But the theme of sin and grace plays a large role in the Exercises and deserves comment. Each of three distinct approaches to sin and grace contributes to the importance of this consideration within the logic of the Exercises.

The salvation history interpretation takes the objective content of the text of Ignatius and locates it within the larger Christian narrative of creation, sin, and redemption. In this scenario Ignatius speaks of redemption in terms of personal forgiveness. In the grand scheme of things sin disrupts God's plan for history; but Satan and his work of sin are conquered by Christ; and each retreatant's subjective history merges into the movement initiated by Christ.[11] Beneath the mythological language lies the drama described by Paul of each person being torn between good and evil. The consideration of one's personal history of sin functions realistically to place one squarely within this existential history.

The anthropological interpretation of what is going on in the Exercises immediately turns to the human subject. The extensive self-examination that Ignatius prescribes becomes an extended process of self-appropriation as creature, as a human being, as a moral agent, as virtuous, and as morally guilty. A person's taking stock of the self before God promotes a clear-headed responsibility for one's life. But something more is going on beneath the moralism. Human behavior always actualizes a striving for being, for enhanced existence, so that the moral character of someone's action raises the question of where lifestyle places the human person in relation to ultimate reality and personal destiny.[12] The consideration of hell, as inappropriate as that may seem to many today, has the function of vividly raising the question of human destiny.

A social/historical perspective on the human provides a major

---

11. Cusson, BTSE, 138-42.

12. Edouard Pousset puts it this way: "in the person who commits it, sin stems from a will to be and not from a will not to be; the sinner does what he does in an effort to realize himself. But what precisely impels him is a resolve to become himself by and for himself." Pousset, *Life in Faith and Freedom*, 30.

index of how anthropology has developed since Ignatius's time: one cannot understand either the human as such or individual persons apart from their social conditions and relationships. This has led not only to a profound social consciousness and conscience but also to reflections on evil social conditions that, because of their moral provenance, share the quality of sinfulness. The history and pervasiveness of innocent human suffering and human indifference to it challenge the meaningfulness of the human enterprise and call for a thorough revision of the Ignatian language of personal sin.[13]

The social/historical perspective contains more questions. The Christian story of creation as well as the language of original sin, Satan, evil spirits, and hell, even when prefaced with the caution that it is symbolic, can be truly alienating. The classical doctrine of creation and its attendant concepts require thoroughgoing reinterpretation in the light of evolution and the scientific story of the universe.[14] The consciousness of sin in the West compared with Ignatius's time has greatly evolved, and many people, including many who are religious, simply do not have a deep sense of personal sin. Spiritual directors are finding that people talk less about personal sins and that "their sense of such sin has been largely lost."[15] The seeker may have no consciousness of standing before God. Christian anthropology has to be proposed as a hypothesis that generates a deeper level of meaning than can be read off the surface of history. It cannot be presupposed as something that will be recognized by most people today.

In the end, Ignatius has inserted the most attractive and generative aspect of the First Week, a profound sense of gratitude, into the colloquies that conclude two of the meditations (SE, 61, 71).[16] This affective response should arise within a personal exchange with God, and Ignatius proposes that its intensity increases in proportion to the depth of feelings of infidelity that accompany a sense of sin.[17] The strategic

---

13. See Peter McVerry, "The First Week and Social Sin," in *The Way of Ignatius Loyola: Contemporary Approaches to the Spiritual Exercises*, ed. Philip Sheldrake (St. Louis: Institute of Jesuit Sources, 1991), 66 –76.

14. Eduardo López Azpitarte, "Ignatius' Meditations on Sin: From Guilt to Gratitude," *The Way* 47.1 and 2 (January and April 2008), 97-105. J. Matthew Ashley cautions against uses of a "creation story" that absorb rather than respect human responsibility vis-à-vis human suffering in "Reading the Universe Story Theologically: The Contribution of a Biblical Narrative Imagination," *Theological Studies* 71 (2010), 870-902.

15. Francisco J. Ruiz Pérez, "Recommendations for Giving the First Week of the Spiritual Exercises," *The Way* 47.1 and 2 (January and April 2008), 86.

16. The Reflections that take up these Ignatian themes of sin, grace, forgiveness, and gratitude are II.7-8.

17. Cusson, BTSE, 161-64. See also Azpitarte, "Ignatius' Meditations on Sin," 109, 113, and Charles Shelton, "Graced Gratitude," *The Way* 42.3 (July 2003), 138-50.

location of these colloquies in the logic of Spiritual Exercises instills the spirituality they promote with a fundamental moral attitude of gratitude. "The dynamic of the First Week leads to gratitude, the result of a deep and personal understanding of one's place in the cosmic order, as well as to a realization of one's use or misuse of God's gifts."[18]

The Call of the Temporal King[19]

The exercise of The Call of the King marks the transition from the First to the Second Week of the Spiritual Exercises: from anthropology to engagement with Jesus of Nazareth. It provides the rationale for the contemplations of the stories of Jesus that follow, just as the Principle and Foundation sets up the First Week and everything that follows it. Most commentators would agree that this consideration encapsulates the dynamics of the Exercises, not least because it turns attention to Jesus of Nazareth, who occupies the centerpiece of the Christian vision of reality.

In this meditation Ignatius compares Jesus to a king embarking on the noblest of missions who invites his knights to join his cause. Several characteristics of the way Ignatius presents Jesus in this exercise deserve close attention. To begin, the Exercises normally do not present doctrines about Jesus. The Exercises present the stories of Jesus from the gospels; he appears in and through the narratives. The Exercises most often introduce Jesus of Nazareth, not a heavenly Christ; the stories tell of a first-century Palestinian Jew performing a religious ministry. The rationale behind this strategy revolves around a conception of Christian spirituality as "following Jesus," which is traditionally called "the imitation of Christ." The unstated premise maintains that to be a Christian entails living like Jesus and doing what Jesus did. This supposition explains why Ignatius presents Jesus for the most part not as divine but as a human being in whom retreatants will find patterns of behavior they can internalize. Jesus, Ignatius insists, shares completely in the hardships of human life. Another distinctive characteristic of this keynote exercise revolves around Jesus' ministry. Ignatius presents Jesus as an activist engaged in his world. This stands out against a background of many spiritualities of withdrawal from society and gives an orientation to the narrative presentation of Jesus. Finally, behind all this and presupposed lies the place of Jesus in the Christian story and imagination: God empowers Jesus, so that Jesus

---

18. Katherine Dyckman et al., *The Spiritual Exercises Reclaimed: Uncovering Liberating Possibilities for Women* (Mahwah, NJ: Paulist Press, 2001), 177.

19. The text of this exercise is found in II.12. The shortened title of this meditation is The Call of the King.

reveals God. So, approaching these stories leads one into an arena that contains the possibility of encountering traces of transcendent reality.

Exactly how one might construe the centrality of this exercise will vary according to different explanations of the logic of the whole program. Distinguishing the three approaches noted earlier helps to communicate the depth and range of this exercise and what it sets up.

When they are viewed in terms of content the Exercises appear to follow the grand narrative of salvation history. The shift to a consideration of Jesus begins the process of drawing those making the Exercises into that story in an existential way; The Call of the King introduces the second part of the Exercises, which focuses on appropriation and identification with Jesus who defines the kernel of the Christian story.[20] Consistent with biblical theology, Ignatius's move in the Exercises corresponds well with St. Paul's view of Jesus Christ as the "New Adam." In this view, Jesus "sums up" a full human life and represents it as the new prototypical human being. It also fits well with the pioneer Christology of the Letter to the Hebrews, in which Jesus assumes the position of leader out in front of others.[21] Jesus reveals a fundamental way of life, and individuals are called to find their niche within this large pattern.

From an anthropological perspective, Jesus in the Exercises reveals God's values and thus the fulfillment of human values. Embracing God's values will fill up the infinite longing underneath all human desires. Jesus, as the archetypal human response to God, models genuine human commitment and authentic exercise of human freedom. The movement of the Exercises toward a life decision supplies the underlying subtext of the contemplations of how Jesus acted. The stories where Jesus consistently acts in service of the values of God in history gradually reveal the character of the option that the Exercises hold out for each person.[22] This anthropological interpretation should be carefully distinguished from moralism. Ignatius does not celebrate the individual acts that Jesus did. He aims at representing what it means to be in the truth by making one's actions resonant with the intention of the universe. One exists in truth by doing the truth. As Jesus was united with the source of being and the life-giving impulse of the Spirit of God, so too the right life decision will set one on a course defined by ultimate values.[23] The anthropological approach

---

20. See Cusson, BTSE, 98.

21. These ideas will be developed further in Part II.

22. Hugo Rahner, *Ignatius the Theologian* (San Francisco: Ignatius Press, 1990), 113-14.

23. Monika Hellwig, "The Call of the King: Conversion to Justice and Peace," *Aspects of the Second Week, Way Supplement* 52 (Spring 1985), 44.

contains a mysticism of action. This will become apparent in the final contemplation.

The social/historical approach of the seeker to the Exercises is defined by a question: what is worthy of the commitment of my freedom? The seeker may be looking for a riposte to the shock of relativity and pluralism: that no position contains all the truth seems to occlude the possibility of truth itself. This approach to the Exercises may not be looking for an absolute way, *the* way, but it does look for some leverage into the question of truth and some ability to cut through society's many layers of inauthenticity and falsehood. The seeker should know that such leverage will not be found on the surface of life or history; to recognize and to grow into acceptance of even a limited perspective on a centering standpoint requires time. But the Exercises presuppose that searching itself is something positive and not a negative, a having in a not-having, and a presence within silence and absence. The Exercises show "respect for God's freedom and for the diversity of times, persons and circumstances."[24] The Exercises present Jesus of Nazareth as a pointer in the direction of meaning for human existence to people whose own stories "do not lie within the conventional, for those whose experience of life and of God drives them somehow beyond the boundaries, beyond what is normal."[25]

The Two Standards[26]

Ignatius introduced the meditation on The Two Standards relatively early in the Second Week, after considerations of the infancy narratives and before the story of Jesus' baptism. Its place in the series of reflections in Part II is a bit later in the Second Week, but it reiterates from a new perspective the direction set by The Call of the King. It expands the imagery of that meditation by dwelling on alternative ways of conceiving human existence so that a person may locate his or her own place.

The two standards are the two banners of Satan and Jesus Christ, leaders of the forces of evil and good. These two warring parties ask retreatants which one they will follow and the degree of their resolve. The meditation provides an almost perfect example of how Ignatius could employ vivid sensible scenes to convey sharply defined alternatives for human commitment. These alternative worldviews, cultures, programs, or lifestyles become internalized in every person, define

---

24. Philip Endean, "The Ignatian Spirituality of the Way," *The Way* 42.1 (January 2003), 9.

25. Ibid.

26. The text of The Two Standards is found at II.17.

the divided self, and create the struggle between egoism and a self-transcending attraction to higher ideals. Ignatius spells out in classical ascetic-moral terms the slippery slope to ruin and the ascending path to salvation. Under the banner of Satan a person moves from wealth, to honor, to pride, and a life of self-seeking and disregard for others. By contrast, the program of the humble king leads from poverty, to humiliation, to humility, and a life of dedicated service to high ideals. The whole program may be described as an ironic but realistic commentary on society's view of upward and downward mobility in which up is down and down is up.[27]

The extravagant pictorial naiveté of this medieval meditation conceals its extraordinary power. The classic character of these alternatives enables them to cut deeply into everyone's experience, whether in a feudal society or in a highly complex neo-capitalist industrial world economy of consumers. Moreover, these considerations transpire in the presence of ultimacy: the questions being addressed here are not merely moral but spiritual, the questions of being and destiny. In entering this meditation a person asks to be able to find a way.[28]

Ignatius inserted two further meditations into the series of contemplations of the stories of Jesus engaged in ministry. They are the Three Classes of Persons and the Three Degrees of Being Humble, seen in the last chapter. Both are introduced in the course of Week Two in order explicitly to stimulate the connection between the motivation of the retreatant seeking light in his or her existence and the narrative of Jesus. They expand the themes and logic of The Two Standards, and both help set up the moment when retreatants are asked to make a life decision.

Three Classes of Persons.[29] Ignatius composed this exercise in Paris, where he learned how real the attractions of wealth and social status were for his talented fellow students.[30] He defines the three classes or

---

27. Dean Brackley, *The Call to Discernment in Troubled Times: New Perspectives on the Transformative Wisdom of Ignatius of Loyola* (New York: Crossroad, 2004), 90-104.

28. It is fair to say that love of God and love of self are too often represented as antagonistic to each other in sixteenth-century spirituality, Protestant and Catholic. But love of God does not include self-hatred, and one should love oneself more because of God's love rather than less. That being said, the antithesis between egocentrism and self-transcendence is always instructive. See English, *Spiritual Freedom*, 164. Attention to the spiritual level of freedom being engaged in The Two Standards does not deny that psychological dynamics are also in play here. For an analysis of The Two Standards in terms of psychological self-actualization, see Kenneth L. Becker, "Beyond Survival: The Two Standards and the Way of Love," *The Way* 42.3 (July 2003), 125-36.

29. The text of this meditation is at II.22.

30. Ivens, USE, 113-14; Cusson, BTSE, 260-62.

types of persons by the way they relate to the acquisition of a substantial sum of money. Will they surrender by degrees to its lure or achieve a genuine internal freedom in its regard? Through the focus upon an instinctive attraction to external possessions that promise security,[31] the meditation becomes a self-examination of the purity of one's freedom from attachments to "things" and through them an imprisoning self-love.

Three Degrees of Being Humble.[32] The context and subtlety of this consideration require far more explanation than these blunt descriptive statements can carry. For example, the humility proposed here has little to do with psychological attitudes, like timidity, that merit disfavor today. By Ignatius's time, the humility spoken of here had a long and deep spiritual pedigree that related it essentially to creature-consciousness, a self-awareness in relation to God.[33] The three degrees of "humility" that Ignatius lays out really refer to "three manners and degrees of love for God and of desire to obey, imitate, and serve his Divine Majesty."[34] The third and highest degree of a love of Jesus expresses itself as a desire so to identify the self with him, for example, in his suffering for his cause, that we imitate him as closely as possible.[35]

These four Ignatian meditations of the Second Week, joined with the Principle and Foundation, form a coherent and powerful set of principles and directions. In fact, many treat them abstractly as constituting a distinctive spirituality. In the Exercises, however, these meditations shape something larger than themselves, a program of imaginatively entering into the ministry of Jesus. If one forgets that,

---

31. Cusson, BTSE, 255-56, with reference to the Two Standards, but the theme is the same.

32. The text of this meditation is at II.27.

33. Brian Daley, "To Be More Like Christ: The Background and Implications of Three Kinds of Humility," *Studies in the Spirituality of Jesuits* 27.1 (January 1995), 1-39, situates the virtue of humility in the ascetic and spiritual tradition up to Ignatius's time. While patristic, monastic, and medieval writers had penetrating psychological insight, the meaning of humility really emerges out of the spiritual or free self-disposition of a person toward the creator. Philip Endean, "On Poverty with Christ Poor," *The Way* 47.1 and 2 (January and April 2008), 47-66, shows how poverty, humility, and an identification with Jesus describe the progression that is illustrated in the meditation.

34. The words of Pedro Ortiz, Legate of Emperor Charles V to Pope Paul III, who made a forty-day directed retreat with Ignatius in 1538 and kept careful notes. Cited in Cusson, BTSE, 264.

35. Beyond obedience to God's commands and the ideal of complete spiritual freedom posed in the Principle and Foundation, the third degree of "humility" adds a radical identification with and accompanying of Jesus wherever it leads. This is no natural inclination and has to be asked for as gift. Cusson, BTSE, 269.

the consideration on humility, which proposes complete identification with Jesus, will make no sense.

The Discernment of Spirits

From the very beginning, Ignatius wrestled with discernment, and people moving through the Exercises toward a life decision may experience considerable pressure along the way. Over a period of time Ignatius developed some expertise in discerning what was going on inside himself. On the basis of these experiences he developed fourteen rules, or principles, that are more applicable during the First Week and another eight for the Second Week (SE, 313-336). He was addressing "motions" within his experience that came either from within himself or through the influence of what he believed were angels or demons. It is not possible to introduce in a short space an analysis of everything Ignatius was doing with these principles. But they demand some commentary up front on the premise that the topic will come up again in the consideration of "The Election," which follows, and again in Part II.

The discernment of spirits refers to understanding and dealing with what happens within a person in the course of intense spiritual engagement.[36] Judging where interior movements come from and what they mean can be distinguished from making judgments about what they reveal about God or God's will or the content of one's decisions in life. Discernment of spirits is linked to the decision-making process that will be discussed shortly but is distinct from it.[37] The following comments deal only with interpretation of the rules themselves.

Discerning and intelligently appropriating one's moral and religious experience have enormous relevance for life then and now, and Ignatius's treatment of this topic has occasioned a good deal of criticism. For example, on a fundamental level, the projection of the sources of evil outside humanity and the self could undercut human responsibility generally, and particularly for social injustices and oppressions.[38] More positively, looking at other religious methods of spiritual discernment with the help of a community can offset what in the Exercises sometimes looks like the solitary individual locked in a battle within the self.[39] Most important of all, on a practical level, advances

---

36. A selection from the Ignatian text on the discernment of spirit is found in II.28.

37. See Connor, *Dynamism of Desire*, 321-52.

38. Ignatius Jesudasan, "Angels of Light and Darkness," *The Way* 43.3 (July 2004), 71-79.

39. Alan Kolp, "The Clearness Process: A Way Opens," *The Way* 47.1 and 2 (January and April 2008), 175-84. Quaker practices of "clearness circles" can help untie knots of

in psychology help provide a common, tested, and precise language of analysis. Few doubt the astuteness of much of the ascetic tradition from the desert fathers, through Cassian, to Ignatius and beyond. But careful psychological distinctions can be invaluable.[40] Such critical conversation helps in the necessary adaptation of Ignatius's rules to our time.

A deeper theoretical question remains: how can seekers possibly presuppose the influence of God in the complexities of human experience when "ultimate reality" points precisely to what is absent for the seeker? This issue has been addressed extensively, frequently in the context of mysticism, as the possibility of some form of direct contact with God.[41] A language for handling this issue may help an appreciation of these rules for discerning what is going on in religious experience. An openness to and some appreciation of ultimacy form the presupposition for religious and spiritual language, and different thinkers offer many ways of characterizing this appreciation. For seekers, the ultimate refers to that which accounts for the search. This drive or summons forms the horizon for a critical appreciation of what Ignatius called movements within human consciousness. Ultimacy, then, at this primary stage, refers to the horizon of the search for principles and a foundation. Horizons do not appear as objects but precisely as frameworks within which objects are situated. Horizon language should allow people to take interior movements seriously and at the same time subject them to the criticism that any other experience would merit. This solution allows a combination of reverence toward spiritual experience and the critical ability to consider spiritual affectivity as "data for evaluating decisional outcomes" and not as messages from God.[42]

Ignatius throws more light on the process of "discerning spirits" in his outline of ways for making a life decision.

---

confusion within a solitary self and, by interpersonal sharing, offer light and encouragement that releases freedom into agency.

40. Michael J. O'Sullivan, "Trust Your Feelings, But Use Your Head: Discernment and the Psychology of Decision Making." *Studies in the Spirituality of Jesuits* 22 (September 1990), 1-41, gives sound critical advice in the employment of Ignatius's rules.

41. See, for example, Philip Endean, *Karl Rahner and Ignatian Spirituality* (New York: Oxford University Press, 2001), 12-31, 135-53. The meaning of the term "mysticism" is revisited in the discussion of the Contemplation to Attain Love further on.

42. O'Sullivan, "Trust Your Feelings, But Use Your Head," 27. "What we mean by discernment of spiritual consolation is what we know through experiencing, understanding, and judging the movements of consolation." Connor, *Dynamism of Desire*, 352.

The Election

At the end of the Second Week, Ignatius inserts a short treatise on making an election (SE, 169-189).[43] An election is a major decision in one's life, a life decision, either to set the course of one's life in an irrevocable manner or to take hold of it in a new way. The whole course of the Spiritual Exercises leads to such a decision in the purest freedom possible (SE, 21). Every single exercise up to this point, those considered here and all the contemplations of Jesus' ministry, along with the discernment of spirits, aims at freeing a person's freedom from attachments in the face of ultimate reality for this new self-disposition.

Ignatius outlines three methods by which such an election could be made: one in which a person seems gratuitously overwhelmed with certainty, a second in which one comes to clarity by an extensive discernment of spirits, and a third in which a person makes a decision through a marshalling of considerations on every side coupled with clear reasoning in tranquility. With respect to this third method, Ignatius details two distinct procedures for going about these more objective reflections. Because he was convinced that either God as Spirit or angels worked directly in a person, he had more trust in religious affectivity than typically prevails within present secular culture, and he favored the first two methods.

The word *sentire* explains what happens in the "discerning" type of election. It refers to knowing with the heart, a kind of spontaneous knowledge of the divine will by identification with it. Its seeming directness and personal, existential, and engaged character make it a higher form of discernment than the more methodical, objective reasoning process of the third time of election. Other words for this are "prayerful sense," "taste for," appreciation through experience, prayer, and action. Subjective existential engagement with the option being considered is reinforced by positive consolation so that it can be called "affective" knowledge as well.[44] But O'Sullivan, cited earlier, gives reasons for distrusting any uncritical reliance on this form of knowing. In the long run, rather than stressing the distinctions between these "methods," it would be better to notice how they can work together. Methods of discernment should be seen as complementing one another. The reflections on discernment and election in Part II will draw this out.

The Election and the emphasis that Ignatius placed on it in the Exercises raise three large questions that need to be mentioned at this

---

43. A selection from Ignatius's treatise on an election appears in II.29.

44. Hugo Rahner, *Ignatius the Theologian* (San Francisco: Ignatius Press, 1990), 147-51.

point, even though a longer discussion of them has to be postponed: the image of God operative in discernment and making life decisions; the idea of finding God's will for a person's individual life; and the idea of union with God. All three topics involve major spiritual issues.

God was much more accessible to Ignatius than to most reflective people today. The scientific picture of the universe and massive suffering in history do not allow an image of God as a hovering person who intervenes occasionally in the world to work God's will. A naïve image of God as an individual who from time to time acts from the outside has to yield to a more vague "ground of being," or "holy mystery," or "enveloping presence." This infinitely sustaining source of being cannot "intervene" because no place or thing escapes its internal sustenance. In this scheme of things one has to consider the nature of God's accompanying presence and cooperating influence that frequently, in human experience, prompt language of "empowering" or "eliciting" human action. Given the scientific picture of the universe, can a critically reflective language accommodate an experience that God "acts" in the world and draws it forward toward an absolute future?

The sixteenth century, whether exemplified in John Calvin or Ignatius Loyola, drew enormous spiritual stability in the confidence that God had a definite plan for the world and for each person in it, and that one could discern it in some measure. This sense is largely gone today: scientific randomness and the radical experience of contingency have at least seriously modified it.[45] But when Jesus of Nazareth is allowed to point the direction in which spiritual freedom may search, something analogous to what Ignatius understood as providence and the will of God can be retrieved. God's intentions and desires appear more in the form of invitation or solicitation. Jesus holds out to human freedom not a program of God's will but of God's ideals for the human will and the decision to actualize.[46]

The reflections in Part II will develop the idea of a will of God for

---

45. At the same time religious people want and need it in some measure. Reasons for resisting views of evolution lie in a desire that each person's life be embraced by God's providence from the beginning so that each is assigned a role in existence. See Ashley, "Reading the Universe Story Theologically," 873.

46. Joseph Bracken shows that the idea of God's desires is far more fruitful for the spiritual life than a legalistic and objectivist view of God's will. This also fits with a scientific view of the universe and an interpersonal relationship with God. "'God proposes; man disposes.' God, accordingly, is clearly not omnipotent in the classical sense of unilaterally making some *thing* happen. But God is still powerful insofar as God can be and presumably is in many cases persuasive with respect to the self-constituting decision of an independently existing finite subject of experience." Joseph A. Bracken, "God's Will or God's Desires for Us: A Change in Worldview?" *Theological Studies* 71 (2010), 75-76.

human beings in a more existential spiritual context where the topic has more immediate relevance. In the end it makes little sense to speak of God's will for individual persons in a generalized objective way. The meditative portion of this book will introduce concepts of "concrete" knowing, of encountering meaning by "realizing" it through its actualization by freedom in action, and a form of knowing that "possesses" its object through engaged action. All these concepts are crucial for what religious people call "salvation."

Ignatius conceived a life decision that was to be confirmed and lived out as the apogee of the Spiritual Exercises. If the goal of the Exercises was understood as leading to "union with God," that union would consist in a union of wills. In an act of the highest possible freedom a person fuses his or her self with what can best be discerned as the intentionality of human existence portrayed as the desires of its creator. Within the Exercises "the union with God represented by the Ignatian election is not a matter of the extraordinary or the ecstatic, but rather of the whole self's commitment to its relationship with God."[47] Union with God consists in making one's own the rationale of existence itself and making it actual in society by one's behavior.

As noted, Ignatius places his formal consideration of an election or some form of renewed commitment at the end of the Second Week. The Third Week begins by picking up the story of Jesus in Jerusalem before the end. It may be that just as any spiritual resolve will be tested, as Ignatius's certainly was, he wanted the one making the Exercises to accompany Jesus through his ordeal.

Jesus' Death and Resurrection

The death and resurrection of Jesus are not specific Ignatian meditations but topics of the successive Weeks III and IV. Multiple contemplations drawn from the gospel stories fill out each theme. They command a central place in the Spiritual Exercises because they represent a central element of the Christian narrative and Christian self-understanding. On the one hand, the story of Jesus' ministry came to a dramatic climax with his arrest and execution in Jerusalem, an event that left his disciples in confusion and near despair. But the story continued, as some time after his death a group of his disciples experienced him to be alive and raised by God from death. Thus began the Jesus movement, which would gradually part ways with Judaism and develop into Christianity. On the other hand, this story became the basis of a good deal of further theological reflection and interpreta-

---

47. Sylvie Robert, "Union with God in the Ignatian Election," *Ignatian Spirituality and Contemplative Prayer, Way Supplement* 103, ed. P. Endean (May 2002), 110.

tion. Relatively quickly the death and resurrection of Jesus came to be understood together to crystallize the meaning of the whole event of Jesus of Nazareth. By the time of Paul's writings in the 50s Jesus' death and resurrection were understood to capture and reveal human destiny itself and the future of human beings who cling to Jesus in faith. Jesus is the new Adam, the new archetypal human being (Rom 5:12-21). His pattern of life essentially constituted a promise of new life through a death that was faithfully endured (Phil 2:6-11). Gradually Jesus came to be understood as the pioneer, the one who went ahead of human beings showing them the way (Heb 2:10; 6:20).

Ignatius's dwelling on the death and resurrection of Jesus in the Exercises is more striking for its lack of theological reflection than for any theological elaboration. Ignatius of course shared the standard theological convictions of his time, and they implicitly control his contemplations. But he shows far more concern that those making the Exercises form affective bonds with the person of Jesus as the events of his story unfold than for any particular theological construction. Ignatius wants retreatants to be so united with Jesus, as suggested in the third degree of being humble, that they suffer with Jesus' suffering and feel joy with him triumphing over death. In the preludes to the contemplations of Jesus' suffering a person should ask for "sorrow with Christ in sorrow; a broken spirit with Christ so broken; tears; and interior suffering because of the great suffering which Christ endured for me" (SE, 203). In the preludes to the contemplations of Jesus risen the retreatant should ask "for the grace to be glad and to rejoice intensely because of the great glory and joy of Christ our Lord" (SE, 221).

Ignatius's narrative approach to the death and resurrection of Jesus effectively bypasses theological speculation and the doctrines that have grown up around these events. Ignatius wants those making the Exercises to follow the story, to insert themselves into the story, to fuse their own story with that of Jesus' and Jesus' story with their own. Ignatius had an intuitive sense that only when these two stories coalesced in some experienced fashion could the doctrines make any sense. In any case, these two weeks of contemplations are performed within the framework of the life decisions that constitute the Election. They provide a context for those decisions to set and harden.

Mission

The topic of mission is not a distinctly defined consideration in Ignatius's Spiritual Exercises, but a case can be made for inserting it into their logic and presentation.[48] It forms a temporal-historical bridge

---

48. I make this case in Roger Haight, "Expanding the Spiritual Exercises," *Studies*

between the earliest experiences and reactions to Jesus of Nazareth and what an experience of him today might entail.

The symbol "mission" revolves around the idea of sending and being sent. Jesus' ministry implied his being sent by God to proclaim and act out what he called the rule of God. The gospels contain stories in which he sends out disciples to do what he himself was doing. After his death the stories of his appearances, which essentially report the disciples' experience that he was alive in God's sphere, are closely connected with another call to mission. For example, in John's gospel Jesus appears to the disciples who are in a closed room and says, "Peace be with you. As the Father has sent me, even so I send you" (John 20:21). At the end of Matthew's gospel, Jesus appears to the disciples and gives them the so-called missionary mandate to spread the good news to the whole world (Matt 28:19-20). This association of an awareness that Jesus has been raised from death by God, a conviction that this message should be shared among all people, and that people felt delegated to take up this task together represent a deep structure of Christian faith. Without this component in the appreciation of Jesus' ministry, the Jesus movement would never have taken off. So essential is this dimension that some commentators believe it constitutes the resurrection itself.[49]

This analysis of the experience that launched the movement that resulted in the creation of a Christian church contains more than the narrative of a historical development. Something intrinsic to the experience of Jesus and what he stood for is at stake here. In a way the experience that provides the basis for a mission has its origin in the recognition that Jesus' ministry and the values that drove it contain a compelling ideal for human existence. This kind of experience contains within itself an impulse to share it. Such a sharing could transpire in different ways. On the simplest level of response, every real existential embrace of this message will become acted out in some form and degree. It thus becomes implicitly public. A more formal level would entail explicit talk about and formal engagement with the task of communicating and spreading the message.

In fact this mission led to the formation of the church, because an institutional structure was needed to preserve the Jesus movement in history. But being grasped by that mission today may or may not entail joining a church.[50] Rather, this particular offering of the Spiritual

---

in the Spirituality of Jesuits 42.2 (Summer 2010). The Reflections on this topic are II, 38 and 40.

49. This does not represent my view, but I mention it because it illustrates how deep and essential a role this theme of mission plays in the encounter with Jesus of Nazareth.

50. This is a statement of fact rather than principle. On the level of principle it is

Exercises for seekers drives home the point that an authentic encounter with Jesus cannot be reduced to a personal possession but has to elicit some form of action. This gets reinforced in the final contemplation of the Exercises.

Finding God in All Things

The last exercise of Ignatius's Spiritual Exercises is called Contemplation to Attain Love.[51] In this example of creation mysticism Ignatius describes God as suffusing all of creation and, more specifically, acting in it for the benefit of each person. The first meditation of the Exercises, Principle and Foundation, presented creation in metaphysical terms containing principles that describe the coherence in existence. Ignatius returns to creation at the end filled with enthusiasm for the meaning he has found in the story of Jesus. Jesus of Nazareth extends the offer of an interpersonal encounter with God in all things. In many respects providing an analytical account of what is going on in an exercise to promote mystical resonance with the fullness of being intrinsically distorts the desired affect. The following objective description cannot substitute for the existential engagement called for by the exercise.

In this contemplation Ignatius transforms his earlier creation spirituality by setting it in the context supplied by the personal God revealed by Jesus. God cannot be reduced to a metaphysical cause and goal of the processes of being. In contrast to Ignatius, the first principle and foundation of Jesus' teaching has God relating to reality personally. The infinite sustaining ground of being cannot be conceived as *a* distinct limited person, but God is personal nonetheless. This personalism leaves the data of the scientific story of the universe completely intact, but it just as completely transforms its meaning.

From this point of view, God appears as each person's own creator. This perspective redirects the whole story of creation from beginning to its end at this point in time so that it comes to bear on each individual. The cosmic story has brought about everyone's actual standing before God at any given moment. This means that a person can look out on the whole universe and back into the unimaginable time of its evolution and regard the whole dynamic process coming to a point in

---

difficult to conceive a deep, reflective, and serious spirituality that is not public and attached in some way to a community. Without a church the movement would cease to exist in history. But the ways of being a member of a community are many, and participation is always measured by degrees of intensity.

51. The text of this contemplation is found at II.42.

one's own being. The source of this whole process is the personal presence of the creator to the created.

Moreover, because creation refers not to a single initiating act of God but the permanent ongoing dependence of reality on God's creating power, Ignatius presents the world as a medium of interpersonal communication between God and the individual. The world and the things in it are not screens hiding God but media making God present, because God is the within of all that exists.[52]

This contemplative perspective introduces the possibility of what can properly be called mystical experience.[53] It consists in a confluence of what Ignatius calls interior knowledge and a feeling of gratitude for one's being and for being the one who each person is. The meditation is explicitly set up so that a person asks to receive an "interior knowledge of all the great good I have received," so that I will be "stirred to profound gratitude," and this in turn will enable me "to love and serve God's Divine Majesty in all things" (SE, 233). Unlike objective knowledge or erudition, this interior knowledge is subjective, experiential, appropriated, and engaged. This is "felt knowledge, one that identifie[s] with life itself and whose experience [can] only be compared with taste and sensation."[54]

Certain qualities of this interior knowledge seal it as a foundation for a distinctive spirituality. One is its comprehensive character, another its fusion with action, and still another a sense of solidarity and responsibility. Regarding the first, this contemplation does not aim at stirring up a passing emotion but in forming a permanent and fundamental moral attitude. This gratitude cannot be described as a fleeting feeling: the subject matter entirely transcends the here and now to encompass the entire being of a person. The reflective self-awareness of being itself as giftedness elicits a fundamental disposition or durable value response. This becomes a mindset, or a habitual and pervasive outlook, that governs a person's activity, even when it is not formally elicited or explicitly invoked. This enables a person to

---

52. Brackley, *The Call to Discernment*, 216; Ivens, USE, 170; Cusson, SEMEL, 139.

53. Just what is "mystical" experience? This question generates endless debate about its meaning and possibility, all based on different sets of presuppositions. It comes to no resolution. In this work mysticism correlates with any experience of what is truly transcendent. This means that it functions as synonymous with religious experience or formal spiritual experience. This clarifies the meaning of "mystical" here, even though it raises the question of what is "truly" transcendent.

54. Michael Buckley, "The Contemplation to Attain Love," *The Way Supplement* 24 (Spring 1975), 95. For a comparison of Ignatius Loyola's view of contemplation with other Christian masters of the contemplative life, see Josef Sudbrack, "Finding God in All Things," in *Ignatian Spirituality and Contemplative Prayer: Way Supplement* 103, ed. Philip Endean (May 2002), 87-99.

respond out of gratitude "in all things" in response to the intrinsic gift character of a person's whole being.

Turning to gratitude's effectiveness, this new pervasive inclination should shape a person's life: it passes into action. Ignatius lays down the principle: "Love ought to manifest itself more by deeds than by words" (SE, 230). One can go further. Gratitude slides into a response of love in an interpersonal context, and love performs. Love's behavior measures the reality and the authenticity of the virtue. Action makes love pass from being "merely" intentional to being "really" intentional. This pervasive gratitude thus constitutes a mysticism of everyday life by which everyday actions actualize the inner gratitude that governs one's life.[55]

But gratitude in human history can never be pure and undisturbed because of the amount of suffering that marks human life. Individual existence includes personal suffering that leads to death. Each person also exists as a member of the human community, so that integral meaning and gratitude have to incorporate into themselves some kind of reckoning with this history of suffering. An individual cannot really be fully "satisfied" knowing that others are actually suffering in some dehumanizing way. Such is the social character of human existence. Salvation, conceived broadly as integral possession of comprehensive meaning and being, cannot be gained by escape from human solidarity but must be "realized" within it. It is incumbent upon Jesus or any savior figure to hold out meaning to human imagination that can support hope for the self and the human community.

The process of bonding people together extends still further as action forges the union of a person with God. Action, the acting out of a value response, creates a new level of knowing and appreciation which constitutes the "possessive knowledge" referred to earlier. This kind of knowing is analogous to the practical knowledge that comes from handling things, working with them, and thus knowing them from the inside according to how they behave. Through possessive knowledge the objective relationship between knower and known becomes transformed as the object becomes part of the life of the knower. Action promoting the values of the rule of God intimately unites the actors with God.[56]

---

55. "This unity of three moments—interior knowledge or realization, love or affectivity, service or action—constitutes the full goal of the contemplation of the goodness from God." Buckley, "The Contemplation to Attain Love," 96. For Christian believers this spirituality becomes one of service to the reign of God in history. See Jack Costello, "Ignatian Spirituality: Finding God in All Things," *The Grail* 8 (March 1992), 12-32.

56. The idea of "possessive knowledge" is developed by Maurice Blondel, *Action (1893): Essay on a Critique of Life and a Science of Practice*, trans. Oliva Blanchette (Notre

Conclusion

This portrayal of the logic of the Spiritual Exercises of Ignatius Loyola partly explains their status as a classic in Christian spirituality. They have an integral simplicity and integrity. Their depth is such that they continue to generate new experiences that reflect their comprehensiveness. These Exercises are by definition dynamic. Everyone making them embarks on a quest for self-knowledge before the transcendent order. To that searching these Exercises offer in response a mystagogy: that is, they point beyond themselves in a direction toward self-transcendence and ultimacy that can be truly found only through an encounter with the world.

No simple formula synthesizes the logic of the Spiritual Exercises. Several different formulas accurately describe their dynamics in coherent fashion. But they have achieved their status as a classic because their logic includes many aspects and dimensions that interact with one another within the subjectivity of each person who makes them. Surely the Exercises present a Christian spirituality of an imitation of Jesus. They are evangelical in the sense of entering into the symbols and stories of the Bible, especially the gospels, for inspiration on how to live. But such facile descriptions fall far short of what is going on in them. Nevertheless it is hard to resist an attempt to point out in a formal way what the dynamic elements of the Exercises are.

On the level of their large horizon, the most encompassing logic of the Exercises lies in the Christian story. This refers to the holistic vision of salvation history that frequently is presented in the form of a set of beliefs, but whose function in the Exercises is better described as the grand narrative of Christianity. It has a beginning, or grounding, in creation by God, a history of the human race in dialogue with God's intentions and values, and a final goal of return to new life within the very sphere of God. That large narrative has the more particular story of Jesus within it. By an intimate identification with the person of Jesus in his ministry and fate the one making the Exercises encounters the main source from which the larger story was generated and depends. When Christians make the Exercises, this all-embracing metanarrative often tacitly controls everything because it is taken for granted. Proposing these Exercises to seekers throws light on Jesus and brings the inner core of the Christian story out of the shadows.

Dame, IN: University of Notre Dame Press, 1984), 389ff. For example, Blondel says that action mediates and "contains the real presence of what, without it, knowledge can simply represent, but of what, with it and through it, is vivifying truth" (434). How this comes to bear on the Exercises is developed by R. Haight, "Foundational Issues in Jesuit Spirituality," *Studies in the Spirituality of Jesuits* 19.4 (September 1987), 19-20.

Unfortunately, a short study such as this cannot develop the crucial terms of the Christian story in the critical way they should be. Much of this theological reflection has to be left implicit. Nevertheless it is important to notice that when seekers make these Exercises they will enter into dialogue principally with the story of Jesus of Nazareth. In choosing to address the perspective of seekers, the interpretations of the Ignatian Exercises in Part II will not presuppose the transcendent but will allow Jesus of Nazareth to be the place of that encounter.

The second major logic operating in these Exercises was called "anthropological." It finds the distinguishing human characteristic in freedom. It locates the highest form of freedom in active self-appropriation and self-disposition or self-actualization in relationship with value, something good in itself outside the self. Much of the modern and postmodern understanding of freedom, for historical more than reflective reasons, views freedom in competition with a controlling God. By contrast, the Exercises will make sense only when the very idea of God, and thus the Christian story, represent God as the ground and fulfillment of personal and corporate human freedom. Association with Jesus of Nazareth does not restrict human freedom but gives it depth and ultimate importance. The election has the role it does in this logic because it functions as a turning point in which God and God's grace or Spirit support and coalesce with human freedom in an act of self-disposition in relation to the highest possible values available to a person. On this logic the Exercises provide a program for a given person's self-actualization and fulfillment modeled by the person of Jesus of Nazareth, whether or not it transpires within the framework of the Christian grand narrative.

The third logic operative in any making of the Spiritual Exercises stems from the utterly particular narrative that each person brings to the program. It is astonishing that a man of the sixteenth century could be so attentive to the individuality of each person, to his or her uniqueness. More than this, Ignatius also refused to try in any way to predict or control how God's Spirit will work in an individual person. This theme of particularity, in Ignatius's own drama out of which sprang his conversion and the Exercises themselves, and in his almost absolute respect for the freedom of each exercitant, cuts across the first two logics and opens up the direction in which they will take each person. This dimension of particularity, with all its developmental, historical, and psychological depth, does not negate the first two logics but interacts with them to generate new unpredictable insight, imaginative decision making, and the promise of creative and fulfilling action.

CHAPTER FOUR

Interpreting the Exercises for Seekers

The *Spiritual Exercises,* composed by a late-medieval Basque, pro-posed a logic for engaging the stories of Jesus, and it became a classic. This status raises some important questions that need to be addressed in order to clarify the character of the reflections in Part II.

The first issue revolves around the way the Spiritual Exercises are being interpreted in this work. As a landmark in Christian spiritual-ity the Spiritual Exercises contain a world of meaning that scholars and practitioners have shared over centuries. A serious interpretation of such a text has to assume responsibility for the way it goes about its task. This exigency increases with the difference between the cul-tural world of late medieval spirituality and the self-understanding of people in today's secular and religiously pluralistic environment. A rendering that reaches out to seekers will be severely tested. How can an interpretation of the Exercises be faithful to the text and also com-municate with people who do not self-identify as religious?

The second issue, postponed since the Preface, revolves around the idea of spirituality and applies directly to the subject matter of this work. Spirituality encompasses the dimension of human life that the Spiritual Exercises address and the arena in which the seeker looks for meaning. This category has to be specific enough to be able to be called Christian and supple enough to include the seeker in order to define a field for successful communication.

Finally, after developing a method of interpreting the Spiritual Exer-cises that specifically addresses a range of seekers, it will be possible to explain what it means to interpret explicitly religious texts for a par-tially nonreligious audience. It will be possible to explain the strategies of prayer that Ignatius proposes in a way that can accommodate an agnostic seeker.

Interpreting the Spiritual Exercises

How can texts from a distant time and place be relevant to life in the twenty-first century? Many people take for granted that monuments of the past certainly entertain our curiosity, but, because they are embedded in another world of cultural values, they cannot bear normative wisdom for life today. The more deeply one considers this problem, the more serious it gets; the more an interpretation of the past accurately configures its particular horizon, the more it seems to be tied to it and thus loses its moral and spiritual authority in today's very different context. This description of the limited and seemingly restrictive context of all ideas sets up the dilemma of an interpretation of a humanistic text of the past that tries to claim its relevance for life today. On the one hand, a purely historical interpretation of the meaning in terms of the author's intent or the circumstances that generated it binds the text to the past, thereby minimizing its relevance. On the other hand, relating the text to the quite different world of today by definition alters its historical meaning. More pointedly, how can a first-century Palestinian Jew or a romantic sixteenth-century militaristic and patriarchal follower have relevance to present-day life? One has to appreciate the seriousness of this problem for a resolution of it to make sense.[1]

A positive approach to this issue can be discerned in familiar examples. In countries with a constitutional form of government, laws formed in the past, which codify the values and norms of the national culture, are continually interpreted to apply to new situations. What goes on in such interpretation? It always involves change, and yet interpretation can be claimed to remain faithful to the original meaning of the constitution or laws. In any given case such judgment involves complex argument and debate. But some principles can help to clarify in a general way what is going on.

When an idea or a principle becomes written in a text, that objectification breaks the immediate bond it has with the thinker or writer. Meaning takes on a life as a written text in ways that make it in some

---

1. The following sources indicate the world of theory from which the following reflections are drawn: Rudolf Bultmann, *New Testament and Mythology, and Other Basic Writings* (Philadelphia: Fortress, 1984); Dorothee Soelle, *Political Theology* (Philadelphia: Fortress, 1974); Hans-Georg Gadamer, *Truth and Method* (New York: Seabury, 1975); Paul Ricoeur, *Hermeneutics and the Human Sciences* (Cambridge: Cambridge University Press, 1981); idem, *Interpretation Theory: Discourse and the Surplus of Meaning* (Fort Worth: Texas Christian University Press, 1976); idem, *Conflict of Interpretations* (Evanston, IL: Northwestern University Press, 1974); Sandra M. Schneiders, *The Revelatory Text: Interpreting the New Testament as Sacred Scripture* (San Francisco: HarperSanFrancisco, 1991); David Tracy, *Blessed Rage for Order: The New Pluralism in Theology* (New York: Seabury, 1978); idem, *The Analogical Imagination: Christian Theology and the Culture of Pluralism* (New York: Crossroad, 1981); Werner G. Jeanrond, *Text and Interpretation as Categories of Theological Thinking* (New York: Crossroad, 1988). For a fuller account of the conception of theology that is proposed here, see Roger Haight, *Dynamics of Theology* (Maryknoll, NY: Orbis Books, 1990), especially chapters 9-10. And for a brief programmatic essay that applies the principles outlined there to the Spiritual Exercises, see idem, "Foundational Issues in Jesuit Spirituality."

measure independent of the intent of the writer and the context of its original formulation. When ideas and values are written down, they are meant to leave home and travel.

Writing or codification entails a process by which the meaning of the text becomes something of an ideal, a form of thinking and being that enables it to apply to others who may read the text in different circumstances. This describes the intent or purpose of many texts. For example, although Paul wrote his Letter to the Romans precisely to the Romans, in another sense he also wrote it to every Christian because it was passed around and became part of the Christian canon. This ensures its bearing on all Christians into the future.

When people in a distant land or culture read a text from the past, they always grasp its meaning by analogy, that is, as having a meaning that is partly similar and partly different from meanings that they have already experienced and know. When one understands the meaning this way, the text appears both novel and familiar. All communication has analogy in various proportions at its basis. One person would not know what another's fear is without in some measure having already experienced something like it. Communication lives on a transfer of analogous, not identical, meanings.

A classic text from a distant culture, therefore, bears meaning when it is appropriated by the one interpreting it. Appropriation means allowing a meaning that comes from another, from outside the self, to stimulate analogous possibilities of experience and action in one's own life. Appropriation means accommodating oneself to a new meaning and at the same time creatively imagining its appropriateness in the different context in which one exists. Appropriation is interpretation.

The conclusion of these axioms has considerable bearing on the project of interpreting the Spiritual Exercises of Ignatius. Negatively, they forbid Ignatian fundamentalism. The historical study of the Exercises has shed enormous and fruitful light on the text. But the author's intent, the circumstances in which it was written, and what it responded to do not exhaust the meaning of the text. A classic text always bears still more meaning within itself. Positively, its words open the possibilities for new meaning. The Exercises can yield more than one correct interpretation of their import. Different and sometimes opposed meanings, usually based on different suppositions, can be found in the text, and they may be equally true to it. These broad parameters of interpretation situate the following criteria for this interpretation for seekers.

Fidelity to the Exercises. The Exercises may be considered a source for understanding human existence in a manner analogous to scripture.

They provide a set of symbols, of stories, tropes, and especially the person of Jesus, to enable consideration of human life standing before ultimate transcendent reality. Since the text of the Exercises provides the source to be interpreted in this reflection, the first criterion of an adequate interpretation is conformity with the data to be interpreted. A spirituality based on the Exercises has to be faithful to the Exercises. Critical interpretation of the Exercises cannot be based simply on a description of the meaning they mediate to people today without measuring it by the text. In the first instance, historical fidelity is guaranteed by a variety of historical-critical methods of research that have determined the historical context, the intention of the author, and various other indications of the genesis of the text. Here, many of Ignatius's own texts are provided as the basis of the interpretation.

But the meaning of Ignatius's text cannot be limited to what historical analysis can reveal about it. The historical meaning "back then," so to speak, must at the same time be "loosened from" the particularities of that time in order for it meaningfully to address and apply to a set of "receivers" who do not share the same circumstances or suppositions. "Loosened" does not mean "detached." It indicates instead an openness to integral but newly acquired meaning. Interpretation has to work within the tension between the historical preciseness of Ignatius's conceptions, the particulars of his program, and their universality or potential to be appreciated and appropriated by all. It cannot limit the meaning of Ignatius's Exercises to what he thought, to his intentions or his specific worldview, to a sixteenth-century situation or horizon of consciousness, or to how his associates and companions understood him. The historical work on the Exercises is extremely important to ensure fidelity to the Exercises; but any reduction of the meaning of the Exercises to what historians can say about their past meaning effectively negates their relevance to our world today. Those who present the Exercises differently for different audiences know this.

Intelligibility Today. Interpretation is a constructive enterprise: it is meant to transform the meaning of past texts in such a way that analogously they bear the "same" meaning for a present-day audience in a distinctively different historical situation. Beyond but not apart from the historical interpretation of what was meant in the past, interpretation seeks a constructive understanding of reality in the present moment. How then does the meaning from the past come to bear on and remain preserved in the present?

One can understand the process of interpretation that goes on at this point in terms of a dialogue between two people. Imagine them

coming from very different historical backgrounds trying to communicate and share their experiences. Two different cultural "worlds,"
two different standpoints and horizons of experience, two different
sets of presuppositions and premises, encounter each other. Yet there
can be real communication here on the basis of a common humanity
and the commonalities of a shared world to which each can refer. The
freedom of the human spirit is such that it can transcend the self, go
beyond the confines of a person's own limited experience, and appreciate in some measure, at least by contrast, what is other than one's
own experience. But in the end one cannot escape or leave behind
one's own history and the experience that constitutes one's identity.
Rather, what persons learn is drawn into their own consciousness and,
by analogy with elements of their past experience, they make sense of
the others' meaning. The bottom line is expressed well by the principle laid down by Thomas Aquinas: what is received or understood is
received according to the manner of the receiver or knower.[2]

Applying this dialogical principle to the interpretation of texts from
the past, it can be postulated that there can be no appropriation of the
symbols of the past that escapes present-day consciousness. Indeed,
appropriation is interpretation, and it entails drawing the meaning of
the past into a current consciousness of the world. Historical consciousness signifies that every understanding of the past is automatically
reinterpreted within the framework of a present-day understanding
of the world. By the principle of analogy a person's self-transcending
appreciation of the experience of the other as other and different spontaneously becomes translated into terms of his or her own consciousness and thus experience.

This principle is intensified when it is expressed in terms of truth.
Interpretation seeks not only meaning but also truth, not only the
content of ideas but also whether they refer to reality. As a critical
discipline, interpretation casts a questioning eye on two versions of
reality: the world enshrined in the past texts being interpreted and
the world that one takes for granted because it has been internalized
through years of experience. In the dialogue between these two witnesses one must assume that people can understand in some degree
the witness of the dialogue partner in its own terms, as other. But
interpretation cannot affirm as true on the basis of a witness from
another time and place what one knows cannot be the case on the
basis of one's own experience.[3] Surely, too, a genuinely open stance to

---

2. Thomas Aquinas, *Summa Theologica: Complete English Edition in Five Volumes*
(Westminster, MD: Christian Classics, 1961), II-II, q. 1, a. 2.

3. The issues of truth cannot be reduced to items of culture and different ways of
managing life in the world on the surface. Questions of truth subtly draw the inquirer

the voice of the past can confront and change one's own experience. Authentic interpretation requires being affected by the meaning of the text. But at the same time interpretation can construe reality disclosed by a witness from the past only in a way that is analogous and coherent with truth as it is manifested in a person's own historical context. This will have tricky consequences relative to the seeker, who by definition shares a different apperceptive background relative to the Christian story.

Empowerment in Our World. The tension between the first two criteria of interpretation, fidelity and present-day intelligibility, raises the question of how one can discern that a genuinely new interpretation actually is faithful to a past text. This problem finds a resolution in a third criterion of empowerment.

Empowerment for life in the world finds its grounding in an anthropology that views knowledge itself as ultimately pragmatic. The most theoretical kinds of knowledge, even mystical contemplation of ultimate reality and communion with it, are themselves forms of human action that bend back upon human life to enhance it.[4] Theorizing, resting in truth, and meditative communication with God are themselves human activities or behaviors that do not draw human beings out of the world and human history but are the catalysts of a more-fully-human mode of existence.

The principle of applicability, which the interpretation of law exemplifies, illustrates how this works. According to it the applicability of a past law to the present constitutes the law's meaning here and now, so that to determine its applicability is to determine an aspect of the meaning of the law itself. In other words, one does not first decide the meaning of the past law, and then figure out its relevance. Rather the universal meaning of the law is constituted by its diverse applications; continually finding right applications constitutes the internally consistent meaning of the law in history.

The principle of empowerment, when it is integrated into a broad theory of interpretation, reminds the interpreter of what interpretation is for. Like all knowledge, interpretation guides human living, how life is led in the world and concrete history in a present that extends into the future. All interpretation, in its specialized branches

---

into the sphere of ontology, something often shunned but never really escaped.

4. This seemingly utilitarian description does not say all there is to say: it is not meant to exclude the in-itself value of recognizing truth or, by extension, to undermine the intentionality of worship that simply gives God's glory its due. But neither does such worship fail to enhance human existence. Truth, the glory of God, and human thriving do not compete with one another.

as well, is ultimately practical. Its purpose is to open up possibilities for life in concrete history.

When it is applied to interpreting the Exercises, empowerment implies that the point of continuity between the meaning of the Exercises in the sixteenth century and their meaning for anyone today, including a seeker, lies in an analogy between two relationships: between a pattern of life related to the sixteenth century and a pattern of life related to the twenty-first. As the way of life that Jesus preached and lived related to first-century Jewish Palestine, and Ignatius's conception and practice of life related to sixteenth-century Spain and Europe, so too should the interpretation of life proffered by the Exercises today relate to the twenty-first-century world of the exercitant.[5] It is not a question of transposing a past way of life into a new context but of proportionality or analogy between two relationships. Interpretation can never escape from an actual world. Real possibilities today are not the possibilities of the past but of the present and future, not abstract and mystifying but intelligibly coherent with the actuality of our world, not purely individual but in keeping with the real solidarity of each person's life with partners, colleagues, fellow citizens, fellow suffering human beings, and especially the wretchedly poor. Real possibilities are concrete and tied to options that can only be made in a concrete world.

A deep paradox is at work here, one that, because of its subtlety, will undoubtedly continue to generate an equally profound irony. The more interpreters, seeking to be faithful to Ignatius historically and to uncover the original meaning of the Exercises, reduce their meaning to what they meant in the past, the more they cut the Exercises off from our life today and distort the possible meaning they bear for present-day Christians and seekers who remain open to their meaning. But in overcoming this Ignatian fundamentalism, interpretation must keep the three criteria in a constant tension. An interpretation of the Exercises that is intelligible and empowering but not faithful to the inner logic of the text of Ignatius is in that measure a false interpretation. One that is faithful and empowering but not intelligible will, of course, in that measure also be rejected. And one that is both faithful and intelligible but not empowering for life in our world and history today is at best simply irrelevant and at worst counterproductive. But when these three critical norms are held in careful balance, they can

---

5. This analogy and proportionality are discussed by Edward Schillebeeckx, *Church: The Human Story of God* (New York: Crossroad, 1990), 40-45. This description will be amplified considerably by the language of gift, grace, and Spirit drawn from the stories of Jesus and the language of the Exercises, but not in such a way that it undoes the anthropological perspective; grace enhances nature.

produce a wide variety of interpretations that engender an authentic human spiritual life in a host of different historical situations, including the world of seekers who are not Christian.

Conceiving Spirituality

The Spiritual Exercises provided a source for a distinct school of Christian spirituality. But what exactly does "spirituality" refer to? Just as every single person seems to have a distinct spirituality, so too do writers have different conceptions of what the idea of spirituality represents. This plurality is confusing because the many conceptions lack a common denominator. The following is an attempt to circumscribe a conception of spirituality and a description of how it relates to religion. It is not definitive. But it may shed some light on the subject and offer a framework for moving forward. The point is not to establish a single conception of spirituality, but to set up a framework in which to work.

Spirituality may be defined as *the logic, or character, or consistent quality of a person's living insofar as it is measured before ultimate reality.* This conception is described in terms of a person but it can apply as well to a group. The conception remains open and inclusive: according to it, everyone has a spirituality even when they are not conscious of it, as long as they have a relatively consistent character and identity at all. Spirituality points to something like personal identity in action. Even though those with similar spiritualities form groups, still, at bottom, spirituality describes the individual identity of a person. This notion of spirituality rests on the truism that we are what we do, so that the overall character or pattern of our behaviors, their logic, really constitutes the spirituality that in turn defines who we are.

Spirituality in this conception resides most deeply within the sphere of a person's intentional action. The idea that one is what one does should not be understood as a reductionism that collapses spirituality into blind action. The point is not to deny that deeper self-possession and freedom lie behind all truly human action. But with deliberate action the human person constitutes himself or herself; the self-disposition and commitment make a difference; the sum of a person's commitments and actions shapes and reflects the inner self. These reflections lie behind the definition of spirituality as the way a person leads his or her life. This view of spirituality does not reduce it to the notion of a "lifestyle." Specifically human existence consists of intentional and willed action. The sphere of spirituality reaches below the surface of this or that pattern of action to the fundamental option of a person, that pervasive moral attitude or commitment that guides decisions and actions. Taken together, the multiple specific actions of a person fix and define the deepest commitment of that person's will, and ultimately his or her being. A person molds the being of the self through action. In order to assign to spirituality the profound significance it should have in the whole of life, there is no better way than to conceive it as embodied in human action itself.

Working with this conception of spirituality, it appears that every human being has a spirituality. All human beings lead their lives in a certain way. The concrete way of life of individuals and groups makes up their spirituality. Looking at spirituality as action does not result in a limiting or exclusive definition; it implies the very opposite. Action includes and integrates dimensions of the spiritual life that frequently go overlooked. For example, all aspects of secular life in the world are drawn into the sphere of one's spiritual life. The category of action also helps to clarify the interrelationships of some of the elements of spirituality that are often dealt with separately. For example, faith and spirituality can be understood at their deepest points to be synonymous. On the existential level of personal and subjective appropriation, both faith and spirituality refer to the fundamental option and commitment of a person that is actually lived out in his or her action.[6] Hence the quest of people for what is truly ultimate. Spirituality, when recognized as housed in human action, appears as nothing less than the living out of a vision of faith. Action is the actuality of the internalized vision.

The term spirituality can be understood on at least two distinct levels, the one existential and the other reflective and rendered objective through abstract description and analysis. On the first and deepest level of action, spirituality lives within the conscious decisions and actions that make the person to be who he or she is; spirituality is the continuous line of action that fashions a person's identity. On the second reflective level, spirituality refers to a theory or theoretical vision of human life in terms of the ideas, ideals, and ultimate values that should shape it. These two levels constantly interact in the thinking person. Especially when a person's spirituality coalesces with membership in a group, personal spirituality involves a constant interaction between one's being a member and being an individual. It seems obvious that each person has to assume responsibility for his

---

6. Paul Tillich defines faith as "ultimate concern." In this deft characterization "ultimate concern" has both a subjective and an objective sense. Subjectively it characterizes the guiding commitment of a person; objectively it points to that which functions to center a person's life. Tillich insists that what a person takes as ultimate should really be so in order to constitute authentic faith. See Paul Tillich, *Dynamics of Faith* (New York: Harper & Row, 1957), *passim*.

or her spirituality, and that results in a pluralism of spiritualities even within a group. That pluralism extends further to the more abstract realm of distinct schools of spirituality. The Christian movement has generated thousands of distinct spiritualities over the centuries. And the same can be said of other religions. Spirituality is an intrinsically pluralistic phenomenon, and these definitions only harness the idea on a formal level.

The Relation of Spirituality to Religion. One should not underestimate the complexity of either spirituality or religion or the relationship between them. But without some clarification of how these terms function in relation to each other this discussion cannot go forward. For centuries it was presupposed in Western culture that spirituality was so linked to religion that the terms might be used interchangeably. But things have changed in this regard. The signs of this new situation abound: the many different meanings of spirituality broadcast it; the distinction between spirituality and religion has been subjected to endless analysis; and whole groups of people take the difference between these two spheres for granted. The situation demands some formal semantic differentiation.

Working within the framework of the distinction between the two, religion may be defined in this work as a set of beliefs, values, and practices that together define what ultimate reality is and the relationship that obtains between this ultimate reality and human beings. Two elements in this description of religion have particular bearing in this discussion. From one perspective this descriptive definition represents religion primarily in objective social terms. This corresponds with common usage: the word "religion" frequently refers to the public institutions called religions into which people are socialized and become members. On this level religions are larger than individuals and draw people into themselves. But this does not exhaust the meaning of a religion because, from another perspective, it is also internalized and resonates with the deepest religious experiences of the members. On the social level people talk about the religions: Hinduism, Christianity, Islam, and so on. On the personal level it should be clear that religions are constituted by the very lives of the people who live them and would not exist apart from those who bear them in their daily lives. Therefore, although spirituality and religion may be distinct, they are also closely related.

These descriptions of spirituality and religion, especially the distinction between two dimensions of religion, the social and the personally appropriated, can offer some first clarifications about the relationship between the spiritual and the religious. The idea of "spirituality" tends to refer to the deep inner recesses of a person, as, for example, when one says "I am spiritual." This is where each one considers questions of transcendence and looks for ultimate meaning. By contrast, the idea of "religion" often means that one is a member or a practicing participant of a specific religion or religious congregation, for example, when one says "I am (or am not) religious." Religion tends to refer to the external or public sphere, as in organized religion. But this objective meaning does not tell the whole story because on the personal level religion is expected to entail a spirituality or way of life before ultimacy. Thus internalized religion can become the dominant part of one's spirituality, and a person's spontaneous, interior spirituality may find its clearest external expression in the beliefs, values, and practices of a religious community.

The distinction between spirituality and religion, despite their close connection, can result in some awkward terminology, as in the phrase "religious experience." Religious experience refers broadly to human feelings or responses to what appears in consciousness as transcendent and solemn; it elicits responses of reverence and enthusiasm; it comes from a region beyond human control and as a gift. Religious experience cannot be reduced to a single kind. The transcendent appears in many guises and calls forth many different human responses: love, fear, awe and so on.[7] Spirituality and religious experience approach each other at this point. One can easily conceive that some form of "religious" experience may undergird a spirituality when the ultimacy before which spirituality unfolds is transcendent. At the same time much of spirituality revolves around an ultimacy that hardly qualifies as transcendent. Thus, even though "religious experience" and "spiritual experience" at times have synonymous meanings, the term "religious" calls attention to the transcendence of its object.

In sum, this discussion works with a distinction between the ideas of the spiritual and the religious. Spirituality is associated with the individual logic of each person's life that may or may not be learned from and lived within a specific religious community. Religion is associated with a public social institution, a community defined by its public witness to ultimacy. But this distinction would be a distortion if one did not recognize how the categories overlap so that a person's spirituality can become synonymous with a person's religion. One can say that while religion in principle requires spirituality, spirituality does not require religion. In this view of things spirituality is the

---

7. While one could choose many philosophical or theological definitions of religious experience, this thin description borrows from William James's empirical approach to religious experience, which seems appropriate here. See his *The Varieties of Religious Experience* (New York: Collier Books, 1961), 39-58.

deeper and broader category. No one can lack a spirituality, because ultimately spirituality defines individual identity.

Finally, spirituality contains a certain intrinsic inclination to find a public mediation of the ultimacy before which it stands. Given the disorienting plurality of spiritualities and religions that mark human history, it does not seem likely that any individual will find within the self a conception of ultimacy that is complete and adequate in its distinction from all others. Purely individual spiritualities are often unsteady, and the seeker is acutely aware of it. Without public criteria and some norms, private spirituality "imposes no moral authority outside one's own conscience, creates no necessary personal relationships or social responsibilities, and can be changed or abandoned whenever it seems not to work for the practitioner."[8] For this reason it makes sense for seekers to look for guidelines for an authentic spirituality within public religious traditions.

Jesus of Nazareth. Jesus Christ is a public figure who provides a religious and spiritual focus for a good percentage of human beings. Theoretically those people are followers of Jesus Christ who look to him as God's representative, and their spirituality traditionally is called an "imitation of Christ." Ignatius's Spiritual Exercises fall into this classification. Interpreting these Spiritual Exercises for seekers, therefore, requires some introduction to the historical appearance of Jesus and how he came to be inscribed within the pages of the New Testament and the sensibilities of Christians. Because the size, complexity, and subtleties of this subject exceed what can be said in a few words, this discussion aims only at making two points: one is that the stories of the gospels beautifully preserve the memory of Jesus of Nazareth; the other is that Jesus was imaginatively constructed by the authors of the gospels, and imagination is required for any retrieval of him today.

Jesus was a Jew who lived during the first three decades of the Common Era in Palestine, more specifically in Galilee. During the final period of his life he took up a public religious ministry. He presented himself as a prophetic figure, a teacher, and a worker of exorcisms and healings. He gathered a group of disciples, attracted crowds, and during his preaching in Jerusalem during Passover he so antagonized Jewish religious leaders and the Roman occupiers of the city that he was executed by crucifixion. Some time after his execution, however, his followers experienced Jesus to be alive and risen into God's sphere,

---

8. Sandra M. Schneiders, "Religion vs. Spirituality: A Contemporary Conundrum," *Spiritus* 3 (2003), 173.

and they began a movement in his name. Gradually, during the course of the rest of the first century, especially after the fall of Jerusalem and the razing of the Temple in the year 70, the Christian church began to take form as distinct from Judaism.

The memory of Jesus was preserved by the disciples who walked with him and then within the Jesus movement that continued after his death. The stories and reports of his teachings became part of the movement itself, the vehicles of its communication and relevance. In the course of three decades these stories and the stories that Jesus himself told, the parables, his sayings, and his moral teachings, found their way into written forms. Jesus also taught by dramatic symbolic actions such as eating with public sinners, and these stories too were remembered and told, and some of them were written down. As the movement built momentum the meals of disciples provided a venue where these stories could be told and amplified. The stories were useful in preaching. The gospels appeared when editors later gathered these stories into collections that contain Jesus' sayings and actions and portray the ministry that led to his execution in Jerusalem. Added to these are other stories narrating appearances that reflect the Easter experience that "Jesus is alive."

One significant reflection that flows from this brief story of the formation of the gospels has to do with the Jesus that they represent. If the goal is to keep alive the memory of figures of the past, the best vehicle for this consists in telling their stories and writing them down. The narrative captures and preserves the public persona of people vividly in remembered or projected sensory images. Other writings than the gospels in the New Testament proclaim and analyze the significance of the teaching and destiny of Jesus and appeal to him to answer questions in more abstract discursive terms. But the stories about Jesus, even when they were adapted to respond to issues in the communities where they were written, retain a sense of the reality of his person and retrieve him in concrete, imaginative scenarios.

The other important consequence of the way the gospels were generated goes more to their intrinsic character. The writers of the gospels are more accurately designated editors; they composed the gospels from pre-existing stories, either oral or written down. These stories were current because they too were used to communicate the relevance of Jesus and his teaching to the immediate problems of the day. Surely some of the stories may go back to eyewitnesses, but the testimony was anecdotal rather than reportorial and exact. For example, the gospels contain no physical description of Jesus. Sometimes the details of the stories fit better with the later circumstances of the audiences to whom the stories were told than with Jesus' situation. Sometimes a story may have been constructed to make a general historical point or a theological teaching and not to relate an actual series of events. But Jesus healed people, whether or not this or that particular story happened as described. On balance, when the gospel stories seem plausible, they may be taken on the whole to represent Jesus rather well, whether or not the details are exact. The effort to determine as best one can what Jesus actually said and did has been going on for over a century and is fraught with controversy in the details and in principle: believers in Jesus' divine provenance fear historical reductionism, while those who relate to Jesus as a person want accurate knowledge about him.[9] Both parties are aware that the stories of Jesus involve a certain amount of imaginative reconstruction of his ministry; there is no memory without imagination. It will be shown further on that Ignatius prescribed extensive use of the imagination in his considerations of Jesus in order realistically to recreate what he took to be straightforward reports. The person making the Exercises today, who by contrast possesses critical awareness of the imaginative character of these stories, can still feel free to use the imagination to recreate the living Jesus in the way Ignatius suggested, knowing that this is what the writers did as well.

Jesus and Spirituality. The substance of spirituality consists in a person's conduct as measured by ultimate values and concern. The gospels present Jesus of Nazareth in a collection of stories that display his actions relative to his ultimate concern: the way the creator intends the world to be. Jesus called this God's rule of love and justice in the world of the present as well as in an absolute future. The discussion now turns to how the stories of Jesus may be appropriated into a spirituality for the twenty-first century by means of the imagination.

Everyone knows what the imagination is, but few can define it exactly. Because imagination almost defies a substantive definition, it may legitimately be circumscribed by mental functions.[10] First, the imagination binds general, abstract, and notional understanding to the concrete world. The maxim that nothing exists in the mind that was not previously in the senses provides the principle for this function. Sensations are received in the imagination, where human intelligence fashions them into concepts and language that allow thought

---

9. The most comprehensive account of this quest for the historical Jesus is found in John Meier, *A Marginal Jew: Rethinking the Historical Jesus,* vols. 1-4 (New York: Doubleday, 1991-).

10. These reflections are drawn from Aquinas, *Summa Theologica,* I, q. 78, aa. 3-4; q. 79, aa. 1-8, without any commitment to the faculty psychology that lies behind Thomas's description.

and public communication. This makes the imagination a kind of clearing house for the two-way traffic between the human mind and the world of which it is a part. The world imposes itself on us through the senses, and we knowingly relate back to the concrete world referentially through the imagination by language.

Second, imagination combines with memory to store the images gained through encounters with the world within each human subject. Some trace of what human beings experience concretely in their dealing with the world is converted into subjective images that reside in the storehouse of an imaginative memory. These become the markers of our history, the resources of our meaningful conversation, and definers of our identity. The capacity for imaginative recollection enhances human ability to understand and relate to the present by supplying each person with a large field of references.

The third major function of the imagination can be called its creativity. The imagination has an active, dynamic power that enables human beings to create new things. Thomas Aquinas illustrates this in a simple and yet powerful way. The human person can imagine a mountain; we can also have an image of gold; we can then combine them and deliberately imagine a mountain of gold. This fundamental dynamism, something like a pure desire to construct, lies at the bottom of all human creativity, from the curiosity of explorers and the acquisitiveness of bank robbers to the artistic creativity of writers and musicians and the scientific discovery of chemists and astrophysicists.

A particular aspect of this creativity shows up in analogical perception. Things are analogous, it was noted earlier, when they are partly different and partly the same. The analogical imagination is one that can intuitively or spontaneously grasp the similar in the different. Analogy of this kind supplies the basic structure that allows humans to communicate: total difference cannot communicate. "We understand one another, if at all, only through analogy. Who you are I know only by knowing what event, what focal meaning, you actually live by. And that I know only if I too have sensed some analogous guide in my own life."[11] Analogous perception also facilitates new learning. "We begin to grasp what is unfamiliar by moving from what is familiar. If new experiences bore no resemblance whatsoever to familiar ones, they would be unintelligible. There would be no bridges from the actually known to what is not yet clear."[12] In short, analogy with our own experience allows us to learn from others, to understand the language and experience of one another.

---

11. Tracy, *The Analogical Imagination*, 454-55.
12. William C. Spohn, *Go and Do Likewise: Jesus and Ethics* (New York: Continuum, 1999), 54.

The creative analogous imagination also empowers human beings to plan their future. It provides the possibility of grasping the meaningful referential structure of a past narrative and applying it to our own world. A story from the past proposes a different world of meaning, but the imagination "sees" the meaning as bearing reference to present lives. "Analogical thinking discovers similarity within difference by recognizing a common pattern within diversity."[13] The analogical imagination immerses itself in the concrete and particular details of the story and grasps within it a pattern of significance and reference to human existence generally that has bearing on one's own life within its different context and circumstances. For example, Jesus tells the story of a good Samaritan who stopped and cared for a victim of a mugging on the road from Jerusalem to Jericho, and then he tells his Jewish audience to go and do likewise. Today, a Marxist who thinks in social terms realizes that Jesus' command means making the road from Jerusalem to Jericho safe; it means removing the causes of attack; it means justice. For others, it means learning from those who are really different; it means love of enemies; it means reconciliation. The imagination can remain faithful to Jesus' parable and at the same time be wonderfully creative. The analogical imagination bridges the words and deeds of Jesus with the moral and spiritual reflection of people in many different situations.[14]

Still more personally, the imagination can negotiate a fusion of narratives that opens up new possibilities for an individual's or a group's life.[15] "Standpoint" and "horizon" offer spatial and visual metaphors for the framework that helps determine all understanding. The social and cultural situation, the circumstances that influence perspective, personal background and formation, all constitute a person's standpoint and horizon of consciousness. All texts were created in a particular horizon, and they reflect it. When they are interpreted and brought to life in another context, a fusion of the two horizons occurs, the horizon of the text and the horizon of the interpreter.[16] The fusion of narratives with specific reference to the narrative of Jesus operates analogously. It consists in drawing the story of Jesus, and all the stories that make it up, into the present situation. In effect, it consists in retelling the story of Jesus in modern dress. How does the story unfold when it is reset in a present-day horizon to run parallel with other stories today? This operation contains the same questions relative to

---

13. Ibid., 55-56.

14. Ibid., 50.

15. The idea of a "fusion of narratives" is a riff on the phrase "a fusion of horizons," drawn from Gadamer, *Truth and Method*, 271-74.

16. Ibid., 267-71.

truth as in a fusion of horizons. Can one really appreciate the story of Jesus in his own time, and can a transposition retain the authenticity of the original? The answer to the first question is yes, because Jesus is a human being and can be understood by self-transcendence and analogy with ourselves. The second question has to be nuanced according to the principles of interpretation described earlier. The authenticity of the transposition will not lie in the details of situation and culture but in the logic of the human life that is represented. The fusion of narratives can happen existentially only in people who try it out.

In the end the fusion of narratives is a personal existential affair in which one imagines the story of Jesus within one's own story, rather than the other way around.[17] This is so because the result has to unfold in the actual world of today. Such fusions of narratives would be characterized by an infinite number of different degrees of closeness and levels of intensity. At any level, however, the freedom and autonomy of the disciple are not diminished but enhanced. Allowing the story of Jesus into the calculus of one's interpretation of the world and the future opens up new possibilities for human freedom. It would be easy to think of this fusion in Christian terms as a union with Jesus Christ, but that characterization remains ambiguous because in Paul it implies a mystical union. More basically, the fusion of narratives results in a person's dedication today to what Jesus gave himself to in his time, the actualization of the values of God in history. "Go and do likewise." It will be shown in Part II how this can result in a kind of mysticism of existential union with the object of commitment. But this Ignatian mysticism plays itself out in committed action, and attachment to Jesus only becomes real in action. The payoff of this spirituality is forged not in any imaginative sentimentality but in decision. From beginning to end the imagination guiding this fusion of narratives is practical. What it draws from imaginative immersion in the parable that Jesus himself is, it invests in creative action into the world.

To sum up here, although religion and spirituality are closely aligned, spirituality designates the deeper and more comprehensive sphere of life. The actual relationship of a person to ultimate reality is constituted by the overall logic of his or her conscious behavior. It is exactly at this point that both Christian and seeker, or any human

---

17. Christian believers could very well insist that their whole spirituality rests on their story unfolding within the sphere of Jesus Christ as this is stated in the letters of Paul, who does not tell the narrative story of Jesus. This difference could provide leverage for contrasting the relation of the Christian and the seeker to Jesus; it would lead into different formal faith commitments. Here the description remains on the historical level, the following of Jesus, and is focused on where the Christian and the seeker would have something in common, that is, being moved and empowered by Jesus.

being at all, can relate to Jesus of Nazareth. Spirituality always learns from others, and by the sheer fact of being a human person one can meet and respond to the teaching and example of Jesus. In fact this description of a spirituality influenced by Jesus fairly accurately describes the relation of many Christian and non-Christian seekers to Jesus of Nazareth.

A Note on Freedom

The word "freedom" occurs frequently in this work because it lies at the center of the underlying anthropology. Sometimes the formal reflections of Part II hold out freedom to people who are bound by a net of multiple relationships and responsibilities that allow few choices. Some space has to be opened up in which the language of freedom can appear feasible. Although a brief note will not resolve the tensions, it may clarify the language. The word "freedom" overflows with meaning, and a few distinctions will show its different functions in the reflections of Part II.

The primary meaning of freedom equates it with the human person itself: a person is freedom. This substantive use characterizes what distinguishes the human person from other biological forms. It refers to the person's being-present-to-the-self in a reflection that recognizes and assumes responsibility for the self vis à vis reality beyond the self. Søren Kierkegaard appealed to this individual freedom against its absorption by idealistic generality, and Alain Badiou appeals to the free subject as a place where universal truth can be discovered as an event transcending various relativistic social constructions.[18] Freedom is the sphere of being in which a person recognizes the self as self, and subjective freedom gives rise to responsibility and ethics where reality other than the self elicits responses to value. All of this occurs not in some airy space of mere thought but within the heaviness of bodies and the routine of daily obligations. Transcendence does not leap out of the physical but appears as the possibility of spirit within and through it.

The elemental freedom that constitutes the human being exercises itself at a variety of levels, and this tends to make freedom refer to a quality of the human person. The one area in which most people recognize the quality of freedom lies in the ability to make choices. Yet ironically many of the choices people seem to make in freedom are not free at all; and, remarkably, some people, Nelson Mandela springs to mind, appear to be most free when they have been imprisoned. These

---

18. Alain Badiou, *Saint Paul: The Foundation of Universalism* (Stanford, CA: Stanford University Press, 2003), 4-15 and *passim*.

paradoxes show that one cannot simply lay out the meaning of freedom in discursive language. The term "freedom" introduces focused attention to the sphere of the human spirit and puts before it a variety of attractive ideals.

The paradoxical character of freedom gives rise to the idea that freedom assumes a "higher" or "deeper" quality when it represents a person taking more conscious possession of the self. Although it is getting rarer in developed Western societies, something strangely beautiful and humanistically profound appears in a faithful monogamous relationship over 50 or 60 years. Fidelity in commitment of the self to another person or to a lofty ideal does not negate the self-determinations of constant choices but draws them up into another level of freedom's potential. Surprisingly a person can become more free in a comprehensive commitment to a cause, if it is transcendent enough to elicit such breadth and openness.

Because freedom represents the human itself and is not a static essence, it develops with human self-understanding across the history of growing human potential. One of the most dramatic examples of this in the history of Western culture is the rise of historical consciousness, especially during the nineteenth and twentieth centuries. One of the reflections in Part II (10) focuses on the gradual coming to an awareness that movement through time does not include a pre-programmed future, that the human collectivity both has some control over the future and yet repeatedly appears to be bound by a fated destiny. This strange new situation lays heavy social and ecological burdens on a collective human freedom that appears to resist change while it actually continually changes. All this does not add up to a philosophy of freedom. But it may clarify the sometimes jarring language of a spiritual idealism that reaches out to freedom in an appeal for self-actualization.

Can the Exercises Be Offered to Seekers?

The term "seeker" was defined earlier primarily to refer to those with no explicitly developed religious faith, even though it is used more diffusely to include Christians and people of other faiths. This raises the question whether the Spiritual Exercises can be offered to people with no religious belonging, especially in the light of the first principle of interpretation that a presentation of the Exercises must be faithful to the text. A brief discussion of this clarifying question will reveal the tensions involved in this effort and the fact that it is not without problems.

The conception of spirituality operative in this project opens up some new possibilities on this issue. Spirituality refers primarily to the way people lead their lives, with special reference to an ultimate horizon which guides their behavior. In this view of things everyone has a spirituality, and this rescues the term from some esoteric sphere without tying it exclusively to traditional religious behavior. Spirituality may or may not be religious. It may not even be reflectively appropriated. But spirituality consists of more than a conscious flow of activity. It includes the set of ultimate values that constitute a horizon that contains the metrics by which a person measures importance and makes decisions. The way people lead their whole lives in the face of what they posit as ultimate defines their spiritual identity. The most secular of seekers, then, have a spirituality, albeit somewhat unstable, because, by definition, they are looking for more formulation.

The Spiritual Exercises can be addressed to one without religious faith because, in the way that Ignatius set them up, the substance of the Exercises consists in imaginatively entering into the gospel stories of Jesus of Nazareth. Despite the fact that Ignatius had a high Christology, he insists in presenting the gospel stories in a way that actually highlights Jesus' being a human being and thus able to be followed.[19] This humanity of Jesus is the key to his approachability, communicability, and universal relevance. All can appreciate Jesus insofar as he is a human being and thus like them.

But one should be aware that a consistent appeal to Jesus' human life and ministry creates some tension with a Christian sensibility for what Christian doctrine proclaims about his person and his relationship with God.[20] This tension lies beneath the surface of the language employed to reflect on Ignatian meditations. Although it is acute, it can be managed. The problem consists in finding a language that accommodates two different audiences, those used to thinking of Jesus as divine and those approaching him as a fellow human traveler. It should be added as an aside that this is not a theological problem, because the doctrine of most Christian churches preserves the integ-

---

19. This was developed briefly in the last chapter under the subheading of The Call of the Temporal King.

20. For example, William Reiser does not think the Spiritual Exercises can authentically be offered to seekers who remain outside Christianity: the Exercises "have clear and pronounced Christological parameters, and presuppose a certain level of incorporation into the Christian community. . . . At their core the Spiritual Exercises are intended to take people deeper into the mystery of the life, death and resurrection of Jesus." See Reiser, "The *Spiritual Exercises* in a Religiously Pluralistic World," *Spiritus: A Journal of Christian Spirituality* 10 (Fall 2010), 138, 152. I believe that Reiser is operating out of the first holistic framework for the Exercises described early in Chapter 3, which situates them within the Christian story. By itself, this framework is prone to narrowing down of the range of the appeal of Jesus of Nazareth to the Christian interpretation of him. The other two frameworks expand the horizon of vision.

rity of Jesus' being a human being exactly like us. Interpretation for seekers does not reduce Jesus to what a seeker might be able to affirm any more than lack of faith proves the nonexistence of God. The project of this presentation of the Exercises is not reductive. But the intrinsic rhetorical problem of finding the right language remains. It will not be resolved without patience from each side of the issue: tolerance on the part of Christians who expect to hear more about Jesus' divinity, and tolerance on the part of secular seekers who may hear too much of it.

Other tensions arise on different sides when an interpretation of the Exercises envisages a particular audience. It will not hurt to refer explicitly to a number of them. By turning attention to the seeker, the interpretations that are offered in the reflections of Part II gravitate toward some fundamental questions to which human existence itself as a self-conscious phenomenon gives rise: questions of the whence of existence and purpose in life. The Exercises become slanted toward what in some fashion all human beings relate as seekers. For some who are familiar with the Exercises, their immediate relevance for daily living may seem to be siphoned off by a concern for the big questions. How Jesus may speak to this or that family situation and how more commonplace decisions may become matters of discernment do not receive attention. But the Exercises do address this whole range of experience. In answer to the question whether the Exercises are intended only for those making a decision or for those simply renewing their lives, commentators are unanimous about their general application. Thus, all the reflections in Part II could be expressed differently in order to show how each one has bearing on everyday living. The sum of such reflections would show how Ignatian spirituality can accompany a person through the interminable minor decisions that make up life's course.

Some might claim that the essence of Ignatius's Exercises involves a personal affective relationship of the one making them to Jesus Christ. At issue is not a doctrinal commitment but a personal relationship of familiarity. Time and again Ignatius appeals to just such a personal bond with Jesus that the Christian culture of his time invited. This presentation of the Exercises in some degree avoids this appeal because one cannot presuppose that disposition in the seeker from outside the Christian circle. But this allows the New Testament portrait of Jesus to do its work so that people encountering him may grow into a personal relationship. The audience of seekers also shifts the sensibility that is appealed to. One has to assume that an inquiring person has implicit criteria for credibility, that a seeker asks questions, that he or she needs explanation. If the Exercises were completely withdrawn from the realm of affectivity, they would no longer represent what

Ignatius constructed. But when they are addressed to seekers, if they lack a critical edge, they will fail.

From the other side and by contrast, these Exercises may appear to the seeker to be no more than the familiar Christian religion served without formal doctrine. Too much of the traditional and exclusive worldview lives hidden in the apparently open language. Is Jesus really someone that human beings can realistically relate to as a fellow seeker before an unknown future? This sets up the Scylla of the seeker and the Charybdis of the Christian between which this book tries to sail.

Ignatian Methods of Prayer

Finally, attention should be turned to the meditations and contemplations that constitute the building blocks of the Spiritual Exercises. Although Ignatius introduces several methods of prayer in the Exercises, what he called "meditations" and "contemplations" provide the principal parts of the program. These types of interior reflection share a common broad structure. The beginning and end of meditations and contemplations are similar. But the character of the middle or body of the two differ significantly. It will be helpful to represent the structure of a meditation and a contemplation and insert commentary within each. Both of these forms conclude with what Ignatius called a "colloquy," which consists in a direct personal conversation with God. That too requires special consideration when the audience of the Exercises are seekers who may not live with an active consciousness of God.

This is a good place to insist again that the reflections of Part II do not offer spiritual commentary relating verbatim to the texts that are provided by a director to those making the Exercises. Normally a director of the Exercises offers such spiritual commentary in order to help stimulate a meditation or contemplation. This commentary usually relates directly and stays close to the subject matter of the text. It frequently runs parallel to the text and uses primary spiritual language to open up its meaning. The goal of such input never lies in the commentary itself; inspiration springs from engagement with the text, especially when it is a passage from scripture. But the director's commentary tries to represent the texts. By contrast, the reflections in Part II are more general and do not engage the texts so literally. Although these reflections have grown out of engagement with the texts, they use reflective, analytical language to address issues that may block or open up spiritual illumination. While they may be of assistance to directors of the Exercises who design spiritual commentary for particular audiences, they are not meant themselves to be the basis of meditation or contemplation and prayer. They accompany but do not substitute for the Exercises.

The Structure of a Meditation. The substance of a meditation consists in interior reflection on a truth, a moral principle, or a maxim about life that is deep and able to bear unlimited consideration from various viewpoints and in new contexts. Compared with contemplation, the subject matter of a meditation is more abstract, cerebral, or intellectual. It engages intelligent insight and reasoning as one rolls the proposed construct around in one's mind, considers it from different perspectives, and asks about its consequences for life. The key to the substance of a meditation revolves around what medieval thinkers considered the three powers of the soul: memory, intellect or reason, and will or the ability to make a decision. A meditation could be defined as applying these three mental abilities to a specific subject. The full measure of a meditation has an introductory phase, a body, and a conclusion.

Introductory Phase
The introductory phase has an introductory prayer and two preludes.[21]
　　1. *Preparatory Prayer*: "Ask God . . . that all my intentions, actions, and operations may be ordered purely to the service and praise of the Divine Majesty" (SE, 46). The intent of this preparatory prayer is invariable; it remains the same in meditations and contemplations (SE, 49). It reflects Ignatius's purposefulness. One should approach a meditation or contemplation with full attention and fixed concentration.
　　2. *First Prelude*: Create or imagine space for the content of the meditation (SE, 47). Situate the subject matter in a context, or locate it within the specific framework in which it should appear. The point here is to provide a definite focus for the subject matter.
　　3. *Second Prelude*: Ask God for what one wants to gain from this meditation. This too is consistent across meditations and contemplations and shows the pragmatism of Ignatius. He wants people to be goal oriented in undertaking each exercise. Of course one may not get what one asks for. Nevertheless persons entering into the exercise should formulate for themselves what they want to achieve through it.

Meditation
Meditation engages a person's memory, intellect, and will, the three powers of the soul, on successive topics, propositions, phrases, or

---

21. Examples of the "preludes" that Ignatius prescribed are found in the text of Reflection II.17, Two Types of Life (The Two Standards) and Reflection II.22, Three Types of People (Three Classes of Persons).

points that can be distinguished within the subject matter of the text. These will vary with the object of the meditation, but the format can be schematized in a general manner as follows:

1. *The Memory* calls to mind the truth or moral maxim or set of principles or theological passage to be considered and fixes its words or its elements or its components in the mind.
2. *The Intellect* considers the meaning of the text, truth, or principle by slowly considering it from various angles, turning it over in the mind. Two distinct questions are implicitly being entertained, the one after the other:
   a. What does the truth mean in its context, as far as one can tell?
   b. What possible meanings does it have for me, or open up for my future?
3. *The Will* weighs whether this truth or maxim makes any claim on one's moral sense or allegiance and whether it impels any decision or course of action.

Concluding Colloquy

The conclusion of a meditation for Ignatius consists in a colloquy with God. A colloquy is an informal and personal conversation. The character of the colloquy is discussed below in relation to a contemplation.

The Structure of a Contemplation. Although a contemplation shares the same general structure as a meditation, it has a considerably different character because of the different type of subject matter. Whereas a meditation deals with something that is notional and abstract, a contemplation turns to a narrative or a dynamic scenario. The subject matter of a meditation appeals to reason and discursive intelligence, and a contemplation appeals more explicitly to the imagination as the controlling mental function. A meditation looks for light and insight; a contemplation expects to be moved and looks for a resonant affectivity. Compartmentalization such as this, however, never quite succeeds, as a person cannot escape either imagination or intelligence in any form of reflection. But the emphasis falls in a different place, and it gives the exercise a different character.

Introductory Phase

The Introductory Phase begins with the introductory prayer and has three preludes.

1. *Preparatory Prayer*: The preparatory prayer is the same invariable petition as in a meditation.
2. *First Prelude*: Ignatius stipulates three preludes for a contemplation as distinct from the two in a meditation. The second and

third of a contemplation correspond with the first and second of a meditation. But the new "first prelude" helps define the distinctiveness of a contemplation. It consists in "calling to mind the history of the subject I have to contemplate" (SE, 102). This corresponds with the shift of subject matter to a narrative. It can often be accomplished by recalling a scenario or more practically by reading a text and situating the story in a history. This sets up from the outset the narrative character of this kind of exercise. It may be that the story contains moral maxims or a general truth, but the approach to such a reflection begins from below, from a concrete series of events. This becomes clear in the next prelude.

3. *Second Prelude*: "This is a mental representation of the place. It will be here to see . . ." (SE, 103). From one point of view this prelude is that same as the initial prelude of a meditation, but because Ignatius envisages a dynamic scene with players, he uses the word "observe" and the language of "seeing in imagination" (SE, 112). A person is to re-create the scene and the dramatic action in the imagination. The content of the contemplation is a concrete unfolding scenario. "See who is there and hear what they say and notice what they do." In effect a person is putting oneself into the narrative as a participant observer.

4. *Third Prelude*: "This is to ask for what I desire" (SE, 104) and is formally identical with the second prelude of a meditation but with some distinction because of the prominence of the imagination. For example, when Ignatius suggests that one ask for an "intimate knowledge" of the subject matter, this implies an affective response that includes an impulse to action.

The Contemplation

In contrast with a meditation a contemplation is characterized by a shift from the "powers" of a person (memory, intelligence, and will) to the imagination that attaches to the sensible sphere. The imagination relates to the concrete visible world, the audible world, and so on. It also considers the relationship of the subject, the self, to the projected persons and events that make up the scene and the narrative. A variation of the contemplation structures it explicitly around the five senses: "This will consist of applying the five senses to the matter . . ." (SE, 121). The instructions are to see, observe, hear, smell, feel, and taste the characters of the scene, who are involved, and what is going on. One becomes an actor in the scene, and thus something to be considered is the self and how one relates to what is unfolding. The point is existential closeness and engagement to promote an affective reaction.

Concluding Colloquy

There is no substantial difference between the colloquy of a meditation and that of a contemplation other than what the subject matter may suggest. The colloquy, as indicated earlier, consists in a conversation with God. Ludolph of Saxony wrote out formal colloquies for those who took up his *Life of Christ*, but generally Ignatius left the content of this conversation open. The freedom of a spontaneous or unscripted personal dialogue fits with Ignatius's conviction about noninterference with either the retreatant's freedom or the working of the divine Spirit. Ignatius envisaged this as a deeply personal, transparent, and honest conversation, qualities that are in turn the measure of it being a conversation with God.

The Prayer of a Seeker. If a seeker is one who is not religious but agnostic toward religious beliefs in God, a personal colloquy with God represents fairly precisely where he or she cannot go. It makes no sense for a seeker to read a prescribed prayer when the very point of a colloquy requires interpersonal reciprocity. At this point certain spiritual seekers may hit a wall. How can seekers who have had no encounter with a personal God entertain such a colloquy?

No specific response to such a question can apply to all seekers because the category reaches far and no two persons are identical. With that caution registered, it may still be helpful to appeal to language from the recognized mainstream of the Christian tradition that deals with analogous problems. This approach may be relevant for some seekers who embark upon the Exercises and for those who are responsible for offering them to others. This tradition includes "negative theology," which appreciates how God transcends everything we know in this world. It recognizes that one can stand before the mystery that Jesus points to in his ministry and relate to it as the absolute mystery of being in a stance that might be called "apophatic mysticism."[22] The question is, how would one describe the prayer of an apophatic mystic?

---

22. This phrase is drawn from Wesley J. Wildman, who uses it to describe a theologian's relation to God that has been shaped by an encounter with naturalism within the context of the discussion of the relation between science and [Christian] religion. The position grows out of a sense of how deeply anthropomorphism shapes the public language of God and God's action in the world. In contrast to this, it reflects an internalization of the absolute incomprehensible mystery of God, while at the same time experiencing this transcendence of God as a presence that grounds the being of all things that exist. His statement of this position can be found in Wesley J. Wildman, "Ground-of-Being Theologies," in *The Oxford Handbook of Religion and Science*, ed. Philip Clayton (Oxford: Oxford University Press, 2006), 612-32; idem, "Further Reflections on the Divine Action Project," *Science and Theology* 3 (March 2005), 71-83.

A mystical tradition has been a strain of Christian spirituality almost from its inception. It has its roots in an awareness of the God-ness of God. Because the imagination binds all human knowing to the concrete, human beings have no direct access to transcendent reality. Ultimate reality transcends all finitude and all sensible images. Even the idea of God as person acts as a symbol that draws human openness into absolute mystery. In the Thomistic tradition Meister Eckhart had the intuition that God cannot be equated with anything but, as pure act of being, is "no-thing" but the all-encompassing energy of being itself. In his sermon on Paul, who after being knocked to the ground on his way to Damascus, rose, and with his eyes open saw nothing, Eckhart understands Paul encountering God because God is nothing. God cannot be any thing because every thing is limited. To conceive of God as something is not to grasp even the notion of God for God is nothing.[23] The seeker by definition has an appreciation that noth-ing that he or she has found is God. The seeker has a sense of some encompassing reality that appeals to the pure openness of the human quest. That quest implies a basic trust in being itself. Standing before the unknown in silence from within such an openness is a colloquy.

The prayer of a seeker may be described as a prayer to an unknown God. Such a prayer bears an unresolved paradoxical structure of rec-ognizing a presence within an absence. It implicitly responds to an unknown. It attends but does not speak because words do not encom-pass the experience, and all names distort what presents itself only in its being sought. Silence alone expresses this kind of recognition. In this response faith yields to hope, a restless trust that absolute mystery, whether it be called opaque or luminous, by its utter transcendence of all that is, supplies or includes within itself its own appropriate response. Is this prayer? Perhaps it cannot be so named by the firm believer who stands outside the experience. But Ignatius's creation mysticism in his Contemplation to Attain Love, when it is coupled with the new story of the universe, moves people in the direction of such an experience from both ends of a spectrum that runs between doubting belief and inquiring agnosticism.

* * *

Part I has been a lengthy introduction to the Spiritual Exercises of Ignatius Loyola directed at, roughly speaking, three audiences that are quite different. On one side are firm Christian believers, includ-ing those who are familiar with the Exercises and have internalized

---

23. Meister Eckhart, *Meister Eckhart: Teacher and Preacher*, ed. Bernard McGinn (New York: Paulist Press, 1986), sermon 71.

their energy. This group of people may be challenged by the interpretations elicited by an audience of seekers. On the other side, seekers represent an open set of people that share two qualities: they lack the stability that a firm faith can ensure, and they are looking for deeper dimensions of human existence to nurture their spirituality. A good number of people stand somewhere between these two groups; they have faith in transcendent reality but are asking questions; they may have some religious belonging, but it is not satisfying their spiritual longing. The reflections in Part II are directed to people in all three of these groups. They are meant to accompany those who approach spirituality through a Christian framework structured by Ignatius's Spiritual Exercises.

PART II

Reflections to Accompany the Spiritual Exercises

Part II offers a series of reflections on the meditations and contemplations of Ignatius's Spiritual Exercises. The reflections are divided into four weeks and follow the logic of the Exercises described in Chapter 3. In certain cases the reinterpretation of the Exercises for our time calls for a change of the name of the meditation or contemplation. The scriptural passages chosen as the subject matter of the contemplations sometimes correspond with those chosen by Ignatius, but they are all drawn from Luke's gospel for consistency and to show the prominent role of the Spirit in Jesus' ministry. The First Week is entitled "Anthropology"; it does for our time and for the envisioned audience of this work what the themes of sin and grace did for those undertaking the Exercises in the sixteenth century. The Second Week is considerably longer than the others because it deals with the substance of Christian spirituality drawn from Jesus of Nazareth. Ignatius did not envisage a literal division of time assigned to the Weeks, and the length of the Second Week fits his principle of adaptation. In a fairly traditional interpretation, the election has been situated at the end of the Second Week. In preparation for a major life decision or correction of one's life course, a reflection on Ignatius's discernment of spirits prefaces the consideration of the election. The Third Week concerns the execution of Jesus and the Lukan account of his suffering and death. The Fourth Week traditionally turns to the resurrection of Jesus as testified to by the appearance narratives in the gospels. The reflections of the Fourth Week extend the revelations of the Easter experience to a mission of sharing its gifts with others and to the story of the formation of a Jesus movement, from its origin to the present time. The Exercises end with the creation mysticism that Ignatius presents in the final Contemplation to Attain Love.

Anthropology

Ignatius composed the Spiritual Exercises in a late medieval world and intended them for Catholics who shared his culture. In the First Week Ignatius proposed exercises that lead to a number of elementary but profound experiences. One such experience may be a sense of being a part of God's creation, which has a stable structure and is moving toward an intended goal. Another experience revolves around the theme of honest self-knowledge before an omnipotent, all-seeing God. This entails taking stock of one's moral failings. Still another experience, intimately related to the others, goes to the heart of the Christian vision. Ignatius wanted a person to feel God's forgiveness and acceptance of him or herself in particular, despite any sin and precisely as each one is. This experience spills over into a response to God's love with gratitude. These encompassing spiritual experiences penetrate deeply into the foundation of Ignatius's spiritual vision.

The meditations of the First Week function as a preparation for entry into the narrative of Jesus of Nazareth, and they have their own integrity. But the ability to appreciate those fundamental spiritual experiences cannot be presupposed. They depend on some relatively basic ideas that may not be commonly held or whose meaning might not be understood. Most people in our secular world recognize the words "creation," "sin," "God," and "freedom" and may even use them in conversation. But who would argue that they bear a common meaning, let alone one that would be universally accepted as relevant or true, in a randomly selected group? Right at the start of the Exercises, then, we confront the distance between the thoroughly religious late medieval world and our own religiously pluralistic and secular world. Fundamental conceptions of reality vary so radically that it becomes impossible to broach the subject of spirituality without first establishing an elementary vocabulary.

These reflections, therefore, deal with some basic conceptions and questions that are frequently presupposed in Christian spirituality and whose meanings are particularly unstable today. For example, as people internalize the scientific story of the making of the universe, our planet and species, how are they to integrate that knowledge with a spiritual sense of being created? How can the evolutionary story of life reinforce a sense of the sustaining power of God? How a person understands the nature of humanity and character of the human person cannot be taken for granted.

The reflections in the First Week that follow are designed to preserve and represent the experiences of created contingency, honesty before God, and gratitude for God's creation and love. They aim at bridging the culture of Ignatius and the culture of the twenty-first-century developed world. Together these reflections relate to our world the basic conceptions that lie behind the scriptures in a manner proportionate or analogous to the way Ignatius's First Week meditations did to his world. The italicized texts are quotations from the indicated sources.

1. Looking for Principles and a Foundation

Human beings are created to praise, reverence, and serve God our Lord, and by means of this to save their souls.

The other things on the face of the earth are created for the human beings, to help them in working toward the end for which they are created.

From this it follows that I should use these things to the extent that they help me toward my end, and rid myself of them to the extent that they hinder me.

To do this, I must make myself indifferent to all created things, in regard to everything which is left to my freedom of will and is not forbidden. Consequently, on my own part I ought not to seek health rather than sickness, wealth rather than poverty, honor rather than dishonor, a long life rather than a short one, and so on in all other matters.

I ought to desire and elect only the thing which is more conducive to the end for which I am created.

— Ignatius Loyola, *Spiritual Exercises*, 23

Ignatius Loyola possessed what many reflective people in our world do not: a first principle and foundation upon which he could build his life. Even religious people may not enjoy this privilege. But this preface to his Exercises opens up salutary questions for our time: Who am I? Why am I here? Does some larger purpose underlie being itself and human existence? Is it realistically possible in our age to imagine or formulate a comprehensive vision of reality?

When human beings are considered in relation to other forms of life they stand out on the basis of their freedom. While continuity marks evolutionary creation and all forms of life, freedom differentiates the human. A fundamental impulse for life animates all forms of living creatures: they strive to continue living, to grow and flourish. In an analogous manner the human species has a drive for the flourishing of freedom. This can be experienced by each person even though the conceptions of exactly what constitutes such full flourishing vary wildly.

The human freedom experienced by each person within the species carries a tension between a sense of one's own individuality and being a part of a community and society. Paul Tillich described the polarity between being an individual and being a member of a community as part of the structure of human existence. Wide variations exist along a spectrum from autonomy to responsibility to a group, but neither dimension can be reasonably negated. The narrative of one's life reinforces a person's individuality; human beings live in time and become more defined as individuals by their stories. Yet they are always accompanied by others, and no one exists independent of the influences of community. If principles and a foundation for human existence are found, they will have to be such that they are both common and at the same time bear direct relevance for the unique individual.

Ignatius writes of human sovereignty over the world of nature and the things of this world. We live today with a knowledge of the human not available to the sixteenth century: how deeply human existence is immersed in nature and replicates the inorganic and organic strata of evolution; how human existence itself depends on an integrated relationship with nature; how powerfully collective freedom can threaten its own existence by deep damage to the planet. We have learned that the things of this world are not only "created for human beings" but also that human beings are created to tend and care for the "other things on the face of the earth." These points dramatically illustrate how freedom is bound to matter, transcends it, and is responsible for the world on a broad evolutionary scale but with immediate practical consequences. John Calvin captured this responsibility in his principle of stewardship: the things of this world "were so given to us by the kindness of God, and so destined for our benefit, that they are, as it were, entrusted to us, and we must one day render account of them."[1]

When Ignatius distinguishes between ends and means, he engages in a consideration of principles and a foundation. Distinguishing between ends and means provides some sense of an internal order of

---

1. John Calvin, *Calvin: Institutes of the Christian Religion*, ed. John T. McNeill (Philadelphia: Westminster, 1960), 3.10.5.

things. If the distinctive mark of human existence is its freedom, and if freedom contains an inner dynamism for flourishing, the distinction between ends and means establishes a way of speaking about a possible coherence within human existence without an appeal to an externally imposed ideology. The things that are means to foster human freedom appear as good, and those things which suppress human freedom are evil. This is hardly the end of a discussion because there may be little agreement about exactly what constitutes freedom. But a recognition of the possibility of talking about principles and foundations represents ground gained.

Ignatius lays down another basic principle about human freedom when he talks about "attachments" and "indifference." The word "attachments" accurately describes our little addictions, wherein freedom develops dependencies. We pick a thing up, it sticks, and we can't shake it off. Ignatius uses the term "indifference" in a positive and not in its more common negative sense of no reaction at all. Freedom can be cool or passionate, but in either case it remains sovereign over itself. True freedom is light and not weighed down by attachments. Paradoxically, it grows in strength with its lightness, because detachment makes room for reflective decision. And freedom's strength, when it is responsible, engenders freedom's flourishing. The ancient philosophers were right in perceiving the height of freedom as the ability to commit the self. Self-disposition transcends attachments.

The quest for and the exercise of true freedom in our world today elicits considerably more obstacles than in the sixteenth century. Many of these stem from the pervasive pluralism that marks contemporary life. Two consequences deserve mention in the context of a search for principles and a foundation.

Blaise Pascal, the seventeenth-century scientist and Christian apologist, formulated humanity's basic wager in a relatively homogeneous world. At the time of his authorship, spiritual competition from Jews and Muslims was suppressed. He virtually framed the wager between two options as a flip of a coin. On the one side, the option against God, was the status quo, misery in this world, and nothing thereafter. On the other side was a meaningful life in this world and eternal happiness in the next. "Compare the two chances: if you win, you win everything; if you lose, you lose nothing. Don't hesitate, then. Make a bet that God exists."[2] In his context and with those options, the choice seems relatively easy compared with one in our secularized and religiously pluralistic world. Yet Pascal's wager remains instructive in

---

2. Blaise Pascal, *Pensées* in *The Essential Pascal*, ed. Robert W. Gleason (New York: Mentor-Omega Book, 1966), 91.

one respect: one has to choose. In Pascal's formulation the risk was so one-sided that it barely existed at all. Today the factor of risk involved in choosing God has been augmented by a dazzling array of options.

Establishing principles and a foundation for one's spirituality, then, demands the risks of choice and commitment. No storm-free zone exists for those who actively participate in today's world. One must choose, because not to choose is to choose. But assuming responsibility to locate a center of gravity for living is too important a decision to be left entirely to whim or private logic. An individual needs public options and stories to have any chance of finding real principles and anything like a foundation. An ethical assessment and protection of the deepest dimension of one's freedom requires some sort of community or social ratification. A purely idiosyncratic spirituality that makes no appeal to generally reasonable principles and a public story hardly appears accountable. One has to choose, and one should choose responsibly.

One way of taking stock of one's spirituality consists of deliberately measuring it against a common standard. Such a standard should be public, as in the case of the narratives of the world religions. From the very beginning of the human race people have shaped their spiritual lives by the sacred narratives of a community. The public and traditional character of these narratives give them a depth and authority that transcend any individual: they have withstood the test of variations according to time, place, and circumstance.

Seeking principles and a foundation for spirituality requires focus, method, and sustained effort. The Exercises of Ignatius Loyola provide a structure for the search. They unfold within the grand narrative of Christianity and focus on the ministry of Jesus of Nazareth as it was remembered and interpreted by his followers during the decades after his death and resurrection. They facilitate realistic imaginative entry into the logic of Jesus' ministry, guided by the individual gospel stories that preserve his memory. They rest upon an elementary process of learning from Jesus, as a revealer of God and teacher of the fundamental values of being and living before God. The premise of the Spiritual Exercises lies in the conviction that Jesus represents a universally relevant teaching about ultimate reality and a model of human life consonant with it.

2. The Evolutionary Order of the World

Keeping in mind the image of Earth from space, consider four aspects of this planet and its place in the universe. First: it is very old. In billions of years, the key numbers are 14, 5, and 4. The universe originated in a primordial flaring forth, rather inelegantly named the Big Bang, about fourteen billion years ago. . . . From that explosive instant onward to this day, the universe has continued to expand, as galaxies and their stars come into being and pass away. Our own sun and its planets emerged about five billion years ago, coalescing from the dust and gas left by previous generations of stars that exploded in their death throes. On planet Earth about four billion years ago, a new eruption occurred, Life, emerging in communities of single-celled creatures deep in the primeval seas and evolving into the more than one million species present today. . . . Second, the universe is incomprehensibly large. There are over one hundred billion galaxies, each comprising billions of stars, and no one knows how many moons and planets, all of this visible and audible matter being only a fraction of the matter in the universe, which, being not well understood, is called "dark." Earth is a small planet orbiting a medium-sized star toward the edge of one spiral galaxy. We are but a speck. Third, the universe is complexly interconnected, everything being related to everything else to some degree. . . . Quite literally, human beings and all creatures on this planet are made of stardust. The story of biological evolution, moreover, makes evident that we humans share with all other living creatures a common genetic ancestry tracing back to the original single-celled creatures in the ancient seas. . . . Fourth, the universe is profoundly dynamic. Even as you read these words, new space is coming into being as the universe continues to expand outward. Galaxies whirl around their central black hole; our planet revolves yearly around our star and rotates on its axis every day; whole species emerge, thrive, and go extinct, as do individuals whose time span arches from birth to death. No longer, then, can theology contrast nature's static regularity with human history, or oppose the fixed pagan gods of nature with the mobile God of the Israelites on the move in history. Nature itself is historical.

— Elizabeth A. Johnson, Quest for the Living God:
Mapping Frontiers in the Theology of God
(New York/London: Continuum, 2007), 183-85

This account of creation from a scientific perspective frequently stimulates a deeper sense of religious wonder and awe than does the mythic story of Adam and Eve. It displaces that story with a vivid sense of human smallness, contingency, and complex dependency. If religious spirituality begins with questioning and wonder, science has provided a new religious impetus. How does the unimaginable size of the universe, which has evolved through the interaction of stable laws and randomness over an immense period of time, affect an understanding of human existence?

Spirit and matter meet in human consciousness. Human subjectivity provides a theater in which spectacular dramas unfold. We see fatalists take precautions to avoid an accident and thereby contradict their theories of doom. Determinists debate among themselves the relevance of a given scientific experiment and thereby implicitly deny their determinism. The nihilist worries about the appropriateness of a gift to a niece and thereby honors value. The purely self-interested pragmatist enters into a deep personal relationship, experiences moral obligation and perhaps love, and becomes disoriented.

In human consciousness the objective order is framed by self-consciousness and becomes the subject matter of human knowledge. Within human consciousness the whole of matter, the universe of fire, ice, and stone and all chemical and biological processes, becomes transformed into a new world charged with meaning. With the emergence of the human species, evolution ushered in a new dimension of existence.

Human beings observe the world as spectators and interact with it as a set of objects outside the self. So it is with other forms of life. But with intentional reflection human consciousness can penetrate to a deeper level of being in the world. This begins with the recognition that human beings exist as parts of the whole. Human persons do not stand outside the physical world as if it were other in kind. Science has underlined in the strongest of terms this obvious point by demonstrating the continuity of the lines of evolution and the interrelated character of everything that exists. Human existence is worldly existence.

Yet many phenomena account for the tendency of human beings to stand back from the world and project it as something outside the self. As a species, human beings have tried to dominate the non-human sphere by manipulating the things of the world for their own well-being. As a higher form of being, human consciousness appears so transparent to itself that each individual experiences a self-consciousness. This engenders a certain self-possession that allows each person a distinct and unique perspective on a seemingly exterior reality. When the self remains unexamined and operates wholly from within its own spiritual space, its self-absorption tends to draw the entire world into itself. This ability to "look out over" the world and to become an objective observer of the world and user of its objects paradoxically can limit freedom by binding the human spirit to those very objects. Spending spiritual capital on the acquisition of objects frequently restricts freedom by creating attachments that distract the human spirit, weigh it down, and conceal deeper and more expansive levels of meaning.

Evolutionary biology confirms that human subjectivity simultaneously participates in the physical world and stands apart from it, considers it, reflectively differentiates itself from it, freely acts upon it, and intentionally shapes it. Human spirit, consciousness, and freedom are interchangeable terms when they designate a space where reality becomes self-conscious, intentional, and responsible. Human consciousness is the world conscious of itself. Being conscious in the world and of the world thus entails a two-way traffic: the world creates the human subject and fills it with content, and the human spirit deliberately acts in and upon the world in new and creative ways as freedom. This interpenetration of the human spirit and physical world means that to know more about the world and its evolution is to know more about the self: evolution is each person's history. It also means that to know the self is to know the world, for the self is the physical world conscious of itself. The human is spirit of the world.

The reciprocal relationship between matter and spirit provides a premise for human beings to learn about themselves from the world, and about the world from human subjectivity. The human as a conscious part of the world allows its knowledge of the universe to shed light on the human self. The nonseparability of human freedom and the physical world allows the human imagination to find in the natural world resonances of its own dynamic subjectivity. This reciprocity allows human beings to project meaning found in themselves upon the universe of which it is a part. This principle of correlation based on mutual revelation deepens any contemplation of the world.

The effort to imagine the size of the universe, for example, provokes human awe. Yet this world and this history have generated each individual being. Thus, each personal consciousness is a part of this whole universe, constituted by its energy, stardust indeed. Each person is related to all things; the same stuff that constructs the world produces the human subject. This notion of the history of the universe embodied in each individual person forces expansive thinking that approaches the metaphysical. This vision of the universe compels new conceptions of the human that are more humble, dynamic, related, and engaged. The enormity of the theater of human existence, and the momentum behind its production, both diminishes and exalts the human subject.

The randomness and contingency that characterize the genesis of the universe touch the existence of every individual human person. Just as rigid formulas cannot account for the course of trial and error that evolution takes, so too is human freedom unpredictable even on a personal level. As the human subject stands before the world and asks why it is the way it is, the same question may be addressed in exactly the same terms relative to the self: why is being at all? And why is it the way it is? Why am I, and why am I who I am? That these questions generate many different answers does not mean the questions are misguided. It means that the depth of the issues cannot be harnessed in a single perspective or line of thought and that most answers will bear some truth.

The intricate interrelatedness that describes nature reflects as in a mirror the complexity of the human person. Delicately calibrated organization marks large systems in nature from the wing of a mosquito to the complex psyche of a human being. The beauty of these systems utterly transcends sensible delight and draws one into questions of being. Who cannot wonder where the design of such intricate interrelatedness comes from? And when the response comes back, "the steady increment of natural selection over vast periods of time," does that satisfy? Or are there more questions to be asked?

In the human dialogue with the universe, just as the world impresses itself upon human subjectivity, so too does human experience project meaning onto the universe. If the universe reproduces its patterns within human subjectivity, then the meanings discovered within human thought can be affirmed of the universe. If human existence can find within itself meaning, value, and an impulse to trust the future, then these qualities are part of "nature" and can be predicated analogously of the world. Since human spirit is spirit of the world, the purposefulness that human beings spontaneously demand of their own lives can be demanded of the universe that resonates within them. This dialogue never has and never will produce a comprehensive and coherent picture of a universe in full course of its evolutionary process, but it encourages investment in a purposeful universe.

3. Creation

In the beginning when God created the heavens and the earth, ²the earth was a formless void and darkness covered the face of the deep, while a wind from God swept over the face of the waters. ³Then God said, "Let there be light"; and there was light. ⁴And God saw that the light was good; and God separated the light from the darkness. ⁵God called the light Day, and the darkness he called Night. And there was evening and there was morning, the first day. ⁶And God said, "Let there be a dome in the midst of the waters, and let it separate the waters from the waters." ⁷So God made the dome and separated the waters that were under the dome from the waters that were above the dome.

And it was so. [8]God called the dome Sky. And there was evening and there was morning, the second day. [9]And God said "Let the waters under the sky be gathered together into one place, and let the dry land appear." And it was so. [10]God called the dry land Earth, and the waters that were gathered together he called Seas. And God saw that it was good. [11]Then God said, "Let the earth put forth vegetation: plants yielding seed, and fruit trees of every kind on earth that bear fruit with the seed in it." And it was so. [12]The earth brought forth vegetation: plants yielding seed of every kind, and trees of every kind bearing fruit with the seed in it. And God saw that it was good. [13]And there was evening and there was morning, the third day. [14]And God said, "Let there be lights in the dome of the sky to separate the day from the night; and let them be for signs and for seasons and for days and years, [15]and let them be lights in the dome of the sky to give light upon the earth." And it was so. [16]God made the two great lights—the greater light to rule the day and the lesser light to rule the night—and the stars. [17]God set them in the dome of the sky to give light upon the earth, [18]to rule over the day and over the night, and to separate the light from the darkness. And God saw that it was good. [19]And there was evening and there was morning, the fourth day. [20]And God said, "Let the waters bring forth swarms of living creatures, and let birds fly above the earth across the dome of the sky." [21]So God created the great sea monsters and every living creature that moves, of every kind, with which the waters swarm, and every winged bird of every kind. And God saw that it was good. [22]God blessed them, saying, "Be fruitful and multiply and fill the waters in the seas, and let birds multiply on the earth." [23]And there was evening and there was morning, the fifth day. [24]And God said, "Let the earth bring forth living creatures of every kind: cattle and creeping things and wild animals of the earth of every kind." And it was so. [25]God made the wild animals of the earth of every kind, and the cattle of every kind, and everything that creeps upon the ground of every kind. And God saw that it was good. [26]Then God said, "Let us make humankind in our image, according to our likeness; and let them have dominion over the fish of the sea, and over the birds of the air, and over the cattle, and over all the wild animals of the earth, and over every creeping thing that creeps upon the earth." [27]So God created humankind in his image, in the image of God he created them; male and female he created them. [28]God blessed them, and God said to them, "Be fruitful and multiply, and fill the earth and subdue it; and have dominion over the fish of the sea and over the birds of the air and over every living thing that moves upon the earth." [29]God said, "See, I have given you every plant yielding seed that is upon the face of all the earth, and every tree with seed in its fruit; you shall have them for food. *30And to every beast of the earth, and to every bird of the air, and to everything that creeps on the earth, everything that has the breath of life, I have given every green plant for food." And it was so. 31God saw everything that he had made, and indeed, it was very good. And there was evening and there was morning, the sixth day. 21 Thus the heavens and the earth were finished, and all their multitude. 2And on the seventh day God finished the work that he had done, and he rested on the seventh day from all the work that he had done. 3So God blessed the seventh day and hallowed it, because on it God rested from all the work that he had done in creation.*

— Genesis 1:1-2:3

This text is the source for the Jewish and Christian vision of reality as created by God out of nothing, not just in the beginning but continuously, making God the ground or sustaining energy of being itself. This reflection does not aim to make all that fall into place, but it supplies a number of paths along which the mind might travel in the search for light. Such a light can never lay mystery bare, but it can illumine some ways to appropriate these very different scientific and religious stories.

Meditation on creation can be confusing. The last consideration was not religious, but the awesome character of the story of the universe solicits a religious sensibility. The opening chapter of Genesis, by contrast, makes a direct statement about God, creator of heaven and earth, in strictly theistic terms. This stately mythic story has nurtured the piety of Jews and Christians for millennia. But taken at face value this story misleads at several points: it depicts God as a big person who, like a potter, shaped the world as we know it, and this was done "in the beginning" all at once, so that stable order and monarchical rule underlie all reality. The scientific story contradicts this at almost every point and can leave the religious imagination in a state of bewilderment.

God cannot be a big person in the sky. The metaphor of the artist shaping matter into art forms vividly symbolizes the "creative" act: partly free, partly led by the elements, partly intuitive, partly deliberate. With imaginative calculation the artist culls new form out of rough material to give it new meaning. Theistic religions provoke the imagination spontaneously to project such a creator of all reality. The scientific story of the universe interrupts this familiar metaphor mainly by calculating the sheer size of the universe. The mind recognizes the words "infinite creator," and they seem to make sense. But the imagination balks at the concept. Because the reflective mind cannot form a spatial image of the size of the universe, the image of an infinitely large artist collapses. The creator cannot be like anything known; no finite agent supplies a realistic metaphor. The new story of the universe hammers home Thomas Aquinas's conviction: whereas we may know *that* God is, human beings cannot know, and especially cannot imagine, *what* God is.

Creation by God does not refer to an event that took place "in the beginning." Both stories of the universe begin "in the beginning" and thus suggest that creation in a religious sense refers to an action that initiated a temporal process. The imagination provides a simple image of God establishing the players and initiating a chain of events in motion through time. But the contemporary human mind has no real grasp of a temporal event of creation. Such an action of God by definition would utterly transcend human knowledge.

A spiritual or religious approach to creation does not proceed "outside-in" but "inside-out." The mind does not deduce creation from observation but intuits it from within human experience. Because human persons are a part of the universe, each person is a part of the universe that is self-conscious. And people are able to experience within themselves a dimension of their being that is not subject to their control but absolutely dependent on an outside power, not only in the beginning but at any given moment. People do not have power over the source and ground of their own existence. The idea of divine creation, of establishing an orderly world out of nothing, finds its roots in this primal experience. The idea that the world and the human person were created by a transcendent agency does not come from outside but from within the experience of being a finite creature. And despite its size, the universe, like the self who is a conscious part of it, is finite creature. The Genesis narrative comes alive when read as a narrative poem expressing human wonder at this dimension of the self and the world.

God is God and not an idol. This simple saying conceals a complex logic deep within human subjectivity that is overwhelmingly confirmed by both stories of creation. When human beings confront themselves by reflection and recognize the contingency of their being and being itself, their radical dependence contrasts with that power of being from which all is dependent, whatever it be. All beings are dependent; God is the name for the ground of being upon which all things depend. No one has a clear idea of what absolute being really means or refers to other than transcending all limit or finitude. Thus, all human beings theoretically could agree on what God is not, namely, anything that is finite or of this world. For many this is a cliché. For others it supplies leverage to see through the imposters, to recognize false claims, to criticize nation or race when it begins to subordinate human life to itself. The transcendence of ultimate reality, when it is associated with the source and ground of being, cannot be conceived as a human rival but only as the protector and guarantor of what creation is meant to be. The religious story of creation asserts this rather directly in anthropomorphic language. The massive power of the scientific story suggests that whatever the ultimate source of being is, it cannot be simply identified as a piece of the whole. God is inexhaustibly transcendent. Whatever God is, creation signifies that God is not primarily authority over or against the human but as its creator totally the advocate of human flourishing.

God's transcendence does not equal distance but presence. The size of the universe cannot be confused with the transcendence of ultimate reality, or God. But because human beings cannot understand anything without the residue of a concrete image, the new story of the size of the universe tends to push God higher and farther away from our speck of a planet. The story in Genesis actually reflects a small world that the new story has exploded with a big bang into a universe. Yet the religious doctrine of creation complements the explosion of the Big Bang with an implosion of the creator's concern for all of creation, even in the finitude of its infinitesimal parts. When the creator is conceived as creating out of nothing, nothing stands between the creator and the creature. Genesis has been refined by doctrine: in the religious conception, God does not use a medium or elements to fashion the universe. Creation out of nothing means that finite reality exists by the command of the creating power of the creator. Science tends to understand reality itself as energy. The Hebrew and Christian scriptures use an analogous metaphor, "Spirit," meaning energy of life and existence, but in a transformed religious way. Spirit in a religious sense is the immanent presence of the creating and enlivening power of God. These two languages are not the same, but comparative alternating between them generates insight.

The religious story of creation incorporates into itself the scientific and makes the universe sacramental. Some readings mistakenly collapse these two stories into each other and confuse them, taking the religious for the scientific and vice versa. It is important to recognize that they are not the same story because they rest on different sources and have meanings according to different logics. The scientific is extrapolation from empirical data; the religious story is extrapolation from religious experience. Given their different logics, they do not have to interact, but they can. For example, one cannot hold on to the religious story and completely dismiss the scientific story because religious language cannot neglect the very object to which the doctrine of creation refers. In other words, imaginative reference to the universe means that the doctrine of creation has to integrate contemporary understanding of the universe into itself. Done conscientiously, internalizing the scientific account of the genesis of the universe and life into the religious creation story can also be completely transforming. The interacting of the stories should not be understood as confusing or mixing the two. But when they are considered as parallels, the religious narrative transforms the scientific story by turning the universe into sacrament. The energy of God becomes a deeper or primary sustaining force of being and its unfolding: God is the dynamism and momentum of the evolving universe. The immanent presence of God cannot be read naively off the surface of everyday events or world developments, but it can still be experienced as the power of being itself.

The influence moves as well in the other direction, when worldly experience leads to an active naming of ultimacy. Cosmogenesis and the evolution of life raises the question of the name of God or, better, the many names for ultimate reality. Humans have no platform on which to base a comparison. It is a mistake to think that one metaphor gets closer than any other to the reality of God. Everything known about the universe and the human militates against a single name for an absolutely transcendent ultimate reality. But this statement of humility on the part of human knowledge actually enhances what can be said about ultimate reality on the basis of a consideration of the world. For it calls for a human dialogue about perceptions of ultimacy. Because all revelation of transcendent reality occurs within the deep recesses of human subjectivity, one can use that very source as one that provides meaningful names. In other words, various realms of human experience open up to human consciousness levels of meaning that are transcendent. The source of all being can be referred to as the ultimate, the fully real, absolute being, the ground of being, the ontological norm of truth, the guarantor of value, the field or matrix of all finite forces, serendipitous creativity, absolute incomprehensible mystery. Each of these terms, and the meanings that lie beneath the proper names or categories of different religious systems, all lead back to primal human experience of the world, the universe, reality. The search for ultimate reality will never end, even when it grasps an individual person.

4. God: Provident Governor of the Universe

[1]Bless the Lord, O my soul. O Lord my God, you are very great. You are clothed with honor and majesty, [2]wrapped in light as with a garment. You stretch out the heavens like a tent, [3] you set the beams of

your chambers on the waters, you make the clouds your chariot, you ride on the wings of the wind, ⁴you make the winds your messengers, fire and flame your ministers. ⁵You set the earth on its foundations, so that it shall never be shaken. ⁶You cover it with the deep as with a garment; the waters stood above the mountains. ⁷At your rebuke they flee; at the sound of your thunder they take to flight. ⁸They rose up to the mountains, ran down to the valleys to the place that you appointed for them. ⁹You set a boundary that they may not pass, so that they might not again cover the earth. ¹⁰You make springs gush forth in the valleys; they flow between the hills, ¹¹giving drink to every wild animal; the wild asses quench their thirst. ¹²By the streams the birds of the air have their habitation; they sing among the branches. ¹³From your lofty abode you water the mountains; the earth is satisfied with the fruit of your work. ¹⁴You cause the grass to grow for the cattle, and plants for people to use, to bring forth food from the earth, ¹⁵and wine to gladden the human heart, oil to make the face shine, and bread to strengthen the human heart. ¹⁶The trees of the Lord are watered abundantly, the cedars of Lebanon that he planted. ¹⁷In them the birds build their nests; the stork has its home in the fir trees. ¹⁸The high mountains are for the wild goats; the rocks are a refuge for the coneys. ¹⁹You have made the moon to mark the seasons; the sun knows its time for setting. ²⁰You make darkness, and it is night, when all the animals of the forest come creeping out. ²¹The young lions roar for their prey, seeking their food from God. ²²When the sun rises, they withdraw and lie down in their dens. ²³People go out to their work and to their labor until the evening. ²⁴O Lord, how manifold are your works! In wisdom you have made them all; the earth is full of your creatures. ²⁵Yonder is the sea, great and wide, creeping things innumerable are there, living things both small and great. ²⁶There go the ships, and Leviathan that you formed to sport in it. ²⁷These all look to you to give them their food in due season; ²⁸when you give to them, they gather it up; when you open your hand, they are filled with good things. ²⁹When you hide your face, they are dismayed; when you take away their breath, they die and return to their dust. ³⁰When you send forth your spirit, they are created; and you renew the face of the ground. ³¹May the glory of the Lord endure for ever; may the Lord rejoice in his works— ³²who looks on the earth and it trembles, who touches the mountains and they smoke. ³³I will sing to the Lord as long as I live; I will sing praise to my God while I have being. ³⁴May my meditation be pleasing to him, for I rejoice in the Lord. ³⁵Let sinners be consumed from the earth, and let the wicked be no more. Bless the Lord, O my soul. Praise the Lord!

—Psalm 104

This psalm is an extraordinary prayer. In several respects it presents an account of creation that runs parallel to the first chapter of Genesis. But the prayer is in the present tense, depicting the actions of God as ongoing, transforming God's creating into providence and governance of the world. It directs the imagination to the whole world and easily leads to reflection on these traditional symbols of God ruling the universe and guiding history. Yet the violence of nature and of human beings calls God's providence and governance of the world into question. Can these literary symbols, the repetitive submission of creation to God's might, support a contemporary spirituality?

One way of appreciating this psalm consists of surrendering to its flow: it draws one into a panoramic embrace of the physical, organic, and social world. It transports the imagination across land, sea and sky, and descends to the particulars of daily life. The dynamic quality of the picture, for it is filled with action, transforms the picture of God from maker to caretaker. God does not appear as the potter at the wheel turning chaos into order but as the overseer of a well-planned and carefully tended garden. God works in all things. The order and harmony are organic, and everything fits together, because all things work together in an intricately complex way to produce and sustain life. Surely this is an idealized account that does not raise up the rough, wild side of nature that turns cold and ruthlessly violent. But the violence of nature does not negate what the psalmist encounters and feels. A later reflection will consider the damaged universe. This prayer celebrates the harmony that flows from the source of life: God designed the intricate web of life with wisdom and nurtures it by giving each living thing its food in due season. Should God withdraw attention, the breath of life itself subsides. God is the good governor of a good creation.

Two symbols occur in this psalm in a most natural and spontaneous way that belies their future importance in later Christian vocabulary: God's "wisdom" and God's "spirit." God has made all things in and through God's wisdom (v. 24). This term has a large history and too many connotations to list, but the basic sense of it here reflects a conviction that God's intelligence has infused the world with a certain discernible order. Also, the power by which God creates is God's spirit (v. 30). God's energy that bestows and sustains being is like the wind or the breath of life: invisible but real. God as spirit engenders life, and God as wisdom regulates it. These two aspects of God account for the wonderful harmony of creation through time. Even God glories and rejoices in this work. The psalmist invites all into this purely positive appreciation and grateful response.

The symbols of God's providence and governance of the world

respond to inner spiritual requirements that are deeply threatened. One requirement is for meaning. The search for meaning rises especially within the context of time: life unfolds into a future that is becoming less and less predictable. This threatens most people. A good example of how providence supplies meaning to life is found in Calvin's theology in which the sovereign God foresees the smallest event in the universe: "But even the hairs of your head are all numbered" (Luke 12:7). God's governance reinforces the sense of order in the universe and in society and adds a sense of empowerment that enables people courageously to confront the obstacles of life.

These symbols, however, have been so challenged by science, secularization, and a general disenchantment that many have discarded them as empty and others have never entertained them. The evolution of the world proceeds by random event across vast periods of time and not by purposeful design. The patterns that have evolved are ultimately contingent. More and more, the laws of nature are manipulated by human creativity, and humans appear to be taking over the governance of the world, with ominous results. Fewer people than ever appeal to transcendent causes for worldly events: the world is bereft of divine powers. These developments within the cultures of developed societies sharply contrast with the primitive romanticism of the psalmist. Even prayerful and reverent piety cannot abdicate clear thinking. Such are the objections of a postmodern culture.

These complaints represent experiences no less authentic than the enthusiasm of the psalmist. Is there room for equally honest accommodations on both sides? Where does religiously reverent realism lie? The symbols of divine providence and governance follow the same religious logic as the idea of creation out of nothing. They entail religious experience functioning within a field of transcendent inquiry. Divine providence does not interfere with the workings of nature and history but grounds them. Thus, whatever is said of providence and divine governance refers to God as the primary momentum behind the events of time, the evolutionary character of reality, all this-worldly causality, contingency, randomness, and freedom. This ever-present supporting power beneath all that actually happens does not intervene or supplant the empirical world but rather, as its ground, guarantees its autonomy. Providence and governance must be understood within the evolutionary world as transcendently embracing it.

More will be said in the next reflection on the experience of evil. But the two symbols used by the psalmist, God as Wisdom and God as Spirit, open the imagination to ways in which the enthusiasm of this prayer can be appropriated into today's cultural context. The metaphor of wisdom applied to God suggests a plan and design for the universe. Although the universe itself emerged by cosmic chance, each person looking backward and laterally at his or her life can recognize a chain of events that has constituted the self. In retrospect each human subject exists as the result of specific events that converge in the individual. The new story of the universe does not destroy design but reconceives it in constantly dynamic terms. The intelligence associated with a divine source, therefore, should not be imagined as a static, unchanging law or blueprint, but as a practical intelligence that continually recognizes, adjusts to, and transcendently enables interaction with new temporal situations. The factor of time integrated into rationality repositions God in the human imagination as dynamic interactive Wisdom.

The metaphor of spirit suggests the energy of life, the power of existence and growth, the force of creativity itself. When God is thought of as Spirit, the imagination reaches for the infinite source of the energy that flows through the universe, that stimulates life and finally freedom itself. God as Spirit, however, does not operate in the world as a finite actor: the creator God precisely is not a finite agent in history. God does not intervene in the world and act in creatures' stead, but is always present to creatures. A designation of what God as "Spirit" does might be "accompaniment." The idea of accompanying carries personalist connotations. The personal character of the infinite ground of all being completely transforms the abstract quality of God's immanent sustaining presence and power into active caring. God as Spirit symbolizes God, a present, actively accompanying and empowering creation through time and into the future. Representative human agents, such as prophets, provide a place to discern the direction or intention of God's empowerment.

The way one conceives the providence and governance of God has practical implications for spirituality, especially in the area of prayer of petition that asks for God's intervention. Scripture, the whole Christian tradition, and the daily lives of most Christians today exhibit the practice of asking things of God that we cannot provide ourselves. *Benedictus benedicat*: may the Blessed One bless us. Humans praise God, present needs, and ask God to respond. Have science, secularization, and skepticism occasioned a cold rational picture of the world and eviscerated the warm relationship people had with God that allowed them to ask God for the things they need? The answer to this question is a decisive no. Such a conclusion clearly misses the point of reflection, which is not to supplant primary religious language and practice but to clarify them. A religious experience of God's support of human existence remains the constant thread underlying the stories of creation, providence, and God's sovereign governance of the world.

The referent of that experience, God, can only be grasped negatively, as that which infinitely transcends all attempts at domestication. On the one hand, to proclaim what the creator of heaven and earth cannot be or do is self-contradictory. God is unlimited. Thus, the deep logic of petitionary prayer remains. It expresses a realistic dependence and need before God. On the other hand, one should chasten the childish desire for God to intervene in the course of history to satisfy immediate personal desires. Human beings who relate to God have to balance gratitude and hope: gratitude for every thing that augments human life, and hope that God's power of being envelop existence against the forces that destroy life so that it will come to a salutary end.

In the end, one has to hope the psalmist has it right. This prayer correlates with the human situation. Short of a full eschatology, God's providence and governance, that is, God's wisdom and spiritual presence and accompaniment, provide a priori grounds for courage in a complex, dynamic world.

5. The Disordered World

*30¹⁹He has cast me into the mire, and I have become like dust and ashes.
²⁰I cry to you and you do not answer me; I stand, and you merely look at me. ²¹You have turned cruel to me; with the might of your hand you persecute me. ²²You lift me up on the wind, you make me ride on it, and you toss me about in the roar of the storm. ²³I know that you will bring me to death, and to the house appointed for all living. ²⁴"Surely one does not turn against the needy, when in disaster they cry for help. ²⁵Did I not weep for those whose day was hard? Was not my soul grieved for the poor? ²⁶But when I looked for good, evil came; and when I waited for light, darkness came. ²⁷My inward parts are in turmoil, and are never still; days of affliction come to meet me. ²⁸I go about in sunless gloom; I stand up in the assembly and cry for help. ²⁹I am a brother of jackals, and a companion of ostriches. ³⁰My skin turns black and falls from me, and my bones burn with heat. ³¹My lyre is turned to mourning, and my pipe to the voice of those who weep."*

31⁵"If I have walked with falsehood, and my foot has hurried to deceit— ⁶let me be weighed in a just balance, and let God know my integrity!— ⁷if my step has turned aside from the way, and my heart has followed my eyes, and if any spot has clung to my hands; ⁸then let me sow, and another eat; and let what grows for me be rooted out."

38¹Then the Lord answered Job out of the whirlwind: ²"Who is this that darkens counsel by words without knowledge? ³Gird up your loins like a man, I will question you, and you shall declare to me. ⁴Where were you when I laid the foundation of the earth? Tell me, if you have understanding. ⁵Who determined its measurements — surely you know! Or who stretched the line upon it? ⁶On what were its bases sunk, or who laid its cornerstone ⁷when the morning stars sang together and all the heavenly beings shouted for joy? ⁸Or who shut in the sea with doors when it burst out from the womb?— ⁹when I made the clouds its garment, and thick darkness its swaddling band, ¹⁰and prescribed bounds for it, and set bars and doors, ¹¹and said, 'Thus far shall you come, and no farther, and here shall your proud waves be stopped'?"

— Job 30:19-31; 31:5-8; 38:1-11

One can readily imagine the poet who composed Psalm 104 living in relative comfort, perhaps in the royal court. Human life is good. The writer of Job writes from the standpoint of innocent human suffering. Can one person identify with the two visions of reality projected in these primal iconic texts? How can the imagination hold together the order and beauty of the world with the violence, disorder, and injustice that abound?

The way to begin is to listen to the words and the tense interchange between Job and God, which does not resemble the psalmist's language at all. Everyone can enter into this drama because it is a parable of the problematic character of the religious question, whether it be personal or institutional. Here innocent suffering speaks out, and the ardent believer addresses God in confused exclamation. Of course one asks: can Job really be innocent? But such is the premise of the narrative, and there are innocent people. To quibble is to avoid the questions driving this text. Job rightly protests: this is not fair; it is unjust! Despite the degree of his dispossession and physical torture, which is extreme, Job speaks out of faith. But he protests and teeters on anger. He also assumes that God is in control, for it is hard to conceive how the creator of heaven and earth could not be implicated in earthly suffering. To this charge God responds from the whirlwind of transcendence with an irony that reads like cutting sarcasm: you are ignorant; you know nothing of the vast reality of which your suffering is but a tiny part. The creature has no leverage over the creator. In the end Job must confess his unknowing.

But the story cannot end there because it describes too accurately the course of history for a majority of the human race. In absolute numbers the reality of innocent suffering mounts rather than decreases. In contrast to the psalmist, this story suggests that the human world is intrinsically disordered. As far as most people are concerned, despite

Job's appeals to God's presence and power, God does not show up at all. Innocent suffering for many simply confirms the absence of God. Everyday common human experience suggests an alternative contrary to that of the psalmist.

Even a small dose of innocent suffering for those who experience it can cause doubt about God. The blatant amount of it in the world attacks spiritual confidence in God, creator of order and justice. It pushes human response in several possible directions. For some it prohibits faith at the outset. Frequently suffering scandalizes those who already profess faith in God. Religious faith may take various forms, but in every case it stumbles over the incompatibility of suffering with a good, loving, and all-powerful creator God.

Some faithful people cling precisely to that sort of God. This response remains completely absorbed with a loving God and defends God on the basis of God's transcendent mystery, much as does the book of Job. Not to do so surrenders to the negativity of suffering itself. Without the mystery of a loving God the world "becomes the dungeon in which man dies the death of an animal (a clever animal)."[3] A creator God of love promises that the eternal value of each human person will be realized in the end. A person who encounters the transcendent power of God sustaining and empowering the being of the universe probably expects this God to remain constant.

Another reaction to the experience of human suffering is to resist it. God has created human freedom for just such a task, and one cannot expect God to intervene in the world to resolve problems that God has equipped human freedom to handle. These last two believing responses do not contradict each other but describe distinct emphases that require further reflection.

No coherent theory of innocent human suffering makes it intelligible or tolerable. But Pierre Teilhard de Chardin provides an analytical description of the human situation that illumines the relationships between self, world, and God that takes into account innocent suffering.[4] Human existence has to be understood within a universe whose forces interact and sometimes violently collide. Human beings are constituted as part of this evolving reality. Each individual depends on two sources of energy: the creating power of God for sheer being and a seemingly infinite array of finite interactions of the surrounding world that keep the individual alive. These agencies of God and of the surrounding world feed the growth of each person. Then, toward the end of the life cycle, their withdrawal or entropy results in human diminishment. In

---

3. Karl Rahner, *Do You Believe in God?* (New York: Paulist Press, 1969), 72.

4. Pierre Teilhard de Chardin, *The Divine Milieu: An Essay on the Interior Life* (New York: Harper & Brothers, 1960), 45-68.

a striking image Teilhard speaks of humans being hollowed out so that God can completely enter into and appropriate personal existence.

Human existence in this world cannot be understood apart from its immersion in matter and the buzzing forces of nature. In many ways human life mirrors the violent interaction of the elements that characterize all of nature. Human reason spontaneously seeks a cause behind every effect and seeks to assign responsibility for every injury. This healthy critical human response is appropriate. But the evolutionary premise of human existence itself entails that human beings participate in and contribute to the vast confusion of the often violent agencies that comprise nature and the world in process. From that premise, the meaningfulness of such an evolutionary world requires a God-like presence from the perspective of the past, the present, and the future. God responds to the question of the source of being and the origin of the universe. God in the present is the one to whom Job can complain and present his lament. And God in the future provides a possibility of ultimate justice.

The contemplative description of how innocent suffering is a part of the natural world should not dissuade human recognition that it is evil when it destroys human life and freedom. The proper response to such evil is unequivocal outrage on the part of those who suffer and those who witness it. The appropriate response to dehumanization is: "This should not be!" Its existence threatens the worth of all human life. This response also includes a spontaneous impulse of resistance, a desire to negate the negation, to right the situation, and to restore the victim to the extent that one is able. In other words, negativity possesses a positive impulse to resist an evil that should not be.[5] This sets the stage for a more active response to the causes of human suffering.

The believer in God has to stipulate that innocent suffering contradicts God's creative intentions. It makes no sense for a creator God to desire the destruction of what God creates. But at the same time the believer must find God within the world that actually exists. God should not be conceived as the creator of a world other than this one, and this world evolves through processes that involve a good measure of violence and innocent suffering. These principles suggest some large parameters for the possibility of coherent meaning. God creates and sustains a world that by God's design is semi-autonomous in its development. This is another way of saying that God does not operate in the world as a finite cause, and thus not as the cause of particular evils. God acts as the world's sustaining ground, accompanying pres-

---

5. I am describing here a negative experience of contrast, a structure of human response drawn from Edward Schillebeeckx, *Church: The Human Story of God* (New York: Crossroad, 1990), 5-6.

ence, and abiding promise of an absolute future. God's creating leaves space for both randomness and the creative agency of human freedom. Thus, God's intentions for human flourishing and God's desire that dehumanizing suffering be resisted must be carried forward by human agents. Human beings do not have the leverage to read God's specific will in particular events, but can live meaningfully in hope for a time of justice that only God can provide. The God who does show up and addresses Job can be understood in an evolutionary key as saying: "I am not the problem. But I promise a resolution."

This logic sets the premises for what Juan Luis Segundo calls a "project" spirituality.[6] God is creating a world in the making that is as yet far from finished. Read from the past by science and history, this project appears to be open to the future. Read by creation faith, with this project God intends the full flourishing of all that exists, especially of human beings who enjoy reflective consciousness. When human beings participate actively and consciously in this project, the project itself becomes self-reflective. It is primarily through this project that humans become united with the creator in their being and creativity. As Teilhard states: "in action I cleave to the creative power of God; I co-incide with it; I become not only its instrument but its living prolongation."[7]

This vision and its corresponding spirituality represent an extraordinarily positive interpretation of human existence. Does this interpretation depart from the text of Job and cover up a world that is intrinsically disordered and unjust? It may appear so to some. But this spirituality reflects a basic trust in the meaningfulness and goodness of existence. It reacts against the potential scandal of an evil that is no mirage. It discovers in a creator God a hopeful conception of the human enterprise. And it translates faith in the creator of an evolutionary process into a summons to human freedom to participate in that creativity.

6. The Infinite Value of the Individual

11[21]*For it is always in your power to show great strength, and who can withstand the might of your arm?* [22]*Because the whole world before*

---

6. Juan Luis Segundo was himself deeply influenced by Teilhard de Chardin. He outlines what is meant by "project spirituality" in *The Christ of the Ignatian Exercises* (Maryknoll, NY: Orbis Books, 1987), 41-124; "Ignatius Loyola: Trial or Project?" in *Signs of the Times: Theological Reflections* (Maryknoll, NY: Orbis Books, 1993), 149-75.

7. Teilhard, *Divine Milieu*, 31.

you is like a speck that tips the scales, and like a drop of morning dew that falls on the ground. [23]But you are merciful to all, for you can do all things, and you overlook people's sins, so that they may repent. [24]For you love all things that exist, and detest none of the things that you have made, for you would not have made anything if you had hated it. [25]How would anything have endured if you had not willed it? Or how would anything not called forth by you have been preserved? [26]You spare all things, for they are yours, O Lord, you who love the living. 12[1]For your immortal spirit is in all things. [2]Therefore you correct little by little those who trespass, and you remind and warn them of the things through which they sin, so that they may be freed from wickedness and put their trust in you, O Lord.

– Wisdom of Solomon 11:21-12:2

Consider the infinite value of the human individual. This exercise offers a stark contrast between what one observes in everyday social life around the world and the belief of many religions. Is the infinite value of each human life any more than a sentimental moral ideal? Or a pragmatic maxim aimed at self-protection? It seems paradoxical to claim that a finite reality possesses infinite value. This passage of scripture invites meditation to penetrate below the surface of human behavior in a search for the ontological value of the human person.

Everyone tends to value his or her own individual life. The command to love the neighbor as the self presupposes self-love as the baseline of moral appreciation. Even self-hatred is a type of self-preoccupation. A fundamental moral intuition or perception extends the self-love that each person feels to the other. The value that each person places upon his or her self has to be extrapolated to others for all the reasons that one appreciates one's own being. And yet this relatively clear moral formula functions only selectively on an interpersonal level and frequently does not transcend social boundaries. In times of war societies become accustomed to killing enemies, and nationalism inflates the message to "the more the better." In order for soldiers to kill spontaneously, they must be schooled and conditioned, and most learn the lesson well. The customary competitions of social life do not compare to war, but they generate prejudices and biases that lead to hatreds that can resemble wartime mentalities, and frequently enough these are acted out. The larger the social grouping, the more relationships become impersonal, social divisions harden, and the individual lives of those outside the group lose value.

If not the infinite, perhaps the absolute value of the human person can be defended rationally. Immanuel Kant, the eighteenth-century

Enlightenment philosopher, presents concern for the other as an unconditional moral imperative. This inner command does not come as an imposition of external law but from within human reasoning and willing itself. For Kant, the foundation of all morality demands that every human person value all others as persons like oneself and never merely as an object or a means to an end.[8] Yet innumerable ideologies of inequality obscure the clarity of Kant's reasoning by fixing upon the differences among human beings and, in a competitive spirit, lowering the value of others. Examples range widely as arguments appeal to evolutionary biology, expedience in managing society, and a nihilistic pragmatism of power. Even the smallest difference supports a bias that diminishes the other. Prejudices are not always explicitly conscious motivations; they often operate spontaneously as learned reactions that undercut esteem for other people.

Given the deep and pervasive hold that socially mediated values have on the human individual and the relative failure of even pellucid moral reasoning such as Kant's to shape effective social consciousness, few people expect religious values to have a decisive social impact. But the creation spirituality illustrated in the above prayer from the Wisdom of Solomon expresses a compelling vision. It accompanies creation faith and founds a comprehensive and inspiring set of convictions about human existence.

This prayer, a personal address to a personal creator God, slowly unpacks the idea that the creator of heaven and earth loves the things that are created. God's love motivates the full power and effectiveness by which God calls creatures into being in the first place. God's love holds beings in being; it embraces them and envelops them with existence. "For you love all things that exist, and detest none of the things that you have made, for you would not have made anything if you had hated it." This creator God, then, is the God of power and might, the infinite God who transcends the universe. But God, being infinite, radiates a love that is also infinite and subject to no limit. Thus, God can shower love on creatures without division or subtraction. God loves each creature with a love that God would bestow if it were the only creature and God's love for it were exclusive. All creatures are God's in this way, and God relates to them as God's own. Such is the scope of an infinite altruistic love of a creator God.

The implications of this prayer show why creation faith entails faith in the human. Many Christian theologians across time and traditions have recognized that a lack of faith in God really stems from or at least

---

8. Immanuel Kant, *Fundamental Principles of the Metaphysic of Morals*, trans. T. K. Abbott (Buffalo, NY: Prometheus Books, 1988), 57-58.

includes a failure of faith in human existence. Faith in God and faith in the human involve each other. Recognition of finitude and sin should not diminish a basic trust in one's fellow humans. Although Genesis proposes the human as created in God's image, the doctrine of sin is frequently used to tear down human nobility. Due to the prevalence of sin, law becomes regarded less as an expression of intrinsic human values and more as a heteronomous external control over social behavior. But it is one thing to have realistic caution about any exalted human plan, and quite another fundamentally to distrust human aspirations. Christian theology begins talking positively about the human in the light of Jesus Christ and incarnation, but the fundamental rationale for faith in the human begins in creation faith itself, as is beautifully expressed by the author of this prayer. Creation faith reaches out to the creator of heaven and earth. It implies that God has faith in and trusts human existence. Creation love is God's love for creation, and that love is itself creative of a noble human existence.

Søren Kierkegaard illustrates this creative love with a romantic parable of a love that bridges social class: a royal family member takes a spouse of humble origin and status. Surely such a marriage will not work because the equality needed for authentic love will be lacking, and without equality proclamations of love appear as condescension or pity. But if the love is real, it will transform the partners into equals because genuine love has a creative power to raise the other up and establish equality. This story comes out of the Lutheran tradition of justification by pure grace, and Luther's insight also describes the dynamics of the love of God that underlies creation. Luther depicts Christ, who embodies God's love, as a bridegroom who relates to human beings, the bride. The dynamics here are not psychological but ontological: Luther illustrates the status of the human as beloved. For a reflective human being who recognizes God's love and responds, this parable opens up a new sense of the value of the human person. Each human being is God's beloved, and, as God's love is infinite, the beloved has an infinite value.

From creation faith springs forth an ethic rooted in gratitude. A foundational ethic refers to the fundamental moral attitudes that suffuse a person's or a group's response to the world. These moral attitudes are comprehensive; they do not exclude but coexist with other moral dispositions. To be clear on what is meant by gratitude, consider the opposing moral attitude of entitlement, as illustrated by social divisions at their extremes, for example, between the wealthy and the poor. On the one side, growing up in comfort where everything necessary and more is at hand can generate an expectation that things will always be provided. Because possessions are always there and taken for granted, a person or culture can begin to think of them as entitlements: one has a right to life's accessories and expects them to be provided. Poverty can generate another value response that utterly lacks a sense of entitlement, even where it may be proper, because being deprived appears to be the natural state of being. From this perspective the provisions of life are a gift. Living on the edge of nonbeing can engender a pervasive feeling of gratitude for being and the desire to endure if not flourish.[9]

The text from the Wisdom of Solomon illustrates how the merger of a creation faith and spirituality fosters an ethic built on gratitude. Gratitude is a moral response whose defining characteristic entails the recognition that being is a gift. Gratitude lies at the core of Luther's spirituality and ethics. It embodies the doctrine of justification by pure grace. Of course, in Luther this is a spirituality of "redemption," but faith's recognition of God's creating love carries with it an invitation to the same kind of response. The sense of being created invites gratitude for one's being, because creation entails an immediate being-in-relationship to the creator. Gratitude has ethical implications, because it includes an impulse toward a response of love not only for God but for God's intimate friends.

7. Stories of Sin

3[1]Now the serpent was more crafty than any other wild animal that the Lord God had made. He said to the woman, "Did God say, 'You shall not eat from any tree in the garden'?" [2]The woman said to the serpent, "We may eat of the fruit of the trees in the garden; [3]but God said, 'You shall not eat of the fruit of the tree that is in the middle of the garden, nor shall you touch it, or you shall die.'" [4]But the serpent said to the woman, "You will not die; [5]for God knows that when you eat of it your eyes will be opened, and you will be like God, knowing good and evil." [6]So when the woman saw that the tree was good for food, and that it was a delight to the eyes, and that the tree was to be desired to make one wise, she took of its fruit and ate; and she also gave some to her husband, who was with her, and he ate. [7]Then the eyes of both were opened, and they knew that they were naked; and they sewed fig leaves together and made loincloths for themselves. . . . [22]Then the Lord God said, "See, the man has become like one of us, knowing good and evil;

---

9. These correlations are purely illustrative and by no means necessary, because the social conditions can also contribute to the opposite moral dispositions: the rich can be generous and the poor grasping.

and now, he might reach out his hand and take also from the tree of life, and eat, and live for ever"— [23]*therefore the Lord God sent him forth from the garden of Eden, to till the ground from which he was taken.*

11[1]*Now the whole earth had one language and the same words.* [2]*And as they migrated from the east, they came upon a plain in the land of Shinar and settled there.* [3]*And they said to one another, "Come, let us make bricks, and burn them thoroughly." And they had brick for stone, and bitumen for mortar.* [4]*Then they said, "Come, let us build ourselves a city, and a tower with its top in the heavens, and let us make a name for ourselves; otherwise we shall be scattered abroad upon the face of the whole earth."* [5]*The Lord came down to see the city and the tower, which mortals had built.* [6]*And the Lord said, "Look, they are one people, and they have all one language; and this is only the beginning of what they will do; nothing that they propose to do will now be impossible for them.* [7]*Come, let us go down, and confuse their language there, so that they will not understand one another's speech."* [8]*So the Lord scattered them abroad from there over the face of all the earth, and they left off building the city.* [9]*Therefore it was called Babel, because there the Lord confused the language of all the earth; and from there the Lord scattered them abroad over the face of all the earth.*

—Genesis 3:1-7, 22-23; 11:1-9

Christianity contains no greater contrast than one between the essential nobility of the human and its actual condition. Christian experience and doctrine testify to this condition in ways that seem extreme. Human beings are described as fallen, sinful, guilty, damaged, corrupted, and depraved; and preachers frequently represent life as dark and miserable. The churches that make up Christianity estimate this condition in various depths and have different strategies and ritual behaviors that address it. All churches agree, however, that sin is part of the human condition. But what is sin?

The dimensions of sin are many, and any one of them may be emphasized. Sin may refer to an all-embracing human condition of moral introversion that affects the whole of human life. Or sin may be an active egocentric tendency, impulse, or desire that requires constant vigilance and resistance. Or sin may refer to acts that both constitute and arise from the sinful condition, fundamentally injurious to the self and others. All manifestations of sin run counter to the creator's intent for human flourishing. But the question is whether the Christian paradox of human existence as both sinful and infinitely valuable is at bottom obsessive and destructive or honest and productive.

A description of the tensive relationship between the individual person and the community may be helpful background for understanding the preoccupation with sin in Christian self-understanding. On the one hand, each person has an inner self-consciousness, a sense of individuality that can assume responsibility and exercise freedom. On the other hand, from its conception, the self is nurtured by outside forces that continue to shape a person until death. Along the spectrum of this polarity a given individual person always lives in a community, usually more than one, and will become a more or less autonomous, or more or less passive, member of these groups. Reciprocally, the communities or institutions may be more or less demanding of compliant members. The interaction between individual persons and groups describes a fundamental polarity of human existence, and it explains the choice of the two texts for meditation.

These classic stories from Genesis are distinct but run along parallel lines. The narratives are the stories of every person, and both explore the dynamics of motivation. People can check the meaningfulness of these vignettes against their own experience. The first story describes mythologically the first and thus archetypal human sin. Commanded to refrain from a certain action, Adam and Eve think they are being deprived of greater knowledge and power, and, seeking it, they disobey. Reflection on this primal sin usually locates its roots in pride or desire for self-aggrandizement and characterizes the act as disobedience. In the second story the actor is a group which also disobeys the creator's command to spread out and settle in various regions. Instead, it builds a great city, including a tower "with its top in the heavens," symbolizing the pretensions of the group and their quest for power. Like the disobedience of the individuals Adam and Eve, this corporate disobedience springs from overreaching ambition. God's punishment illustrates the power of a social institution such as language. By garbling their single language, God scatters the group in disarray. Reflection on the dynamic relation between the individual and the group will also yield the realization that another primal sin is loss of self through passive self-surrender to the will of others.

More and more people are calling the concept of sin into question. Social sciences describe human behavior simply to be what it is; at best, it may be legal or illegal according to local ordinance. A shrinking world shows that various religions and cultures are not obsessed with, and some do not even possess, a deep concern over sin. Even identifying sin requires some premises. A sense of sin depends on standards, norms, or ideals for human behavior that transcend local culture to define the essentially human. Are there any human characteristics so inherent that to negate or ignore them assaults or demeans human life? Another premise, at least in a theistic tradition, requires the personality of God. Sin consistently carries a connotation of offending

God: it involves disobedience against divine intent, ungratefulness, lack of fidelity, a breach of a personal relationship. This explains why penetrating guilt accompanies sinfulness. Sin is not only objectively wrong but also breaks a transcendent bond of love and trust. The topic of sin extends far beyond doing or not doing this or that. It inspires reflection upon the very character of the human and the status of each person's existence.

These two anthropological stories from Genesis illustrate two intertwined types of sin, one within the individual person, the other in society. The individual person grows through the stages of the life cycle into maturity, one who assumes reflective responsibility for the self. Personal sin may be described as self-actualization that is self-centered and unconcerned with others; or, by contrast, personal sin may consist of a failure to assume responsibility for the self.

The greater part of Christian tradition has examined sin with an individualist lens. But social sin has a far greater destructive scope. Social sin refers to a systematic pattern of social behavior that consistently injures human life or represses human freedom. If socially structured behavior attacks human life, it is evil; if a whole system suppresses human freedom, not of a particular individual but collectively, it is sinful. Most fail to appreciate the sinful character in such social institutions, because social routine renders social responsibility nearly invisible. But social institutions depend on human freedom and can be changed. Many social structures, institutions, and systems damage humanity and destroy human lives, but individuals support them. Slavery and patriarchy are good examples. The destruction of the ecosystem attacks the human because of the symbiotic relationship between human beings and the earth. Social sin is precisely social in character, but individuals share in it by their participation in society.

A deep grasp of the reality of sin will be accompanied by a recognition of its power to restrict freedom and moral growth. A person may grasp sin intellectually, but sin grasps the human person existentially. Luther phrased it forcefully: sin entails a certain bondage of the will. Luther was not the first to say so. Paul confessed to the Romans that he was not fully in control of his own person: "For I do not do what I want, but I do the very thing I hate" (Rom 7:15). No one can fully and freely possess the self. Paul was getting at something deeply frustrating to anyone who wishes to assume responsibility for the self. This entrapment binds even more tightly on the social level. Human beings largely think as their language allows, value as their community dictates, and walk in the direction the group points. Even when people do not choose their groups, they usually fall into step. Groups, however, inherently tend to be selfish; by definition they divide by their boundaries; and they inevitably favor members over outsiders. Human beings cannot escape implication in the social policies and actions of their memberships. Exit society and you become implicated by omission before the bar of social responsibility.

Yet the idea of sin is losing ground in developed Western societies, certainly by comparison with the degree to which it formerly had a grip on Christian consciousness. What is required for a contemporary recognition of sin and acknowledgement of its existential meaningfulness as an operating principle? The issue has to be addressed in a narrative way: sin reveals itself in narratives of contrast. One kind of contrast was described in the contemplation on a disordered world (Reflection 5), where a negative confrontation with a disordered world that inflicts human suffering demonstrates that something is wrong and implicitly suggests the way things should be. One can recognize behaviors that are simply evil, and one can recognize sin when the agent is the self. The demonstration also operates in the other direction, when narratives reveal an inherent attraction to virtuous, constructive behavior. William James shows how the saints demonstrate for society a level of human virtue that it would not recognize as possible without them.[10] Most cultures still prize fundamental virtues and eschew vices, even in the face of a pluralism that threatens traditions. But the insistence on tradition alone will not mediate virtue; only an existential experience can move people to recognize the virtues and vices for which they are accountable.

Finally, because sin is an existential reality, a knowledge of what "sin" means does not really constitute a spiritual exercise. Ignatius Loyola understood this. In fact his world required no explanation of the concept of sin, and so he plunged himself and his retreatants directly into a review of their lives. He did so by focusing on sin. Today many retreat directors encourage a more balanced recapitulation of both the virtues and the vices of one's personal story. The point of such a narrative review is directed toward assuming personal responsibility for one's life in honesty before ultimate reality: a conscious spirituality.

8. Jesus' Story of Divine Forgiveness

[11]Then Jesus said, "There was a man who had two sons. [12]The younger of them said to his father, 'Father, give me the share of the property that will belong to me.' So he divided his property between them. [13]A few

---

10. William James, *The Variety of Religious Experience: A Study of Human Nature* (London and Glasgow: Collins, 1960), 347.

*days later the younger son gathered all he had and traveled to a dis-
tant country, and there he squandered his property in dissolute living.
¹⁴When he had spent everything, a severe famine took place throughout
that country, and he began to be in need. ¹⁵So he went and hired himself
out to one of the citizens of that country, who sent him to his fields to
feed the pigs. ¹⁶He would gladly have filled himself with the pods that
the pigs were eating; and no one gave him anything. ¹⁷But when he
came to himself he said, 'How many of my father's hired hands have
bread enough and to spare, but here I am dying of hunger! ¹⁸I will get
up and go to my father, and I will say to him, "Father, I have sinned
against heaven and before you; ¹⁹I am no longer worthy to be called
your son; treat me like one of your hired hands."' ²⁰So he set off and
went to his father. But while he was still far off, his father saw him and
was filled with compassion; he ran and put his arms around him and
kissed him. ²¹Then the son said to him, 'Father, I have sinned against
heaven and before you; I am no longer worthy to be called your son.'
²²But the father said to his slaves, 'Quickly, bring out a robe — the best
one — and put it on him; put a ring on his finger and sandals on his feet.
²³And get the fatted calf and kill it, and let us eat and celebrate; ²⁴for
this son of mine was dead and is alive again; he was lost and is found!'
And they began to celebrate. ²⁵Now his elder son was in the field; and
when he came and approached the house, he heard music and danc-
ing. ²⁶He called one of the slaves and asked what was going on. ²⁷He
replied, 'Your brother has come, and your father has killed the fatted
calf, because he has got him back safe and sound.' ²⁸Then he became
angry and refused to go in. His father came out and began to plead
with him. ²⁹But he answered his father, 'Listen! For all these years I
have been working like a slave for you, and I have never disobeyed
your command; yet you have never given me even a young goat so that
I might celebrate with my friends. ³⁰But when this son of yours came
back, who has devoured your property with prostitutes, you killed the
fatted calf for him!' ³¹Then the father said to him, 'Son, you are always
with me, and all that is mine is yours. ³²But we had to celebrate and
rejoice, because this brother of yours was dead and has come to life; he
was lost and has been found.'"*

— Luke 15:11-32

In this text Jesus tells a story about God as a loving, forgiving, accepting father. One of the most popular passages in the Bible, this short
story has three acts: the younger of two sons takes his inheritance,
leaves, squanders it, and hits bottom; then, coming to his senses, he
returns home and is welcomed by his father beyond all measure;
finally, the older loyal son becomes resentful, having never been

rewarded for his steadfastness. The story is a parable that Jesus uses as a device to open human imagination to the transcendent territory of the values of God. The parables frequently contain surprising reversals or contrasts. This story reveals how divine forgiveness relates to human sin. For Ignatius, the entire First Week leads to this plateau, a personal encounter between honest self-knowledge and recognition of the total love and acceptance of God.

Of the many things that can be said regarding contrasts in the story, one stands out: after the son's self-seeking behavior that inevitably leads to ruin, he receives outsized joyous welcome upon his return. No trace of grudging reception or conditional acceptance, but rather a spontaneous all-out party of celebration. The contrast clearly shows the preposterous ease and limitless dimensions of the love of God for one who in fact had betrayed the family. This interpretation stands right at the center of the whole story, and the story's structure intensifies the meaning: the worse the betrayal, the more expansive and deep the welcoming home appears. The graver the sin the more profound and unfathomable does the father's response appear. This tension dominates the story, and to make this point plain the father states it in a sharp paradox: "this son of mine was dead and is alive again; he was lost and is found!" Just in case anyone might miss this obvious point, the parable says it twice. The contrast looms, as stark as death and life, between estrangement, destitution, and failure in an alien land, and being established and connected as a son in a prospering family. The contradiction between being completely alone and alienated from oneself and becoming utterly secure and honored in one's position, the center of attention in a well-established family supported by friends, is rendered irrelevant by the unfathomable resource of the father's love.

No two individual people bear the same relationship to God, because each person and each story has unique qualities. An experience of the love and acceptance that God has for each person will take on the different modalities that each person brings to the relationship. The last act illustrates this, and many people entering this story may relate to the older brother. On one level, his response seems quite reasonable for the very reason he gives. But the response of the father, without rebuke, invites his other son to a higher plane. Surely the older son was correct in never asserting his entitlement over against the family. But has he not been too passive and immature in his dependence? The father's love has invited him to a status of equality of shared responsibility and ownership, which until now he has not seen. Here the father's love raises up the loyal son from dependence to equality, from passivity to partnership: "Son, you are always with me, and all that is mine is yours."

In Christian language, the term "grace" often substitutes for the love of God. Grace takes on countless accents in different scriptural contexts, the history of theology, and the churches, but its significance may be concentrated in a common essence: grace refers to God's love and the effects or blessings that God's loving presence and activity bestow on human beings. When grace is coupled with a theology of creation, it enriches the religious relevance that is displayed in this parable. A dominant note of the father's love lies in its constant expectation of the son's return. The prior concern of God for people combined with the complete gratuitousness and comprehensiveness of God's love begins to describe the permanent embrace in which human beings live. God's accompanying presence throughout all of creation sets the stage on which the human story unfolds. Creation as gift flowing from God's love defines the presupposition of all human entitlement. The love of the creator father is spontaneous, extravagant, unrestricted, unconditional, unreasonable, unmerited, and illogical, and it makes the difference between death and life. Does this mean that the mercy of God prevails over the justice of God? Probably not in such a clear opposition. It would be better to say that with this parable human imagination is being drawn to a whole other and new sphere of love and its power. Conceived in ontological terms, this parable makes a statement about the character of being.

What is required for this loving acceptance? Human suspicion and perhaps our era's litigious sensibility have complicated the clear, direct Christian response to this question: it comes by pure grace, and nothing is required for its being there. That stark simplicity says that human beings cannot so remake themselves as to deserve God's love, and are not expected to do so. From beginning to end God's love creates creatures and sustains them; it does not respond to human worth but constitutes it. Lutheran theologians such as Dietrich Bonhoeffer warn that free grace should not be turned into cheap grace, that acceptance of it has to be real acceptance. Luther recognized the gospel principle that the fruit reveals the character of the tree, and Ignatius reinforces that with the gospel maxim that true love shows itself in deeds rather than words. But forgiveness, like grace, is always there. It requires only acceptance, something impelled by God's Spirit of love, to work its way into conscious living.

Real acceptance of real forgiveness results in real affects. Forgiveness reconstitutes a person in moral wholeness through the healing love of God. The interpersonal character of love transpires in a unique way in each individual. The two sons illustrate this: the moral breach of the younger son was egocentric hubris; the older son never gained a sense of independence, and his resentment appears as immaturity, a loss of self, and a lack of agency. Divine love prunes the excesses and fills up the holes within a human person, restoring the self to itself and righting its relationship with the source of human existence.

God's forgiveness, when it is consciously accepted, results in what has to be called liberation. The degree or intensity of this cannot be measured, but its character can be described. The liberation that accompanies a conscious relationship with a God of love who completely understands, forgives, and accepts leads to a reconstitution of integrity on the most fundamental level of being. This involves a loss of the burden of guilt; the past that drags down the conscience is lifted from one's life. God's love does more than change a negative psychological self-image or counter the opinions of others. God's forgiveness penetrates a person's being and touches the roots of the feelings of guilt. It effaces real guilt, something that may not be available through even the most sincere and complete human forgiveness. Divine acceptance can radically reverse a true bondage of the human spirit and recreate a new lightness, openness, and freedom. God's love does not bind human freedom; it re-creates and releases it.

Recognition of divine forgiveness presupposes an active relationship with transcendence. Gratitude for forgiveness should stimulate a spontaneous desire to grow in one's attachment to God. In classical language this is called "change of life" and "sanctification." The experience of being loved and accepted by God may generate a spirituality of acting out God's values in the world. Dedication to a transcendent ideal in life, something that draws the self out of the self, evidences the empowerment that has followed the catharsis of forgiveness and acceptance. The metaphor in the parable of a transition from death to life does not exaggerate the radical character of such a transition.

Ignatius proposes a number of colloquies at the end of the meditation on sin that dwell on the contrast between human sinfulness and divine goodness, shown in God's love, mercy, and forgiveness. At one point he sets a dramatic scene: "Imagine Christ our Lord suspended on the cross before you, and converse with him in a colloquy" (SE, 53). Then, in this context, he asks that the person probe his or her relation to God: what have I done, what am I doing, and what ought I do for God, whose love and forgiveness is seen as represented by Jesus on a cross. Jesus' death will be the subject of a later reflection; but Jesus' story of divine love and acceptance makes the point. The seeker may not find that the Christian story of the cross has the leverage that Ignatius presupposed. But Jesus' story of the love of a creator God communicates a parallel message. The logic of the First Week of the Exercises comes to an emotional peak at this precise point, and no one better than Luther explains what is going on here. Human existence in its deepest moral dependence meets acceptance from the ground of being itself. This drama of acceptance of the human is not general but is individually proportioned to and experienced by each person, *pro me*, as Luther put it. Luther captures exactly the logic of Ignatius's First Week in the tensive and dynamic mutual reinforcement of being sinful and of being loved, accepted, and forgiven.

9. On Freedom and Gifts

[14]"For it is as if a man, going on a journey, summoned his slaves and entrusted his property to them; [15]to one he gave five talents, to another two, to another one, to each according to his ability. Then he went away. [16]The one who had received the five talents went off at once and traded with them, and made five more talents. [17]In the same way, the one who had the two talents made two more talents. [18]But the one who had received the one talent went off and dug a hole in the ground and hid his master's money. [19]After a long time the master of those slaves came and settled accounts with them. [20]Then the one who had received the five talents came forward, bringing five more talents, saying, 'Master, you handed over to me five talents; see, I have made five more talents.' [21]His master said to him, 'Well done, good and trustworthy slave; you have been trustworthy in a few things, I will put you in charge of many things; enter into the joy of your master.' [22]And the one with the two talents also came forward, saying, 'Master, you handed over to me two talents; see, I have made two more talents.' [23]His master said to him, 'Well done, good and trustworthy slave; you have been trustworthy in a few things, I will put you in charge of many things; enter into the joy of your master.' [24]Then the one who had received the one talent also came forward, saying, 'Master, I knew that you were a harsh man, reaping where you did not sow, and gathering where you did not scatter seed; [25]so I was afraid, and I went and hid your talent in the ground. Here you have what is yours.' [26]But his master replied, 'You wicked and lazy slave! You knew, did you, that I reap where I did not sow, and gather where I did not scatter? [27]Then you ought to have invested my money with the bankers, and on my return I would have received what was my own with interest. [28]So take the talent from him, and give it to the one with the ten talents. [29]For to all those who have, more will be given, and they will have an abundance; but from those who have nothing, even what they have will be taken away. [30]As for this worthless slave, throw him into the outer darkness, where there will be weeping and gnashing of teeth.'"

—Matthew 25:14-30

Forgiveness liberates freedom for freedom, freedom to realize human potential in the exercise of human agency. This raises more questions. If freedom defines the core of human existence, how should freedom be understood? How does freedom relate to the gifts at its disposal? What measures the quality of its exercise? Spirituality revolves around these fundamental issues. This meditation takes this parable of delegated agency and opens it up to a reflection on the meaning of human gifts considered as investments of the creator. This could lead to a reorientation of some basic convictions about human life.

This parable tells the story of someone with position and power investing his servants with money that he expects they will turn into gain. The word "talent" refers to a unit of money unrelated to the idea of a human "skill," but the phrase "to each according to his ability" suggests the analogy with natural gifts. The parable bears on how human beings are to use their "talents." Trustworthy agents work the money, take risks, and earn more. Conservative servants play it safe, in effect do nothing, and thus are of no use to the one who delegates them. The shocking part of the parable comes with the harsh conclusion that echoes an aphorism of Jesus in Mark: "For to those who have, will more be given; and from those who have nothing, even what they have will be taken away" (Mark 4:25). Not only that, the overly cautious slave is condemned. At the very least the parable implies that God views human freedom as a sacred trust to be exercised.

Narrative lends itself to moral interpretation. This story suggests that humans should be responsible for carrying out what they are sent to do. Human beings should use their talents in the service of those authorized to assign the tasks of life. The stakes of the story are raised when its meaning is applied to the sphere of the nature of human existence and its purpose. Two considerations open up that line of thinking. The first recalls the earlier premise that the human person be defined by its most basic characteristic: spirit. Although imbedded in matter, spirit is freedom; it transcends and cannot be reduced to the physical. Spirit is experienced as the presence of the self to the self, or self-consciousness, the bending back of human consciousness on itself. The second point imagines human individuality as a bundle of talents. Each individual person consists of a unique package of abilities that define potentialities for distinctive performance. The question of the purpose of human existence is how this particular set of gifts is to be used. Each person wraps his or her talents with the freedom that he or she is summoned to exercise. Do people have their own niche in existence? Does faith in a creator God shed light on the purpose of this freedom? The earlier idea that forgiving grace sets freedom free suggests a positive answer to these questions.

This interpretation goes beyond the issue of right and wrong behavior to an existential appreciation of the purpose of human freedom and the different ways in which it is exercised. The parable suggests that basic norms govern how human beings are called to exercise their talents. On this issue Søren Kierkegaard provided meticulous analyses of the personal exercise of human freedom and left some distinctions that can help sort out these issues. His appreciation of human existence as a narrative allowed him to see how different dimensions of the exercise of freedom develop into lifestyles or spiritualities that define a person's being. These levels are described as aesthetic, rational, and transcendent.

A first level of freedom is the ability to consider options and choose. Called "free choice," this level of freedom lies right on the surface of consciousness. Negatively, it entails a lack of external restraint; positively, it is the very power of making decisions and carrying them out. Everyone recognizes this possibility and exercises it constantly in various areas of life. But this elementary power can be radically curtailed by material, social, and cultural bondage: some people have no options. When people do have options, choice can define a lifestyle or a spirituality of acquiring and reveling in the possession of things. Such a consumerism represents a relatively shallow ideal. More often than not a pleasure principle or an aesthetic desire impels constant choosing. In its purest form this mode of living resembles the butterfly that bounces along from flower to flower or pleasure to pleasure, or the dog that follows its nose. Attraction to the beauty of sensible objects arises from an aesthetic inclination more than rational or widely recognized objective goals. Ironically such a social lifestyle may appear gloriously free and yet merely skim the surface of freedom's potential.

By contrast, intentional commitment to a single idea, goal, person or cause represents a deeper form of freedom. This depth is measured by the ability of personal freedom to define the self. When choice simply responds to aesthetic attraction, the self becomes passive before the object; in commitment, a person shapes the self by deliberately disposing it toward a single more stable ideal. This rational level of freedom goes deeper, because at this level a person exercises more inner control over the self in focused attention and considered self-discipline. If the object of freedom possesses worth, that worth becomes internalized. In such a transaction, freedom recreates itself deliberately by taking hold of the self and committing it to something of considered value and appropriating it. This level of free self-disposition and commitment results in a firm and steady lifestyle.

A third level of freedom transcends the bonds of earthly logic and reason and occurs when one is grasped by a transcendent reality that may lead along uncharted paths. Here freedom, as a personal commitment to God, or more generally to ultimate reality that transcends society and reason, gives a person another perspective on life in this world. The call experienced by some of the prophets in the Hebrew scriptures illustrates this. In this experience of freedom, a recognition of what is truly transcendent desacralizes the world and elicits the commandment against idolatry, that is, treating something of this world as ultimate. Luther spoke of one's attachment to the God of history making each person lord over all in order to be in service of all. He thus saw how this level of freedom's attachment to ultimacy releases the prophetic dimension found in religion that gives it leverage over idols. If commitment grows from the depths of freedom, this prophetic dimension measures its height. The prophetic imagination displayed in the Hebrew Bible shows a freedom free of all fear of the world. In a grotesque way, Abraham, mythically called by God to sacrifice his son, provides an archetype of this faith commitment of freedom. In faith a person attaches the self to God and God's cause, as best this can be discerned, and follows the path that it provides as one that comes from the author of life itself and thus completely fills up freedom's potential.

The aesthetic, rational, and transcendent dimensions of freedom are distinct, but they may intersect. It is possible to imagine someone whose only aspirations revolve around aesthetic choice and superficial pleasure. The commitment to a universal ideal, by contrast, takes hold of the self and enhances it with the value that freedom embraces. But transcendent spiritual commitment establishes a self-possession that includes aesthetic and rational values and draws them into a more complex synthesis within freedom. Transcendent spiritual commitment does not undercut the other schemes of value but orders them by suffusing them with the value of a transcendent reality. A formal spiritual commitment establishes a center of gravity that helps to sort out other relative values and priorities for freedom's agency.

Reading this parable in these social existential terms, where human talents are understood as gifts of the creator, and asking how one's own talents should be freely deployed help to clarify an undertaking of the Spiritual Exercises. Ignatius proposed the Exercises as a method for making a major decision in one's life in an objective manner after sorting things out (SE, 21), or more generally as a way of taking hold of one's life in a new and deliberate way. This involves knowing and assessing one's talents. But more importantly it requires a framework in which to understand one's own freedom in order to align one's talents toward the goal of one's life. A consistent spirituality would include measuring one's commitment by some ultimate value, in this case, God's creative intention. From this perspective the first aesthetic level of freedom by itself seems wasteful of talents, because none are consciously developed; reason calls human beings to exercise their freedom on the second intentional level of commitment; and response to transcendence defines an explicit spirituality. In this parable Jesus steers spiritual commitment toward the values of the rule of God. People get the point when they pose the question: "What am I doing with the gifts that I have been given?"

10. Human Freedom in History

Up to now human beings lived apart from each other, scattered around the world and closed in upon themselves. They have been like passengers who accidentally met in the hold of a ship, not even suspecting the ship's motion. Clustered together on the earth, they found nothing better to do than to fight or amuse themselves. Now, by chance, or better, as a natural result of organization, our eyes are beginning to open. The most daring among us have climbed to the bridge. They have seen the ship that carries us all. They have glimpsed the ship's prow cutting the waves. They have noticed that a boiler keeps the ship going and a rudder keeps it on course. And, most important of all, they have seen clouds floating above and caught the scent of distant islands on the horizon. It is no longer agitation down in the hold, just drifting along; the time has come to pilot the ship. It is inevitable that a different humanity must emerge from this vision.

—Pierre Teilhard de Chardin,
Activation of Energy (New York:
Harcourt, Brace, 1971), 73-74

Pierre Teilhard de Chardin was a Christian, a Jesuit priest, a paleontologist, a theologian, a poet, and a spiritual writer. Early in his life he developed a love for the earth in its physical form that merged with his religious sensibilities. He committed his life to the study of the evolution of the human species. This text illustrates the emergence of historical consciousness and the recognition of human involvement in evolution and care of the planet. The Spiritual Exercises helped to shape Teilhard's spirituality, and he in turn situates the Exercises in the context of an evolving world that is now entrusted to human hands. The transition to a global historical consciousness described in this allegory represents a transition in human perception that can completely transform a spirituality that lacks a sense of historicity.

Historical consciousness raises this question: if freedom is a narrative in history, does an evolutionary world offer it a project?

One way to begin to appreciate this little paragraph might be to compare it with the allegory of the cave in Plato's *Republic*. There prisoners in a cave were allowed to see only shadows on a wall, with the result that all reality became reduced, in their minds, to shadowy figures without substance. Such are human lives lived on the surface of everyday life, ignorant of essential values and ideas. When released into the world outside, the prisoners are at first blinded by the brightness of the sun, but finally, by its light, they slowly perceive substantial, meaningful reality. Teilhard's allegory is no less profound but moves in an opposite direction. He benefits from cumulative insights of thinkers such as Karl Marx and Charles Darwin. Marx read human nature as creative freedom in history. He defined the human as *homo faber*: the freedom given to humans is constructive; it works, makes new things, and creates even social systems that in turn shape the people who live within them. He valued work as an authentic human activity and resented its enslavement by the masters of the industrial revolution. He realized as well that knowledge and valuation reflect the position in society the knower occupies. Human beings condition their own knowledge, freedom, and selves by the spheres of meaning they construct. When all this is fitted into a Darwinian framework of process and emergent life-forms, a new set of norms for knowledge, agency, and self-appreciation appears: "the time has come to pilot the ship."

New perspectives and currents of thought such as these do not necessarily negate one another but reveal aspects of reality that swirl around in the imagination to shape new interpretations and understandings. Marx's view of freedom offers a dynamic creative perspective on human existence; he recognized that the human person has a social dimension whose influence on individual perception and action is far more complex than common sense reveals. These fundamental appreciations of human freedom also throw new light on religious symbols. A good example of this is Jesus' symbol of the reign of God either in this world or in an absolute future. If Jesus' preaching is understood as revealing the creator's intention for how the human world should operate or is destined to become, it provides human freedom with images and ideals that attract human energies and talents. Such a scenario broadly describes the way many churches, theologians, and faithful understood the Christian vision at the beginning of the twentieth century.

Teilhard brings fundamental anthropological premises to spirituality. One is evident in the sheer scope of his thinking. He forces those reading him to situate themselves within the universe, an evolving world, and the movement of all history. An individual cannot seriously conceive of glimpsing God's creative intention by simply examining personal consciousness. Teilhard encourages his readers to venture imaginatively into the dynamics of emergent creation itself. He postulates that the story of cosmogenesis, the evolution of human life, and the dynamics of history contain clues to the intent of the creator. This does not negate individual experience; recognizing process and change enhances individual initiative by realistically representing context and possibility. Human freedom is individual and personal; it is social in its formation and in the exercise of responsibility; it is also a part of the world, both distinct from and integrated into matter.

Teilhard also teaches that the symbiotic relationship between human freedom and the material world means that people cannot enter into a conscious relation with God apart from the world, but only in and through the world. Love of God and love of the world are not competitive: the idea of love of God does not correlate with withdrawal from the world. Spiritual freedom does not negate aesthetic consciousness but injects it with transcendent value. As part of the world, human freedom has to find its way to God within the world.

Finally, this attachment to God in and through the world unfolds mainly through action or activity within the world. Because the creative power of God permeates the world, God becomes the milieu within which and by whose power finite existence subsists. Building on this incarnational principle, Teilhard proposes that the way people truly solidify a union with God consists of uniting their activity with the broader thrust of evolutionary history in the direction of God's values or, as Jesus termed it, the rule of God. This activist dimension of spirituality arises from a tradition far removed from that of Marx, and yet they share a remarkable coincidence in some fundamental premises.

Juan Luis Segundo, who comments on Ignatius, takes up the impulse of Teilhard's thought and applies it directly to the kind of spirituality he wants the Exercises to generate. Using a contrast between a "trial" and a "project" spirituality referred to earlier, he illustrates the change of thinking to which Teilhard's allegory points. A "trial" spirituality unfolds within the first dimension of freedom, which consists mainly of choice between alternatives. A theory of human destiny offers human freedom the finality of heaven or hell. In this theory, earthly life consists of a trial; and, on the basis of the choices made in this world, human beings will ultimately decide their destiny of either heaven or hell. This entails a spirituality of caution, of fear of making a mistake. This world has little value other than being the site of this drama; human beings are foreigners on earth, and their true home lies ahead in heaven. By contrast, a "project" spirituality consists of action that collaborates with divine creativity, and human freedom really contributes something to the absolute end of the "project" of life itself. The human person appears as a potential "collaborator in a *plan* common to God and myself."[11] This view rests on the premise that evolutionary creation continues; as a spirituality, it relies on a conception of creative freedom cooperating with God's Spirit that goes back to Augustine.

This distinction shows that spirituality can be seen as an exercise of creative freedom. It addresses the posture of the free self within society: passive or active, withdrawn or engaged, being safe or creative. Certain principles stand out in Segundo's contrast of trial and project spirituality. In a trial spirituality two directions are offered to the first level of freedom, human choice: transitory things here below or eternal values above, ultimate failure or salvation. Attractions and options compete in a zero sum game: the more one loves God the less one loves the world and therefore shuns it. The world constitutes a temptation against one's love of God. Thomas à Kempis's late medieval *The Imitation of Christ* gives classic expression to this spirituality. A project spirituality, by contrast, appeals to the second level of freedom, commitment, and injects it with transcendent value. For this spirituality human dedication to the kingdom of God in history "is something on which the general plan or reign of God depends."[12] Motivation in life shifts from the desire to save one's soul apart from the world to the desire to serve God's project in history. A person finds and identifies with God by engaging the world.

The role of Jesus Christ in the Christian imagination appears differently in the two contrasting spiritualities. In a trial spirituality Jesus is the exemplar of one who successfully passed the test. He made all the correct choices in an archetypal way. Jesus' suffering becomes an asceticism of self-negation rather than commitment to a cause. In a project spirituality Jesus appears as one who preached and acted out the kingdom of God in history. He remains the exemplar, but in this case of a life lived in history completely dedicated to implementing the values of the rule of God within his realm of influence. Following Jesus aims not at self-negation but at self-gift to the cause represented by Jesus' ministry.

The societies and cultures of the developed world have internalized much of the scientific worldview that lies behind Teilhard's allegory.

---

11. Juan Luis Segundo, "Ignatius Loyola: Trial or Project?" in *Signs of the Times: Theological Reflections* (Maryknoll, NY: Orbis Books, 1993), 153.

12. Ibid., 171.

From a secular point of view it simply describes the gradual shift to a deeper historical consciousness and an evolutionary worldview. When this becomes coupled with a religious imagination, it constantly releases new meaning for life in the world and for understanding Christian spirituality.

11. The Kingdom of God in the End

[31]*"When the Son of Man comes in his glory, and all the angels with him, then he will sit on the throne of his glory.* [32]*All the nations will be gathered before him, and he will separate people one from another as a shepherd separates the sheep from the goats,* [33]*and he will put the sheep at his right hand and the goats at the left.* [34]*Then the king will say to those at his right hand, 'Come, you that are blessed by my Father, inherit the kingdom prepared for you from the foundation of the world;* [35]*for I was hungry and you gave me food, I was thirsty and you gave me something to drink, I was a stranger and you welcomed me,* [36]*I was naked and you gave me clothing, I was sick and you took care of me, I was in prison and you visited me.'* [37]*Then the righteous will answer him, 'Lord, when was it that we saw you hungry and gave you food, or thirsty and gave you something to drink?* [38]*And when was it that we saw you a stranger and welcomed you, or naked and gave you clothing?* [39]*And when was it that we saw you sick or in prison and visited you?'* [40]*And the king will answer them, 'Truly I tell you, just as you did it to one of the least of these who are members of my family, you did it to me.'* [41]*Then he will say to those at his left hand, 'You that are accursed, depart from me into the eternal fire prepared for the devil and his angels;* [42]*for I was hungry and you gave me no food, I was thirsty and you gave me nothing to drink,* [43]*I was a stranger and you did not welcome me, naked and you did not give me clothing, sick and in prison and you did not visit me.'* [44]*Then they also will answer, 'Lord, when was it that we saw you hungry or thirsty or a stranger or naked or sick or in prison, and did not take care of you?'* [45]*Then he will answer them, 'Truly I tell you, just as you did not do it to one of the least of these, you did not do it to me.'* [46]*And these will go away into eternal punishment, but the righteous into eternal life."*

—Matthew 25:31-46

This last meditation of the First Week deals with the end of time. "End" has a double sense, one of goal or purpose and the other of stopping or reaching a climax when God brings things to a close.

Consideration of the end completes a creation faith and gives a fuller perspective on human existence in time. Just as meaningful narratives have a beginning and an end, so too each person inescapably faces the question of his or her destiny. Can hope in an end-time deepen creation faith, support a project spirituality, and stimulate hope in a comprehensive meaning of human existence?

This remarkable passage that Matthew's gospel puts in Jesus' mouth is called an apocalyptic revelation, that is, a simulation of the end-time in a cosmic pictorial panel. The Son of Man is a mythic emissary of God appearing in the clouds; this is referred to in the Book of Daniel in the Hebrew scriptures. The Christian movement in the first century used it to help interpret the identity of Jesus. Here, Jesus the Son of Man functions as a ruler and God's judge of all nations. Two elements in particular make it appropriate at this stage of the Exercises. The scenario endorses the practical project spirituality considered in the last reflection. It affirms a faith where discipleship of Jesus essentially includes service of those in need. The passage also takes a practical quotidian spirituality and inserts it into a context of finality in which the life of all nations will be gathered up. Here in a scene from a mystery play is a metaphysical account of the whole of human history. The story contains a judgment, closely aligned with the charge to serve the neighbor, in order to address the question of whether cosmic history is meaningful and ruled by justice.

Many of the practical spiritualities of social engagement that have revitalized theology since the nineteenth century have turned to this passage in Matthew. It addresses the mutual relationship between love of God and love of neighbor in a way that concerns and responds to people in need, and as an intrinsic dimension of Christian faith as distinct from an outcome of it. This is no esoteric debating point, but a fundamental conception about a being in relationship with God that potentially interrupts contentment with an individualist religious identity. Satisfied religious faith often rests on the supposition that God is readily available, usually in and through the churches, synagogues, temples, and mosques. By contrast, the working premise of practical spiritualities, frequently unstated but implied, postulates that one finds God within the neighbor. The neighbor here means every person in need who crosses one's path. Sometimes Jesus put it more strongly: the neighbors are those in need whom we are to seek out.

The logic of how love of neighbor can be equal to or actually be love of God does not seem immediately apparent because neighbor and God are not the same thing, and acts addressed to different objects are different actions. One logic governs relationships with creatures, and another with God, who is not something of this world.

But because God transcends this world, conscious contact with God can have content only on the basis of some this-worldly medium, contact point, or representative, at least in the form of an image of God. The solidity of one's response to God is thus measured by a representative. The person in need, a friend of God, is that representative. The First Letter of John puts it strongly: "If anyone says, 'I love God,' and hates his neighbor, he is a liar; for he who does not love his brother whom he has seen, cannot love God whom he has not seen" (4:20). Read positively, this saying implies that when one does love the neighbor, one also loves God, because the closest representatives of God are human beings. And closest among these are those who suffer. Like the one handicapped child among many draws a distinct supportive love of parent and sibling, so do those who suffer attract God's egalitarian love in a special way. In the absence of a tangible God in history, then, one loves God most concretely and actively in and through God's own most intimate friends or loved ones. On the one hand, one cannot love God without loving God's friends. On the other hand, the *identity* of loving God's friends and loving God lies in the act of self-transcending love that, in going out of the self to the neighbor, reaches the God who is present in neighbors as their creator and lover.

But where does an act of love of neighbor lead? Does it have lasting or only immediate meaning? These big questions are addressed in eschatology, that is, reflection on the end-time, as depicted in the scene from Matthew's gospel. This end-time refers to that which awaits each person and, in the larger framework, how one might imagine the culmination of human history. With the parable of a final judgment, the discussion of spirituality expands to include the consideration of human destiny. The Christian response to these questions comes framed in the language of resurrection and eternal life. Both of these terms, resurrection and eternal life, express a fundamental hope in an absolute future. A consideration of resurrection awaits the case of Jesus of Nazareth, but something has to be said now about the hope it fuels. Is hope merely an easy optimism? Realistic hope in an absolute future requires some kind of honest rationale. Such a rationale would also reinforce the project spirituality already outlined.

Optimism hovers on the surface of things and always expects the best possible outcome. Christian hope operates on a different plane. Hope consists of a fundamental moral attitude that regards reality as good, even though our temporal existence leads inevitably to death. All other positive responses to life spring out of this confidence in being. This basic human conviction correlates with time. Hope characterizes temporal existence, where the future in its social historical forms always remains out in front but relentlessly crashes in unexpectedly. Despite all planning, the future always arrives in surprising new forms; it always carries both promise and threat, and in the end it always brings death. Yet hope takes account of the temporality of being and relates to time positively and constructively. Hope contrasts starkly with despair, which either short-circuits or closes down the power of constructive meaning-making. Hope can be described as creation faith extended forward into the future. The open character of an expanding universe into an unlimited future beckons the infinitely capacious character of human hope.

But hope has to confront the negativities of existence. Devastation by natural disasters, systematically planned historical atrocities, and oceans of innocent suffering have to be reckoned into the calculus of human existence. It is not so easy to talk about hope or the meaningfulness of human existence in the concentration camps or in any social situation that systematically depersonalizes and dehumanizes whole groups of people. Only when all vision of God or possible presence of God is occluded does the really radical character of hope assert itself meaningfully for our time. Only when human life is actually experienced as dead ended and when, in that experience, a basic trust in being rather than nonbeing asserts itself does the absolutely foundational character of hope appear. Only when the very meaning of hope reflects the dialectical tension found in the claim that value and worth are perceived from within negativity itself does the category of hope take on honest and realistic meaning. Then it does not eclipse human suffering; then human suffering spurs it on. Hope is trust, despite the tides of meaningless negativity that contaminate historical existence, that human life is worthwhile. Hope, rooted in the sheer desire to exist, testifies to a deeper undercurrent of meaning in being.

If, as Ignatius said echoing Jesus of Nazareth, love manifests itself more in deeds than in words, then hope manifests itself more in resistance to evil and in constructing new and better situations than in waiting for evolution or God to right a wrong. Realistic hope does not mean or imply inactivity or passive expectation. Hope is neither mindless optimism nor limp acceptance of one's own or another's or society's suffering. That false brand of hope does not take seriously the gravity of human suffering, nor does it recognize that hope is a dynamic impulse to activity. Real hope in the future does not block out the memory of innocent suffering, but keeps that memory alive, so that hope can face suffering and engage it with responsible activity. Taking negativity seriously cannot mean surrendering to it and handing it victory; only hope can aggressively deal with suffering and negate the negation by transforming it into a stimulus for constructive action in personal life and in history. At bottom, hope constructs meaning within the self and in society.

This leads to two final reflections that are essential to an honest account of what Christians call the end-time. These concern what cannot and can be said about what this end-time looks like. It takes only one or two critical questions to reveal the fact that we know absolutely nothing about such an end-time. Hope in an absolute future does not translate into knowledge of it or about it. Assertions about an end-time are projections of creation faith into the absolute future of the Godhead. This confession of agnosticism by comparison with knowledge of this world does not undermine faith and hope but simply acknowledges their character. But something straightforward and positive can be said about how this hope in an end-time transforms human self-understanding. If God's creativity is still at work in an evolutionary universe and human history, and if human beings are most in communion with God when positively exercising the creative freedom that God has bestowed upon them, then one must conclude in faith that human beings are meant to contribute as co-creators of the absolute future that God is bringing into being. If such were not the case, the tremendous human impulse to be creative, along with what is actually produced in a positive vein, would be hollow and ultimately meaningless. Here too human beings have to surrender to unknowing. But one can hope that what human beings construct in love and for the benefit of other people will, in the end, comprise part of all that is ultimately real.

Human hope is embedded in the Matthean parable of a final reckoning. It reflects an elementary human desire. The story of Jesus, on which Matthew relies and to which the Exercises now turn, will offer more ground for such hope.

Jesus of Nazareth and His Ministry

The Second Week of the Exercises turns to the story of Jesus of Nazareth. It covers scenarios of Jesus' ministry up to his entry into Jerusalem. The first meditation on the Call of the King provides the basis of the whole program because it establishes the platform of the spirituality of the Exercises in the ministry of Jesus of Nazareth. The interpretation here builds on this by inviting people, no matter what their own stories have been up to this point, imaginatively to enter into the story of Jesus and see what it offers.

The gospels contain many stories of Jesus, and some were selected rather than others. All of the contemplations of Jesus' ministry are drawn from the Gospel of Luke. One reason for this is consistency, the desire to have a unified source for the portrait of Jesus or a single version of the Jesus story. Because Luke wrote a two-volume work, his gospel and the Acts of the Apostles, using him enables one to extend the narrative of Jesus and Jesus' disciples into the early decades of the gradual formation of a church. A certain concern for history governed the selection of the Lukan scenarios. Not all of the stories that Luke tells of Jesus have the same degree of historical authenticity. Therefore, when Ignatius calls for the use of the imagination, it is good to have an idea of the character of the story one is dealing with. Imagining Jesus behind the text is not the same as taking the text as itself a literal report. These stories are not literal reports, but they broadly reflect the kind of things that Jesus did. Finally, Luke gives a quite prominent position to God as Spirit in both his works, and this fits well with contemporary exigencies for spirituality.

Some of the vignettes gathered here have been selected because they represent or illustrate some basic element in the logic of the Exercises. For example, since the Call of the King proposes a spirituality of following Jesus, it seems natural to include a story of Jesus soliciting followers. Other stories represent substantial dimensions of Jesus' ministry. For example, because Jesus healed people and performed exorcisms, a story of Jesus' healing represents many instances of the same kind of activity. Virtually all scholars of the New Testament find

Jesus' conception of the rule of God at the heart of his whole ministry. Stories of Jesus himself telling parables to illustrate the rule of God form an essential part of the Jesus story and get close to the central content of his message.

During the course of his contemplations of Jesus, Ignatius inserts a series of meditations that give them all a particular Ignatian character, direct the flow of energy, and stimulate motivation. Ignatius's axioms for discerning the internal movements that these contemplations stir up are most important. They are not formally taken up until Reflection 28, but they can easily be considered when they seem to be needed. Ignatius also explains ways of going about making a life decision that in one form or another is crucial to the whole enterprise. That decision is considered late in the Second Week but can be entertained at another time.

12. Jesus as Leader: Following Christ

The Call of the Temporal King, As an Aid
toward Contemplating the Life of the Eternal King

The Preparatory Prayer will be as usual.

The First Prelude. A composition by imagining the place. Here it will be to see with the eyes of the imagination the synagogues, villages, and castles through which Christ our Lord passed as he preached.

The Second Prelude is to ask for the grace which I desire. Here it will be to ask grace from our Lord that I may not be deaf to his call, but ready and diligent to accomplish his most holy will.

The First Point. I will place before my mind a human king, chosen by God our Lord himself, whom all Christian princes and all Christian persons reverence and obey.

The Second Point. I will observe how this king speaks to all his people, saying, "My will is to conquer the whole land of the infidels. Hence, whoever wishes to come with me has to be content with the same food I eat, and the drink, and the clothing which I wear, and so forth. So too he or she must labor with me during the day, and keep watch in the night, and so on, so that later they may have a part with me in the victory, just as they have shared in the toil."

The Third Point. I will consider what good subjects ought to respond to a king so generous and kind; and how, consequently, if someone did not answer his call, he would be scorned and upbraided by everyone and accounted as an unworthy knight.

*The Second Part of This Exercise Consists in Applying
the Above Parable of a Temporal King to Christ our Lord,
according to the Three Points Just Mentioned.*

The First Point. If we give consideration to such a call from the temporal king to his subjects, how much more worthy of consideration it is to look on Christ our Lord, the eternal King, and all the world assembled before him. He calls to them all, and to each one in particular he states: "My will is to conquer the whole world and all my enemies, and thus to enter into the glory of my Father. Therefore, whoever wishes to come with me must labor with me, so that through following me in the pain he or she may follow me also in the glory."

The Second Point. This will be to reflect that all those who have judgment and reason will offer themselves wholeheartedly for this labor.

The Third Point. Those who desire to show greater devotion and to distinguish themselves in total service to their eternal King and universal Lord will not only offer their persons for the labor, but go further still. They will work against their human sensitivities and against their carnal and worldly love, and they will make offerings of greater worth and moment, and say:

"Eternal Lord of all things, I make my offering, with your favor and help. I make it in the presence of your infinite Goodness, and of your gracious Mother, and of all the holy men and women in your heavenly court. I wish and desire, and it is my deliberate decision, provided only that it is for your greater service and praise, to imitate you in bearing all injuries and affronts. And any poverty, actual as well as spiritual, if your Most Holy Majesty desires to elect and receive me into such a life and state."

—Ignatius Loyola, *Spiritual Exercises*, 91-98

This consideration sets up the essential logic of a spirituality with Jesus of Nazareth as the focal point. On the surface the metaphor on which Ignatius builds the meditation compares Jesus' call for followers to the invitation or summons of a king to a cause so noble that no one of good will could refuse. The reflection that follows probes the deeper structure of human experience that allows the meditation to open up a searching perspective on the entire gospel story of Jesus. This consideration asks that the persons making the Spiritual Exercises appreciate the logic of Ignatius's presentation of Christian spirituality and be attentive to their initial response to it.

Human beings have no direct access to ultimate reality. Although what Christians call God sustains reality itself by a creating presence, no one knows God directly or can even conceive of ultimate reality apart from the world in which each one exists. Because human beings subsist in the world and history, religious experiences occur in contexts and situations; they are connected with particular persons, things, or events that focus attention and provide content and meaning. In their turn, revelatory symbols, like theophanies, prophets, and sacred objects and places, draw the consciousness of those who encounter them into a sphere of transcendent mystery that offers meaning and liberating power. Revelatory experience that begins a tradition or continues within one elicits different descriptions: enlightenment, gift, existential encounter, personal communication, communion with ancestors, salvation, liberation. Different images name the character of what is experienced across a spectrum that stretches from sheer emptiness to fullness of being. Because revelation always has some mediating focus, one can approach a particular tradition of revelation and spirituality through the central medium, symbol, or lens that floods human consciousness with grace, meaning, and empowerment. In Christian spirituality Jesus is that lens.

The experience of transcendence that occurs through particular historical symbols possesses a tensive character. The tension lies between the particular revelatory symbol and the transcendent reality it makes present. Revelation carries this tension, and spiritual consciousness shares its dynamic character. For example, the fleeting beauty of a daffodil, or a vast field of them in morning's sunlight, can evoke a sense of a transcendent source of beauty that repeats itself in the species and their individual units year after year across time. Negative experience especially can be powerfully revelatory: for example, innocent human suffering and dehumanizing events stimulate a simultaneous reaction on the basis of transcendent convictions about the way things should be. These different kinds of experience draw human consciousness into a sphere of meaning "below" and "above" the operational surface. In negative experiences human beings can encounter a transcendent ground for better possibilities; in ecstatic experiences human beings can encounter a transcendent invitation for hope.

Anyone can have these experiences at any time. For example, after a bitter argument, one needs to talk to a friend to retrieve the positive acceptance that ratifies one's worth. After a particularly joyful experience, one needs to share the object that elicited it. These experiences open up a sphere of light, value, responsibility, morality, and still more deeply of spirituality and response to something that bears a claim on human being itself. Symbols of transcendence draw human response down into created reality even more deeply where the reasons for being at all may be involved. Only within that region can one discover the height and breadth of an inner possibility for a fullness of being that can serve as a ground for hope: that is, transcendent reality.

This background provides a context within which to introduce Jesus of Nazareth, who will be the principal subject matter of the rest of the Spiritual Exercises. Jesus represents the core of Christian spirituality. The pivotal character of this meditation, then, lies in the way Ignatius introduces the consideration of Jesus. What is the rationale for his view that Jesus as a leader king can supply a foundation for spiritual meaning?

Jesus of Nazareth was not a king. Comparing him to a king represents a personal and cultural appropriation of Jesus by Ignatius into his own life. Generally, people find the literal imagery of a king leading a religious campaign of violence repugnant, and writers typically reference the crusades to suggest moral failure or cultural relativism. The metaphor of a military leader does not invite a positive appraisal of Jesus' ministry. But the military metaphor of kingship can be bypassed, and people can direct their imaginative gaze to Jesus straightaway. But notice how Ignatius's metaphor sets before us the qualities of a leader that can attract one's attention. Jesus of Nazareth, a fellow human being, offers an irresistible cause that appeals to a human quest for transcendent value. Jesus appears in the gospels in a narrative form. The stories portray how he exercises his leadership by actions meant to be followed. The content of the action always bears a relation to the character of ultimate reality. What Jesus does in the stories of his ministry become mediations of God. And, finally, the stories of Jesus invite fellow human beings to a moral and spiritual appreciation of reality that can support an authentic spirituality. People today have different models for moral idealism in action than the noble king, and, when they look at Jesus, they should look for these qualities. Each of them deserves comment.

First, this meditation on Jesus the leader contains the radical tension of revelation: finding transcendence within a finite created symbol. Ignatius had a classic high Christology and related to Jesus as divine. Yet he resolutely presents Jesus of Nazareth as a human being, the way he appeared in history, as a leader who shares the hardships of those who would follow him. Jesus will be presented as revealer of the transcendent sphere precisely as a this-worldly medium that is comprehensible to human beings but points them toward and draws them into the values of God. Kingship provided Ignatius with the closest analogy for someone who can elicit total absolute loyalty. To such loyalty Jesus offers a set of transcendent values that attracts a free commitment.

Second, the king in the story models Jesus by proposing a project, a cause that elicits a course of action. Jesus of Nazareth reveals the cause of God by what he says and does; doctrines about him arose later. Jesus represents a proposal for human action, a project. Classic Christian doctrines are the results of second-order questions about the inner metaphysical character of Jesus of Nazareth that, through speculation and debate, evolved into Christian doctrine. Behind and beneath the doctrines lies the event of Jesus, the story of Jesus that each gospel tried to capture in its own way. Nothing communicates Jesus of Nazareth better and more forcefully to human imagination and consciousness than the stories that tell what he means by telling what he said and did.

Third, the deeper content of the narrative of Jesus supports human flourishing. All Jesus' sayings refer to a God who supports human life and its development to its full human potential. All Jesus' actions work toward making what he calls the values and will of God actual in his ministry. The metaphor of a crusading king fails right here: the desire to conquer by force contradicts the purpose of Jesus' ministry. That ministry responds to such questions as these: Is there any ultimate value to human existence? What is its source or ground? Where and how does it manifest itself? Jesus offers God as the response to these questions. But Jesus does not just say that God is like this or like that. Rather, Jesus acts out the response, so that one looking at Jesus says, "God is like Jesus." Jesus reveals the being of God by embodying actions typical of God in his ministry to release human freedom and promote its positive and constructive agency.

Finally, Ignatius proposes Jesus on the analogy of a leader issuing a summons or invitation to enter into this sphere of meaning and action. One reason why narrative most accurately represents Jesus of Nazareth, as it does any human life, lies in its moral and spiritual appeal. The gospel stories provide the best way to hear his moral and spiritual call. The gospel stories show that Jesus was dedicated to the cause that he called the reign of God. This moral objective represents God's desires and possesses an intrinsic spiritual dimension of ultimacy. This moral and spiritual cause thus makes an appeal to the sensibilities of all human beings: Jesus is an invitation into a new experience and exercise of life.

In a typical move Ignatius presents this Jesus spirituality as a call to distinctive service. People will respond to Jesus as they are moved and as they can. But these Exercises present Jesus to those who are willing to show "greater devotion" and want "to distinguish themselves in total service." This theme of giving "more" and being of ever-greater service appears at first sight as competitive language, but it intends to solicit the hearer's full personal potential in the service of the external project. This becomes clear in the words of the colloquy. Ignatius rarely formulates the words for an individual's address to God. In this case the words are radical and can only be elicited from a profound experience that has taken hold of a person. Such an experience may or may not occur in this meditation. For this prayer is itself a gift that will be spoken in different circumstances with different degrees of commitment now and as people return to it along the way.

13. Incarnation

¹In those days a decree went out from Emperor Augustus that all the world should be registered. ²This was the first registration and was taken while Quirinius was governor of Syria. ³All went to their own towns to be registered. ⁴Joseph also went from the town of Nazareth in Galilee to Judea, to the city of David called Bethlehem, because he was descended from the house and family of David. ⁵He went to be registered with Mary, to whom he was engaged and who was expecting a child. ⁶While they were there, the time came for her to deliver her child. ⁷And she gave birth to her firstborn son and wrapped him in bands of cloth, and laid him in a manger, because there was no place for them in the inn. ⁸In that region there were shepherds living in the fields, keeping watch over their flock by night. ⁹Then an angel of the Lord stood before them, and the glory of the Lord shone around them, and they were terrified. ¹⁰But the angel said to them, "Do not be afraid; for see—I am bringing you good news of great joy for all the people: ¹¹to you is born this day in the city of David a Savior, who is the Messiah, the Lord. ¹²This will be a sign for you: you will find a child wrapped in bands of cloth and lying in a manger." ¹³And suddenly there was with the angel a multitude of the heavenly host, praising God and saying, ¹⁴"Glory to God in the highest heaven, and on earth peace among those whom he favors!" ¹⁵When the angels had left them and gone into heaven, the shepherds said to one another, "Let us go now to Bethlehem and see this thing that has taken place, which the Lord has made known to us." ¹⁶So they went with haste and found Mary and Joseph, and the child lying in the manger. ¹⁷When they saw this, they made known what had been told them about this child; ¹⁸and all who heard it were amazed at what the shepherds told them. ¹⁹But Mary treasured all these words and pondered them in her heart. ²⁰The shepherds returned, glorifying and praising God for all they had heard and seen, as it had been told them. ²¹After eight days had passed, it was time to circumcise the child; and he was called Jesus, the name given by the angel before he was conceived in the womb.

—Luke 2:1-21

This and the next three scriptural stories from Luke's gospel depict the appearance and beginnings of the ministry of Jesus of Nazareth. Together they propose in narrative form aspects of what Jesus communicates: God's personal presence within this world, the baptism of Jesus as God's commissioning him for his ministry, the announcement by Jesus of the content of his ministry, and his choosing disciples to follow him.

The idea of incarnation almost defines Christianity for many, and the Christmas scene portrays it in a vivid imaginative narrative. This traditional Christmas story has little or no historical value. But the point of the story penetrates to the heart of Christian self-understanding. The story centers events leading up to it and away from it. Together they show that God designated Jesus to be God's representative in history. Luke reflects the Christian conviction that God was present to Jesus in an extraordinary way so that the power of God animated his whole life. Incarnation means that God was active in the person of Jesus. This spiritual exercise asks whether a person can retrieve and resonate with the spiritual power of this story even though it does not depict actual historical events.

For many people biblical criticism has altered a naïve approach to the infancy narratives. But the fact that these stories do not report actual historical events as they occurred but are works of a corporate imagination working within a tradition should, in turn, release the imagination of those who interact with them. Taking up the New Testament narratives directly evokes sensory images; these stories were imaginatively written, and they draw the readers into the scenes they create. Once his Spiritual Exercises begin focusing attention on scriptural accounts of scenes from Jesus' ministry, Ignatius proposes much more active use of the imagination: picturing the scenes and placing oneself in them in order more directly to appreciate or feel their sensible unfolding. This does not work for everyone. Each person has to make adjustments on this point and approach the stories in ways that feel comfortable and effective.

For Ignatius these scenes were quite literal and historical. Today, no single reconstruction of their meaning and relevance would work for all. One person might want to stay with the traditional scene as Luke or Ignatius depicts it: imaginative constructs communicate truth in their own way. Christians all over the world recreate this scene at Christmas time, and it bears tremendous affective significance. Another person can make up his or her own scene, realistic or abstract, because Jesus was born somewhere, or use another strategy to focus the imagination. But the point remains, namely, to fix attention upon and engage an encounter with the event of Jesus' appearance personally and deeply. Such a consideration cannot fail to note the historic and even cosmic importance that people over centuries have assigned to Jesus' birth and its representation of the theological idea of "incarnation." The way a person imagines the meaning of that theological symbol, incarnation, should have metaphysical power. The following reflections arise out of a contemplative exercise.

God is not distant, but present to and at work in the world and within human existence. Much could be said about the notion of incarnation from the perspective of creation. A creator God sustains reality in being from within. Thus, the Bible is full of incarnations. Angels represent God incarnate by reflecting God's presence while preserving God's transcendence. God as Spirit affects prophets and charismatic leaders; God speaks to Moses as the "within" of a burning bush; as wisdom, God appears in the world's order. One can depict incarnation in Jesus in terms of God as Word, as in the Prologue to the Fourth Gospel. Luke and the other synoptics depict God's incarnation in Jesus in terms of God as Spirit. Incarnation means that God's presence is effective in the being and life of Jesus, not only in the way he lived, empowering him, but also in his being itself.

It is not that the world assumes the character of the divine: an infinite difference (but not distance) distinguishes created reality from the creator. The world is not God, and God creates the world precisely as something other than God. God is not distant from the world but present to it as sustaining energy and in the intimate way that a personal creator would love what God created as God's own. The doctrine of incarnation in Jesus thus opens up the wider significance of God's immanence within and presence to all of creation in a personal way. Christians have encountered an intensified presence of God in Jesus, that which makes him God's representative. Because they encounter Jesus as God's representative, people can draw associations from him to God, all history, and the relationship between God and history. This marks the very point of the idea of an incarnation of God in Jesus.

God should not be projected as an alienating power, a heteronomous authority. When human freedom becomes more intensely engaged with God, the more free and empowered that freedom becomes. This axiom arises from the notion of incarnation; God should not be imagined over against human freedom but as immanent and at work in human freedom, in Jesus and in all human beings. The principle involved here bears repeating: the more God empowers human freedom, the more free and capacious that freedom grows. Christians imagine Jesus as the height of God's incarnation in human freedom, making him, because of it, not less but more fully human.

The principle follows from an understanding that God cannot be imagined as a being among many. Too often language depicts God as a large, powerful creature who competes with human freedom for place and status. By contrast, when the imagination depicts God as the power of being, when human consciousness becomes grasped by God's presence, and then deliberately takes hold of this source of its own being, it participates intentionally in the power that sustains freedom. Incarnation contradicts the view that religion, closeness to God, and especially God's closeness to human existence, suppresses or usurps freedom. The God whom Jesus represented in his ministry does not suppress or oppress freedom but precisely releases it, from servitude to the false gods of this world and for the service of God's values.

The presence of God to and within the world by God's creative agency also has bearing on the way one relates generally to life in the world. The theological idea of incarnation in the life of Jesus bears analogies to God's presence to the world of nature and to human existence. Internalizing the idea of creation weans human imagination away from a world filled with divine spirits. The importance of this revelation stands in contrast to the idols that society proposes in a language of ultimacy and a power that alienates. Of itself the world does not exhibit a sacred character. The creation of the finite world defines its secularity as other than and different from Deity, who alone is the holy one. Whatever sacrality is found in the world draws on the power of its creator which is both within it and mediated by it as something other than itself. Creation by God of a radically finite world other than God's self posits a truly secular world; it is not the home of spirits or demons or gods, but the place where the human spirit exercises its freedom.

When incarnation refers to the immanent creative presence and power of God as Spirit, as in Luke's usage, it cannot be entirely restricted to a reference to Jesus of Nazareth. It bears a larger analogous meaning than is carried by what Christians encounter in Jesus of Nazareth. All creation and all human beings analogously participate in God's being present and active within them. This conviction gives the nature of reality a fourth dimension of depth, of eternity encompassing time, and of infinity supporting contingency. These corollaries flow from God's presence that pervades all reality and constitutes Christianity's spiritual interpretation of the world. Incarnation thus expands and intensifies the possibilities of genuine religious experience. Incarnation points to God at the center, always and everywhere available.

This incarnational view of the world is brought to a focus in the story of Jesus' birth. God's intentional presence and empowerment are depicted in the "wonderful" or numinous events that lead up to, accompany, and follow this scene. The story is told in a series of panels, which, if they were examined carefully, would appear fanciful. But the story can transform otherwise secular existence with spiritual meaning. It brings Jesus into precise focus as one who was so filled with God's presence and power, referred to in biblical language as Spirit, that he came to represent the character of God and God's relation to human life. The narrative communicates this in the simplest possible way. In an impossible contrast, the power of the infinite creator Yahweh becomes tied up with the nascent human life of a newborn. The story thus makes the deepest of conceptions about reality accessible to all. It opens up the great narrative of creation and God's immanence to it in interpersonal terms of human relationships that remain classic no matter how they are covered over by commercialism and sentimentalism. This scene predicts that Jesus of Nazareth will exercise his freedom in such a way that he becomes Emmanuel and represents God with us.

14. The Baptism of Jesus

²¹Now when all the people were baptized, and when Jesus also had been baptized and was praying, the heaven was opened, ²²and the Holy Spirit descended upon him in bodily form like a dove. And a voice came from heaven, "You are my Son, the Beloved; with you I am well pleased."

– Luke 3:21-22

The story of the baptism of Jesus depicts him being commissioned as a representative of God. It is usually included when, using a series of criteria, exegetes offer an opinion on whether a gospel story may refer to an actual historical event. That does not authenticate the details of the story, only the probability that Jesus had some relationship with John the Baptizer and was baptized by him. Some exegetes recreate an association between John and Jesus; Jesus may have been a disciple of John before he began his own ministry.

The story relates to the beginnings of Jesus' ministry. It leaves to the imagination unanswered questions about how Jesus discerned his vocation. Assuming that spirituality may be understood as the logic of a person's whole life in the face of ultimate reality, how do people know what shape their lives should take? How do persons decide what they should do? Christianity has known a variety of indices to measure the will of God for each person. Not least was the supposition that an all-knowing, creating, and provident God had a plan for each person's life, and each one could use a variety of means to discern it. An open evolutionary view of the universe, a deep historical consciousness, and the sometimes shocking experiences of contingency can seriously undermine any idea that God has programmed the life of each person. This seems to undermine the basic Christian sense of vocation, the idea that each one has a specific calling in life. This story of Jesus taking up his ministry, one that Paul described as obedience to his Father in heaven, raises this question of vocation, even though it tells nothing of how Jesus actually came to the decision that he should undertake the ministry he did.

The reflection that follows sets up a principle that opens up a way of considering the stories about Jesus. It then reflects on Jesus beginning his ministry in the power of the Spirit. It concludes with the question of how human beings can discover a sense of vocation by looking within themselves.

This is the first consideration of an incident in Jesus' ministry. The New Testament contains a wide range of theological interpretations of who Jesus Christ was and what he did. Among them Paul's conception of Jesus as the new or second Adam has particular relevance for a consideration of these scenes in Jesus' life. Paul's Letter to the Romans contains one of the most concise expressions of this idea: "If, because of the one man's trespass, death exercised dominion through that one [Adam], much more surely will those who receive the abundance of grace and the free gift of righteousness exercise dominion in life through the one man, Jesus Christ" (Rom 5:17). In contrast with the first human who failed, Jesus got it right; as Adam was the archetypal human being, now Jesus is; Adam marked the beginning of human existence, but Jesus becomes the source of new being. Although the biblical framework of creation and fall has been displaced by the scientific story of human origins, the metaphor of a new human archetype has imaginative power. It provides a premise for looking at Jesus as one to be followed.

The previous contemplation of the nativity and the idea of incarnation that surrounds it gave rise to the idea that God's presence was so profoundly at work in Jesus that he can be considered God's representative: Jesus reveals the character of God. The idea of Jesus as the new Adam releases a further idea: Jesus reveals what human existence should be. Looking upon Jesus as Adam preserves his human status, for Adam was precisely a human being. But God's presence to him is such that, although a human being, people can look to him for guidance and illumination concerning the nature and character of human existence. At the same time, what happened to Jesus analogously happens to all; what Jesus was, all human beings can be: Jesus reveals the potential of human existence.

These two ideas, that Jesus is the new Adam and that he models human existence, are implicit in the role the Spirit of God plays in this brief recounting of the baptism of Jesus. The symbol of the Spirit of God expresses encounter with the power of God working in the world. Like the wind, the Spirit goes unseen but is experienced as a present and effective power in the works of prophets and leaders who perform above their capacities. The Spirit of God instills life and enables ability of an extraordinary kind. The Spirit makes this scene a key moment in Luke's narrative interpretation of Jesus. For Luke, God as Spirit plays a major role in the story of Jesus. The Spirit acted in Jesus' conception and birth. Now Luke presents the Spirit of God visually and physically as a dove and experienced as a voice from God appointing Jesus to a mission. This Spirit will support his preaching and ministry with divine power; the Spirit will be sent after his death and will animate Jesus' community in its world mission. In some respects, the Spirit of God plays the major role in the whole story of Luke's gospel and his Acts of the Apostles. Jesus and later the disciples appear as the agents of the Spirit of God. In this "agency Christology" Jesus Christ does something in history and in so doing releases a movement. The force behind the action comes from God as Spirit, and Jesus is the divine Spirit's free instrument.

The gospel story of Jesus' baptism by John represents in narrative form the commissioning by God of Jesus for his public ministry to the kingdom of God. God speaks from heaven appointing or naming or identifying Jesus as God's anointed one, a Son of God. This implies that Jesus has been chosen by God and is beloved of God. His commissioning means, in the eyes of the primitive Christian movement, that Jesus in his ministry represented in a forceful and defining way God's values.

As far as Jesus is concerned, it is practically speaking impossible to have access to his inner thoughts or his psychology. But one has to imagine that his baptism was a moment of empowerment, of internalization and appropriation of a commitment to preach the kingdom of God. Luke's story need not be considered a detailed report on Jesus' baptism: the brief statement expresses the theological motifs that were indicated. But Jesus obviously at one point decided to take up his ministry, and his baptism along with others provides a plausible point of departure for his assuming his ministry.

Paul's second and new Adam interpretation of Jesus sets the goal of this contemplation and most of what follows. All of the contemplations on Jesus' ministry appeal to some kind of self-reflection. They present Jesus' story as revelatory of how God relates to human existence. The stories about Jesus provide occasions or touchstones for finding dimensions of the basic meaning of human existence. They function as narrative icons that release potential for self-evaluation and emulation. In short, insofar as Jesus offers revelation of God and human existence, consideration of the incidents of his life that have been remembered and recorded amounts to an invitation to follow in the power of the same Spirit.

Ignatius gave a lot of thought to a sense of vocation. He developed sets of principles and axioms to guide people along a path of discernment of God's plan for their lives. This will be considered later. Much of this material was framed in a manner that today appears naively supernaturalistic. Some interpreters simply transfer the dynamics of Ignatius's language into the sphere of psychology. Both of these strategies could be useful, but there is a middle way that is both psychological and spiritual.

When a person accepts the idea of creation and has a sense that existence itself and all its modalities are gift, this conviction promotes a sense of gratitude and responsibility. Each person has responsibility for his or her own life. Not everyone shares this obvious and yet profound conviction in the same degree. In fact, many people are so busy responding to immediacy that they never quite assume personal responsibility for their own being. But when a person does come to a sense of obligation in the disposition of the self in freedom, he or she will be on a path that leads to a sense of "vocation."

The first place to look for an answer to the question of what a personal vocation might be lives within each person. There one finds the collection of talents that make up each individual. Each person's set of gifts is his or her own. As gifts they elicit a response of gratitude; as a distinct and personal collection they lay out possibilities for a future that will be literally unique; as a unique package of gifts they should be construed as coming from the creator God; they also need to be matched with a goal worthy of the gift and the person they define. This set of gifts is one's vocation. It opens up a historically conditioned, contingent, and open path by which a person can create his or her future and at the same time be called to it. Vocation is not a set plan but an openness for one's own specifically creative freedom.

A person's vocation has never been missed or lost by decisions in the past or training that foreclosed possibilities. It always exists now. This counter-intuitive judgment recognizes how every decision opens up new possibilities that can become real and actual, compared with roads not taken or earlier dead ends. The higher freedom of possible self-disposition is always actual, and this signifies that people can always participate now in the creation of the gift of their own vocation.

15. Jesus Preaching at Nazareth

[14]Then Jesus, filled with the power of the Spirit, returned to Galilee, and a report about him spread through all the surrounding country. [15]He began to teach in their synagogues and was praised by everyone. [16]When he came to Nazareth, where he had been brought up, he went to the synagogue on the Sabbath day, as was his custom. He stood up to read, [17]and the scroll of the prophet Isaiah was given to him. He unrolled the scroll and found the place where it was written: [18]"The Spirit of the Lord is upon me, because he has anointed me to bring good news to the poor. He has sent me to proclaim release to the captives and recovery of sight to the blind, to let the oppressed go free, [19]to proclaim the year of the Lord's favor." [20]And he rolled up the scroll, gave it back to the attendant, and sat down. The eyes of all in the synagogue were fixed on him. [21]Then he began to say to them, "Today this scripture has been fulfilled in your hearing." [22]All spoke well of him and were amazed at the gracious words that came from his mouth. They said, "Is not this Joseph's son?" [23]He said to them, "Doubtless you will quote to me this proverb, 'Doctor, cure yourself!' And you will say, 'Do here also in your home town the things that we have heard you did at Capernaum.'" [24]And he said, "Truly I tell you, no prophet is accepted in the prophet's home town. [25]But the truth is, there were many widows in Israel in the time of Elijah, when the heaven was shut up for three years and six months, and there was a severe famine over all the land; [26]yet Elijah was sent to none of them except to a widow at Zarephath in Sidon. [27]There were also many lepers in Israel in the time of the prophet Elisha, and none of them was cleansed except Naaman the Syrian." [28]When they heard this, all in the synagogue were filled with rage. [29]They got up, drove him out of the town, and led him to the brow of the hill on which their town was built, so that they might hurl him off the cliff. [30]But he passed through the midst of them and went on his way.

—Luke 4:14-30

Luke uses this dramatic story as a programmatic statement inaugurating Jesus' ministry; it provides an initial statement about Jesus' spirituality and the God he serves. Jesus appears as teacher and prophet in the name of the God of justice and concern for the poor, sick, and marginalized. Jesus' cause begins to take shape. The story invites re-creation by the imagination, and the text of Luke gives plenty of material with which to work.

Jesus is in the synagogue in Nazareth where he was raised. He stands up to read the lesson and is handed the scroll of the prophet Isaiah from the Hebrew Bible. The themes chosen reflect Luke's interpretation of Jesus. Isaiah tells of the one coming, anointed by the Spirit, to proclaim healing and liberation. Jesus sat down with all eyes upon him and he said, "Today this scripture has been fulfilled in your hearing." The word "today" in this context may not refer to Jesus here and now, an equivalent of "I am the Messiah," but has the more general sense that this is going on in our time. Whether it happened in this way during his actual ministry or after his death in the course of the Jesus movement, many people came to recognize Jesus as the Messiah. Whether Jesus is interpreting himself in Isaiah's words or the community used Isaiah to understand Jesus, it gradually became clear that Jesus had relevance that extended beyond Israel.

This story of Jesus defining his ministry in terms of the prophet Isaiah is either Jesus' own definition of his ministry or the community's recollection of its fundamental intent on the basis of light shed on the matter by the prophetic tradition. In the latter case, the community saw a correspondence in the Isaiah passages and used them to interpret Jesus. But this required some basis for the correlation. Either way, then, this story can be seen as a vivid narrative that condenses into a synthesis and formula the character of the ministry of Jesus of Nazareth. When asked the question who was Jesus of Nazareth and what did he do, this programmatic story offers a short comprehensive account of his ministry and the tradition out of which it arose.

Jesus' ministry defines his spirituality; his spirituality is his ministry. On that equation one would have to describe this as a project spirituality, a spirituality of social engagement. In this story Jesus stands up and states that what Isaiah described as the effects of God's Spirit restoring God's reign in society is going on in Israel as he speaks. Jesus sees himself as part of this movement of the reign of God. The story does not present Jesus as one primarily seeking personal communion with God in private prayer, even though that was definitely a part of his spiritual life, but as being God's servant in history. The story does not propose that ideal spiritual behavior is governed by the intent to seek God's favor upon oneself. This story has Jesus putting before his audience then and now a spirituality of service. Jesus' relationship to God entails moral response to the ethical demands raised by classes of people: the poor, those in paralyzing debt, those in prison perhaps because of intractable debt, those physically sick, those who needed a new start with a Jubilee Year where debts were forgiven and a restoration of society was attempted. This story offers a programmatic statement in narrative not analytical form, and the rest of the stories of Luke's gospel consistently carry it forward. Jesus of Nazareth has generated an enormously diverse range of spiritualities suited to different ages and cultures. But none should be allowed to overshadow this statement of Jesus' mission and the spirituality entailed in it.

When the narrative content of this story is presented in this way, and then situated in the context of the role that Jesus plays in the Christian construal of God, it also conveys some relatively clear characteristics, however general they may be, of God's desires for human behavior. It provides some relatively clear ideas about God and God's will. If "God is like Jesus," the content of this story emphatically indicates that God's reign counters injustice in society and all unjust repression of human potential. The foundational intention behind this prophetic text of Isaiah correlates neatly with the movement of creation itself. God's creating promotes wholeness of life, *salus* or human flourishing, overcoming everything that negates the full potential of existence from being realized. The opposite of creation is nothingness; withdraw the power of God and one has death. This foundational antithesis of creation over death in the story defines Jesus' mission in service of a God of life, life to its fullest against the forces of death.

The story communicates clearly in terms of the tradition of the prophets the content of Jesus' cause: sight to the blind, health for the sick, freedom for the oppressed. The content of Jesus' ministry falls within the scope of Jewish kingship in the sense that the king had responsibility for the well-being of all who were subject to his reign. So too with the rule of God: God is concerned for all, especially those whom society neglects. This explains why the rule of God dictates justice and compels attention to all those who suffer because they fall through the cracks of society. Jesus announces his mission as the reign of God, which consists in God's values ruling society and providing the pattern for life in this world. God's rule thus symbolizes God's project for the world and for history and society. The blueprint has to be human, always adjusted to new situations; but the project is God's, written into the intention of creation itself. Jesus' whole ministry and all his words, parables, and sayings can be and should be interpreted within the context of the rule of God.

The story lays out in general terms the fundamental moral attitudes that provide a direction for a virtuous human life. When Isaiah's words are taken to define Jesus' mission, and Jesus is allowed to influence one's personal life, this story will recommend a set of fundamental moral attitudes. The phrase is almost self-explanatory and refers to permanent dispositions toward the world, other human beings, and life itself that embrace one's whole being and spontaneously lean a person toward a number of characteristic responses in particular situations or to actual events. All human beings develop a set of fundamental patterns of response to the world. On this understanding, this story portrays the mission and spirituality of Jesus as entailing the fundamental moral attitudes of compassion and responsive love to those in need. Compassion, as the word indicates, presupposes a free human subject who allows the suffering of others to affect the self. "Suffering with" supposes a bond between human subjects through which the suffering of one or many draws others out of themselves in feeling and response. Responsive love translates compassion into action. Ignatius said love shows itself in action rather than words, an axiom that expands in practical terms the dynamics of responsive love. Such fundamental attitudes, therefore, easily develop into social consciousness and responsibility. They describe the fertile ground within which other virtues are rooted. In the course of considering other aspects of Jesus' ministry, the stories of Luke's gospel will fill out these fundamental moral attitudes in greater detail.

How does Luke's story of Jesus announcing his own ministry compare with Ignatius's story of Jesus' kingly leadership? First of all, the very idea of a medieval king, when it is compared with Luke's servant of God's rule drawn from Isaiah, invests the notion of Jesus as a king with irony. Ignatius compared Jesus to a king, but as the meditation progressed, it became clear that Ignatius's king became a servant of God's cause. The point of the metaphor was leadership in a cause that calls forth a radical commitment and loyalty. In the kingdom of God, God is the sovereign ruler, and the servant of God comes to implement God's creative intent. Thus the title "king" when applied to Jesus is intrinsically ironic. In Ignatius its content no longer refers to autonomous authority and power but, as in Jesus' appeal to Isaiah, leadership in service of the higher values of God. This irony resembles the many reversals in Jesus' own parables and aphorisms: "the last will be first, and the first last." Jesus as royal leader can communicate only by irony: the king is servant of God; the king represents the poor against the powerful who would exploit them. Jesus represents God's intentions in his service: in teaching, healing, social critique, and building up.

16. The Call of Disciples

¹Once while Jesus was standing beside the lake of Gennesaret, and the crowd was pressing in on him to hear the word of God, ²he saw two boats there at the shore of the lake; the fishermen had gone out of them and were washing their nets. ³He got into one of the boats, the one belonging to Simon, and asked him to put out a little way from the shore. Then he sat down and taught the crowds from the boat. ⁴When he had finished speaking, he said to Simon, "Put out into the deep water and let down your nets for a catch." ⁵Simon answered, "Master, we have worked all night long but have caught nothing. Yet if you say so, I will let down the nets." ⁶When they had done this, they caught so many fish that their nets were beginning to break. ⁷So they signaled their partners in the other boat to come and help them. And they came and filled both boats, so that they began to sink. ⁸But when Simon Peter saw it, he fell down at Jesus' knees, saying, "Go away from me, Lord, for I am a sinful man!" ⁹For he and all who were with him were amazed at the catch of fish that they had taken; ¹⁰and so also were James and John, sons of Zebedee, who were partners with Simon. Then Jesus said to Simon, "Do not be afraid; from now on you will be catching people." ¹¹When they had brought their boats to shore, they left everything and followed him.

—Luke 5:1-11

This is a story of Jesus inviting people to follow him. It marks the conclusion of the Lukan version of what Ignatius proposes in his meditation on "Jesus the Leader," namely, Jesus laying out a project and then making a summons for disciples who would follow him and join him in the project. Were they actually called by Jesus in such an explicit way? Or did people who heard Jesus speak spontaneously follow him? It does not matter in the end. These gospel stories are imaginative constructs. Luke's story of Jesus choosing disciples in some respects corresponds with stories in other gospels, but is elaborated by conflating the recruitment of disciples with another story of a marvelous catch of fish. It is thus a product of a creative storytelling imagination. The climax of the story is that, like Ignatius himself, "they left everything and followed him."

The idea of being called has two sources: a person's internal gifts and talents that push, and a perception of external possibilities or goals that attract. This story asks that a person consider the attractiveness of Jesus' aims as a personal call.

Jesus' baptism suggested reflection on how anyone can decide his or her specific path in life. Such a choice confronts many as they enter adult life. But demands for radical decisions of readjustment frequently interrupt established careers in complex developed societies where people are constantly in motion. Reflection on Jesus' baptism turned to the way human beings decide the particulars of their lives on the basis of the talents and gifts that make them who they are. In the light of a creator God, these talents appear as elements of the grace of life itself given to each individual. One knows the desires of God by knowing the self. This story of Jesus, when he chooses disciples, enters into the same terrain, but the dynamics of finding one's way are quite different. Here one experiences an invitation toward a way of life that comes from outside the self. In Ignatius's Jesus, the appeal came from the leader and his cause. In this story, Jesus issues a direct invitation. The story presents him teaching and then dramatizing his authority by a wondrous manipulation of nature. The appeal of the charismatic leader overwhelms the chosen. The reflection that follows probes ways in which such a story might find some traction today.

Vocation in this story consists in an appeal from outside the self. Jesus intervened in the lives of these fishers, and they set off on a new way of life. The various ways in which external values exercise their attraction and awaken human desire can create a confusing jumble of opportunities. But it would not be difficult to imagine a scale of values that stretched between lower and higher, or between goods that were less or more noble. Some values and goals to which people are attracted are generally recognized as being more lofty while others are ordinary or low or even base. Although such values will always be deeply affected by cultural conditioning and circumstance, not to mention personal preference, there is no reason why analysis cannot penetrate to something like shared or common appreciations of some basic values, because they intrinsically and directly entail a constructive practice of living, just as their opposites are destructive.

Another way of comparing values and their appeal lies in the kind of response they elicit. Some values and projects appear to be good in themselves and demand respect: altruistic projects of social value have this quality. Other values and human endeavors are egocentric: they are desired not for their own sake but insofar as they respond to various needs at some physical or psychic level. Higher values draw a person out of the self; lower values are desired for the satisfaction they provide.

The appeal of a way of life can be examined further in terms of the affect that such a choice holds out to the person considering it. A thorough description of a human commitment to certain values or projects would show that the object of one's commitment bends back and lends its value to the person committed to it. People participate in the value of the object to which they are committed. This sets up a symbiosis between personal freedom and its objects, especially when central and centering projects such as vocational commitments are concerned. Self-esteem correlates with the values to which people have committed their lives. This may or may not match social approval. Many people transcend social measures of success and fix on the value of the project because of the way it defines the self. At the opposite end of the spectrum, cultures generally recognize that some objects, projects, and ways of life demean the human subject who engages in them. These cultural norms illustrate by contrast that a whole range of options are laid before persons for their choice, and that these commitments are not neutral but potentially affect deeply the very being of the one who embraces them.

The story of Jesus choosing disciples raises the question of how one positions the self in relation to God's values of the kingdom and the invitation of Jesus Christ to follow him. At this point, this is a somewhat abstract question, because the program that Luke's Jesus announced at Nazareth was not described in detail. The many stories about Jesus yet to be considered will reveal more detail in the picture of how Jesus went about interpreting the reign of God in history. These stories will illustrate the teachings of Jesus and some of his symbolic actions that show what he meant by the rule of God. But before considering specific aspects of Jesus' ministry, it may helpful to distinguish two ways of relating to Jesus' call.

People can respond to stories about Jesus in two different ways. One person may relate to Jesus in a direct personal way that is passive in character; Jesus affects the person who is taught or healed. This person relates to Jesus as a client and beneficiary. Another person may relate to Jesus as an exemplar. The accent of the relationship lies less in being affected by Jesus and more in an active response to it; Jesus shows the way for people to follow, so that they relate to Jesus as an apprentice. In the first case, the disciple remains in a dependent relationship to Jesus and is constantly supported by that relationship. In the second case, followers are directly related to God as identified by Jesus and, without breaking the tie to Jesus, do for others what Jesus did for them. The first case correlates with a classic spirituality of the "imitation of Christ" that ends in a continual dependence on Jesus Christ. The second case correlates with a more autonomous following of Jesus; it internalizes the patterns of Jesus' service and adapts them to new situations. The second seems more plausible and appropriate in a complex secular world.

In the end, holding on to both of these relationships can be constructive. The tension between the two need not be exclusive; it suggests shifting points of view, each of which can be helpful. This tension subsists within the corporate Christian imagination. By definition the Christian views the world through the lens of Jesus of Nazareth. But Jesus points to God and by representing God sets human freedom free.

At the end of the meditation on "Jesus the Leader" Ignatius asks the one making that exercise to turn and talk to God in a personal way, and he even puts words in the person's mouth. He provides an example of how one may conclude all of the meditations and contemplations of the Exercises. What is going on in that particular colloquy holds a more general lesson. The reflection in which one engages during or after these exercises resembles the way Luther thought about the doctrines of what God does for human beings in Jesus Christ. Such thinking and reasoning should not be reduced to abstract and objective consideration. Any self-conscious reflection on God implicates the person doing the thinking, because the subject matter, God, draws that person consciously into a sphere that relates to him or her. A person cannot think about Jesus as in some sense God's address to human existence without specifically underlining an existential dimension of its being *pro me*, "for me." So too, the whole drama of Jesus' public ministry, whose inauguration is displayed narratively in this series of considerations, is *pro me*, and one has to react. Ignatius supplies a set of words in the meditation on "Jesus as Leader," but each person's own words would be more appropriate and responsive to the situation and subject matter.

17. Two Types of Life

*A Meditation on Two Standards, The One of Christ,
Our Supreme Commander and Lord, the Other of Lucifer,
the Mortal Enemy of Our Human Nature*

The Preparatory Prayer will be as usual.

The First Prelude. This is the history. Here it will be to consider how Christ calls and desires all persons to come under his standard, and how Lucifer in opposition calls them under his.

The Second Prelude. A composition, by imagining the place. Here it will be to imagine a great plain in the region of Jerusalem, where the supreme commander of the good people is Christ our Lord; then another plain in the region of Babylon, where the leader of the enemy is Lucifer.

The Third Prelude. It is to ask for what I desire. Here it will be to ask for insight into the deceits of the evil leader, and for help to guard myself against them; and further, for insight into the genuine life which the supreme and truthful commander sets forth, and grace to imitate him.

The Standard of Satan

The First Point. Imagine the leader of all the enemy in that great plain of Babylon. He is seated on a throne of fire and smoke, in aspect horrible and terrifying.

The Second Point. Consider how he summons uncountable devils, disperses some to one city and others to another, and thus reaches into the whole world, without missing any provinces, places, states, or individual persons.

The Third Point. Consider the address he makes to them: How he admonishes them to set up snares and chains; how first they should tempt people to covet riches (as he usually does, at least in most cases), so that they may more easily come to vain honor from the world, and finally to surging pride. In this way, the first step is riches, the second is honor, and the third is pride; and from these three steps the enemy entices them to any other vices.

The Standard of Christ

Similarly, in contrast, gaze in imagination on the supreme and true leader, who is Christ our Lord.

The First Point. Consider how Christ our Lord takes his place in that great plain near Jerusalem, in an area which is lowly, beautiful, and attractive.

The Second Point. Consider how the Lord of all the world chooses so many persons, apostles, disciples, and the like. He sends them throughout the whole world, to spread his doctrine among people of every state and condition.

The Third Point. Consider the address which Christ our Lord makes to all his servants and friends whom he is sending on this expedition. He recommends that they endeavor to aid all persons, by attracting them, first, to the highest degree of spiritual poverty and also, if his Divine Majesty would be served and pleased to choose them for it, to no less a degree of actual poverty; second, by attracting them to a desire of reproaches and contempt, since from these results humility.

In this way there will be three steps: the first, poverty in opposition

*to riches; the second, reproaches or contempt in opposition to honor
from the world; and the third, humility in opposition to pride. Then
from these three steps they should induce people to all the other virtues.*

*The First Colloquy should be with Our Lady. I beg her to obtain for
me grace to be received under the standard of her Son and Lord; that is,
to be received, first, in the highest degree of spiritual poverty and also,
if his Divine Majesty would be served and if he should wish to choose
me for it, to no less a degree of actual poverty; and second, in bearing
reproaches and injuries, that through them I may imitate him more, if
only I can do this without sin on anyone's part and without displeasure
to his Divine Majesty. Then I will say a Hail Mary.*

*The Second Colloquy. It will be to ask the same grace from the Son
that he may obtain it for me from the Father. Then I will say the Soul
of Christ.*

*The Third Colloquy will be to ask the same grace from the Father,
that he may grant it to me. Then I will say an Our Father.*

—Ignatius Loyola, *Spiritual Exercises*, 136-147

Ignatius appropriated the moral dualism of scripture made famous
by Augustine's two cities, the city of Satan and the city of God. This
allowed him to expand The Call of the King (Jesus as Leader) in a
dramatic visual and programmatic contrast between the strategy of
Satan for a life of vice and that of Jesus Christ for a life of virtue. This
reflection appropriates the logic and aim of the text in a straightforward contrast between two types of life and asks whether they clarify
options proffered by society today. The contemplations that follow it
take up the program of Jesus in more concrete, specific terms.

Ignatius wanted to be clear about how he was using gospel values
as criteria for measuring the quality of life responsive to the appeal of
Jesus Christ. To do this he contrasted two "standards" or banners that
essentially symbolized two strategies or logics of life that are respectively bad and good, destructive and life-bearing. He saw the lure of
wealth as a main source of human ruin; it leads to honor and then
pride from which all evil flows. Against this he pitted the example of
Jesus as poor, the subject of contempt, which gained him the humility
relative to God that enabled him to accept a death that gained salvation. This picture needs to be refocused. Besides the questionable
theology, it is not helpful to elevate a life of voluntary poverty as a
higher form of spirituality or to posit money as a suspicious entity in a
complex industrial world where one has to earn money simply to live,
raise a family, and participate in society. But that in its turn does not
lessen the classical dangers of wealth and the desire to acquire it.

This reflection uses the analogous term, "type": a constructed ideal of something, such as an organization, that serves as a template to calculate how an actual social group is performing, whether it is measuring up. A type functions as a diagnostic tool. Types do not exist, but as fictive models they are useful in judging actuality by comparison with an ideal form. They supply abstract criteria for stimulating understanding, motivation, and decision by a review of how behavior should be oriented to goals.

This reflection employs another shift of language to preserve Ignatius's intent. The new names for the types are "Anti-Christ" and "Jesus Christ." This moves the emphasis from personification of the principle of evil in Satan and makes the type more clearly a type. It can but does not necessarily demythologize Satan. The type of Jesus Christ is not a personification but points to the ministry of Jesus of Nazareth.

Although types are constructed and not real, they bear a reference to actuality that they measure and criticize; they are applicable precisely as clarifying questions about the real. This raises the question of what the subject matter of this meditation is: what is being considered? This exercise refers simultaneously to aspects of the social structures in which human beings live and to individuals who participate in society and internalize its values. The types refer to various social groups and the members who share their corporate values. This follows the idea seen in the First Week that a main source of temptation and sin in human life comes not from evil spirits whispering in human minds, but from patterns of society that have built into them sets of negative values. As social individuals, everyone is shaped by the worlds he or she inhabits. In classical language, to resist temptation and sin one has to understand their provenance. This meditation rests on the supposition that one of the major sources of sin, though certainly not the only one, lies in the world that shapes individuals. This sin of the world shares all the deceits that Ignatius attributes to Satan. The object of this meditation, then, is simultaneously social system and personal motivation. The contrast of the type of life set forth in Jesus' ministry with that of Anti-Christ stimulates constructive spiritual energy.

The goal for this meditation remains as Ignatius defined it in the prelude that asks "for insight into the deceits of the evil leader, and for help to guard myself against them; and further, for insight into the genuine life which the supreme and truthful commander sets forth, and grace to imitate him." "Insight" means spiritual penetration and appropriation, because Ignatius clearly explains the logic of the deceits of the evil leader and of the genuine life proposed by Jesus. But Ignatius's explanation works within an individual personalist framework, and this too needs adjustment to comprehend the power that society and culture have over the behavior of individuals. Ignatius proposed the existential path of wealth, honor, arriving at pride as the source of the destructive action of people. Several formulas could be employed to update but not replace the logic of the social mechanisms of sin and grace. But the following seems quite descriptive: sin is enabled by hierarchy, which fosters competition and leads to either success or failure within that system. The logic of Christ will be the opposite of this.

Consider Anti-Christ: this is an organized way of life that is hierarchical, leading to competition as a way of life, resulting in either a loss of self before or within the system or a successful self-assertion over others.

The course of this structure is just as straightforward as that of Ignatius. Hierarchy does not mean any ordered social stratification. Bureaucratic organization of life structured by law is a given in the world; the world cannot run without it. But organizations are not sacred. Hierarchy refers to a *hardened* order that so approaches the objective and impersonal that it loses its subjectivity, freedom, and thus humanity. Hierarchy is not only impersonal; it tends to depersonalize and thus dehumanize individuals. It also dominates; it positions some people over others and encourages the objectification of both those "below" and those "above" by the very functionalism it needs to perform adequately, that is, to generate the corporate outcome. Social objectification enables competition, which also promotes effectiveness of the whole organism, but along the way strengthens the tendency to treat other members of the organization as units of performance.

Note too how these three stages, hierarchy, competition, and self-definition, do not represent a progressive development but simply mark three qualities or possible characteristics of organized social life or a subculture. But these elements also become qualities of the persons in the system. The characteristics of the system become internalized in the members and, depending on the depth to which they shape the personalities and behavior of participants, become a "second nature" or social-habitual way of acting and being in the world. It is difficult for persons to extricate themselves as individual persons from the groups in and through which they live or work.

One should also attend to the two possible outcomes of hierarchy. On one side lies the loss of freedom or autonomous self-actualizing power. On the other side success within the system consists in a dominating control over others. Both are dehumanizing qualities at opposite ends of the spectrum that the system encourages. This structure of Anti-Christ is found throughout society, not only in business, education, politics, but in elementary life forms, in language and various levels of culture. Human beings have no values that are not socially mediated: thus racism, sexism, every social and cultural bias, and every social hatred is mediated through social systems.

Anti-Christ is any social system to the degree that it dominates, depersonalizes, and generates a competitive spirit among persons with the promise of achievement. Those who fall under its sway will either win success by dominating others or lose themselves by becoming submissive to the will of others.

Consider Jesus Christ: this is, by contrast, an organized way of life that is egalitarian, leading to dialogue and mutual understanding as a way of life, resulting in both a possession of oneself and an ability to transcend the self in commitment to a worthy cause on behalf of others.

The course of this structure is just as straightforward as that of Ignatius. This second scenario, or type of life, is the photographic negative of the first; that is, being the opposite, it negates the negatives of the first. As the countertype to sin, it is the result or effect of grace and mediates it in turn. Egalitarianism does not mean leveling all to the same level of talent and ability, the same role or even social status: it means treating others as persons. Personalism within a social structure does not negate distinct roles and purposeful cooperation toward a goal, but resists the depersonalization that leads to treating others merely as means. The point is that respect for persons becomes written into a culture and social interaction. The result of socialization into this type of groups, for everyone has multiple memberships, is learned self-respect, a sense of autonomy and agency, and a set of ideals rooted in the fundamental moral value of respect and compassion for other human beings and the world.

One should note the two outcomes of the concluding quality of this type of social system: it stimulates both a possession of oneself and an ability to transcend the self in commitment to something outside the self. This lesson is partly taught by reception and gratitude. This self-possession and self-transcendence at the same time seem so rare socially that they appear to be a gift, or what Augustine and Ignatius would call the influence of God's Spirit in human lives.

Because types are fictive models and not themselves entities, one organization or society can in various degrees embody both types at once in tension with each other. This makes consideration of these types, relative to the actual organizations in which human beings live, a form of diagnosis of society and the self. This second abstract type, Jesus Christ, will become more concrete when attention is turned to the gospel portraits of Jesus of Nazareth, who inspires this type of human existence.

18. Following Jesus

⁵⁷As they were going along the road, someone said to him, "I will follow you wherever you go." ⁵⁸And Jesus said to him, "Foxes have holes, and birds of the air have nests; but the Son of Man has nowhere to lay his head." ⁵⁹To another he said, "Follow me." But he said, "Lord, first let me go and bury my father." ⁶⁰But Jesus said to him, "Let the dead bury their own dead; but as for you, go and proclaim the kingdom of God." ⁶¹Another said, "I will follow you, Lord; but let me first say farewell to those at my home." ⁶²Jesus said to him, "No one who puts a hand to the plough and looks back is fit for the kingdom of God." 10¹After this the Lord appointed seventy others and sent them on ahead of him in pairs to every town and place where he himself intended to go. ²He said to them, "The harvest is plentiful, but the laborers are few; therefore ask the Lord of the harvest to send out laborers into his harvest. ³Go on your way. See, I am sending you out like lambs into the midst of wolves. ⁴Carry no purse, no bag, no sandals; and greet no one on the road. ⁵Whatever house you enter, first say, 'Peace to this house!' ⁶And if anyone is there who shares in peace, your peace will rest on that person; but if not, it will return to you. ⁷Remain in the same house, eating and drinking whatever they provide, for the laborer deserves to be paid. Do not move about from house to house. ⁸Whenever you enter a town and its people welcome you, eat what is set before you; ⁹cure the sick who are there, and say to them, 'The kingdom of God has come near to you.' ¹⁰But whenever you enter a town and they do not welcome you, go out into its streets and say, ¹¹'Even the dust of your town that clings to our feet, we wipe off in protest against you. Yet know this: the kingdom of God has come near.' ¹²I tell you, on that day it will be more tolerable for Sodom than for that town."

—Luke 9:57–10:12

This passage begins with three proverb-like sayings of Jesus meant to test the desire of those who would follow him. Ordinarily, proverbs represent conventional wisdom, common sense in an orderly world. These aphorisms say that following Jesus in his commitment to the kingdom of God requires extraordinary dedication and utter single-mindedness. Luke combines this with a story of Jesus sending his followers to bear witness as he did to the rule of God in the neighboring towns. In a rough and hostile world, this is to be a mission of peace and reconciliation; it consists in witnessing to new being and healing those who suffer. If this project runs into conflict or rejection, followers are to deliver their message and leave. The text provides an occasion for further consideration of what following Jesus might entail.

The reflection on Jesus gathering disciples distinguished between two distinct ways in which the person called might relate to him. Some relate to Jesus primarily in the passive way of the beneficiary, while others relate primarily as active fellow workers. Although the two are not exclusive but overlap, they can represent quite different styles of Christian life. Without excluding the first, Ignatius built the Exercises around the second path with The Call of the King and The Two Standards. Both position Jesus as a leader to be followed. This story of the demanding character of a commitment to the rule of God and of Jesus sending disciples on mission supports an active spirituality. A person commits to God's cause as revealed and exemplified by Jesus because it is worthy and promises to fill freedom to the full.

The aphorisms at the head of this vignette suggest that the stakes of following Jesus are high. Does "let the dead bury the dead" mean that persons who choose to delay response to the kingdom of God in order to perform basic family duties are already spiritually dead? Not at all. These sayings communicate one point clearly: following Jesus entails commitment to the values of God that completely absorb a person's attention and becomes all-encompassing. With these sayings Jesus seems to go out of his way to shock his hearers into a recognition that something radical is going on here.

Reflection on this point has to show that what is asked is not impossible, without taking the edge off the passage. One way of doing this understands the commitment to follow Jesus as so fundamental that it cannot be compared with the concrete and specific obligations entailed in social life. Rather than compete with them, this dedication to the rule of God subsumes or sublates them into itself as an enveloping commitment to larger, more comprehensive meaning. All other duties are influenced, modified, and even regulated by it. Commitment to the values of God's rule does not exclude other decisions, commitments, or ways of life, because all of these are taken up into this fundamental moral and spiritual dedication. Particular decisions that do seem to challenge discipleship fall out of the reckoning: they do not enter into the calculus of decision making. This also means that the kind of absolute singularity and totality of what a commitment to following Jesus entails cannot be limited to a single lifestyle or professional calling but can be played out within a wide range of secular ways of life. This formula shows that this following Jesus points to a manner of living that is always developing, because it constantly intersects and commingles with other engagements within society and history.

What is the object of this commitment? Exactly what is the kingdom of God that formed the center of Jesus' mission? The metaphor of the kingdom of God comes from the idea of God as ruler, governor, or king of the universe. Jesus' many approaches to the kingdom of God fill the phrase with specific content and associations. But its formal meaning refers to the way things would be or will be under God's rule. Reductively, it is the will of God for the world, or the way God designed the world to be, or the desires of God for human existence as distinct from purely self-interested and worldly values. The first answer to the question then is abstract and formal: the kingdom of God refers to God's values and God's sovereign rule as creator of heaven and earth, the way society would be according to God's intent.

To know what these values are more specifically and concretely requires closer examination of Jesus' ministry, because he did not represent them discursively but manifested them in the many facets of his activity. Jesus spoke at greatest recorded length about the rule of God in parable, but he also defines it through aphorism, as in Luke's text, and in symbolic actions, that is, actions such as healings, which actually render it present. The lack of a precise description of the idea of the rule of God corresponds with its transcendent character: it is not quite available for exact human description. In philosophical language it resembles a utopian ideal that bends back and judges human relations and society as they appear in actuality.

The various antitheses revolving around the kingdom of God need not be understood as exclusive or canceling each other out. Did Jesus conceive of the rule of God as breaking into history during his time or in the future as the end of history? Would it be a supernatural cosmic event or mediated through human agents? Did God's rule refer to God's sovereignty over each person within the human heart or more objectively over the world and society? And how is this kingdom of God to be brought about? The rule of God can come about only through God's agency. Yet Jesus preached moral responsibility and not passive waiting. It is possible to line up evidence for each side of these antitheses and to make a case that one side has more weight than the other. But it is far more intelligent to be inclusive in judgments about what is going on here. The kingdom of God is a religious symbol that points to and makes present a sphere of reality that transcends clear human perception and yet resonates with spheres of meaning that lead down multiple paths taking different directions. One has to get used to a fullness of transcendent meaning released by the ministry of Jesus that generates a legitimate pluralism of interpretations.

The kingdom of God in Jesus' ministry was also a mission. This idea of being sent, of being commissioned and delegated to do something, becomes very prominent in the Christian interpretation of Jesus and in the development of the Jesus movement into a church and a religion. The theme becomes prominent in the Fourth Week of the

Exercises. But its roots lie in Jesus' own ministry. It would be impossible to understand Jesus' ministry without recognizing that he did not assume an exclusive responsibility for it. His words and actions indicate that he acted as a servant of what he understood to be God's values and desires for human beings and their society and history. His language reflects one who experienced himself as one sent to serve a transcendent cause in history. It is quite possible so to enter into the stories about Jesus that the transcendent appeal of what he stood for is also experienced as an impelling empowerment for mission.

It is important to clarify early in this regard that one cannot read in Jesus' ministry a formula for the reform of society or anything like a social or economic plan. Such an idea confuses transcendent power with political planning of life in society. These spheres should not be separated, but they are utterly distinct. God provides transcendent goals and motives for living and not historical plans. It is better to think of following Jesus as establishing a basis for a comprehensive spirituality. It combines the ethical and the spiritual without compromise of either. Ethics in this broad sense includes critical political and social reflection and a prudential calculus of moral right and wrong. Spirituality draws these essential components of human living into the horizon of transcendence and absolute worth. Spirituality thus integrates knowing and doing within a sphere where a person is connected with a ground of being that provides a direction within the flow of existence. It falls to human responsibility to determine how best the values of the rule of God can be made effective in any given historical context and concrete situation. But the stories about Jesus and the stories that he himself told provide a relatively clear narrative grounding for a spiritual commitment to follow Jesus.

19. Jesus as Healer

[14]Now he was casting out a demon that was mute; when the demon had gone out, the one who had been mute spoke, and the crowds were amazed. [15]But some of them said, "He casts out demons by Beelzebul, the ruler of the demons." [16]Others, to test him, kept demanding from him a sign from heaven. [17]But he knew what they were thinking and said to them, "Every kingdom divided against itself becomes a desert, and house falls on house. [18]If Satan also is divided against himself, how will his kingdom stand?—for you say that I cast out the demons by Beelzebul. [19]Now if I cast out the demons by Beelzebul, by whom do your exorcists cast them out? Therefore they will be your judges. [20]But

if it is by the finger of God that I cast out the demons, then the kingdom of God has come to you."

—Luke 11:14-20

The next three contemplations turn to stories about Jesus that help fill out the "type" Jesus Christ as it was set up in Two Types of Life. They illustrate by example three aspects of Jesus' ministry which scholars agree represent historical characteristics of Jesus' activity. In other words, Jesus assumed these familiar roles: he was a healer, an itinerant teacher, and a prophet. This story presents Jesus as a healer in a world where demons were often thought to be the cause of sickness; in it Jesus healed by the higher power of God working through faith. He was what in some cultures today is known as a faith healer. The story invites anyone who would follow Jesus to consider the various human places, personal and social, that need healing today. But the story also tells of conflict with those who would not accept the implied authority of Jesus or positively resisted him. This theme of conflict remains consistent across all three forms of his ministry. From this one can generalize that Jesus' ministry generated conflict and reflect on how Jesus dealt with it.

These stories unfold in a religious culture distinct from that of the developed world in the twenty-first century. This culture bore traces of animism; space was filled with angels and demons, with powers and principalities that rivaled then the electronic signals that saturate earth's atmosphere today. Life was hard and short; people construed the reasons for health and sickness crudely and were largely mistaken. But absolutely certain are the facts that life was precarious and that for the living it was frequently sickly. This is a world of popular religiosity, of unknown powers but a firm belief in the reality of spirit causality. This is the culture in which Jesus lived, which he shared, and in which he acted. He has first to be situated there before he can be read as revelatory in another particular culture. Transposing him as he overtly behaved into another culture without formal interpretation results in nonsense.

The world of first-century Palestine was also one of binary thinking. Many polar tensions structured perception: life and death, good and evil, moral light and darkness. In a complex world of grays, this may seem simplistic. But binary thinking possesses some salutary dimensions. For example, it allows one to look for and be clear about the positives in a world filled with negatives. In a damaged world and a history filled with conflict, one asks what forces are trying to nurture life? This was Jesus' retort to his critics in the story, and its force lay in the actions themselves. How can one doubt the positivity of exorcising evil spirits? Binary thinking also allows one to ask the critical question: is this form of activity a promotion of human flourishing or is it at bottom predatory, seeking the good of some at the expense of many others? This penetrating question tries to cut through the use of complexity as a cover to hide the obvious; it reveals in the maze of detail what is really going on; it challenges presuppositions. For example, does human life always have to be competitive? Does conflict always have to resort to physical violence so that it will always have a destructive edge and cause collateral damage? If courses of action do harm to others, can they really represent the kingdom of God? Straightforward questions often penetrate colossal social hoaxes.

One of the main problems for appropriating Jesus today lies in his being imbedded in a culture so technologically distant from the present. The problems with exorcisms are compounded by "miraculous" cures and restorations to life. This behavior in its overt presentation provides no model for the present; in fact, it alienates Jesus from the present age. And the strategy of explaining or arguing against Jesus' actions, literally conceived in present-day rational or scientific terms, is embarrassing. Jesus as a healer, as well as a teacher and a prophet, can only release meaning relevant to the present time when he first appears as a person of his own time. Only then can he stand for and communicate meaning that illumines life in other times and cultures, including the twenty-first century.

For example, the gospels present the wonderful healings of Jesus not as actions against the laws of nature but as wondrous examples of the creative power of God as Spirit. Jesus communicated a sense of God's immanent, enveloping power of being, and he mediated that power in response to different singular negative sets of circumstances and cases. The actual concrete actions of Jesus as they unfolded historically are not chronicled in these stories, nor is the metaphysics of what transpired. To look for or even try to imagine such things could completely miss the point. Those issues remain mysterious in any age. The questions for today that will release meaning from these stories have to be formulated in other more directly relevant terms. What kind of spiritual power did Jesus plausibly exercise in his time and according to the standards of his culture that responded to possession, sickness, and death?

The point of this story in Jesus' ministry lies in the power of God for life against death. Jesus' ministry carried God's creative power forward in the centuries-long tradition of the charismatic figures in Israel's history of the covenant. It is impossible to analyze the metaphysics of this mediation from the texts. That is not the point. But the finger of God is the power of God: it is synonymous with the Spirit of

God, and it comes to bear in this or that case. The power of God communicates life; God provides the power of being itself. It represents wholeness and *salus* or health against the forces of sickness and death. If Jesus' presence drives out demons, it happens by the power of God, which Jesus represents, symbolizes, and sacramentally brings to bear. What is revealed in this story is that where there is genuine healing, there is the power of God. The story does not primarily intend a revelation of Jesus but of the kingdom of God that Jesus mediates. The Christian community will say something about Jesus on the basis of the story, but the exorcism primarily communicates life and indicates where the rule of God can be found. Jesus' presence and action make God's power felt in history.

Although the story of Jesus' ministry is filled with what are called his "miracles," he was not a singular worker of healings and cures. Stories tell of other healers who dotted the landscape in the same period, and this story refers to other exorcists. These figures too responded to human suffering, to sickness and disease of various kinds. The pattern of the stories of Jesus' responses to human suffering tend to objectify and thus hide his personal human response to individuals. The gospel stories themselves suggest that Jesus spent most of his time responding to all sorts of human dilemmas. One has to suppose that he responded out of sympathy and love and in each case did what he could.

This gives rise to an obvious question: what needs healing today and what forces are responding to the human suffering that marks such a staggering percentage of human lives? What kind of human energy and resources known to present culture, analogous to what was mediated by Jesus in his, can contribute to enhancing human life? Where in the world is the power of the rule of God today? What institutions provide a healing force in society today? What agencies stand committed to react against the dealers of death and diminished life? What kinds of needs are so prevalent that they are taken for granted, breed cynicism, and sap the energy of hope? What specific movements reassert explicit life-giving energy and thus implicitly in Jesus' name hold out an invitation for one's commitment to the rule of God in the world today? When these questions are asked in a quiet, contemplative mode, they will yield answers.

What can one expect with regard to healing in Jesus' name? What if faith healing does not work? This blunt question clarifies the context and is best answered by other questions. What does one think when a medical procedure fails? Or a social program? When a social strategy for the common good makes things worse, we try again. Healing in Jesus' name does not mean God intervening and usurping human responsibility. It refers to God's grounding and sustaining whatever can be done in a concrete situation.

Jesus reveals the Spirit of God that acts in human agents. He bears witness that wherever healing and restoring of wholeness or *salus* takes place, there also will one find the kingdom of God. This insight presents the key that unlocks the significance of this story and all the stories of Jesus the healer. Jesus-like positive resistance to human suffering exists in multiple forms, from medicine to social reconciliation, from faith healing to religiously motivated voluntary associations and nongovernmental relief work. These corporate actions respond to the critics that the finger of God is here. Jesus was a healer in his small world that called out for healing; the power of God becomes manifest wherever the power of healing and human reconciliation asserts itself in response to human suffering and in resistance to its causes.

20. Jesus as Teacher

¹He was praying in a certain place, and after he had finished, one of his disciples said to him, "Lord, teach us to pray, as John taught his disciples." ²He said to them, "When you pray, say: Father, hallowed be your name. Your kingdom come. ³Give us each day our daily bread. ⁴And forgive us our sins, for we ourselves forgive everyone indebted to us. And do not bring us to the time of trial." ⁵And he said to them, "Suppose one of you has a friend, and you go to him at midnight and say to him, 'Friend, lend me three loaves of bread; ⁶for a friend of mine has arrived, and I have nothing to set before him.' ⁷And he answers from within, 'Do not bother me; the door has already been locked, and my children are with me in bed; I cannot get up and give you anything.' ⁸I tell you, even though he will not get up and give him anything because he is his friend, at least because of his persistence he will get up and give him whatever he needs. ⁹So I say to you, Ask, and it will be given to you; search, and you will find; knock, and the door will be opened for you. ¹⁰For everyone who asks receives, and everyone who searches finds, and for everyone who knocks, the door will be opened. ¹¹Is there anyone among you who, if your child asks for a fish, will give a snake instead of a fish? ¹²Or if the child asks for an egg, will give a scorpion? ¹³If you then, who are evil, know how to give good gifts to your children, how much more will the heavenly Father give the Holy Spirit to those who ask him!"

– Luke 11:1-13

The story of Jesus preaching at Nazareth portrayed Jesus as a teacher. People frequently called or addressed him as teacher in the gospel stories. Historically, Jesus went from village to village as an itinerant teacher to communicate moral and religious lessons. To be called teacher ascribes a certain status and authority to Jesus, but little or no hard data establish whether Jesus prepared himself to be a teacher as an apprentice or had credentials other than his charismatic authority. At Nazareth he taught from the scriptures, thus indicating an ability to read and a knowledge of his Jewish tradition. To be a teacher often entailed having disciples, and Jesus did have a group of followers and associates.

In this story Jesus teaches his disciples how to pray in terms of content, and then he urges them to pray with perseverance and confidence. The selection forms part of a larger passage dedicated to the theme of prayer. But Jesus' teaching had a larger scope. He addressed many topics particularly related to the kingdom of God: who God is and the "ethics" of God's rule. He taught fundamental moral responses to self, others, world, and God. Beyond communicating verbally in sayings and parables, he taught by doing, and one can read many of his actions as symbolic.

The Lord's Prayer is the classic Christian prayer largely because, as most exegetes believe, Jesus himself taught it in some version probably close to Luke's formula, and because its content reaches into daily life across the ages. This prayer, also called the "Our Father," lends itself to *lectio divina*, that generic name that includes a variety of ways of reading and rereading texts in ways that stimulate affections toward God and free-form personal address to God. Ignatius suggests some methods of this kind of prayer in his Exercises (SE, 249-260), such as saying each word of the prayer and allowing it to release meanings through considerations and contrasts before passing on to the next. Other scriptural prayer forms, such as the Psalms, lend themselves to improvised patterns of *lectio divina*. But how or what does the language of the Lord's prayer communicate to a broad audience in today's world?

The prayer that Jesus taught his disciples seems simple and straightforward. It is typically Jewish and follows traditional patterns. It begins with an address of the sovereign God of power and might, Yahweh, as "Father." It then addresses five petitions to this personal God who is father of all. Each petition is distinctive and can become a topic of reflection in itself because it relates to aspects of human existence that are perennial and deep.

Jesus addresses God as Father. This is not entirely original to Jesus, for the Hebrew scriptures contain such forms of address. Yahweh was a personal God. But it is worth dwelling on the way that the picture of the universe today and the conception of God as creator enter into some tension with the very process of personification: the unimaginable size of the universe does not facilitate thinking of God as a person of any kind. Other specific issues surround this form of address, such as a gendered metaphor for God, or cultural experiences of fathers that may be antithetical to what Jesus intended. No universal solution to these existential issues presents itself. But the problems emphasize the meaningful tension that arises when personhood and intimate, caring love are imagined in dimensions that can encompass a universe. Such considerations can stun the imagination into worshipful awe and elicit experiential images of God relative to one's own life.

The first petition can also be understood as an exclamation, an expression of praise and hope that God be recognized as God. The idea that God be praised gathers much into itself: it expresses the desire that creation itself reflect back to the creator the creator's due. The psalms are full of the song of the universe, all of nature, praising God. The psalms recognize God's being God: God is holy and no words can catch up with the reverence that reality itself owes God. Human beings have to find their voice in the hymn that the immense choir of the universe sings to God.

"May your kingdom come" advances the sentiment of the previous petition but not greatly. In a way, this petition acknowledges that God's name and being are not revered the way they should be, not just in a lack of fitting worship, but more importantly in the very condition of the human world. This petition and this desire set the premise of Jesus' ministry: that God's kingdom come. This wish or hope incorporates the earlier reflection about the conceptual polarities of the rule of God, such as "in the present" and "in the future," into the existential sentiments of prayer. Who does not experience the absence of God's rule in the world around them or in their lives? This prayer may become routine for some, but it can also express the anguished situation of a person losing hope. This petition could be elicited out of an anthropological emptiness that God's address to humankind can fill with meaning and purpose.

Although the next three petitions are more practical, they also penetrate to existential issues. For example: give us food. This may be an expression of reverent gratitude of those who have food on the table: God save us from feelings of entitlement. Or it may be the prayer of the desperate: "give us food!" Those who are destitute may more reasonably be tempted to a sense of entitlement. Few illustrate this better than Job. But this prayer is probably most meaningful when it is spoken with the common voice of the community: give *us* food. This praying of the prayer should engage the responsibility of all for the nurture and well-being of all and promote a sense of solidarity.

The prayer for forgiveness is not addressed to other persons but to God. The rationale for this bears much reflection and still remains mysterious. Our sin for the most part offends other people, and they can forgive us as we promise to forgive others. But this transaction leaves a remainder, some vestigial need to make things right before the ultimacy of God who, as present to history and personally concerned with it, has a stake in its affairs. Against a backdrop of ultimacy, every serious injury of the neighbor requires understanding and forgiveness from God, and only some kind of assurance of forgiveness can fully handle that kind of guilt. This dynamic runs deep within the Christian imagination.

So too does hope in some absolute future, a hope that the seriousness of existence itself is not illusory, a cosmic fraud, so that "nothing matters" in the end. Thus the prayer: "do not allow us to fail." If God by the creation of the species elicits a promise of life, then the only way this can fail is by human failure. Self-knowledge or honesty about one's own human weakness, then, prompts this prayer.

Jesus' teaching included many other matters besides prayer, and it would be a mistake to limit even his verbal teaching activity to the subject of prayer. His parables provide rich lessons about the kingdom of God, and some of these will be considered later. A major part of Jesus' teaching also consisted in communicating by example through symbolic actions. This becomes especially important because the majority of followers of Jesus will not conceive of themselves as teachers, and yet they can bear witness to a message in much the same way as Jesus did. For example, two stories show Jesus letting his or another's action make the point: the story of the woman who anointed Jesus' feet and dried them with her hair and the story of the woman caught in adultery.

In the first story (Luke 7:36-50) a Pharisee is honoring Jesus at a banquet, and a woman who was a sinner enters the room, anoints Jesus' feet, and dries them with her hair. Jesus raises her up with praise for the love that she has shown. She is a public exemplar of virtue, in contrast to his host, whom Jesus faults for not extending him the common courtesies that she did. In the story of Jesus being confronted by Pharisees with a woman caught in the act of adultery (John 8:1-11) and asked whether she should be stoned as the law prescribed, Jesus counsels mercy over the letter of the law. Then, in a striking gesture, he invites those without sin to challenge him. These are examples of many actions of Jesus that communicate moral and spiritual truths.

Considering Jesus as a teacher and reading the stories about him with this in mind shape an apperceptive attitude to the narrative that allows relevant meaning to be appropriated in circumstances that are significantly different. Most people, in fact, will hardly look upon themselves as teachers in their following of Jesus. But if teaching includes behavior that simply bears witness to a set of values, then much can be learned and internalized by comparing personal resonances with Jesus' witness to what he called the kingdom of God. People can be "teachers" by being doers of the word in a thousand public roles within a thousand different social contexts.

21. Jesus as Prophet

³⁷While he was speaking, a Pharisee invited him to dine with him; so he went in and took his place at the table. ³⁸The Pharisee was amazed to see that he did not first wash before dinner. ³⁹Then the Lord said to him, "Now you Pharisees clean the outside of the cup and of the dish, but inside you are full of greed and wickedness. ⁴⁰You fools! Did not the one who made the outside make the inside also? ⁴¹So give for alms those things that are within; and see, everything will be clean for you. ⁴² But woe to you Pharisees! For you tithe mint and rue and herbs of all kinds, and neglect justice and the love of God; it is these you ought to have practiced, without neglecting the others. ⁴³Woe to you Pharisees! For you love to have the seat of honor in the synagogues and to be greeted with respect in the market-places. ⁴⁴Woe to you! For you are like unmarked graves, and people walk over them without realizing it." ⁴⁵ One of the lawyers answered him, "Teacher, when you say these things, you insult us too." ⁴⁶And he said, "Woe also to you lawyers! For you load people with burdens hard to bear, and you yourselves do not lift a finger to ease them. ⁴⁷Woe to you! For you build the tombs of the prophets whom your ancestors killed. ⁴⁸So you are witnesses and approve of the deeds of your ancestors; for they killed them, and you build their tombs. ⁴⁹Therefore also the Wisdom of God said, 'I will send them prophets and apostles, some of whom they will kill and persecute,' ⁵⁰so that this generation may be charged with the blood of all the prophets shed since the foundation of the world, ⁵¹from the blood of Abel to the blood of Zechariah, who perished between the altar and the sanctuary. Yes, I tell you, it will be charged against this generation. ⁵²Woe to you lawyers! For you have taken away the key of knowledge; you did not enter yourselves, and you hindered those who were entering." ⁵³When he went outside, the scribes and the Pharisees began to be very hostile towards him and to cross-examine him about many things, *⁵⁴lying in wait for him, to catch him in something he might say.*

—Luke 11:37-54

Prophecy played an essential role in Jewish religion. The great prophets recorded in the Bible shaped the imagination of the Jews and Jesus among them. The prophet communicated God's view of reality: God's thoughts, desires, and will. Prophets usually did not assume the office on their own but were drafted by God through some religious experience or dream, sometimes against their will. Most prophets were charismatic figures who operated publicly as the conscience of the people or the king. Rather than as a straight-out predictor of the future, the prophet acted as God's religious and social critic, warning of the disastrous consequences of social infidelity. Prophets assume God's perspective on reality, relate to religion ambivalently, and cause conflict all around.

In various scenes in the gospels people react to Jesus as a prophet, and Jesus probably thought of himself as playing a prophetic role. Luke understood Jesus as a prophet whose message led him to Jerusalem: "Yet today, tomorrow, and the next day I must be on my way, because it is impossible for a prophet to be killed away from Jerusalem" (Luke 13:33). This story about Jesus in conflict with Pharisees and lawyers occurs in a context in which Jesus had just accused his generation for refusing to hear him the way the Ninevites had failed to attend to the prophet Jonah. While preaching, he was invited to dinner by a Pharisee, and this clash ensued.

Prophecy assaults both religion and society; no one really escapes its charges. In Jesus' Judaism, these two spheres were intertwined and complicated by Roman occupation. This story directs Jesus' prophetic outburst to the religious establishment. The passage shows Jesus challenging the Pharisees and the lawyers. They should not be imagined according to stereotypes. The Pharisees and scribes held respected religious authority; one should not assume the discredited status assigned to them by later Christian interpretation. Jesus confronted legitimate authority, so that understanding the dynamics of his prophetic criticism requires analogies that deal publicly with respected authority. It was not their office that was at stake but this particular "generation" whom Jesus accused of corruption.

More particularly, Jesus used a distinction between outward observance and the inner heart to accuse the Pharisees of hypocrisy and the keepers of the law of a legalistic promotion of external observance that burdened people rather than served their religious needs. The prophet criticizes the public life of a religion that claims formal righteousness in its rituals but manages to kill inner spiritual life. Jesus aggressively insults the Pharisees and lawyers for oppressing people rather than supporting, nurturing, and encouraging them. He condemns external religious practice that does not reflect integrity. He also ranked the lawyers with those who had refused to attend to the prophets who came before him. The passage falls within the tradition of the prophets who called for social justice and people's care for one another before sacrifices or other objective observances. This raises the question that appears frequently in the gospels themselves; where did Jesus get the authority and the courage to challenge established religious authority?

Jesus had to have had a spiritual sense of being called in order to possess the moral leverage he needed to confront the religious authorities of Israel. One can imagine the elements of that calling in terms suggested earlier: the push from within and the pull from without. Jesus had to have had an inner sense of what the rule of God entailed, a feeling of being empowered by it, and implicitly an urging of the Spirit of God within himself to take up this prophetic ministry. But this was matched by the negative objective religious and social situation in which he found himself. Prophecy entails a negative experience of contrast, a recognition that a prevailing objective situation intrinsically and aggressively contradicts and damages human life, so that it should not be. A religious establishment that imposes burdens on the human spirit rather than freeing the human spirit and lightening its load cannot represent the rule of God. Religious organization exists precisely to encourage and strengthen spirituality, not repress it.

Prophecy is also a critique of society. In Jesus' day the boundary between religion, society, and state were in some instances nonexistent, confused, or present but tenuous. But religion's ability to criticize society and the state still obtains where a separation between religion and state government prevails. To some extent, the very distinction or 'separation" of spheres of competency and influence strengthens a role for prophetic religious communities in democratic societies. Internalizing the values of God communicated by the prophet that represent the protection, promotion, and flourishing of human freedom should stimulate a criticism of any organization in which they are ignored or overridden. This does not entail assuming a stance of moral superiority, because identification with God's values mediated by Jesus always includes self-criticism.

The perennial questions that have to be addressed at any present time are twofold: how may this prophetic spirit be experienced by the follower of Jesus? And how and where may this prophetic dimension of Jesus' ministry be credibly exercised today?

Following Jesus as prophet has to reckon with the idiosyncratic character of this role. Few are called to the public role of prophecy in the same way that Jesus challenged the religious institutions of his day or the way the term is commonly understood today. The solitary prophets of this world are few. But following Jesus has to include being attentive to his critique of organized religion and recognizing that the content of his prophetic teaching has universal relevance. Everyone can appreciate the critical leverage emanating from the rule of God. Following the prophet Jesus, then, means aligning oneself with groups that criticize religion in the name of the inner core of a spirituality derived from the values of the kingdom of God. In what church are Jesus' words not applicable: woe to you pastors, preachers, and bishops. You love "the seat of honor." "You load people with burdens hard to bear, and you yourselves do not lift a finger to ease them."

Churches should be critics of society. Although only few individuals become recognized as prophets, people at large can adopt a prophetic style and become involved in voluntary associations that promote the welfare of those without social power or agency. Whole churches, as communities of followers of Jesus, should have a prophetic edge that measures their fidelity to Jesus of Nazareth. Christian churches should contain groups that criticize society on the basis of God's values. But prophetic communities can credibly engage society with the moral leverage of Jesus and the prophets only when they have felt its pressure on their own behavior.

Martin Luther expresses well how clinging in faith to Jesus of Nazareth liberates human freedom from fear and endows a person with a prophetic sensibility. It was noted earlier how the commitment of freedom to a lofty value enables participation in that value. Analogously, the commitment of one's freedom to Jesus the prophet establishes a bonding with God's values through Jesus that gives a person prophetic leverage. Committed people can distinguish between genuine spiritual values and idolatry. They can become so freed by their attachment to God through Jesus that they no longer fear with mortal fear the disapproval of either religious or civil power. They become sensitive to a larger perspective on human and spiritual values and disvalues. Communication with God through Jesus instills a share in the prophet's insight and liberty.

The situations that demand prophetic critique are usually obvious and strategically challenging. The point does not require a list of social cancers. Social agents are exercising social power to promote social evils all the time. Of course, prophetic critique that makes things worse is not helpful, and individual prophets without moral leverage are fairly useless and sometimes ridiculous. Yet in complex societies the prophetic charism should in some measure be shared by all followers of Jesus. This will best be exercised in voluntary associations that have credibility and some power. The prophetic behavior of Jesus challenges moral relativism. People always accept prophetic critique when it favors their own interests. But can Christians provide the grounds for a moral discernment that applies universally and consistently across the board? Authentic prophecy goes beyond a partisan spirit and appeals to a transcendent authority. Jesus' conception of a rule of God creates a groundwork for the conviction that some things are simply wrong, and it provides a basis for a morally urgent response that resists them.

Jesus was a prophet. Accepting him and allowing the values of the rule of God that shaped his ministry to influence one's own life require responsiveness to the dynamics of prophecy. Essentially this consists in recognition that God and God's word stand in judgment on the various ways in which human beings have corrupted the creator's values and desires for the world. Prophecy entails interruption, a confrontation with the way things are usually carried forward, because of their inherent injustice or arrogant perversion of God's intent for human beings. The prophetic spirit continually forces recognition that everything is not all right, that this is a damaged world, that human beings are largely responsible for this situation, and, finally, that these are not just "those people," because everyone is implicated.

22. Three Types of People

The Preparatory Prayer will be as usual.

The First Prelude. It is the history, that of three classes of typical persons. Each of them has acquired ten thousand ducats, but not purely or properly for the love of God. Each desires to save his or her soul and to find God our Lord in peace, by discarding the burden and obstacle to this purpose which he or she finds this affection for the acquired money to be.

The Second Prelude. A composition, by seeing the place. Here it will be to imagine myself as standing before God and all his saints, that I may desire and know what will be more pleasing to his Divine Goodness.

The Third Prelude. It will be to ask for what I desire. Here I will ask for the grace to choose that which is more to the glory of his Divine Majesty and the salvation of my soul.

Persons Typical of the First Class would like to get rid of the attachment which they have for this acquired money, in order to find God in peace and be able to save their souls. But these persons do not take the means, even to the hour of death.

Persons Typical of the Second Class also desire to get rid of the attachment, but in such a way that they will keep the acquired money, so that God will come to where they desire. These persons do not decide to relinquish the money in order to go to where God is, even though that would be the best state for them.

Persons Typical of the Third Class desire to get rid of the attachment, but in such a way that they have no inclination either to keep the acquired money or to dispose of it. Instead they desire to keep it or dispose of it solely according to what God our Lord will move their will to choose, and also according to what they themselves will judge to be better for the service and praise of his Divine Majesty.

Meanwhile they strive to imagine that, as far as their attachment is concerned, they have abandoned all of it. They strive earnestly not to desire that money or anything else, except when they are motivated solely by the service of God our Lord; in such a way that the desire to be able to serve God our Lord better is what moves them to take or reject any object whatsoever.

Colloquy. The same three colloquies should be made as in the preceding contemplation on the Two Standards.

Note. When we feel an inclination or repugnance against actual poverty, or when we are not indifferent to poverty or riches, a great help toward overcoming this disordered inclination is to beg the Lord in the colloquies to choose oneself to serve him in actual poverty (even though it is contrary to our lower nature); and further that one desires it, begs for it, and pleads for it, provided only that it would be for the service and praise of his Divine Goodness.

— Ignatius Loyola, *Spiritual Exercises*, 149-157

This meditation introduces a pause in the contemplations of Jesus' ministry to the rule of God. It deals with three people who feel they have to make a decision in their lives. The decision, however, has been complicated by the possession of a large sum of money. Considering each of these cases thus becomes a mental analysis of how motivation works in the lives of anyone making a serious decision. Placing this meditation at this point within the flow of the Exercises does two things: it holds up a mirror to anyone who feels the attraction of the values of God's rule as Jesus portrays them and helps sort out motives for a decision; it also refers back to earlier meditations such as Looking for Principles and a Foundation, Jesus as Leader, and Two Types of Life. In so doing it recalls principles that can drive this simple comparative consideration to the deepest and highest levels of the meaning of human existence. In sum, the meditation amounts to personal probing of the motivation behind true freedom. Considering the three types generates light that illumines the self.

The premise of the three cases is simple but dynamic. Each of three people has come to possess a large sum of money. All are deeply spiritual in the sense that they want their lives authentically to correlate with ultimate reality. At this point in the Exercises this means more precisely an attraction to the values of the rule of God as manifested in Jesus' ministry. But the magnetism of the money attracts desire and complicates commitment to these values. In each case the existential dilemma revolves around three factors: the freedom and motivation of the person making a decision, the lofty values displayed by Jesus as the primary object of potential commitment, and the money that awakens an attaction that rivals or otherwise affects the way one relates to the higher values. Ignatius dramatizes the depth and seriousness of the consideration by asking a person to imagine the self before God and the court of heaven, thus encouraging total honesty and transparency. He then recommends that one force the issue and ask for help to appreciate and desire the higher object.

The first case dramatizes the tension between dedication to high value and the lure of wealth. The power of each appears in the stalemate. All have experienced versions of these dynamics. Freedom becomes paralyzed between two conflicting values, and the dilemma is resolved by indecision. The problem is that a higher level of freedom has been compromised because this person could not shake off the attachment to the status, power, privilege, and security symbolized by money. The issue goes beyond this or that choice. Because of the attachment to possessions, the person has backed away from the human act of making a decision. One can easily say that not to decide is to decide, but a higher level of deliberate self-appropriation has been avoided.

The second person decides but makes the decision without total freedom, because freedom has been intrinsically affected by the desire for the money in a way that has not been acknowledged. The case itself stipulates this: the desire actually to get rid of the money unfolds within the envelope of a resolve to keep it and rid oneself of only the attachment to it. This person is self-deceived and fails to see or appreciate the possibility that the higher value really is higher. This condition releases rationalization, ways in which human addictions influence seemingly objective but actually distorted or dishonest thinking. Attachments can thus subtract from one's ability to dispose the self with full freedom. This case has wide relevance because bias is so difficult to discover on one's own. Frequently it cannot be recognized without a mirror, a medium that reflects the self back to itself.

The third case illustrates freedom in control of itself, a stage where one can exercise unimpeded agency in an act of self-disposition. Through self-reflection the person reaches a platform where he or she can make a self-transcending decision. A theological doctrine is at work in Ignatius's wording. Theology presupposes that such an ability to act with self-transcending freedom could only be a gift of God's internal empowerment called grace or divine Spirit. This giftedness does not decide the actual choice but frees the person involved from desires beyond his or her control so that freedom reaches an equilibrium. This becomes manifest in the quality of the person's motivation. Equanimity here stands not for passionless passivity but passionate objectivity. The person sees clearly and desires objects according to their inherent value as distinct from being led compulsively.

These cases illustrating the seductive power of money reveal how human freedom can become so captivated by possessions that it loses a dimension of its own inherent self-transcending potential. Using the distinction between "being" and "having," one can appreciate how "having" can so come to control "being" that a person cannot imagine the self without certain possessions. Another tension lies buried still more deeply within the dynamics of freedom: in Christian tradition this has been framed as a tension between self-possession and self-gift, or self-love and self-transcendence. Recasting this meditation by considering one's talents in place of money opens up this even deeper crisis when it comes to responding to values that transcend the self and invite commitment.

In the case of the first person, the high ideals set forth by Jesus of Nazareth for service to a common human flourishing so dominate the picture that cultivation of one's own talents seems to be placed in jeopardy. One's talents are not external possessions; they define the specific identity of a given individual person. Self-love and neighbor-love can thus engender conflict. On the empirical levels of ordinary life with its everyday decisions, this person makes no centering decision that gives life a focused direction but goes with the flow, sometimes dedicated to self-improvement and at other times to service. These persons remain on the first level of freedom; they guard their options.

The second person decides, and that decision, in degrees of more or less, sets up the self, defined by his or her talents, to be the criterion for responses to appeals from outside the self. Self-care, self-possession, self-development, self-promotion, all of which are virtues without which a person's life in a complex world would be scattered and diffused, create the filter through which every summons from a value outside the self must pass. This does not create a complete barrier to self-transcendence, as in Augustine's conception of freedom inescapably curved in upon itself, but it modifies response and prevents real self-sacrifice, denial of self, and full and selfless commitment of one's talents to aspects of society greater than the self. The worth of the world ultimately becomes reduced to the sphere of this person's subjectivity.

The third person recognizes talents as gift and is willing to give them to others or to a cause larger than the self. There is so much going on in this commitment that it becomes difficult to sort out. Earlier anthropological considerations reflected on the distinctive character of the human to recognize one's being itself and all one's talents as gift. First, human beings have nothing on which to base an entitlement to being. Second, the elementary freedom that allows self-reflection in the first place also gives humans an ability to recognize values outside the self, especially normative social values that protect life, which are higher than the individual person and call it out of itself. Third, human freedom can give itself to some aspect of that set of values without giving itself away. Søren Kierkegaard was so mesmerized by this paradox that it suffused all his thinking. Self-emptying fills one with value, strength, and renewed self-possession; giving one's life to something greater than the self *is* a new being and not a mere condition for gaining it as a consequence. This increment of being comes from participation in the "deeper" or "higher" sphere of value and being to which one attaches the self. Later in these Exercises this paradox of detachment from the world and the self will be the basis of finding the supreme value of God within the autonomous world and the self.

This meditation prepares the way for further consideration of what Jesus proposed as the sphere of God's rule and the values it contains. It provides as well a framework in which to consider possibilities for decisions about one's life. The versatility of the three versions of this simple case lies in the ability of each story to release relevant meaning at various depths: of making a choice, of a life decision, of understanding human freedom, of a vision for the human. At each of these levels the objects of choice, money or higher value, symbolically represent dimensions of human freedom and motivation that in turn correspond to levels of importance or value that are written into the social structures of the world. And deep within those structures lies a paradox that occurs in the exchange between self-possession and self-gift. One has to possess the self in reflective freedom in order to give the self in commitment. But that gift of self, in the very process of the giving, reestablishes the self within new grounds of being.

23. Jesus on Ultimacy

[16]Then he told them a parable: "The land of a rich man produced abundantly. [17]And he thought to himself, 'What should I do, for I have no place to store my crops?' [18]Then he said, 'I will do this: I will pull down my barns and build larger ones, and there I will store all my grain and my goods. [19]And I will say to my soul, Soul, you have ample goods laid up for many years; relax, eat, drink, be merry.' [20]But God said to him, 'You fool! This very night your life is being demanded of you. And the things you have prepared, whose will they be?' [21]So it is with those who store up treasures for themselves but are not rich toward God."

—Luke 12:16-21

Jesus communicated his most explicit teaching about the rule of God in the form of parables. These resemble very short stories that often make it emphatically through a reversal of ordinary or expected human response. Generally one can understand this as showing that the rule of God does not follow the social norms that are in place: God's ways are not human ways. The next four contemplations do not represent the full range of the many parables in the New Testament but are interpreted to respond to some big questions.

Entering into the narratives in which Jesus himself tells a story affects the perspective of the contemplation. Exegetes agree that many of the parables in the New Testament represent to a greater or lesser degree Jesus' actual teaching. This does not make these stories verbatim repetitions of his teaching, but it licenses a person approaching them today to use a realistic imagination. One can imagine hearing Jesus offering these parables and ask, "What is this kingdom of God that he is referring to?" The meditations that follow offer highly interpretive reflections responding to that question.

Over the centuries the parables of Jesus have gained titles: this one is usually called "The Rich Fool." In short and graphic terms the narrative introduces the listener into the sphere of ultimate meaning and reality. It states clearly that the rule of God encompasses life and death.

If someone enters into this story told by Jesus and follows the line of thought that it suggests, it should expand consciousness with new appreciations of human existence. Usually this is not a matter of learning new facts but of appreciating where Jesus' narrative leads. The premise stipulates that these parables were Jesus' way of communicating what he called the kingdom of God. The stories open up ideas about what human life would be like if God's will and values prevailed. In most cases Jesus' message contrasts sharply with human behavior.

Here the contrast lies in the dramatic irony: the rich fool formulates his plan for storing his wealth toward years of the good life and then dies that very night. And lest the symbolism be lost, Jesus states it plainly: this man measured his life by his treasure instead of by his relationship with God, that is, the rule of God. The man's whole plan unfolded within the sphere of building security and comfort for his physical life, but completely neglected the sphere of ultimate meaning.

Generally it makes good sense to prepare for the future. For the most part the behavior of the rich farmer appears sound; he takes care to provide for the future, to lay up stores as insurance for old age. His action may appear individualist in some societies; it represents an option possible for some people (wealthy) more than others (dispossessed). The story may contain an implied criticism of individualism at the expense of others. But Jesus takes this seemingly normal behavior guided by a set of values that make good sense for life in this world and contrasts it to life lived for values that concern a person ultimately and absolutely as one stands before God. The deeper and more substantial values relate to a sphere of transcendence that makes the program look like hoarding and reflect a narrow self-concern at the expense of everything and everyone else. The bad sense, then, consists in ignoring the different levels of reality. In itself the plan appears completely positive, but it effectively displaces a concern for ultimacy. It represents a blindness to other dimensions of reality, to questions of the nature and purpose of human existence. The kingdom of God in no way denies the values of life in this world, but it censures blindness to deeper levels of reality, human responsibility, and accountability that override the demands of immediacy. The point lies in the contrast between life as it unfolds in its quotidian events and the height and depth of the meaning of existence itself. Recognizing the contrast gives a person the power to make decisions in daily life that connect with a depth of meaning within existence.

The notion that Jesus' message of the rule of God refers first of all to a deeper range of meaning helps to explain how it relates to life in this world. In the parable the question of the kingdom of God comes crashing into human life with an abrupt and unplanned death. Human existence exhibits no starker reality than death; death terminates life. To this the parable says that the rule of God refers to the sphere of meaning and reference that transcends time to embrace both life and death. Sickness and death forcefully mediate this sphere of meaning because they call the coherent meaning of life in this world into question. In the face of this general pattern, only human beings can recognize ultimacy. The behavior of the farmer indicates that he either ignored or had forgotten this dimension of life. But in one stroke all the planning for a fruitful and full life in terms of eating one's full, sleeping late, and merriment in between suddenly evaporated. This little parable opens up the universal issue of ultimate meaningfulness of life in the face of death. The message of the rule of God in turn only makes sense within a framework of questions about transcendent meaning in the face of that which calls that very transcendence into question.

Other human experiences, both positive and negative, can open up the sphere of ultimacy. Ecstatic experiences of being transported by the sublime can contain an invitation into transcendence. Kinship bonds that cannot be broken, positive experiences that one does not want to end, intimate constructive relationships of love that carry people into the future, certain experiences that are so solid that they promise eternity, all suggest an importance that intimates the sphere of ultimacy. Yet, because these positive experiences are finite and passing, their transcendent dimension can easily be ignored. And the voice of God may appear more radically in the whirlwind than in comforting experiences. The negativity of sickness and death communicates the contingent character of life in this world like no other, and the sphere of ultimacy appears in the contrast as an object of hope. Ultimacy promises meaning within and beyond the negativity. Negative experiences add a pointed relevance to this sphere of meaning. Ultimacy is a dimension of real life.

The parable also provides clues for thinking about how the sphere of ultimacy relates to the sphere of immediacy that occupies so much of life's attention. Without allegorizing the parable,[1] one can still consider different aspects of God's rule. Does the parable suggest ways of talking about this sphere of ultimacy in more concrete terms? Imaginatively projecting a perspective from God's side, God's rule encompasses heaven and earth, time and eternity. The rule of God is the prerogative of the creator of heaven and earth who provides the ground of being itself. In the affairs of this world, God has ceded control over events to human freedom. Given human limitations, the structures created by people will inevitably fail to reflect the full flourishing of life intended by the creator. Jesus faults the fool not for planning to secure his future but for neglecting a whole range of other relationships. In other words, the kingdom of God addresses human beings not to draw them out of the sphere of immediacy, but to envelop

---

1. The logic of the parable is such that generally the narrative makes a single point. Meditating on a parable, however, often gives rise to allegorizing certain elements in it. A person gets distracted by a detail and follows it, thereby giving it a semi-autonomous semantic value as in an allegory where various details or persons represent meanings in a parallel story of life itself. There is evidence that Jesus' parables were sometimes allegorized by the communities in which they circulated before appearing in the gospels.

the concerns of this world with a wider context for a meaningful life. The kingdom of God appeals to a more penetrating awareness of the depths of reality and a loftier consciousness of the heights of meaning it can reach. Jesus uses the metaphor of the kingdom of God as an instrument of prophetic critique in order to communicate a consciousness that will enhance and validate human life.

The point of Jesus' story may be phrased in terms of misplaced ultimacy. The rich farmer did not obey this moral maxim: investing ultimate concern in the less than ultimate is inappropriate. This insight becomes obvious when the whole plan dissolves in the man's death. The proper order of reality and its corresponding wisdom stipulates that value responses should correlate with the kind of value being responded to. This becomes a fundamental principle of the spiritual domain: to assign ultimate importance and worship to finite objects amounts to idolatry. In the language of the parable, idolatry is stupid. Idolatry in this sense correctly describes a great deal of human behavior, and Jesus' parable exposes it.

The higher character of ultimacy means that in the proper order of things the rule of God should not be considered a rival of worldly values. Ultimacy criticizes worldly values when they take on an importance more than their due. The kingdom of God represents transcendent values, so that the sphere of ultimacy does not replace or even compete with immediacy but envelops it. In addition to critique, higher values subsume or draw the lower values up into themselves and transform their meaning with a surplus of significance. The kingdom of God means that the positive values of this world, when they correspond with the rule of God, may make an eternal difference.

Because the sphere of ultimacy embraces and enfolds both life and death within itself, it contains a promise of fulfillment that the finite or immediate values of life in this world cannot offer. One need not measure ultimacy against a whole range of this-worldly values in order to make the point; it is enough to recognize the difference and the relation between the two spheres. The parable, then, urges the listener to recognize that the ultimacy symbolized by Jesus' God protects the secular values of this world. Ultimacy guarantees the values and overall meaning of this world precisely against the bleak reality of annihilation. It is almost certainly true that for the most part the hearers of Jesus' parables already knew the meaning of transcendence and ultimacy over against the confusion of idolatry. Thus, his teaching was an appeal to an existential life that corresponded with those basic beliefs. When transposed into a secular world, this parable can release transforming insight. If it penetrates the walls of immediacy, it can open up new dimensions of reality.

24. Jesus on Justice

²⁰Then he looked up at his disciples and said: "Blessed are you who are poor, for yours is the kingdom of God. ²¹Blessed are you who are hungry now, for you will be filled. Blessed are you who weep now, for you will laugh. ²²Blessed are you when people hate you, and when they exclude you, revile you, and defame you on account of the Son of Man. ²³Rejoice in that day and leap for joy, for surely your reward is great in heaven; for that is what their ancestors did to the prophets. ²⁴But woe to you who are rich, for you have received your consolation. ²⁵Woe to you who are full now, for you will be hungry. Woe to you who are laughing now, for you will mourn and weep. ²⁶Woe to you when all speak well of you, for that is what their ancestors did to the false prophets."

—Luke 6:20-26

The primary text for this contemplation is not a parable but Jesus' teaching of the Beatitudes, or blessings. In Luke these are accompanied by the Woes, which were more likely constructed by Luke than spoken by Jesus. These sayings of Jesus point to a sphere of absolute justice and are closely related to the point of his parable of The Rich Man and Lazarus. Both stories tell of an immanent ground and overarching canopy of final justice that encompasses the evolutionary world of violence and the innocent suffering of human beings. Human existence longs for this; Jesus said it is there; can one believe it?

Jesus announced these blessings as coming from God in the form of good fortune; the woes speak God's warnings of the negative consequences of behavior injurious to others. The woes are less condemnations of a situation than invitations to recognize the lack of moral substance in the benefits of wealth as contrasted with the substantial human relationships that prevail under God's rule. Wealth actually endangers moral character. The blessings do not make their promises on the basis of a law of nature or history. Jesus makes no appeal to naturalism, nor to some logic or fate that controls the course of history. Behind his assurances of blessing stands a personal God, sovereign ruler of the universe, who is both the source and the executor of justice. The universe, the world, and history therefore are suffused with subjectivity and intentionality, and God intends justice. Today it is difficult to translate "God" into the idea of a big person because of the obvious anthropomorphism that this entails and its utter incongruence with today's story of the genesis of the universe. At the same time the God of Jesus resists a reduction of the universe to sheer matter with no remainder. Jesus' teaching holds out a world of justice constituted by transcendent and intentional subjectivity.

The kingdom of God is a moral sphere. While recognizing that one cannot quite circumscribe the exact meaning of what Jesus meant by the phrase, it helps to recall the working shorthand formula used here: the kingdom of God refers to the way things would be if all people followed God's desire that human beings flourish in community and in individual life. It applies not only to the way this world should be, but also, in terms of hope, to the way things will be in the end-time. Because human history remains radically broken and marked by disorder, dehumanization, and horrendous suffering, the fullness of the kingdom of God refers to a utopian condition that only God could bring about in some absolute future. But even now, in the present time and in this world, certain fragmentary signs of the kingdom of God appear in events such as the ministry of Jesus, so that his words of promised blessings gain plausibility within human hope.

This teaching of Jesus about a just universe may be the most difficult of all his teachings to accept today. This picture of a God of justice reigning in this world seems to be flat-out contradicted by enormous blocks of evidence. The most historically shocking experiences of all have occurred in the twentieth century, the most enlightened of all in terms of knowledge. The scandalous waves of massive innocent social suffering effected by deliberate human policy are matched in the cumulative histories of individuals. Nature is neither personal nor merciful; it works its way independently of subjective response. Because a considered affirmation of a just universe cannot easily rely on overt evidence, the very idea of the rule of God has lost much of its traction. That human beings desire justice and are willing to fight for it remains a given. But the fight is frequently waged at the expense of others. Thus, the confident proclamation of blessings and woes does not even begin to describe our actual world. The contradiction between the ways of the world and the rule of God that Jesus emphasizes seems to run even deeper today. And people are so used to massive injustice that Jesus' teaching simply appears incredible.

Jesus' parable of The Rich Man and Lazarus (Luke 16:19-31) presents the desire of the human heart for divine justice in a morality play. Jesus' warning, "woe to you who are rich, for you have received your consolation," could have been the conclusion of this story. The rich man was clothed in splendor and feasted; outside his gates Lazarus languished in hunger and disease. Lazarus died and was carried to heavenly bliss; the rich man was transported to the tortures of hell. Here the God of justice evens things out, not with vengeance but by simple accounting: straightforward reckoning of cosmic justice. Is there a way of providing some plausibility to this teaching, or is such faith reduced to emotional clinging to impossibilities?

The question of a just universe represents one of the measures of the distance between Jesus' world and the world today. Jesus stood on solid common ground when he challenged his audience to moral responsibility. They shared his belief in God the creator of heaven and earth, the one who attended to the lilies of the fields and the sparrows in the air. This personal protector would guarantee justice in the end. By contrast, the world today trembles with so much innocent suffering, such severely unequal distribution of fundamental resources, and the inalterable destiny of destitution for so many that injustice has become the statistical norm. Only the most naive of people expects or counts on justice in the world at large. Whoever God is or whatever name ultimate reality bears, it cannot convert to an expectation of a moral universe in an empirical historical sense.

The theologian Johann Baptist Metz coined the phrase "dangerous memories," referring to the searing images of innocent suffering from our common human history. He believes that the danger lies in the spontaneous human reaction to resist and seek redress against the causes of such injustice. Dangerous memories release the desire within human beings for a God of justice to make things right. The endangered are all those who live off such human exploitation. But the danger of these memories goes deeper to endanger all human beings, because they undermine the very idea of the righteous character of the universe and its ground. Innocent suffering among humans simply extends the violence of nature in the course of emergent life and the competition of species. Its prevalence tends to make people take it for granted. Basic trust in the moral coherence of human history and society has been corrupted.

These objective considerations force a return to elemental human desires and a reflection on whether they yield any light. The profound gap between human expectations and reality may point the way to a revision of how the seeker might approach Jesus' teaching of a world framed in justice. The searching impulse residing within many convinced believers might also benefit from this prayerful reflection.

The desire for justice has a firm hold on the human spirit. It lives in the same house as love of self: each person requires justice in his or her own regard. This same fundamental instinct reaches out to others in society, because a moment's reflection yields the conclusion that the common good bears implications for the fate of each one. This primitive sense of solidarity explains why wholesale human outrages such as pogroms, massacres, and genocides disorient and ultimately can scandalize. This fundamental desire appears to be much more than a wish on the surface of human consciousness. It might be better described as a structure of human consciousness that is aligned with a desire for life itself as well as for coherence and meaning. From this premise it is not unreasonable to think that these inner demands of human existence arise out of the very stuff that gave rise to human being, so that, in turn, these inner exigencies correspond with an elementary character of being itself. In other words, human persons can read and discover the character of being itself within themselves because they are nothing less than a conscious participation in that very being. From this perspective the teaching of Jesus regarding a finally just universe symbolizes and reveals the deepest inner demands of being itself. The coherent character of the universe reveals itself within human existence precisely as a moral imperative. Human beings know a just universe, not outside themselves, but within themselves.

In the end, Jesus teaches that human beings live their lives in a sphere that has a moral coherence that demands justice in the very face of a history that betrays it. But this teaching corresponds with a fundamental spontaneous reaction of human existence itself. The name of God points to the source and ground of that human demand and the possibility of its final accomplishment. Remove God from the equation and the world loses its fundamental moral structure, and human beings live in a sphere whose morality lies no deeper than human convention. But this general reflection also takes on a more intimate and personal character when aligned with Jesus' teaching. Granted the new view of the universe virtually forbids a conception of God as a big person in the sky. Yet as the ground and source of being itself, God is not less than the free personal form of being that each person knows within the self and in intimate relationships with others. This conviction makes the inescapably anthropomorphic language humans use in relation to God more than just necessary. It is appropriate, not because its finite form represents God's infinite being, but because it represents a human relationship with a God who can only be symbolized in our terms.

25. Jesus on Morality

[25]Just then a lawyer stood up to test Jesus. "Teacher," he said, "what must I do to inherit eternal life?" [26]He said to him, "What is written in the law? What do you read there?" [27]He answered, "You shall love the Lord your God with all your heart, and with all your soul, and with all your strength, and with all your mind; and your neighbor as yourself." [28]And he said to him, "You have given the right answer; do this, and you will live." [29]But wanting to justify himself, he asked Jesus, "And

who is my neighbor?" [30]*Jesus replied, "A man was going down from Jerusalem to Jericho, and fell into the hands of robbers, who stripped him, beat him, and went away, leaving him half dead.* [31]*Now by chance a priest was going down that road; and when he saw him, he passed by on the other side.* [32]*So likewise a Levite, when he came to the place and saw him, passed by on the other side.* [33]*But a Samaritan while traveling came near him; and when he saw him, he was moved with pity.* [34]*He went to him and bandaged his wounds, having poured oil and wine on them. Then he put him on his own animal, brought him to an inn, and took care of him.* [35]*The next day he took out two denarii, gave them to the innkeeper, and said, 'Take care of him; and when I come back, I will repay you whatever more you spend.'* [36]*Which of these three, do you think, was a neighbor to the man who fell into the hands of the robbers?"* [37]*He said, "The one who showed him mercy." Jesus said to him, "Go and do likewise."*

—Luke 10:25-37

The title of this parable is "The Good Samaritan." One of the best known of all the parables told by Jesus, it announces in clear terms that the fundamental moral attitude of human beings toward one another should be love, an attitude so all-embracing that it includes enemies. It points to another area of difference between the kingdom of God and actual human society.

One can easily imagine Jesus telling this story, perhaps for the first time, or improvising to respond to a questioner. But one cannot use Jesus' own language today and recreate the jolting character of the story, because the reversal in the parable was lost when the story entered the tradition. For Jews, the Samaritans, who occupied their own region within Palestine, were a despised people. The very idea of a "good" Samaritan contained an impossibility, something like "the good Hitler," although that may be a bit strong for a social opprobrium. The parable, therefore, neatly illustrates two qualities of the genre. On the one hand, the reversal of expectation and value in the parables of Jesus could sometimes shock and scandalize people. This one proposes an enemy of the Jews as a model for Jewish life. The contradiction interrupts, brings people up short, and makes them react. This one could have made some people angry. On the other hand, Western culture has completely lost a sense for this reversal, because the Samaritan has become a good and loving person. All are supposed to be like the Samaritan, because he exemplifies an exceptional degree of self-transcending love. Jesus was saying that even those who are looked down upon can exemplify the values of the kingdom of God, and they should be imitated when they do.

In ordinary human situations the values of the parables, when they are raised up, will cut against the grain. So it is with love as a basic virtue. For example, priests and Levites were the holy men of the established temple cult. They alone, in a hierarchical division of labor, were able to enter holy spaces and touch the sacred objects of rites and services. They undoubtedly passed by the stripped and beaten man for fear of defilement. But that makes the implied criticism penetrate more deeply, through these two individuals, into established religious values. This parable, when Jesus told it, was radical and shocking in its attack on the symbols of piety; it subverted respect for the clergy and those who held religious authority in the name of basic love of neighbor.

The reversal of the story results in the teaching of the love of enemies. All people are neighbors and thus solicit human love. This represents a breaking open of an ethics whose boundaries are marked by tribe, nation, or religion. Although the idea occurs in the Hebrew scriptures, Jesus emphasizes an essentially universal ethic. It matters little whether Jesus was the first to break open the boundaries of morality, because this teaching has revolutionary consequences for all people all the time. It interrupts the practical ethics of every culture, subculture, and group that spontaneously maintains boundaries to distinguish insiders and outsiders. Love in principle should be universal in scope. The expanse of love's demand cannot be contained by kinship or group, according to the parable, but only by the requirements of the neighbor in question. In sum, enemies become the criterion for the breadth of this basic love toward others in the teaching of Jesus, and its degree corresponds with their needs. An earlier meditation on the allegory of the last judgment in Matthew showed how in Jesus' teaching this love of neighbor in the poor, the naked, and those in prison became a measure of the authenticity of one's love of God. This teaching too has become a commonplace, but a little reflection reveals its radical implications.

This parable contains another reversal. The lawyer asks who is the neighbor and Jesus responds with an answer to another question, Who is neighborly, or what does it take to be a neighbor to others? The shift of ground is deliberate. It is as if the lawyer asking the question wanted a clear legalistic definition of the boundaries of what is being asked of a person. In describing a neighborly disposition of love, Jesus removed all the boundaries and stripped external religion of all its legalistic power over a morality of love. But Jesus' teaching relentlessly goes further, because the parable has neighborly love not just responding but looking for objects of its concern. One should be proactive in love of neighbor, seeking out the neighbor who needs help, reaching out to one's enemies if they are genuinely in need. Do good to those who hurt you. This kind of love disarms and finally tames the energy within the tornado of hatred and evil among human beings. According to the pacifist theology of John Howard Yoder, this is the logic of how Jesus redeemed humankind, by giving the absolute example of not striking back but of loving in return.

The idea of a "sphere of morality" understands the term morality as pertaining to the personal responsibility of the agent. Jesus proposes love as the fundamental moral attitude or virtue that governs the responses that individuals make to other human beings. A fundamental moral attitude refers to a basic disposition out of which many different actions flow. Love means that one wills the good for the other. Jesus also lays out the rationale for this understanding: this is the way God acts, or this logic governs the sphere of the rule of God. The idea of the kingdom of God includes this. God and God's rule are such that no enemies exist in God's ken or under God's rule. Jesus did not argue to this all-embracing vision but taught it as something familiar to him; human beings are invited to be imitators of God and to enter into this sphere of moral behavior.

The shocking character of this teaching shows in the fact that the majority of Christians do not accept it in practice. Some argue against it as impossible in complex societies within an interdependent world. At best, this love ethic can provide plausible ideals for individual persons in their relationships with other individuals, but it cannot be a regulator for the relations between groups or societies. The reason lies in the fact that groups possess no focused center of consciousness, so that corporate freedom cannot be exercised by a single will; groups always gravitate toward self-interest. While love pertains to the private sphere, social issues have to be negotiated on the basis of objectively reasoned policies that ensure a balance of power among the self-interested parties. Ultimately, although social relations depend on a corporate freedom, they can only be set in place and manipulated by impersonal reasoning and power. Thus, love has little place in public life and policy.

Although love does not dictate social policies, it can have a greater influence on such policies than this stark realism allows. As a fundamental moral attitude, love does not tell anyone what to do, but it invites all to a common spirit with which everything should be done. Love crosses the barriers that forbid or limit participation in public life; love questions a fiercely competitive framework of thinking and tries to replace it with a more inclusive sense of solidarity; love sets as the goal that all the participants in a given group and its subgroups seek the common good or the good of the whole. This fundamental moral attitude does not provide any positive programs, but love can operate critically and negatively. It can recognize systems that isolate, marginalize, and in some cases discriminate against and dehumanize whole segments in society. It can prophetically judge as wrong systems that positively corrupt the common good. Love as a commonly shared moral attitude seeks the best policy in which the most flourish rather than the one in which my group flourishes the most.

A practical attitude toward society might assume that policies based on love rather than justice will either be ineffective or disastrous. But this sheerly pragmatic judgment should not be the only or last word. Love as a fundamental moral attitude translates into the social arena not as a technical principle for deducing policy but precisely as a premise for social discernment and authentic public service. Love of all including enemies recognizes and creates solidarity. And the promotion of solidarity of all, a common "we" consciousness, truly affects society. Through solidarity love welcomes pluralism and coexistence with others, even those who appear to be rivals or enemies because of different roles or interests. Beyond that, love of one's fellow human beings so embraces solidarity that it can defy differences and stand against social policies that deny the rights of some and exclude or actually punish others for being different. In this view, behind every critique of injustice lies a more fundamental love of human beings because they share the common grace of God's love. God rules out of love.

26. Jesus on Hope

¹On one occasion when Jesus was going to the house of a leader of the Pharisees to eat a meal on the Sabbath, they were watching him closely. . . . ¹²He said also to the one who had invited him, "When you give a luncheon or a dinner, do not invite your friends or your brothers or your relatives or rich neighbors, in case they may invite you in return, and you would be repaid. ¹³But when you give a banquet, invite the poor, the crippled, the lame, and the blind. ¹⁴And you will be blessed, because they cannot repay you, for you will be repaid at the resurrection of the righteous." ¹⁵One of the dinner guests, on hearing this, said to him, "Blessed is anyone who will eat bread in the kingdom of God!" ¹⁶Then Jesus said to him, "Someone gave a great dinner and invited many. ¹⁷At the time for the dinner he sent his slave to say to those who had been invited, 'Come; for everything is ready now.' ¹⁸But they all alike began to make excuses. The first said to him, 'I have bought a piece of land, and I must go out and see it; please accept my apologies.' [19]*Another said, 'I have bought five yoke of oxen, and I am going to try them out; please accept my apologies.'* [20]*Another said, 'I have just been married, and therefore I cannot come.'* [21]*So the slave returned and reported this to his master. Then the owner of the house became angry and said to his slave, 'Go out at once into the streets and lanes of the town and bring in the poor, the crippled, the blind, and the lame.'* [22]*And the slave said, 'Sir, what you ordered has been done, and there is still room.'* [23]*Then the master said to the slave, 'Go out into the roads and lanes, and compel people to come in, so that my house may be filled.* [24]*For I tell you, none of those who were invited will taste my dinner.'"*

—Luke 14:1, 12-24

This parable of Jesus is called "The Great Banquet." The banquet, where guests reclined and ate their fill with good food and wine, frequently symbolizes the fulfillment of Israel's history, the completion of human life, where God displays God's power and glory before all nations, God rewards the elect for their fidelity, and human existence is complete, filled, saved. The banquet, then, represents final salvation, where all lives will be vindicated. It is promised to Israel, and, like an aura, it appears on the horizon of history to draw it forward. Jesus' parable uses this imagery and symbolism to speak of human destiny. He teaches that this object of hope has moral obligation attached to it. He asks whether transient successes in this life can satisfy the demand that life be meaningful, or whether meaning requires hope in an absolute future.

A single reflection cannot consider the many factors that complicate the story of Jesus telling this parable to this audience. He is at the house of a leading Pharisee, on the Sabbath, and they are watching him closely. But Luke recounts this story decades later, and his preoccupations are also operative: concern for the poor, the lame, and the blind that defined Jesus' ministry from the outset, prophetic announcement of a new rule of God in Jesus' ministry, confrontation with hollow religion, reversal of expectations and of things taken for granted. All of these themes can carry the imagination into relevant meaning for human life today. This reflection, however, enters into the banquet as a symbol of the absolute future that this parable so deliberately exploits. This symbol and the human hope that clings to it have pointed meaning in today's world.

Blessed is anyone who enjoys the banquet of salvation in the kingdom of God! This exclamation prompts Jesus' parable. But the story within the story has different meanings in its own context and in

Luke's authorship. Jesus tells those at the dinner that, although they are people of the covenant, this does not mean they have automatic entry to the final banquet. The three people who found excuses for not coming show that they do not take the invitation seriously; the final kingdom of God makes moral demands. The poor, the lame, and the blind prove to be more worthy than those who do not conscientiously embrace the kingdom of God. It is hard to imagine Jesus threatening Israel with loss of its covenant election since he was so focused on announcing the kingdom of God precisely to Israel. By contrast, it is hard to think that Luke was not thinking about Gentiles: in Luke's time, the Jesus movement was attracting Gentiles in cities around the Mediterranean. In Luke's telling, this parable had become doubly shocking to Jews. It not only threatened exclusion on moral grounds but also opened the banquet of salvation to Gentiles and made it inclusive.

Now the story forms part of the New Testament. How should the parable be read today in such a way that, like the story of the "good" Samaritan, it retains its meaning? It must retain its reversals. Christians may not presume that merely being a Christian entitles them to salvation. God's promise of and invitation to salvation comes gratuitously but not cheaply; it addresses human freedom with moral expectations.

And it reaches all people. As Jesus ultimately opened up Judaism to Gentiles, so too Christianity and Islam should open up their peoples' recognition of God as operative within the whole of history. God's invitation to salvation remains gratuitous, a gift, but it is not rare. God's salvation suffuses the very atmosphere of creation so that nothing comes into existence outside of God's invitation to completion and final flourishing. Those of other religions who live conscientiously are invited to the banquet and will be filled. The parable of Jesus breaks open a narrow christocentrism to the theistic vision of God inviting all creation to a new fullness of being.

What does this parable have to say to people who live with a vivid consciousness of the birth of the universe in a big bang, an evolutionary biological conception of the emergence of the human species, and a suspicion of the anthropomorphism that describes a God who forms covenants with certain groups of people and promises them salvation? Just as the biblical story of creation has been replaced in contemporary imagination with the enormously long and complex story leading to human existence, so too the story of the future of the earth and human life in it has to be placed in a new and expansive imaginative framework. This cannot involve mixing and confusing a scientific and a religious view of human beings. But the whole story of the genesis of the universe and human life on earth can itself be placed in a context of the human search for coherence and thus yield significant spiritual meaning. That meaning appears within the sphere of hope.

Hope may be understood as another fundamental moral attitude. As a moral inclination, hope remains undifferentiated and forms a basic trust. It refers less to specific acts of expecting this or that, and more to a disposition of the human subject that lies open to the future. The active desire that the poor, the lame, and the blind enjoy this banquet expresses this undifferentiated hope and is sustained by it. This openness itself can be described as transpiring on different levels, but as a fundamental moral leaning it includes a positive conviction that being and human existence in particular are good despite their damaged condition. This moral disposition transcends a biological will to live; it combines a receptivity to what is given and an aggressively constructive energy that wants to contribute to, rather than take from, reality by an exercise of creative freedom in the particular historical situation in which it finds itself. Because so much could and does affect human beings that can dampen human hope, it appears as a particularly positive human trait, more like a gift than an instinct of nature. Hope does not reduce to an optimism that remains on the surface of existence. Hope does not expect good things to happen at every turn, but hope is convinced in the face of death that life still remains ultimately valuable. Hope comes into its own when it is shaped by belief in God.

Hope transforms the openness of human subjectivity and consciousness into a conviction of the positive outcome of human existence and of being itself. One could say that such hope implicitly includes the idea of God within itself as its ground. But hope does not convert to any explicit knowledge of God; hope supplies no data and no positive concept of God. Since the future itself does not yet exist, the very idea of an object of hope bears a searching character and only extrapolates an unknown future. The power of human hope becomes clear when it stands in contrast with despair, also a fundamental moral attitude of a negative kind that should not be confused with the clinical disability of depression. The opposite of hope, despair appears far more intentional than an uncontrollable condition. Despair is perhaps engendered by negative experiences and supported by beliefs, but it is clearly not a generative outlook. Hope, by contrast, generates positive virtues and stimulates creative action into the future. Human beings need hope in order actively to contribute vitality to history and society and thus thrive in the world.

The language of the banquet is the language of hope. The banquet provides a symbol for beginning to name the object of hope without knowing it. It precisely "symbolizes" in the sense of objectifying in language an unknown reality and giving it a meaning that represents what hope promises: to fill up, to give satisfaction, to fulfill, to sum up existence, and to bring it to completion. On the one hand, the symbol is ridiculously out of proportion with what it has to encompass in our day: the recapitulation of the evolution of the universe. On the other hand, it has a simple material existential meaning that most people have experienced and even the destitute can dream of. The experience of hope implicitly gives rise to the idea of God as that which or the one who lies behind, or makes possible, or guarantees the outcome. Is God responsible for human hope, or does hope produce the idea of God? This question yields no demonstrable answer because hope and God as the ground of being reciprocally entail each other. Jesus does not argue the case to the twenty-first century. He offers it as a narrative possibility to human freedom and thus as a way of life.

The language of hope, when God is conceived as its ground, becomes spiritual and metaphysical. Without knowing about God, hope reaches out to that which can supply fulfillment, and this openness provides the space for faith in God. This God sustains human flourishing because, as the ground of hope, God gives the creativity of freedom its final rationale. Hope does not conflict with a scientific imagination but can in fact find support in the new story of the universe. That story is one of creativity. Beneath the struggles of life and death, encompassing the conflict and even violence of nature that marks subhuman and human life together, lies the vector of creativity, of new being constantly arising. Hope for an absolute future is not a scientific belief. But the story of the universe encourages hope, and hope in turn drives human creativity. Jesus' rule of God draws the energy of the universe into itself.

27. Three Ways of Commitment

Three Ways of Being Humble

The First Way of Being Humble is necessary for eternal salvation, and consists in this. I so lower and humble myself, as far as is in my power, that in all things I may be obedient to the law of God our Lord.

Consequently, even though others would make me lord of all the creatures of the world, or even though to save my temporal life, I would not enter into deliberation about violating a commandment either human or divine which binds me under mortal sin.

The Second Way of Being Humble is more perfect than the first. It is what I have when I find myself in this disposition: When the options seem equally effective for the service of God our Lord and the salvation of my soul, I do not desire or feel myself strongly attached to have wealth rather than poverty, or honor rather than dishonor, or a long life rather than a short one.

Furthermore, neither for all creation nor to save my life would I enter into deliberation about committing a venial sin.

The Third Way of Being Humble is the most perfect, and consists in this. When I possess the first and second ways, and when the options equally further the praise and glory of God, in order to imitate Christ our Lord better and to be more like him here and now, I desire and choose poverty with Christ poor rather than wealth; contempt with Christ laden with it rather than honors. Even further, I desire to be regarded as a useless fool for Christ, who before me was regarded as such, rather than as a wise or prudent person in this world.

Note. One who desires to obtain this third way of being humble will profit much by making the colloquies of the meditation on the Three Classes of Persons, as presented above. In order to imitate and serve our Lord better, he or she should beg him to be chosen for this third, greater, and better way of being humble, if the service and praise to his Divine Majesty would be equal or greater.

—Ignatius Loyola, *Spiritual Exercises,* 165-168

This meditation interrupts the flow of contemplations of the scenarios of Jesus' ministry and allows Ignatius to steer a person toward a practical goal. Ignatius did not conceive this consideration as a formal meditation but as a subject for reflection during the days leading up to serious decision making. Here it becomes the first of three meditations that form something of a unit leading in the direction of an election or life decision, which figures so prominently in the purpose of the Spiritual Exercises. The three consider the motivation behind making a spiritual decision, techniques for sorting out inclinations and feelings that Ignatius called discernment of spirits, and the process itself of making such a decision.

Analysts of the Exercises see a definite progression leading from the Two Types of Life, through the Three Types of Persons, to this consideration. These three meditations emphasize knowledge of the spiritual way of Jesus, and then a commitment to following him, and they conclude in this exercise with a loving attachment to and identification with him. This helps situate this meditation as beginning a bridge from the Second to the Third Week.

The idea of "humility" in this deliberation does not correspond with a current everyday meaning. When spirituality is considered within the context of secular society in a post-Enlightenment industrial age, humility appears as a passive, alienating virtue in a dynamic culture and an activist society. But here humility refers less to a psychological personality trait and more to a person's relationship of openness to transcendent value or to God. It has more to do with conscious self-disposition than to personal characteristics. As was seen in the meditation on Two Types of Life, poverty and contempt lead to humility, which there means one's dependence on God and consequent response. When the rule of God appears countercultural, obedience to God can generate an activist and even a subversive spirituality. People can open themselves to God in varying ways and degrees, and the conscious motivation behind this commitment forms the subject matter of this meditation.

The three degrees of humility describe three distinct kinds of responsiveness to God with corresponding levels of intensity. Characterizing the distinctiveness of each provides a map ordering them in an ascending pattern. The first case describes a love of God appropriate to any creature. The second relationship with God corresponds with the dedicated servant; it responds more proactively to the demands of the rule of God than the first. The third spirituality explicitly relates to God through Jesus for whom one develops a personal affection that can be described as friendship. There are no negatives here; each defines positive relationship to the rule of God.

The first level of humility represents a baseline openness and responsiveness to God that is defined almost juridically. Imagine a loyalty to God in a way that will never break the fundamental relationship of obedience to God's order of things but will remain faithful to God's values in all matters that are serious. In a Christian view of things, this represents a bottom line standard of behavior. A person intends never to compromise what is essential in his or her relationship to God as creator of heaven and earth. Positively, this converts to fidelity to God according to the rudiments of God's law as expressed, for example, in the Ten Commandments. In Catholic moral teaching, "mortal" sin means deliberate self-alienation from God that is knowing and free.

The second mode and degree of humility describes a more intense degree of committing oneself to God's desire for human life. This intensity is measured by the equilibrium in one's self-control and self-disposition, the idea seen in the meditation Seeking Principles and a Foundation that Ignatius calls "indifference." This attitude relativizes all ordinary attachments to the things of this world and represents a complete surrender to God's desires as they appear in the discernment of each one.

The third transcends the already extraordinary second attitude. This scenario reveals a person who actively seeks to be so identified with Jesus as to imitate him even in his suffering. Love and affection drive this person to imitate Jesus in a way that does as he did. This leads to the radicalism shown in the language. Such radical behavior is usually predicated of public models of the Christian life, but many do the same thing quietly. It may lead to distinctive behavior such as joining a specific spiritual community or some other distinctive form of spiritual life.

The equivalent of humility in today's world appears in commitment to a cause that transcends the self. In the sixth century, Benedict, whose rule became a standard for Western monasticism, had a clear conception of humility as dependence on and responding to God in love in contrast to pride. Humility consisted in responsiveness to God, and in the Benedictine Rule obedience to the abbot ensured it. When culture means human ways over against God's ways, the rule of God in Jesus' ministry carries a strong countercultural edge. While Benedict's spirituality gathered people in community, Jesus' preaching also cut deeply into his Jewish culture and society. He intended his message of God's rule to insert God's values into human society, not to define a way of life outside of society.[2] Thus, the meditation on the Two Ways of Life showed how life committed to the rule of God leads to self-possession and a commitment to a noble transcendent cause. The three ways of humility described by Ignatius can be restated as kinds or degrees of commitment to the cause of the rule of God within society.

How would a person respond to the rule of God in the first degree of commitment? Paraphrasing the words of Ignatius, a person expressing this commitment would say, "I commit myself, to the best of my ability, actively to live my life according to the values which the wisdom of ultimate reality has written into nature and the fabric of human society." This need not be formulated as a spiritual commitment, but it actually defines a lofty spirituality. It may follow a humanistic or naturalistic impulse, or possibly a creation faith. The universe has produced human life that strives to find the wisdom that will allow its societies to flourish. In response to the constantly dynamic reordering of society, this person dedicates his or her life to the cause of the common good and the flourishing of human life.

The second level of commitment suggested by this meditation focuses explicitly on the rule of God and equates the wisdom of the

---

2. This should not suggest that Benedict's communities were not deeply engaged in the agricultural societies of their time.

universe and flourishing of humanity to the will of God. Besides giving this level of commitment an explicitly spiritual dimension, Ignatius describes a distinguishing mark that makes this commitment near total. He stipulates "indifference." This means that, all things being equal, the person is completely open to what existence has in store for him or her. This implies further that no other thing in this life will interfere with being committed solely or principally to the rule of God. Everyone can refer to examples of such single-mindedness: it so thoroughly focuses motivation that even slight egocentric distractions are excluded. Complete and permanent service to the values of the rule of God envelop and control a person's life in the course of carrying out ordinary and specific social responsibilities. This commitment does not neglect practical responsibilities but folds them into this fundamental orientation.

The third level of response to the rule of God possesses the distinguishing marks of an all-embracing personal relationship to Jesus of Nazareth. One's actions are dictated not simply by the rule of God but also by the sense of loving emulation of the action of Jesus, an imitation that unites a person with the person of Jesus. The affective bond to Jesus distinguishes this dedication, defines it as uniquely Christian by the personal relationship with Jesus, and gives it an all-absorbing affective intensity not found in the others. This attachment to Jesus suffuses the language of Christian spirituality.

This transposition of Ignatian ideas into the secular sphere helps to emphasize the universal scope of his spirituality and to differentiate more sharply than Ignatius imagined the differences between these three ways of commitment and the breadth of their scope. The three motivational logics of commitment are all deeply spiritual in the sense of an appropriation of ultimate reality into the conscious intentionality that directs a human life. The first could be called secular and naturalistic spirituality, because it describes people directing their lives within the framework of the order of human society in a way that maintains the common good. This ideal provides the orientation of their lives. The second is spiritual in the more formal sense of recognizing an ultimate reality that grounds the values of the social order. This represents a step beyond absolute respect for the common good, toward assuming a personal relationship to God, or ultimacy under a different name. This commitment to God, in turn, grounds a passion for and a commitment to promoting the common good. Ignatian indifference reveals the intensity of this motivation: nothing else in this world will stand in the way of this project. The third spirituality is particularly Christian because of the mediation of Jesus. Jesus determines Christian spirituality by defining the meaning of the rule of God. The commitment to Jesus is personal and not simply an acceptance of the ideas he stood for. This personal attachment to Jesus gives this spirituality its distinctiveness and accounts for its comprehensive character: it rules not only mind and action but also the affections.

28. Discernment of Spirits

Rules to Aid Us toward Perceiving and Then Understanding,
at Least to Some Extent, the Various Motions
Which Are Caused in the Soul

In the case of persons who are earnestly purging away their sins, and who are progressing from good to better in the service of God our Lord, . . . it is characteristic of the evil spirit to cause gnawing anxiety, to sadden, and to set up obstacles. In this way he unsettles them by false reasons aimed at preventing their progress.

But with persons of this type it is characteristic of the good spirit to stir up courage and strength, consolations, tears, inspirations, and tranquility. He makes things easier and eliminates all obstacles, so that the persons may move forward in doing good.

About spiritual consolation. By consolation I mean that which occurs when some interior motion is caused within the soul through which it comes to be inflamed with love of its Creator and Lord. As a result it can love no created thing on the face of the earth in itself, but only in the Creator of them all.

Under the word consolation I include every increase in hope, faith, and charity, and every interior joy which calls and attracts one toward heavenly things and to the salvation of one's soul, by bringing it tranquility and peace in its Creator and Lord.

About spiritual desolation. By desolation I mean everything which is the contrary of [consolation]; for example, darkness of soul, turmoil within it, an impulsive motion toward low and earthly things, or disquiet from various agitations and temptations. These move one toward lack of faith and leave one without hope and without love. One is completely listless, tepid, and unhappy, and feels separated from our Creator and Lord.

During a time of desolation one should never make a change. Instead, one should remain firm and constant in the proposals and in a decision in which one was on the day before the desolation, or in a decision in which one was during a previous time of consolation.

It is taken for granted that in time of desolation we ought not to change our former plans. But it is very helpful to make vigorous changes in ourselves as counterattack against the desolation, for example, by insisting more on prayer, meditation, earnest self-examination, and some suitable way of doing penance.

Only God our Lord can give the soul consolation without a preceding cause. For it is the prerogative of the Creator alone to enter the soul, depart from it, and cause a motion in it which draws the person wholly into love of his Divine Majesty. By "without a preceding cause" I mean without any previous perception or understanding of some object by means of which the consolation just mentioned might have been stimulated, through the intermediate activity of the person's acts of understanding and willing.

With or by means of a preceding cause, both the good angel and the evil angel are able to cause consolation in the soul, but for their contrary purposes. The good angel acts for the progress of the soul, that it may grow and rise from what is good to what is better. The evil angel works for the contrary purpose, that is, to entice the soul to its own damnable intention and malice.

It is characteristic of the evil angel, who takes on the appearance of an angel of light, to enter by going along with the devout soul and then to come out by his own way with success for himself. In the case of those going from good to better, the good angel touches the soul gently, lightly, and sweetly, like a drop of water going into a sponge. The evil spirit touches it sharply, with noise and disturbance, like a drop of water falling onto a stone.

In the case of those who are going from bad to worse, these spirits touch the souls in the opposite way. The reason for this is the fact that the disposition of the soul is either similar to or different from the respective spirits who are entering. When the soul is different, they enter with perceptible noise and are quickly noticed. When the soul is similar, they enter silently, like those who go into their own house by an open door.

—Ignatius Loyola, *Spiritual Exercises*, 313-336, edited

Ignatius's rules for the discernment of spirits were not meant to be a meditation. He clearly states their purpose, to analyze and understand the various movements that go on in a person in the process of making a serious spiritual decision. These rules reflect a premodern European worldview that included spirits, good and bad, that had access to human subjectivity. The anthropomorphic supernaturalistic language that so dominates the rules can conceal their psychological sophistication. The rules reflect a world in which personified good and evil battle for control of people. This cosmic struggle goes on within the self, which is already torn by a tension between a higher freedom and a lower self-interest and unruly passions and attachments. One cannot say the late medieval world was simple.

Ignatius's rules for the discernment of spirits have their roots in the process of his own conversion and early formation: they come out of his lived experience. They serve two functions in the Exercises. Generally, they give guidelines for a person who encounters too many ideas and feelings about the self and the future to control. These rules provide some prudent counsel and offer some leverage over the push and pull of emotions. More particularly, these rules relate to making decisions, so they will come into play in the next reflection on spiritual decision making. This reflection aims at preserving the importance of the discernment of spirits by refining the gold of Ignatius's rules into plausible language. This language should have both psychological and metaphysical resonance; because it describes both human consciousness and the relationship of people to ultimate reality, it should not be reduced to either one.

An educated person living in a Western secular society will be amazed at the graphic depiction of angels and demons competing for the human soul displayed in this text of Ignatius. Isolating certain essential themes in the picture offers a way of assuring some continuity between this text and its reappropriation. A first step in appreciating it would demythologize the text to discover the acumen with which it describes various psychological feelings that well up in anyone making a relatively serious decision about his or her own life. Should this be a life decision, the unpredictable future weighs heavy and augments the pressure. The gold within this mountain consists in the various maxims that Ignatius uses to sift through what may be a confusion of possibilities and emotions. Ignatius's own strategy in the Exercises favors the feelings and affections that grow out of a personal relationship with Jesus of Nazareth. Attachment to Jesus defines the project of the Exercises. In the previous meditation Ignatius describes a place where decisions are made on the basis of a personal attachment to Jesus. But such feelings may compete with other strong attachments, and Ignatius's rules provide some guidelines for sorting them out. Inner peace and tranquility as opposed to turbulence and confusion, play a large part in the dynamics of consolation and desolation.

Another feature of Ignatius's depiction of discernment of spirits appears in the antithetical and antagonistic tension between the evil spirit and the good spirit. One can translate this antithesis out of the cosmological sphere and into an understanding of the human person and arrive at the anthropological configuration offered in the meditation on Two Types of Life. The internal struggle between light and darkness and good and evil has been a fixture in Christian anthropology. The antithesis pits self-love against self-gift. In the language of Paul and Augustine, the human spirit can curve in on itself or open itself to value outside the self. Human freedom can engage the world and use the world to enhance the self; or freedom may recognize and respond to autonomous value outside the self. This fundamental tension may become a dynamic conflict, and this possibility underscores the usefulness of processes of discernment. This antithesis carries subthemes: on one side the biases, attachments, addictions, and vices that control freedom and inhibit self-transcendence; on the other side the ideas, values, and worthy projects that draw freedom out of itself. These transcendent objects arm freedom with criteria to measure and transcend its obstacles, and thus release the human spirit to ever more freedom. The concrete terms of this abstract antithesis, however, are not always easily recognized, so that the maxims for sorting out deeper desires and goals proposed by the Exercises can be helpful.

Of particular interest in Ignatius's views on the discernment of spirits is the principle that God is directly present to the human subject and operates in the human person in a way that can be discerned: "For it is the prerogative of the Creator alone to enter the soul, depart from it, and cause a motion in it which draws the person wholly into love of his Divine Majesty." The complete lack of a perceptible previous finite cause suggests the divine origin of such an impulse. While that view would be seriously questioned by some theologians and most psychoanalysts today, it serves to mark a difference between spiritual discernment and making an otherwise ethical judgment and moral decision. Dealing with the self as standing within the world and before God makes a difference. A spiritual decision includes moral reasoning but also possesses the added dimension of being accountable to ultimate reality. Within the context of the Spiritual Exercises, this discernment process unfolds after considerable self-analysis and, more importantly, immersion into the pattern of the revelatory ministry of Jesus of Nazareth. However, the point here is not to gather up all the strands of this story, but to situate and characterize the nature of this particular process of discernment. It consists in following Jesus as revealer of God.

Ignatius placed considerable emphasis on directly reading one's own subjectivity in order to discern the provenance of the movement of a given spirit in one's life. Desolation and consolation, antithetical subjective states and sets of experiences, dominate Ignatius's approach to discernment. At the same time it should be clear from the development of the Exercises to this point that the public life of Jesus, as it is preserved in the gospel texts, serves as an external criterion for discerning the spirits. Subjectively, Ignatius imagines the evil spirit Satan or his cohorts of evil spirits competing with the Spirit of God or angelic spirits within the human spirit. These rules reflect how he gained some mastery over this internal struggle. But the clearer and more objective criterion for discerning the spirits comes from Jesus of Nazareth precisely as Ignatius has placed him in opposition to the program of Satan in the meditation of the Two Types of Life. The rules for the discernment of spirits have their Christian foundation in Jesus of Nazareth because he provides the public historical criterion, codified in gospel stories, of what is and what is not of the Spirit of God.

The meditation on Two Types of Life contains a more objective set of criteria for discerning the spirits than the subjective appeal to desolation and consolation. Without rehearsing the antithetical projects of Satan and Christ, one need only recall that the two dynamics involve respectively human freedom trying to draw the world into itself for self-aggrandizement, on the one hand, and human freedom dedicating the self to transcendent values outside the self, on the other. The way the value of that to which one commits one's freedom affects a person should lead to self-knowledge. One does not have to appeal to angels and demons. It is enough to analyze human motivations to see whether a desired object promotes a human freedom curved in on itself or a freedom reaching out to value beyond the self. With Jesus of Nazareth as the norm, much of Ignatius's language of discernment can be reappropriated. A person striving within the pattern of Jesus Christ should count tranquility, satisfaction, and joy as consolation, that is, a positive ratifying feeling of being filled up by the service of others. This consolation accompanies self-transcendence and grows as it becomes more costly. By contrast, feelings of alienation from others, jealousy, competition, and desires for self-assertion that disrupt constructive patterns of service should be counted as Anti-Christ. Ultimately they generate desolation.

The difficulty in spiritual discernment lies less in understanding the criteria and more in applying them to actual human dilemmas. Frequently Ignatius tended to simplify the crises that required discernment: should one follow Christ as a celibate minister or live life as a married lay person? The narrowing down of discernment to making a choice between two life decisions allowed him to magnify the role of feelings and emotions in such a discernment. The present world presents a considerably more complex picture both in the variety of the situations of the people making the Exercises and the frequently impossible problem of wedding talent with myriad possibility and opportunity. The problem of constructive spiritual planning today cannot escape risk. But Jesus' commitment to the rule of God provides a framework and certain criteria for finding or creating a constructive path.

29. Making Decisions before God

In every good election insofar as it depends on us, the eye of our intention ought to be single. I ought to focus only on the purpose for which I was created, to praise God our Lord and to save my soul. Accordingly, anything whatsoever that I elect ought to be chosen as an aid toward that end, without my ordering or dragging the end into subjection to the means, but with my ordering the means to the end.

It happens, for example, that many first choose to marry, which is the means, and in the second place to serve God our Lord in marriage, which service of God is the end. Similarly, others first seek to possess benefices, and afterward to serve God in them. Hence these do not go directly to God, but desire God to come to their disordered affections. As a result they transform the end into a means and the means into the end; and what they should fasten on in the first place they take up in the last. For I ought to take up first my desire to serve God, which is the end, and in the second place the benefice or marriage, and whether it is more suitable for myself, which is the means to the end.

Three [Kinds of Processes] for
Making a Sound and Good Election

The First [Kind] is . . . when God our Lord moves and attracts the will in such a way that a devout person, without doubting or being able to doubt, carries out what was proposed. This is what St. Paul and St. Matthew did when they followed Christ our Lord.

The Second [Kind] is present when sufficient clarity and knowledge are received from the experience of consolations and desolations, and from experience in the discernment of various spirits.

The Third [Kind] is one of tranquility. I consider first the end for which I was born, namely, to praise God our Lord and save my soul; then, desiring this, as the means I elect a life or state of life within the bounds of the church, in order to be helped in the service of my Lord and the salvation of my soul.

By a time of tranquility I mean one which the soul is not being moved one way and the other by various spirits and uses its natural faculties in freedom and peace.

I should consider and reason out how many advantages or benefits accrue to myself from having the office or benefice proposed, all of them solely for the praise of God our Lord and the salvation of my soul; and on the contrary I should similarly consider the disadvantages and dangers in having it. Then, acting in the same manner in the second part, I should consider the advantages and benefits in not having it, and contrarily the disadvantages and dangers in not having it.

After I have considered and thought out every aspect of the proposed matter, I should see to which side reason more inclines. It is in this way that I ought to come to a decision about the matter proposed, namely, in accordance with the preponderating motion of reason, and not from some motion arising from sensitive human nature.

When that election or decision has been made, the person who has made it ought with great diligence to go to prayer before God our Lord, to offer him that election, and to beg his Divine Majesty to receive and confirm it, provided it is conducive to his greater service and praise.
—Ignatius Loyola, *Spiritual Exercises*, 169-188, edited

This meditation is drawn from an extensive section in the Exercises in which Ignatius considers an election, a major choice in life, or a life decision. The guidelines also apply outside the context of the Exercises and in less important decisions. Bringing these considerations to a formal meditation finds warrant in the rationale of the Exercises, which "prepare for a Christian life lived according to a spirituality characterized precisely by the concern to integrate the decisions of life into a person's relationship with God."[3] Ignatius intended the Exercises to help people make decisions that order their lives (SE, 21) and on this basis act differently, because people's actions ultimately constitute their relation with ultimate reality. His language about spiritual decisions reflects his late medieval world. This reflection aims at finding a more plausible language that respects the importance of decisions and the logic that the Exercises contribute to making them.

Every major decision is spiritual. Making a decision specifically for one's spiritual life, and thus during the Spiritual Exercises as well, does not go behind the back of ordinary human decision making. Decisions require experience and knowledge and thus data gathering. A spiritual election should not be considered as being made on the basis of being lifted out of the natural sphere. Making a spiritual decision has to correspond with the various ways in which human beings scan

---

3. Ivens, USE, 129.

their past experience, consider their present situation, calculate where various options will lead, and marshal evidence that will insure a correct decision.

The Exercises are preoccupied with finding God's *will* for one's life. This reflection uses the language of trying to shape one's own life according to God's *desires*. A couple of reasons motivate this terminology. One is that it may be too anthropomorphic to assume that God has a specific or particular will for each person. Thinking about the future and making decisions in life seem to be actions contained within the region of human intelligence and freedom. In the language of God's desires, as distinct from God's will, human beings "retain their own power of self-constitution with or without the active assistance from God."[4] God's general plan for humanity can be discerned in Jesus' ministry; it intends that all human beings realize their full potential and that individuals cooperate to bring this about. God's desires, by contrast, refer to something that God has not determined, namely, the way individual persons internalize the values of God's rule in their lives to the best of their abilities and act on them.

Another reason the phrase God's "desires" seems more appropriate lies in the character of the relationship between the human person and God who is also subject. This interpersonal relationship may be better served by "desires" than by the more definitive and less pliant language of God's "will." "God's will" often suggests that a set pattern of behavior has been determined by God before time itself, so that discernment essentially seeks to discover it: like a hunt for hidden treasure. Too much contemporary experience renders this conception implausible. The terminology of God's desires loosens this conception, lessening God's actual control of history and opening up more range for human responsibility. Discernment consists less in discovery and more in assuming responsibility for the path that best fits personal talents, God's general intention for human flourishing, and God's desires that individuals participate in this project to the best of their abilities.

Ignatius indicated three methods that are suitable for making a sound life decision.[5] These times vary according to individual persons, the life situations of each one making such a decision, and his or her ability to gain enough clarity to feel confident in a course of action. "Times" thus converts to different ways or processes by which a person comes to a subjective conviction about what is to be done and its degree

---

4. Joseph A. Bracken, "God's Will or God's Desires for Us: A Change in Worldview?" *Theological Studies* 71 (2010), 78.

5. In Ignatius's text these are referred to as "times" for making such a decision; they can also be regarded as "methods" for arriving at a decision, and thus also as "kinds" of decision making. In the text as it appears here "kind" has been substituted for "time."

of correspondence with the general will of God. The experience and practical realism of Ignatius disallow a mechanical translation and correlation of a human decision with a particular desire of God. A better way of understanding what is going on here would see it as Ignatius's description of how different people are able to find some clarity about the way their own lives might be directed so that they fit the pattern of God's rule for human beings as revealed in Jesus' ministry.

Ignatius's didactic language describing three different ways of making a decision can be shifted into something closer to a narrative by imagining a person wrestling with something like his or her vocation in life. All this applies in less dramatic terms to other decisions as well. Standing at some crossroads this person asks questions like these: What really is the object that is most worthy of human freedom, and can I do something with my life that will respect that logic? What particular courses are open to me, given my talents, and how do they fit with the values Jesus of Nazareth holds up as representing the intentions or rule of God, the ground of being? In what direction do I feel called to move by the congruence of my being led to this present situation and the lofty project of promoting human flourishing proposed by Jesus' ministry?

The first kind of decision that Ignatius considers does not really require any work because the decision, as it were, comes to a person. Unfortunately, the two examples he gives are not only very particular but also "supernaturalistic" in character. As such they seem to escape the boundaries of ordinary human decisions. But this kind of decision can be understood in everyday terms. Many people in different situations but facing dilemmas with serious consequences for the whole of their lives testify that they decided with absolute certainty: "I never doubted for a moment." "I simply knew this was the right thing to do." It is not rare that values, talents, situation, and circumstances meet in a constellation that seems to decide an issue for a person. John Henry Newman, the nineteenth-century theologian, described well how a convergence of probabilities can deliver practical certitude.

The second kind of decision was the subject matter of the last meditation. Here things do not fall into place without considerable effort, including frequent appeals to imaginative trial and error. This process requires patience as a person wades through the comparisons between value and possibility, and measures the affective responses to a variety of projected scenarios. "What decision, what concrete course of action, feels overwhelmingly right in bringing together my relationship with God, the highest possible values, and the fullest possible exploitation of my freedom and talents?" The project of Jesus Christ as contrasted with its antitype provides the background for this prayerful method of coming to a decision. One cannot prescribe the amount of time and struggle this method will require of a particular individual. Ignatius's own story provides the clearest example of this kind of decision.

Compared to the first two sets of people, the person using the third kind of decision-making process seems like a plodder. Imagine this person awash in the confusion of desires, possibilities, times, places, concrete options, other variables, and unknowns, all crowding in and causing a state of paralysis. What can such a person do? This method is the answer; it appeals to cool reason, in quiet thoughtfulness, making the premises explicit on paper, setting out the realistic options, and under each one listing the values and the disvalues of each prospective choice. "If I do this, that will likely follow. And if I do this other thing, I'll probably end up there." Everyone can recognize what is going on here because this is the ordinary way of making even little choices. This process does not have to be described at length because the point appears in the difference in approach from the other two. Here clear thinking takes precedent over genuine enthusiasm. One states the values and the reasons in the clearest possible way and, once objectified, they can be tamed by practical reason.

Historians note that Ignatius favored the second process over the third. But the second works best when a person can narrow down the possibilities to a choice between alternatives. Given the many options and values the present world holds out to freedom today, the mere idea of having to make a choice that constitutes a real self-determination seems to many either impossible or a source of anxiety. Thus many spiritual directors today will favor the third method over the second. Other considerations might help tip the balance in this direction. For example, these distinct methods are not so separable that a person shuts down affective response in the cooler method of practical reason; nor does affective experience turn out the light of intelligence. Elements of the second method enter into the third and vice versa. Also, further reflection indicates that it would be good to check a decision made according to the second method by an application of the third method. Ignatius tended to confirm a spiritual life decision by setting it before God in prayer. Relative to the importance of any given decision, the cool reasoning of the third method might serve as a penultimate process confirming the first and second methods.

Ignatius placed his considerations on decision making at the end of the Second Week of the Exercises. He thus envisaged a person entering into the Third Week's contemplations of Jesus facing suffering and death with a decision having been made. But each one making the Exercises moves at his or her own pace.

The Suffering and Death of Jesus

The Third Week of the Exercises focuses on the passion and death of Jesus of Nazareth. The Weeks in the Spiritual Exercises do not necessarily represent the amount of time spent on the four topics, and only three contemplations are dedicated to the events in Jerusalem that culminated in Jesus being put to death. The third contemplation of Jesus' actual crucifixion is the relatively long account of Luke. This text can, of course, be broken up into smaller units as considered appropriate. The fourth meditation considers the import or meaning that Christians have found in this history.

The death of Jesus by crucifixion has from the beginning been a focus of intense Christian feeling and theological interpretation. Everything about that sudden event countered expectations and seemed unintelligible when measured by the religious hopes he had aroused. Explanations had to be provided. Some Christians see the death of Jesus as the very core of the whole meaning of Christian faith, while others see it as part of a larger picture. The final reflection on the significance of Jesus' death should not be read as the only possible interpretation but only as one of many.

30. Jesus Enters Jerusalem

²⁹*When he had come near Bethphage and Bethany, at the place called the Mount of Olives, he sent two of the disciples,* ³⁰*saying, "Go into the village ahead of you, and as you enter it you will find tied there a colt that has never been ridden. Untie it and bring it here.* ³¹*If anyone asks you, 'Why are you untying it?' just say this: 'The Lord needs it.'"* ³²*So those who were sent departed and found it as he had told them.* ³³*As they were untying the colt, its owners asked them, "Why are you untying the colt?"* ³⁴*They said, "The Lord needs it."* ³⁵*Then they brought it to Jesus; and after throwing their cloaks on the colt, they set Jesus on it.* ³⁶*As he rode along, people kept spreading their cloaks on the road.* ³⁷*As he was now approaching the path down from the Mount*

of Olives, the whole multitude of the disciples began to praise God joyfully with a loud voice for all the deeds of power that they had seen, [38]*saying,"Blessed is the king who comes in the name of the Lord! Peace in heaven, and glory in the highest heaven!"* [39]*Some of the Pharisees in the crowd said to him, "Teacher, order your disciples to stop."* [40]*He answered, "I tell you, if these were silent, the stones would shout out."*

[41]*As he came near and saw the city, he wept over it,* [42]*saying, "If you, even you, had only recognized on this day the things that make for peace! But now they are hidden from your eyes.* [43]*Indeed, the days will come upon you, when your enemies will set up ramparts around you and surround you, and hem you in on every side.* [44]*They will crush you to the ground, you and your children within you, and they will not leave within you one stone upon another; because you did not recognize the time of your visitation from God."*

[45]*Then he entered the temple and began to drive out those who were selling things there;* [46]*and he said, "It is written, 'My house shall be a house of prayer'; but you have made it a den of robbers."* [47] *Every day he was teaching in the temple. The chief priests, the scribes, and the leaders of the people kept looking for a way to kill him;* [48]*but they did not find anything they could do, for all the people were spellbound by what they heard.*

—Luke 19:29-48

The interaction of two perspectives in these narratives deserves particular notice. On the one hand, historical events transpired in Jerusalem; on the other hand, Luke, writing from the 80s, represents them on the basis of a tradition of interpretations and his own theological vision of their significance. On entering into these narratives, it would be fruitful imaginatively to recreate this implicit dialogue by going back and forth between the two perspectives. "What do I imagine actually happened back then?" "How is Luke using these events to make a point?" This implicit internal dialogue recreates the actual dialogue, both past and present, in which the communities of disciples of Jesus have been engaged across centuries.

Another tension underlies this contemplation and all the events of the Third Week. This tension can be characterized as a structure of irony that arises out of the fact that the meaning of these events does not lie on the surface of history; in fact, nothing can be reduced to the way it appears. For Luke, these events involve ultimate reality, so that, as they unfold before God and God's rule, they contain a deeper meaning for human appreciation. The irony of this history, and of human history in the light of it, shines through this narrative and appeals to a human response to God.

Luke has depicted Jesus as gradually making his way from Galilee to Jerusalem over many chapters leading up to this point. The destiny of his ministry will be sealed there. The narrative provides many leads for the imagination to follow. Jesus enters the city riding on a colt and "the whole multitude" of his followers pays homage to him and says the words of the Psalmist: "Blessed is the one who comes in the name of the Lord" (Ps 118:26). Luke knows that Jesus was no king or, in an ironic religious sense, the kind of king he was. All of Jesus' followers after his death know where this story is leading. Its power lies in the radical contrast between the overt activities of these followers and what is really happening. Jesus is approaching crucifixion.

Luke tells this incident and the whole story of Jesus entering into a situation that would consume him as if it were scripted in advance. Jesus sends two of his followers ahead to fetch the colt, knowing exactly what they would find. The events follow a divine master plan, and Jesus knows it. From his grand theological perspective, Luke understands Jesus acting out a historical arrangement that corresponds with a larger conception of God's rule and sovereignty, one that envelops all of history. Such is the scope of his theological vision. But historical realism today does not easily allow human beings such clear knowledge of the future, and this applies both to Luke and to Jesus. For Jesus to be one who can be followed, he must be a human being, and this goes to the essential character of human knowledge and freedom. In this particular story, whose historicity is not clear, and more generally in Jesus' ministry and decision to go to Jerusalem, one must imagine that Jesus was acting freely with the freedom of a human being. An intrinsic element of that historical freedom lies in its having to cope with an unknown future. Such a historical realism allows this story of Jesus to open up possibilities for everyone facing a dangerous future. And the perspective of two millennia of consequences gives these events enormous significance.

In the second panel of the story of Jesus' entry into Jerusalem Luke has Jesus approaching the city, coming to a place where he has a panoramic view of it, and in a dialogue with the city pronouncing a prayerful lament over its future fate. Disaster lies in Jerusalem's future because of what it is going to do to him. Here Luke appeals to what he knows happened in the year 70, how the Romans besieged the city and, on entering it, destroyed the temple. The interplay of future and present is brought to the surface, and the irony is laid bare. The religious leaders will protect Israel from Jesus and his followers, and in so doing they will destroy the temple, Jerusalem, and Israel itself. The events of history are not what they seem to be; one cannot read the true deeper meaning of anything off the surface. The essential character of historical reality is thus ironic; it contains a deep contrast between what is happening, in the empirical sense of the events that transpire, and the substantial meaning of what is really going on. The deeper meaning can be discovered only by reflection over time, and it is not stable.

In the third panel of the story Jesus abruptly appears before the temple and enters into its precincts. Luke wastes no time as Jesus' first reaction seems to be directed against the commerce that was going on in the courtyard. It is not clear whether this buying and selling was secular or sacred or both. What is clear is that Jesus prophetically contrasts the temple as a place of prayer and the activity actually going on. Was it the business itself, or were the exchanges corrupted and the merchants crooks? Trying to decide such things may be a distraction. The story illustrates how Jesus interrupted business as usual in the name of God. Exegetes see historical substance in Jesus' preaching in the temple, causing friction with Jewish leaders, being noticed, offering some prophetic gesture relative to the temple that gained public attention. These things appear to be plausible and are required to bring to a head the conflict between Jesus and the religious leaders needed to explain his arrest and crucifixion.

The story leaves Jesus coming to the temple daily in order to teach. Here historical realism and the theological message of Luke come close together. Jesus has come from Galilee, and the first thing he does is act out the words of Malachi: "Behold, I am sending my messenger to prepare the way before me, and the Lord whom you seek will suddenly come to his temple" (Mal 3:1). Jesus now stands at the center of Judaism. The story represents Jesus being at home there and teaching God's word with authority. By his prophetic gesture of disrupting the merchants, Jesus has staked a claim to this authority. Luke has him citing the words of the prophet Isaiah: "My house shall be called a house of prayer for all peoples" (Isa 56:7). A realistic imagination can easily embellish this whole scenario. On the one hand, the people who listened to his teaching were "spellbound" by what they heard; and, on the other hand, the leaders' resentment grew deeper. Luke foreshadows what will come: they "kept looking for a way to kill him."

Ignatius approaches these contemplations from the perspective of a personal relationship with Jesus; he wants them to elicit sorrow, confusion, and a sense of personal brokenness and interior suffering as one witnesses what happens to Jesus. In his medieval theology Ignatius experienced the passion as engaging him not only affectively but also metaphysically, for Jesus was going to a death because of Ignatius's sins (SE, 193). But there are other ways of engaging this story personally. One can simply follow the story of how Jesus encountered the forces that resisted his teaching, preaching, and prophetic activity, turned on him, and led him to an innocent death. The story of anyone approaching and reacting to death is intrinsically gripping. But this story has a deeper religious bearing on the meaning and substance of human life. This dimension lies "within" the story, not "above" it, and not as "pre-scripted," but in the sense that these events carry and reveal an inner logic of something happening beneath the surface. No single interpretation of this logic excludes all the rest. This initial contemplation, however, poses the question of the significance of these events as Jesus embarks on his journey toward death.

Luke has his own particular slant on what is happening here. This entry into Jerusalem serves as a set-up for Luke's conception of Jesus' departure from this world. Jesus is beginning his exodus, or departure from this life, which was planned to pass through Jerusalem. This passing will be the turning point of history. God as Spirit, that is, God's accompanying presence to these events, plays a major role in Luke's story. Jesus was conceived by the power of God's Spirit, commissioned and empowered by the Spirit in his ministry, and led by the Spirit to Jerusalem to complete his mission. From the temple his life will continue through suffering, death, resurrection, ascension, and a sending of the Spirit on his disciples so that the mission will extend to the ends of the earth. The large metaphysical story takes a crucial turn here in the temple. Here too begins the story of every Christian life. All the disciples of Jesus after his death and resurrection participate in this story.

31. The Last Supper

⁷Then came the day of Unleavened Bread, on which the Passover lamb had to be sacrificed. ⁸So Jesus sent Peter and John, saying, "Go and prepare the Passover meal for us that we may eat it." ⁹They asked him, "Where do you want us to make preparations for it?" ¹⁰"Listen," he said to them, "when you have entered the city, a man carrying a jar of water will meet you; follow him into the house he enters ¹¹and say to the owner of the house, 'The teacher asks you, "Where is the guest room, where I may eat the Passover with my disciples?"' ¹²He will show you a large room upstairs, already furnished. Make preparations for us there." ¹³So they went and found everything as he had told them; and they prepared the Passover meal. ¹⁴ When the hour came, he took his place at the table, and the apostles with him. ¹⁵He said to them, "I have eagerly desired to eat this Passover with you before I suffer; ¹⁶for I tell

you, I will not eat it until it is fulfilled in the kingdom of God." ¹⁷Then
he took a cup, and after giving thanks he said, "Take this and divide it
among yourselves; ¹⁸for I tell you that from now on I will not drink of
the fruit of the vine until the kingdom of God comes." ¹⁹Then he took
a loaf of bread, and when he had given thanks, he broke it and gave it
to them, saying, "This is my body, which is given for you. Do this in
remembrance of me." ²⁰And he did the same with the cup after supper,
saying, "This cup that is poured out for you is the new covenant in my
blood. ²¹But see, the one who betrays me is with me, and his hand is on
the table. ²²For the Son of Man is going as it has been determined, but
woe to that one by whom he is betrayed!" ²³Then they began to ask one
another which one of them it could be who would do this.

—Luke 22:7-23

This story of Jesus hosting a Passover meal with his disciples on the eve of his arrest, torture, and execution occupies a deeply sensitive place in Christian consciousness. During this last meal with his disciples and friends Jesus communicates his parting words. The story also plays a strategic role because during it he leaves final instructions for his followers. The story contains discrepancies across the four gospels, leading one to believe that there must have been something behind it despite conflicting details. Yet it is practically impossible to escape the confines of the perspective of the gospel writer because every detail comes laden with later interpretation. Whatever actually happened, the story releases profound symbolic meanings that resonate with humanity before God as seen through the lens of Jesus.

The reflections that follow presuppose that Jesus on many occasions had common and more festive meals with groups of his disciples of various sizes in different places. The meal was a time for Jesus and his followers to gather and engage in blessing God, sharing thoughts, teaching, listening, singing, lamenting, relaxing, mourning, celebrating, reviewing, planning, praying, and eating. What went forward after Jesus' death did not develop exclusively out of this particular meal. The movement remembered not just a last supper but a tradition of Jesus' meals with his disciples. All this, however, has been concentrated in the supper depicted in this story and in the other gospels. Across the centuries it has become enveloped with new creative meanings that are remembered in different ways by different traditions, denominations, and churches. The reflections that follow stay close to Luke's story and fix on themes that could be shared by different individuals and communities of interpretation.

Western Christians may imagine the Last Supper as a private meal of Jesus and his band of leaders along the lines of the scene proposed by Leonardo da Vinci. But exegetes think Luke imagined a larger community meal. The language in the longer narrative is not consistent, and some indications point to a larger venue and a more ample community of disciples, men and women. This simple change of premise releases the imagination from several implicit institutional constraints and points it in new directions.

Luke, along with other gospels, proposes that Jesus hosted a Jewish Passover meal. Luke associates what would happen to Jesus with the traditional Jewish story of Passover in which the Jews departed from Egypt and began their journey to liberation. As the Israelites left Egypt after consuming the newly slaughtered lamb, so too the passage of Jesus through death to resurrection marks the beginning of the Christian journey out of Jerusalem and into the Gentile world. This tradition gave the followers of Jesus a language to understand the death of Jesus, and by the time of Paul's letters in the 50s the common meal of the Christian movement was interpreted in connection with the death and resurrection of Jesus. The idea that the last meal of Jesus with his disciples was a Passover meal also gave it a structure of ritual cups of wine before, during, and after the meal proper, which is reflected in Luke's version.

This last meal of Jesus with his disciples provides the occasion for a farewell discourse which begins in this text and continues beyond the verses cited here. The supper forms a literary bridge to Jesus embarking on the series of events that lead directly to his death. In all of this Jesus appears as one who knows what will transpire and deliberately moves along the predetermined course of action. He uses this meal to speak of his death when he will enter into the final banquet of the eternal kingdom of God. The story of the Last Supper combines ritual elements of Passover and those of the early Christian community.

The Last Supper story implicitly reflects the way later communities would emerge out of the band of Jesus' followers. At the meal the disciples are asked to remember him, follow him, and become, like him, agents of God's rule in the world. From Luke's perspective, remembering Jesus surely includes the meal itself. But the deeper substantial meaning refers to Jesus' dedicating himself to the rule of God. "Remember my ministry as a commitment to the values of God and take up this ministry." The farewell discourse that Luke puts in Jesus' mouth tells those in Luke's time how they should be Christians and follow him. Presumably in earlier meals together the disciples were also charged to be a community of followers after his departure. The fact that this story is placed just before Jesus goes to his death gives it penetrating emotional intensity.

The story of the Last Supper suggests to the imagination how a

Jesus movement got started after Jesus' death on an organizational level. The common meal was a socially established way for groups to gain and maintain an identity: they came together for meals in which they established and retained their common purpose. The meal thus became a vehicle of continuity between Jesus' band of followers in the ministry of the rule to God and those who would remember and follow him after his death and resurrection. The point is not that Jesus planned this development. But looking back on these events through the eyes of the writers of the story of the Last Supper allows a person to see that meals with Jesus were in fact part of the founding events that led to the formation of the church and Christianity. The common meal of disciples provided the venue and the structure for the community of the followers of Jesus to evolve: to pray together, to sing hymns, to interpret the scriptures, to strive to understand better who Jesus was, what he did, and who they were, to read letters from other new communities, to welcome prophets and apostles, to have a meal together, and to share what they had to share. It quickly became a ritual sacrament of the community, in which the assembled bonded with Jesus and, in him, with one another. The common meal of disciples plays the same role today.

A common element in the accounts of the Last Supper that Jesus hosts, and presumably earlier meals that Jesus shared with disciples, and the meals of the later communities as they are depicted in other New Testament writings is the presence of Jesus who binds people together. Jesus unites the people at the meal in the flesh or later in memory as a presence within the experience of God as Spirit. Jesus in his ministry mediates God's rule and establishes a connection between people and God. He also binds the community together. He acts as an agent of reconciliation. This supper has thus been associated with the way Jesus can unite people who are different into a community of acceptance and love.

One of the deepest ironies of Christian history lies in the contrast between the central meaning and power of this story of Jesus and how Christian communities have interpreted and used it over time. This meal at bottom celebrates the fellowship between Jesus and his followers. The meal acts out a communion of reciprocal love, where the love not only goes back and forth between Jesus and each of his followers, but also becomes a love that binds all Christians together as one, united in love within God's love. As John put it in his gospel, the Christian community is called to be distinctive on the basis of their love for one another (John 13:35). Acting out this fundamental value of the kingdom of God in this meal, in the wide variety of ritual forms of different church traditions, has had untold religious power in individual lives. Across all the ritual differences the common and binding love should hold all Christians together. Yet nothing has divided Christians in the course of history and nothing divides them more today than their divergent understandings and celebrations of the meal of Christian fellowship.[1] This is one of the sorrows that people have to feel as they contemplate this story of Jesus. The narrative lifts up the spiritual promise of a community of love and mutual understanding and occasions lament at the systematic rejection of this promise by the churches.

But nothing is as it seems. God's ways are not human ways, and God prevails where humans fail. The seemingly natural tendency of human beings to differentiate among themselves, to divide, to compete, and finally to hate and wage war, conceals something that Jesus reveals and actualizes by fragments in Christian communities that unite around him in word and sacrament. Jesus appeared as prophet–revealer of God's rule, and in that rule human beings have their being within the love of God. That deeper reality subsists below the level of interpersonal conflict and nations waging war. The common meal thus provides the great metaphor that describes the ontological status of the human race. Occasionally that reality becomes actualized in conscious practice. And these fragments of human life together help to keep alive hope in the promise of the unity of all in all in the end-time.

32. Jesus' Torture and Execution

[1]Then the assembly rose as a body and brought Jesus before Pilate. [2]They began to accuse him, saying, "We found this man perverting our nation, forbidding us to pay taxes to the emperor, and saying that he himself is the Messiah, a king." [3]Then Pilate asked him, "Are you the king of the Jews?" He answered, "You say so." [4]Then Pilate said to the chief priests and the crowds, "I find no basis for an accusation against this man." [5]But they were insistent and said, "He stirs up the people by teaching throughout all Judea, from Galilee where he began even to this place."

[6]When Pilate heard this, he asked whether the man was a Galilean. [7]And when he learned that he was under Herod's jurisdiction, he sent him off to Herod, who was himself in Jerusalem at that time. [8]When

---

1. This large generalization entails many different rationalizations that include explanations of the sacrament of communion and how it is connected with orders of ministry.

Herod saw Jesus, he was very glad, for he had been wanting to see him for a long time, because he had heard about him and was hoping to see him perform some sign. *⁹He questioned him at some length, but Jesus gave him no answer. ¹⁰The chief priests and the scribes stood by, vehemently accusing him. ¹¹Even Herod with his soldiers treated him with contempt and mocked him; then he put an elegant robe on him, and sent him back to Pilate. ¹²That same day Herod and Pilate became friends with each other; before this they had been enemies.*

¹³Pilate then called together the chief priests, the leaders, and the people, ¹⁴and said to them, "You brought me this man as one who was perverting the people; and here I have examined him in your presence and have not found this man guilty of any of your charges against him. ¹⁵Neither has Herod, for he sent him back to us. Indeed, he has done nothing to deserve death. ¹⁶I will therefore have him flogged and release him."

¹⁸Then they all shouted out together, "Away with this fellow! Release Barabbas for us!" ¹⁹(This was a man who had been put in prison for an insurrection that had taken place in the city, and for murder.) ²⁰Pilate, wanting to release Jesus, addressed them again; ²¹but they kept shouting, "Crucify, crucify him!" ²²A third time he said to them, "Why, what evil has he done? I have found in him no ground for the sentence of death; I will therefore have him flogged and then release him." ²³But they kept urgently demanding with loud shouts that he should be crucified; and their voices prevailed. ²⁴So Pilate gave his verdict that their demand should be granted. ²⁵He released the man they asked for, the one who had been put in prison for insurrection and murder, and he handed Jesus over as they wished.

²⁶As they led him away, they seized a man, Simon of Cyrene, who was coming from the country, and they laid the cross on him, and made him carry it behind Jesus. ²⁷A great number of the people followed him, and among them were women who were beating their breasts and wailing for him. ²⁸But Jesus turned to them and said, "Daughters of Jerusalem, do not weep for me, but weep for yourselves and for your children. ²⁹For the days are surely coming when they will say, 'Blessed are the barren, and the wombs that never bore, and the breasts that never nursed.' ³⁰Then they will begin to say to the mountains, 'Fall on us'; and to the hills, 'Cover us.' ³¹For if they do this when the wood is green, what will happen when it is dry?"

³²Two others also, who were criminals, were led away to be put to death with him. ³³When they came to the place that is called The Skull, they crucified Jesus there with the criminals, one on his right and one on his left. ³⁴Then Jesus said, "Father, forgive them; for they do not know what they are doing." And they cast lots to divide his clothing.

³⁵*And the people stood by, watching; but the leaders scoffed at him, saying, "He saved others; let him save himself if he is the Messiah of God, his chosen one!"* ³⁶*The soldiers also mocked him, coming up and offering him sour wine,* ³⁷*and saying, "If you are the King of the Jews, save yourself!"* ³⁸*There was also an inscription over him, "This is the King of the Jews."*

³⁹*One of the criminals who were hanged there kept deriding him and saying, "Are you not the Messiah? Save yourself and us!"* ⁴⁰*But the other rebuked him, saying, "Do you not fear God, since you are under the same sentence of condemnation?* ⁴¹*And we indeed have been condemned justly, for we are getting what we deserve for our deeds, but this man has done nothing wrong."* ⁴²*Then he said, "Jesus, remember me when you come into your kingdom."* ⁴³*He replied, "Truly I tell you, today you will be with me in Paradise."*

⁴⁴*It was now about noon, and darkness came over the whole land until three in the afternoon,* ⁴⁵*while the sun's light failed; and the curtain of the temple was torn in two.* ⁴⁶*Then Jesus, crying with a loud voice, said, "Father, into your hands I commend my spirit." Having said this, he breathed his last.* ⁴⁷*When the centurion saw what had taken place, he praised God and said, "Certainly this man was innocent."* ⁴⁸*And when all the crowds who had gathered there for this spectacle saw what had taken place, they returned home, beating their breasts.* ⁴⁹*But all his acquaintances, including the women who had followed him from Galilee, stood at a distance, watching these things.*

—Luke 23:1-49

The narrative of Jesus' passion and death stands on its own; no need to review the events of the story. This narrative does not release its power in the details but as a whole. This reflection envisages a person doing this exercise by reading the story slowly, perhaps more than once, getting into the flow of the events, and allowing the story to speak. All the gospels tell it, and it came to represent the heart of the message. It should not be covered over with commentary. This reflection offers a framework for being affected by the story.

This story of Jesus' suffering and death contains a tension between the perspective of the narrator and of the events themselves. The story is told by a community of faith that lives decades later in resurrection faith. This entails the belief that Jesus is alive on the other side of death, in the sphere of God. The narrative contains multiple allusions to texts of the Hebrew scriptures that helped the community interpret who Jesus was. Yet the story unfolds with remarkable objectivity. Entering into the successive events of the story as they unfold requires a certain placing of one's beliefs in parentheses and imagining how what happened was experienced by Jesus and others who participated in the story or witnessed it. It bears repeating that Ignatius looked for a personal relationship between the person making this exercise and Jesus as the premise for the kind of reaction he thought the story would evoke: sorrow, confusion, and pain at what someone who had become a personal inspiration and friend had suffered *pro me*, precisely for the retreatant. This reflection does not presume such an intimately personal connection with Jesus. But it suggests how what is happening in this story has implications for the meaning of human existence and thus how everyone can relate to it.

The passion narrative is the story of how Jesus died. Some natural impulse pushes people to ask about how a person died and, for people close to one who died to tell the story of the causes of the death, what led up to it, and how it transpired. For Jesus' followers this desire to figure out what happened must have been a heavy burden that was never quite relieved. Life and death are not simple facts that can be explained, but mysteries. And this was not a peaceful death after a full life cycle, but an execution of a person who had gone around doing good. The full range of the gospel stories of Jesus attending to people's needs presents him as an agent of human flourishing. This narrative, by contrast, represents a first attempt to understand this death, circumscribe it with causality, wrap one's mind around it, and be able to live with it.

A framework that is useful in understanding negative events has been called a negative experience of contrast. It has been appealed to before in these reflections. It provides an outline for appropriating what is going on in this story. A negative experience of contrast refers to a recognition of a situation or an event that is negative, wrong, unjust, usually but not necessarily in a deep and serious way. Such an experience always presupposes an implicit grasp of the way things should be, positively, for otherwise one would not be able to know a situation or event was wrong. This accounts for the inner contrast, the dialectical or tensive structure of the experience. This experience also contains an implicit desire to right the wrong, to change the situation, to negate the negation, or at least to cope with it.

Such an experience describes the recognition of innocent suffering. The story of Job, for example, is driven by the knowledge that he is innocent and that therefore something is radically wrong. The passion narrative of Jesus' suffering and death is a scandalous story of innocent suffering. The contrast gains larger dimensions with various appreciations of the status of Jesus, and it fuels deep experiences of mystery and compassion. Ignatius's intention for these contemplations fits the subject matter: to "ask for heartfelt sorrow and confusion, because the Lord is going to his passion for my sins" (SE, 193).

This narrative of Jesus being led to his death does contain positive features that can be read off the surface. One of them that did not escape the notice of later interpretations of Jesus' death in the New Testament tells of Jesus' commitment to the rule of God to the very end. This positive commitment provides a major element in the interpretation of the significance of Jesus' suffering and death in the next meditation. In Luke's account Jesus lived out a steady commitment to God's rule from his baptism to his death.

Another positive interpretation of Jesus' suffering and death, in the past and consistently today, reads this death as symbolizing Jesus' and God's identification with those who suffer. Jesus, by standing for the rule of God and bearing witness to it in the face of death, represents God's commitment to those for whom Jesus suffered, the beneficiaries of the rule of God. Of course, a Messiah was not supposed to be executed; the Messiah was to mediate the triumph of God's rule. It was not easy for the followers of Jesus to arrive at an interpretation that made sense of this fiasco. The mode of Jesus' death truly embarrassed his followers and ultimately presented them with an impenetrable mystery. But through reflection on the texts of scripture, especially the prophet Isaiah, people came to see that Jesus' whole ministry entailed God's concern for and identification with those whose deaths seem to leave their lives with no meaning or value. Relative to the cross, however, this perception seems counterintuitive: how does Jesus' cruel death manifest God's concern for those who suffer innocently rather than scandalize because of the lack of it? The question shows how difficult it is to find positive meaning in this tragic outcome of Jesus' ministry. It will bear further reflection.

The negative character of this story dominates and seizes human sensibility. There is something radically wrong here; this should not have happened; the justice of the order of being itself seems threatened. Every death does not provoke this sense of wrong and injustice. It does not attach to a death in old age or from natural causes, which fits the ordinary course of things. But here evil has entered the scene. The causes of this wrongful death are human and intentional. And assigning blame or guilt to this or that person or party does not assuage the biting negativity. In the end, one simply has to recognize that such forces exist. These evil tendencies in the human heart are hard to accept. Resistance to them can be seen in attempts to explain this negative power by personifying it as sin or demons, or imagining a cosmic dualism with a principle of evil contending with creativity. But this mythic thinking does not explain; it simply expresses the problem.

When Jesus and his story are taken as an icon for ultimate reality, however, this story begins to take on cosmic proportions. To the extent that Jesus represents and reveals God's rule, this story entails recognizing that suffering is written into the substance of history and human existence itself. Ignatius had no problem at all internalizing Augustine's moral dualism, the conflict between good and evil, personified, with each contending party seeking human allies. Although the present age does not entertain these mythic terms, this story of Jesus' crucifixion resists being reduced to ordinary human disagreements. At the very least, these conflicts are not ordinary but are the symptoms of some permanent negative condition that infects human existence itself. The twentieth century has shown that the power of this negative self-destructive force knows few boundaries. It contains a potential for humanity to destroy itself.

The human reactions to the story of Jesus' execution can be many and varied, but two deep affects on human sensibility can represent a broad human response. The first is disorientation, and the second is hope. Regarding disorientation, the gospels stories show that the reactions of the followers included confusion of this kind. This judgment probably includes some reading into the situation. This was not supposed to happen to the historic Messiah, if people were beginning to think of Jesus in those terms. If not, many still found religious meaning, salvation from God, in his ministry, so that his execution would have been devastating. This disorientation could run shallow or deep. The more deeply people were won over to Jesus' message, the emptier was the hollow space that was carved out of them by his sudden and unexpected execution. The same is true today.

The other aspect of a reaction to this story of Jesus' punishing death is more positive but can only be appreciated dialectically, that is, in a strict mutual relationship with shock and disorientation. The very perception that Jesus' death was wrong, an outrageous chain of events that should not have happened, manifests precisely by contrast that a positive order of things does exist and that it was violated. The negativity itself presupposes that there must be justice and some order in the universe that grounds the negative valuation of these events. This does not appear on the surface of things; the rule of God is not apparent. But it must be there in order to validate the sense of outrage at the evil that human beings can inflict on others by spontaneous and thorough protection of their own interests in the immediate affairs of life. This hope militates against surrender to negativity and enables human beings to perceive Jesus' resurrection.

33. The Significance of Jesus' Death

⁵Let the same mind be in you that was in Christ Jesus, ⁶who, though he was in the form of God, did not regard equality with God as something to be exploited, ⁷but emptied himself, taking the form of a slave, being born in human likeness. And being found in human form, ⁸he humbled himself and became obedient to the point of death—even death on a cross.

⁹Therefore God also highly exalted him and gave him the name that is above every name, ¹⁰so that at the name of Jesus every knee should bend, in heaven and on earth and under the earth, ¹¹and every tongue should confess that Jesus Christ is Lord, to the glory of God the Father.
—Philippians 2:6-11

This reflection recapitulates the Third Week of the Exercises, concludes the contemplations of the earthly ministry of Jesus, and sets up a transition to the Fourth Week. The idea of the "significance of Jesus' death" is deliberately ambiguous. It refers to the implications of what happened to Jesus as well as the meaning his followers and anyone else may draw from it. Although these questions approach the large theological discussions of redemption and salvation, this consideration stops short of that. It addresses those making the Exercises and not engaged in theology: it seeks to draw the significance of Jesus out of the experience of their encounter with his story.

The text from Paul reflects an early hymn. Some exegetes understand Paul's use of it as an expression of a "second Adam" view of Jesus: the first archetypal human failed; Jesus reran his course and got it right. As such, it expresses the significance of Jesus.

This reflection builds on two premises that provide the foundation for everything else. The first envisages a person relating to Jesus as to one in whom can be found a reliable representation of ultimate reality. The character of ultimate reality is personal God and loving creator—an infinite sphere of power and love. In some ways that stipulation already decides the significance of Jesus, and the question gets focused on the relevance of this for human existence. The second premise implicitly draws the resurrection of Jesus into the mix. The Easter experience of his followers, that Jesus had been saved from ultimate death and was raised to new life, provides the reason why Jesus was remembered: subtract the resurrection and Jesus' death cannot be distinguished from those of millions of others'. Jesus' death by crucifixion thus provides another instance of a tensive present–future perspective on the events of Jesus' ministry. They are all presented from a later perspective, and all who consider them relate to them from their own time. Trying imaginatively to bracket out one's own perspective today in order to enter back into the time of their unfolding by itself would artificially limit perception and short-circuit understanding. Resurrection colors this interpretation of Jesus' death. The cliché that Jesus' passion and resurrection cannot be separated expresses a recognition that speaking of Jesus' death in an isolated way so limits a spiritual perspective that its significance will be curtailed if not simply misunderstood. These premises encompass all that follows.

When one steps back and takes in the execution to which Jesus was subjected, one cannot say that this suffering was good. Human beings are not helped by Jesus' suffering; the torture of Jesus supplies no human rescue. People are inspired by Jesus despite or in the face of his suffering. The God that Jesus preached could not positively will human beings to suffer or ordain that Jesus suffer. The reasons for Jesus' passion are entirely human. One cannot reconstruct them perfectly, but one can imagine them. By contrast, many interpretations of Jesus' suffering depict it functioning in such a way that its violence appears as a good, by being the positive means in a plan by which he won salvation for humanity. Some interpretations implicitly say, "He bore a suffering that others deserved." Others hold, "His suffering satisfied in justice for the injury to the creator God caused by human sin." These naïve anthropomorphisms distort the efforts of the early community to decipher at a deeper level the tragic end of Jesus' life. They leave the earthly events behind and project a drama unfolding in another sphere. These interpretations have resulted in various world-denying spiritualities and ascetic self-punishing practices that are unbalanced by the measure of human flourishing. These spiritualities of the cross somehow imagine self-negation to be an imitation of the suffering of Jesus and thus implicitly turn suffering into a good. While self-control and discipline are virtues, suffering in itself should always be resisted. The ministry of Jesus for God's rule fought against all suffering that in any way diminished people's humanity by being inflicted on freedom. The implications of the contrary are deeply scandalous.

The last contemplation noticed the steady commitment of Jesus that began with his baptism by John and ran through the whole of his ministry even to his death. Jesus dedicated himself in the power of the Spirit of God to a ministry of proclaiming and acting out the rule of God and maintained that commitment "to the point of death— even death on a cross." Jesus' suffering fits into the story of his being savior as the measure of his positive commitment to the kingdom of God. He never abandoned his mission to preach the reign of God in the face of the threat of death, actual torture, and finally death itself.

He actively surrendered his life for the rule of God. In this protracted event dying becomes an act, an intentional final commitment of freedom to the values that a person holds as ultimate. Not all people have such deaths; they may die suddenly in mid-course or be so diminished by sickness that the power of self-disposition has slipped away. But the story of Jesus tells of one who was able to sum up his life, gather up the length of his commitment, and offer his whole self in death to the God who ruled his life. The narrative of Jesus' death presents him as fully in control of himself and intentionally giving his whole self to God's desires for human fulfillment. The metaphysical message in this is unmistakable. It says, "The rule of God is salvation."

Jesus faced his suffering in faith and hope. This facet of Jesus' death reveals the inner logic of being human and standing before ultimate reality. God for Jesus was creator of heaven and earth, and also personal and loving. The story of Jesus depicts him as a person of faith in that God, who went to his death in a course in which he must have felt abandoned or alone, but who persevered in a faith and hope that his death like his life would ultimately be meaningful. All people suffer and die; Jesus reveals how one can faithfully negotiate externally imposed, unjust, and terminal suffering right through to death.

Faith in Jesus as God's representative expands the scope of this revelation of human existence before God. The human race bears the scars of widespread poverty and destitution. The prevalence of crude systemic injustice that directly causes whole groups of people to be smothered by subhuman conditions and to live their whole lives trapped within them directly attacks any easy faith. But Jesus aligned himself with this innocent suffering. His suffering and death identify him with the most severe test of the ultimate meaningfulness of human existence. Being destroyed unjustly by outside forces cannot be identified with salvation in any way; it is the cause of despair. Yet this identification with the project of God to resist innocent suffering is something that can be vindicated by God.

The deepest significance of Jesus for human beings rests on his being a revelation of human existence and God. Jesus reveals humanity to itself by being attached to God, by preaching God's word and God's rule, and by steadfastly acting out that faith to the end. Jesus' actions embodied the content of his faith and thus manifested it concretely. The other side of Jesus revealing what it means to be human before God lies in the character of the ultimate reality to whom he relates. The reflection on Jesus' suffering asked why Jesus' suffering does not reveal a God who is unconcerned with those who suffer innocently, as the religious leaders scoffed while he hung on the cross. We know today that God does not overtly act in our world, that such objections are childish. The action of God does not appear on the surface of history but operates within historical agents and as meaning perceived in the deeper recesses of empirical causality and human subjectivity. It can only be appreciated by the human spirit that desires it. Jesus' death bears witness to a loving God because his fidelity so united him to God's rule that his actions for others represented God.

In sum, Jesus' significance lies in his revelation of how human beings can commit themselves in faith to an ultimate reality, in this case God, before whom they can die in hope. His representation of what it means to be human also throws light on a God who, as the creator, guarantees that faith and hope. In his suffering and death, Jesus' commitment and actions correspond with his message and give it credibility. In this way the significance of Jesus gets located not in this or that teaching, as in some kernel of truth that grounds everything, but in the whole course of his concrete ministry, which he lived consistently to its unjust and punishing end. Jesus is significant because he embodied the rule of God in the world, and his story testifies to that revelation.

Jesus died in Jerusalem, but his story did not end there. The hymn that Paul made his own and seamlessly integrated into his Letter to the Philippians links Jesus' death to his resurrection. The Easter experience is the name for his followers coming to recognize Jesus being alive and thereby transforming their lives once again.

Jesus Risen and His Mission

In the Fourth Week of the Spiritual Exercises Ignatius directs attention to the completion of the Christian story of Jesus Christ, his being taken into the sphere of God. Life through death, since the writing of Paul, names the very center of the meaning of Jesus Christ and of Christianity itself. Ignatius thus brings his narrative spirituality to conclusion with considerations of the resurrection of Jesus Christ and its impact on the Christian life. He provides two sets of contemplations for the Fourth Week: a series of stories of Jesus' appearances from the New Testament (SE, 218-25, 299-312) and The Contemplation to Attain Love (SE, 230-37). The contemplations presented here expand the range of those proposed by Ignatius, and the reflections incorporate a series of presuppositions he did not share.

First, with regard to the scope of these contemplations, they begin with the Easter experience and then go on to show where this experience led in the formation of a Jesus movement that eventually became a church. This expands the narrative of Jesus by continuing the story in the effects that the Easter experience had on Jesus' disciples after his death.

Second, theologians debate different theories of what Jesus' resurrection entailed. In this presentation resurrection means that Jesus really died and yet that Jesus lives anew on the other side of death in the sphere of the God of life. "Bodily" resurrection means that the entire creaturely reality of Jesus of Nazareth lives a new life within God's creating power.[1] This view is not reducible to Jesus living on in human memory.

Third, whereas "resurrection" refers to what happened to Jesus, the "Easter experience" bears reference to the disciples of Jesus. What enabled the earliest followers of Jesus to break out of the disorientation and ontological depression of shattered hope and pass into a new faith that Jesus is alive? Ignatius and many Christians today consider the stories of Jesus' appearances as recountings of events substantially as

---

1. Brian D. Robinette, "The Difference Nothing Makes: *Creatio ex nihilo,* Resurrection, and Divine Gratuity," *Theological Studies* 72 (2011), 545.

they happened and thus as the answer to this question. Yet exegetes today more generally understand the appearance narratives as later literary testimonies to the faith, already in place, that Jesus was really raised. This view underlies these reflections, and it subtly shifts the focus of attention in the story from Jesus, now raised, to the followers of Jesus.

Fourth, reflection then turns to the effects that such an Easter experience had on Jesus' original disciples. Resurrection faith spawned a public Jesus movement that would itself develop historically into a church and Christianity. The formation of a movement of communities provides a historical link between Jesus and Christians today, and it shifts a narrative spirituality from the private sphere to the public sphere where the story of Jesus has an impact not only on individual persons in history but also for history itself. In the last contemplation of the Exercises Ignatius brings the whole narrative of Jesus to a conclusion in an expansive spiritual vision, which can be called a creation mysticism.

34. Emmaus: The Easter Experience

13Now on that same day two of them were going to a village called Emmaus, about seven miles from Jerusalem, 14and talking with each other about all these things that had happened. 15While they were talking and discussing, Jesus himself came near and went with them, 16but their eyes were kept from recognizing him. 17And he said to them, "What are you discussing with each other while you walk along?" They stood still, looking sad. 18Then one of them, whose name was Cleopas, answered him, "Are you the only stranger in Jerusalem who does not know the things that have taken place there in these days?" 19He asked them, "What things?" They replied, "The things about Jesus of Nazareth, who was a prophet mighty in deed and word before God and all the people, 20and how our chief priests and leaders handed him over to be condemned to death and crucified him. 21But we had hoped that he was the one to redeem Israel. Yes, and besides all this, it is now the third day since these things took place. 22Moreover, some women of our group astounded us. They were at the tomb early this morning, 23and when they did not find his body there, they came back and told us that they had indeed seen a vision of angels who said that he was alive. 24Some of those who were with us went to the tomb and found it just as the women had said; but they did not see him." 25Then he said to them, "Oh, how foolish you are, and how slow of heart to believe all that the prophets have declared! ²⁶*Was it not necessary that the Messiah should suffer these things and then enter into his glory?"* ²⁷*Then beginning with Moses and all the prophets, he interpreted to them the things about himself in all the scriptures.* ²⁸*As they came near the village to which they were going, he walked ahead as if he were going on.* ²⁹*But they urged him strongly, saying, "Stay with us, because it is almost evening and the day is now nearly over." So he went in to stay with them.* ³⁰*When he was at the table with them, he took bread, blessed and broke it, and gave it to them.* ³¹*Then their eyes were opened, and they recognized him; and he vanished from their sight.* ³²*They said to each other, "Were not our hearts burning within us while he was talking to us on the road, while he was opening the scriptures to us?"* ³³*That same hour they got up and returned to Jerusalem; and they found the eleven and their companions gathered together.* ³⁴*They were saying, "The Lord has risen indeed, and he has appeared to Simon!"* ³⁵*Then they told what had happened on the road, and how he had been made known to them in the breaking of the bread.*

—Luke 24:13-35

Ignatius must have noticed that the New Testament contains no account of Jesus' resurrection, but only stories that announce that he had been raised and narratives of Jesus, already risen, appearing to his disciples. Resurrection means that Jesus died into God's continuous loving, creating, and life-sustaining embrace. It refers to God's action relative to Jesus as he died and, more generally, relates to human death the way God's creating relates to the empirical beginnings of the universe. Creation and resurrection are not apprehended and affirmed in the same way we perceive worldly events. Resurrection is not something that human beings *know about*, but an object of faith and hope. On that premise, the Fourth Week, dealing with the story of Jesus after his death, continues the narration in and through the experience of the disciples. The stories of Jesus' appearances do not say whether they portray actual sensible events or dramatize literarily the reality that Jesus is risen. These reflections treat the stories as literary statements that Jesus is alive with God.

Some Jews in Jesus' time believed in a resurrection of the dead. In Jesus' case, resurrection designates what must have happened, because Jesus was alive with God and present in their midst. The phrase "Easter experience" refers to the disciples of Jesus coming to the new faith conviction after his death that Jesus was alive. Even though the New Testament provides no information about how Jesus' resurrection occurred, it is legitimate to ask the how the disciples came to this recognition of faith. Luke tells the most detailed and plausible story of how that Easter experience came about in his narrative about two disciples traveling from Jerusalem to a neighboring town two days after Jesus' execution. The story is carefully crafted, clearly organized to be used as a teaching device. The two are still stunned by the incomprehensible event of Jesus' sudden execution. They meet a stranger who explains all that happened by an appeal to the Hebrew scriptures. They prevail upon the man to remain with them for an evening meal, and, as he hosts the meal with familiar words, they recognize that the stranger is Jesus, alive and present to them. They immediately return to tell others of their Easter experience.

This story can also be understood as telling in the terms of two people the story of how the body of the followers of Jesus, over a longer period of time, came to the conviction that Jesus had been ushered into eternal life with God. From this perspective, the story has six stages that represent in a somewhat abstract but coherent way how the community of the disciples of Jesus came to the recognition that Jesus was raised by God. This is the story of the whole community's Easter experience; it is Luke's literary way of depicting the actual history of how the followers of Jesus, absolutely discouraged by his death, came to faith in Jesus' resurrection. This deeper story presents no details, only the broad logic of how that faith was generated. The retreatant can easily imagine being a person who participated in this process that has been repeated across the ages. The story of how the first disciples came to faith that Jesus is alive shares many similarities with how people today come to and maintain the same faith.

Imagine the situation. The two disciples represent all of them. Disorder and discouragement pervade the whole lot of Jesus' followers, each one according to the measure in which he or she had been affected by his ministry to the rule of God. The little phrase, "we had hoped," communicates at once how deeply religious hope had penetrated, reaching to the depth and breadth of his being the Messiah, and how thoroughly execution on a cross destroyed it. Not only had the movement ended abruptly, but also the way Jesus was killed scandalized his followers.

Imagine the discussion of the followers of Jesus during the weeks after his violent death. The disciples of Jesus discussed intently the things that had happened relative to Jesus, his suffering and being put to a shameful death. How long was this period of discussion, this searching reflection, the endless conversation, the effort to figure things out? In the story, the time is compressed. In the actual history of the followers, one could imagine various lengths of time: weeks, months. Where and how did these gatherings take place? In Galilee or in Jerusalem? Or in both places simultaneously among different groups? One can easily imagine various groups of disciples gathering in smaller or larger groups for some time after Jesus' death. One would expect that some form of the meals of disciples would continue simply in order for the followers of Jesus to process the events.

Imagine how the community must have combed the scriptures for enlightenment about what had happened in the whole Jesus event. Included in the discussions were appeals to the Hebrew scripture to find some clues about what was going on. The New Testament shows how the scriptures were the main way in which the disciples came to understand what had happened to Jesus, who he was, and how these two things fit together. The actual course of Jesus' ministry provided new lenses to read the scriptures, and they in turn took on new relevant meaning. New questions opened up new understanding of meaning, already there but now strikingly apposite to the new situation.

This process obviously generated insight and illumination. Somewhere in the course of this extended period of time, at one point or another, in this person or those persons first and then among others, in the course of days or weeks, however it happened will never be known, but somewhere in the course of these conversations it became clear that Jesus had been raised to life by God. This was not proved; in the end, this was not a product of human inference; it was rather a revelation of God, a light perceived by faith. Many things flowed into this new conviction: the memory of Jesus, the language of the scriptures, the reawakening faith and hope of the disciples, and the Spirit of God commonly felt within the community of followers. This collective illumination, insight, and conviction shaped the followers into a new community of positive faith, hope, and mission.

Imagine how, in the course of the meals that various groups of Jesus' followers shared during this period, they gradually came to a recognition that Jesus' presence to them in memory was actually a presence with them in the power of the Spirit of God. This story builds a strong connection between the recognition that Jesus was alive and thus raised and the meeting of the followers of Jesus for meals of remembering. At those meals they talked; they also read the scriptures and prayed. The idea that they recognized him in the "breaking of the bread" is an allusion to the meals that Jesus had with his disciples and is associated with the Last Supper. On the likely supposition that these meals were continued, it is not difficult to imagine that such meals, involving conversation and discussion, became the venue for the illumination and recognition that Jesus was risen.

Through such reflective routes, probably through the assemblies for meals, the followers of Jesus came to the experience that became crystallized in the kerygma. "Kerygma" means "message" and refers to the kernel of the meaning of the gospel. It can be expressed in different aphorisms, and one of these was "Jesus is risen." The end of the Emmaus story, its conclusion, occurs back in Jerusalem with the statement of this primal belief of the Jesus community. Luke was preoccupied with Jerusalem. But whether the Easter experience originated in Galilee or in Jerusalem, it became broadly shared as gradually the community of disciples came to a common conviction of faith–hope: "The Lord has risen indeed" (Luke 24:34).

This contemplation fruitfully could end with an explicit consideration of one's own place in this story. Like all the others, it invites participation. But at this pivotal juncture the invitation may be more momentous. This contemplation transcends both the two disciples and, more generally, the first disciples in the time immediately after Jesus' passion and death. The story potentially includes all Christians at all times and in every situation. This kerygma does not represent the simple coming to believe a fact. Belief in the resurrection of Jesus involves a comprehensive appreciation of human life: its purpose and its destiny. This revelation and coming to faith describes the fundamental orientation of all who take part in the Jesus movement: they live in a faith conviction that God raised Jesus out of death and into God's own sphere of being. The logic of the Easter experience of the earliest community corresponds with the logic of the lives of Christians thereafter. Initial reaction to this response could be the subject of a searching address to God in the words of prayer, whether or not one can internalize resurrection faith.

35. The Meaning of the Resurrection of Jesus

[1]*In the first book, Theophilus, I wrote about all that Jesus did and taught from the beginning* [2]*until the day when he was taken up to heaven, after giving instructions through the Holy Spirit to the apostles whom he had chosen.* [3]*After his suffering he presented himself alive to them by many convincing proofs, appearing to them over the course of forty days and speaking about the kingdom of God.* [4]*While staying with them, he ordered them not to leave Jerusalem, but to wait there for the promise of the Father. "This," he said, "is what you have heard from me;* [5]*for John baptized with water, but you will be baptized with the Holy Spirit not many days from now."* [6]*So when they had come together, they asked him, "Lord, is this the time when you will restore the kingdom to Israel?"* [7]*He replied, "It is not for you to know the times*

or periods that the Father has set by his own authority. ⁸But you will receive power when the Holy Spirit has come upon you; and you will be my witnesses in Jerusalem, in all Judea and Samaria, and to the ends of the earth." ⁹When he had said this, as they were watching, he was lifted up, and a cloud took him out of their sight. ¹⁰While he was going and they were gazing up towards heaven, suddenly two men in white robes stood by them. ¹¹They said, "Men of Galilee, why do you stand looking up towards heaven? This Jesus, who has been taken up from you into heaven, will come in the same way as you saw him go into heaven."

—Acts 1:1-11

The previous contemplation on Luke's beautiful story of the awakening of two disciples to Jesus being alive allowed penetration into the gradual process by which the followers of Jesus came to a corporate Easter experience that bound them together as a movement. This contemplation turns attention to the resurrection itself: what does resurrection mean and to what exactly does it refer? These questions sound abstract, analytical, and theological, and not the subjects of prayer. Yet resurrection marks a threshold in Christian self-understanding that many cannot cross because it calls up something unimaginable and, in fact, impossible. Instead of attracting spiritual sensibility, it confuses or repulses. A prayerful and searching contemplative appreciation of these narratives provides the key to their spiritual relevance. Resurrection refers to something that happened to Jesus of Nazareth, but all people are implied in this story.

Only Luke tells the story of the disciples on the road to Emmaus; he is also unique in representing Jesus' exaltation and passage into God's life in two stages. The first stage is Jesus' resurrection to a transformed kind of spiritual bodily existence on earth, and the second stage is his departure from this world and a journey into heaven. There were no witnesses to the first stage, but this second stage, called the ascension, transpired as the disciples stood by. Luke even emphasizes the visibility of Jesus' ascension as if he were a materialist in the sense that something not sensible would not be real. Jesus was lifted up in the air, and a cloud transported him like a heavenly chariot. Luke associates Jesus with a celestial Son of Man who was to come on the clouds and who would be given glorious dominion in an everlasting kingdom (Dan 7:13-14). Just so was Jesus borne up on the clouds to come again in the future. The brief mention of Jesus' ascension at the end of Luke's gospel serves to bring Jesus' story on earth to a conclusion; in this account it sets up a new story in which Jesus leaves history, and, in his absence, the disciples begin a new phase of the story in the power of the Spirit that Jesus will send. Luke's account of an ascension is a theological construct and does not have historical value.

Focusing a contemplation on Jesus' resurrection through a text describing Jesus' ascension dramatically poses the problem of whether Jesus' resurrection can be imagined at all. Resurrection means that God drew Jesus as a person into God's own transcendent sphere and life: Jesus lives as the individual person Jesus in God. To express this the New Testament uses the term "resurrection." The metaphor suggests reawakening, standing up, being restored to life, and thus continuity with his former self. The New Testament also speaks of Jesus' "exaltation" and "glorification," which point to a more direct entrance into a new sphere and phase of transcendent existence. No standard language captures this. The condition is transcendent and not a this-worldly reality, a function of God's transcendent power and being beyond this world, and therefore literally unimaginable. This means that every sensible image of what happened to Jesus distorts it precisely in the measure that the image renders it a worldly event able to be imagined. Luke's story of the second stage of resurrection, Jesus' exaltation, illustrates well how a consideration of his narrative in the literal or visual terms that a witness might use renders Jesus' resurrection incredible. The same applies to various spontaneous images of Jesus' corpse being resuscitated or quickened again and his occasional passing through locked doors. The resurrection of the body should not be reduced to or equated with pictorial representations; it does not refer to human bodies floating off to some place. Such literalism voids the Christian message for an increasingly large section of humanity.

This problem, which seems insurmountable given the nature of how the Christian story is told, virtually disappears when it is recognized that all human understanding employs the imagination but that the sphere of God transcends this world. These two convictions, once they are internalized, allow people to read the story of Jesus being lifted up and, drawn by this symbolic language, to open their minds to a reality that utterly transcends the visual depictions. A person can freely enter into the narrative, imaginatively follow the succession of events, and be drawn into the transcendent sphere that is offered through them. The meaning of the story transcends the earthly narrative. In this view "transcends" does not translate into something far away and unrelated. God's sphere, while completely other, thoroughly embraces the finite and is found within it.

The existential meaning or significance of resurrection reaches out and embraces all human existence. A commitment to Jesus as representative of human existence and revelation of ultimate reality makes his resurrection a promise of the resurrection of all human beings and thus the guarantor of an ultimate value to human life itself. The proposition can be stated as simply as that. But accepting and entering into this proposal as true completely rearranges all the empirical data about human life and gives it a dimension of inestimable depth and consequence, nothing less than holy mystery. Human life can no longer be conceived as ordinary: life that, after a brief period, withers and dies into nothingness, leaving not even a long-term memory. Given the history of our universe, can a human being really count his or her life as having more than ephemeral value? Even eternal value? The resurrection of Jesus says Yes and thereby completely alters the appreciation of human existence itself. The resurrection of Jesus reveals something that was always the case. To accept it transforms the world.

A paradoxical contemplation of the unimaginable resurrection of Jesus undoubtedly raises this question: why was it Jesus who was raised out of death in this kind of "public" way? Such a line of thought is speculative because it points in the direction of the reasons or motives of God's action and is laden with anthropomorphism. But one can say haltingly that Jesus' resurrection forms an integral part of God's self-disclosure in him as the ratification of his kind of life. God absorbs the seemingly discrediting effect of Jesus' execution, and sets Jesus up precisely as an authentic revelation of the character of God. In other words, resurrection helps constitute the very revelation of God that Jesus' ministry mediated; it is not simply added on but encompasses and ratifies that revelation. This is the ontological climax of the saying of God in the story of the baptism of Jesus: "You are my Son; the beloved; with you I am well pleased" (Luke 3:22). Resurrection validates Jesus' person, his ministry of the rule of God, and his teaching. In Jesus' resurrection, Holy Mystery confirms Jesus as God's revelation of God's self and of authentic human existence.

Jesus embodied values that should not die. Most people have caught glimpses of lives that so overflow with goodness that they simply should not pass into nothingness; their value should last forever. Such analogies help to guide thought about God. On this reasoning, Jesus lived out and made actual a degree of commitment that helps explain why his human existence was ratified by eternal life. But given the unique value of each human person, this calculation extends to all.

Resurrection, however, is not something that human beings can earn on their own. The bare statement of such an idea shows how ridiculous it is. No human person could possibly be "owed" eternal life; its possibility appears only within the overarching and all-pervasive atmosphere of pure gift and the completely contingent and gratuitous event of existence itself. The most fundamental of questions, "Why is there being at all rather than nothing?" shapes the character of all spiritual searching and prohibits religious answers from becoming entitlements. Human existence unfolds in gratuitous dependence, and this condition defines how all relate to resurrection. Why was Jesus raised? In the end the response, "Because of the way he lived," is true but not in itself adequate. Jesus was raised because of God and who God is.

In the end, then, the resurrection of Jesus constitutes an integral part of Jesus' revelation of God; it recapitulates the whole ministry of Jesus and defines it as saving. Jesus' resurrection completes and provides the climactic meaning of Jesus' communication of the rule of God. This proposal flows from viewing Jesus from the perspective of what is revealed in and through him, that is, ultimate reality as personal God. This perspective enables a recognition not only that Jesus did this or that but also that God was doing something in Jesus. Jesus mediates a self-revelation of God. Because the Spirit of God was present and at work in Jesus' ministry, the character of God, the way God is, has been revealed in his life. Jesus' resurrection means that God's concern for all human life reaches through death itself. The resurrection of all means that the significance of Jesus extends far beyond an exemplary human life. Jesus defines the character of reality.

36. Resurrection and Christian Life

36While they were talking about this, Jesus himself stood among them and said to them, "Peace be with you." 37They were startled and terrified, and thought that they were seeing a ghost. 38He said to them, "Why are you frightened, and why do doubts arise in your hearts? 39Look at my hands and my feet; see that it is I myself. Touch me and see; for a ghost does not have flesh and bones as you see that I have." 40And when he had said this, he showed them his hands and his feet. 41While in their joy they were disbelieving and still wondering, he said to them, "Have you anything here to eat?" 42They gave him a piece of broiled fish, 43and he took it and ate in their presence.

44Then he said to them, "These are my words that I spoke to you while I was still with you — that everything written about me in the law of Moses, the prophets, and the psalms must be fulfilled." 45Then he opened their minds to understand the scriptures, 46and he said to them, "Thus it is written, that the Messiah is to suffer and to rise from the dead on the third day, 47and that repentance and forgiveness of sins is to be proclaimed in his name to all nations, beginning from Jerusalem. 48You are witnesses of these things. 49And see, I am sending upon you what my Father promised; so stay here in the city until you have been clothed with power from on high."

—Luke 24:36-49

People who accept Luke's construction of Jesus withdrawing from the world by an ascension after his resurrection will take this contemplation as backtracking. But introducing ascension "early" allowed consideration of how complicated the use of imagination can be in these contemplations. The order here reflects the view that Luke's story of an ascension is theological and has no historical value. The scene for this contemplation occurs immediately after the story of the disciples walking to Emmaus; they have returned to Jerusalem. It simultaneously engages the world of the disciples after the death of Jesus, the world of Luke with his ready catechesis, and implicitly the world in which a person lives today. The interplay of these different perspectives may stimulate fruitful ideas around the theme that this passage raises: what is the character of a response to the ultimate reality of God that faith in Jesus entails?

The reader of this scene has to be struck immediately by the tension the story sets up around the appearance of Jesus. He suddenly appears in the midst of many disciples who were listening to the report of the two describing their experience at Emmaus. The group is terrified, thinking Jesus was a ghost, and he demonstrates he is not by eating. How can one picture this scene today? No normative way can be prescribed. But reading this as a literary device to affirm the reality of Jesus being alive, precisely not in the physical form of his former life but within God's being, allows one to see the disciples relating to Jesus as really alive and present to them through memory and an interior experience of God as Spirit.

As in the story of the disciples on the way to Emmaus, here too Jesus explains how everything that happened to him leading up to and including his death and resurrection was foretold in the Hebrew Bible; everything made sense in terms of the law, the prophets, and the Psalms. Jesus was supposed to die and rise so that the master plan of God could unfold. And here Jesus digests that plan as it is meant to go forward in four elements: (a) the word of God concerning repentance and forgiveness (b) in Jesus' name, (c) is to be proclaimed to all nations, (d) beginning in Jerusalem (v. 47). This represents exactly the kernel of Luke's theology, his version of the catechesis of the young churches as they were gaining an identity distinct from the synagogues. The different elements tease the imagination. This was the message that the earliest followers of Jesus, just getting over their disorientation at Jesus' death, took months and years to discover. But Luke, in full possession of the master narrative, places it in Jesus' mouth as a way of summing up Jesus' ministry and pointing to the future.

People could be struck by the simplicity of the content of the proclamation in Jesus' name. It consists in repentance and forgiveness, something of a contrast to the Christian doctrines, beliefs, and attendant cultic practices that have developed over centuries. Repentance and forgiveness in Jesus' name. The bare statement does not develop the meaning that attaches to each of these elements, especially how forgiveness relates to Jesus' name. But what Luke does not amplify carries qualitative depth. The need for repentance can be considered part of the human condition due to consistent moral frailty. The ontological and moral finitude of each person reaches out for transcendent acceptance. Thus, God's personal forgiveness and acceptance release a person from bondage to self-interest and establish what Luther called the freedom of the Christian. Reduction of the scope of the effects of faith to a formula that eliminates and pares down by definition diminishes; but finding an inner core of God's rule relative to individual persons that is not exclusive expands understanding and self-appropriation.

Luke's narrative continues with essential elements of his theology. He has Jesus say, "You are witnesses of these things." One can easily imagine how important the witnesses became as the time after Jesus' actual ministry lengthened and one needed to preserve his memory. More important, however, a certain responsibility came with faith in Jesus' person and ministry; it entailed more than simply receiving and implied an active response, in this case, bearing witness. The dynamics of this response do not resemble a military command-and-obey kind of authority, but flow out of gratitude in return for a self-communication of God that engenders life, indeed, an entirely new quality of life. The need to respond comes from within the recipient who looks for ways of expression. In this relationship obligation becomes easy and every burden light (Matt 11:30). This obligation leaves the disciple feeling neither dominated nor entitled, but actively grateful.

The question of the relationship between resurrection and mission raised in this story needs to be highlighted, but this must wait for the next contemplation. Here the "sending" is something that Jesus says he will do from his exalted place with God: I will send the Spirit upon you. These few words encapsulate other elements of Luke's theology. As the Spirit of God provided the inner source of Jesus' authority in his mission, so too the Spirit will continue God's presence and activity in history through these new agents of the rule of God. From Jesus the disciples will evolve into the Jesus movement by the power of the Spirit of God. Luke neatly ties together his Gospel and Acts into one story of the Spirit of God at work first in Jesus and then his disciples in a world-historical movement.

It may be fruitful to reflect on this story of the memory of Jesus recharging the motivation of his disciples after his death and resurrection in relation to today's context. What kind of answer can the question of the responsibility of the Christian believer elicit in contemporary Western society? Everything in today's situation seems different if not the opposite of Luke's. Luke describes Christian faith just beginning in a world of other religions; today established Christian faith in the West seems to be fragmenting into privatized nonrelevance. Only a relatively tiny group of people make a professional commitment to being a witness; others seem lost in a general secularized population. Yet the depth of present-day commitment and witness cannot be measured in overt and quantitative terms. There is more quiet Christian witness to the rule of God than meets the public eye.

How can a person manage the tension between what one has received through faith, the grace of forgiveness and acceptance by God, and a realistic exercise of grateful responsibility in bearing witness to this grace within contemporary secular life? One significant difference in context may open different ways of responding to this issue. Luke's conception and description of the leaders of the incipient Jesus movement, Jesus' own disciples, tend to measure this total commitment of self-gift to the movement in quantitative terms. From the beginning Jesus gathered disciples who "left everything and followed him" (Luke 5:11, 28). This is not a realistic description of a broader social response to Jesus in any age. It is more reasonable to think not in quantitative but qualitative terms. Instead of a totality of time, the witness today may respond with a totality of depth. He or she will live out of the new sacred narrative encompassing the whole of life in absolute fidelity in the midst of other social responsibilities. The commitment takes the form of a fundamental disposition that orders all penultimate obligations and choices.

The other question for Christians in Western culture today has to do with the content of the message to which they are being asked to witness. What would be an appropriate translation of Luke's story of repentance and forgiveness in Jesus' name from first-century Mediterranean culture to the twenty-first-century West? The new situation highlights three elements of Christian witness. First and foremost, the rule of God sums up Jesus' ministry; it defines that for which he gave his life. This rule of God cannot be fully captured in terms of content, but only formally as what should be according to God's values as Jesus presented them. This story states well the second element: repentance and forgiveness mean acceptance by a personal God. The personal character of God, however, seems challenged today. More and more Western life is losing the radical personalism of Jesus' revelation of God. Portrayal of intentionality and love as the ground of being has to guard against slipping into shallow and incredible anthropomorphism. Resurrection names a third essential element of Christian faith. This means that God does not abandon personal life in death. For many, this belief has been closely tied to imaginatively depicted historical events. But this is not the only way to conceive the resurrection. One can transcend that to recognize how the resurrection of Jesus bears meaning because his is the story of every person: the destiny of Jesus, the representative of God and of human existence, incorporates everyone. Resurrection is promised to all. And the continuity between Jesus of Nazareth and the risen one that Jesus tries to demonstrate to his disciples in this story refers to the continuity between one's personal life and that which is raised. This belongs to a later consideration of eschatology, but it shows here how directly Jesus' resurrection bears meaning for life today. What people do with their lives and thus who they are with the support of God's Spirit will constitute the absolute future.

37. Pentecost: Resurrection and Mission

¹When the day of Pentecost had come, they were all together in one place. ²And suddenly from heaven there came a sound like the rush of a violent wind, and it filled the entire house where they were sitting. ³Divided tongues, as of fire, appeared among them, and a tongue rested on each of them. ⁴All of them were filled with the Holy Spirit and began to speak in other languages, as the Spirit gave them ability.

⁵Now there were devout Jews from every nation under heaven living in Jerusalem. ⁶And at this sound the crowd gathered and was bewildered, because each one heard them speaking in the native language of each. ⁷Amazed and astonished, they asked, "Are not all these who are speaking Galileans? ⁸And how is it that we hear, each of us, in our own native language? ⁹Parthians, Medes, Elamites, and residents of Mesopotamia, Judea and Cappadocia, Pontus and Asia, ¹⁰Phrygia and Pamphylia, Egypt and the parts of Libya belonging to Cyrene, and visitors from Rome, both Jews and proselytes, ¹¹Cretans and Arabs—in our own languages we hear them speaking about God's deeds of power." ¹²All were amazed and perplexed, saying to one another, "What does this mean?" ¹³But others sneered and said, "They are filled with new wine."

—Acts 2:1-13

Luke foreshadowed this story in his gospel and the first chapter of Acts; it became a very significant event. It occupies a neat place in his larger story of the Jesus movement by providing another linkage between Jesus' ministry and the expanding Christian mission to the nations. It also has an exalted place in the liturgical cycle as the climax of the Easter celebration. Pentecost was a harvest feast celebrated fifty days after Passover; it had other associations as well and became a time of pilgrimage, which provided the occasion for this story. Most exegetes consider this a Lukan dramatic event, like the journey to Emmaus, in which he makes a theological and perhaps a large historical statement through a representative story. Pentecost thus refers to a collective event that did not occur at a single point in time but gradually over the period after Jesus' death. This reflection treats it as a literary unit that offers a key that opens up a spiritual appreciation of the origins of the Christian movement, however they actually transpired.

The short narrative unfolds in two scenes. In the first, the disciples are assembled in a room when a sound like a powerful wind fills the whole house and a tongue of fire rests on each person. The flame represents the power of the Holy Spirit of God, which so energized each one that they were able to speak in other languages. In the second scene, the disciples are outside, surrounded by a crowd of Jews from many different places and speaking about God's powerful actions. Whatever language the disciples used, each person heard them in his or her own native language. Like a miracle story, it has strong supernatural elements.

Luke has gathered into the narrative all the elements he needed to make his point. Jesus has withdrawn as the central character, for the ascension signifies his absence in corporeal form. Of course, Jesus sent the Spirit, sometimes called the Spirit of Jesus (Acts 16:7), and Jesus is the subtext of the whole story. Jesus therefore does not disappear. But the Spirit of God that empowered Jesus now occupies front stage. The story is about the Spirit, and the Spirit is the main actor. The disciples who were with Jesus and are now his witnesses replace Jesus as the overt actors in the narrative. The idea of mission, connected with Jesus' resurrection and a main theme in the whole story of Acts, becomes prominent in this episode. Out in front of this story lies the church, whose origins are being accounted for. Each of these elements deserves consideration.

Recall that the idea of the Spirit of God derives from a recognition of God working within the world as an unseen power, like the wind to which the story alludes (Reflection 14). The story tells of the power of the Spirit dividing to become a unique flame for each individual.

Rather than imagine the Spirit up there and coming down or being sent anthropomorphically, one might see the Spirit embedded within the dimensions of transcendence that accompany religious experience. God as Spirit correlates with the power of creation sustaining all being from within. Spirit language springs from Hebrew sources to express energy within persons and history that comes from transcendence and cannot be reduced to human initiative. The symbol "Spirit" says that otherwise natural events contain the quality of a gift coming from a transcendent source. Jesus' life was charged by it, and now the same power of God that was in Jesus flows within the disciples of Jesus. At this point the Spirit becomes associated with mission.

The disciples' coming to an awareness that Jesus had died into life within the sphere of God included a dimension that has come to be called "mission." The word means "sending" and "being sent" and expresses an essential dimension of the Easter experience. Many of the stories of Jesus' resurrection appearances to disciples have the idea of mission written into them in terms of witnessing. In others it is explicit. In John's gospel Jesus appears to the disciples and says to them: "'As the Father has sent me, so I send you.' . . . he breathed on them and said to them, 'Receive the Holy Spirit'" (John 20:21-22). The association of the appearances and explicit sending corresponds with the logic of coming to an awareness that Jesus is alive. Whatever the depth and resonance of the Easter experience, it includes a desire to share it. The antithesis of a private experience, the discovery that the one in whom the rule of God had been encountered was then vindicated by God has to be communicated. Locating the roots of mission in the Easter experience itself rather than in a purely external command implies that it may be experienced today.

This mission has no boundaries. Historically, Jesus' ministry seems to have operated within the boundaries of Judaism. His was an announcement of the inbreaking of the rule of God in Israel. And it is hard to imagine that the disciples were thinking of a mission beyond Israel very soon after the death and resurrection of Jesus. But Luke has a later perspective, and from this distance he deliberately announces the universal relevance of the message mediated by Jesus. On the one hand, the new messengers begin to speak in a variety of languages so that they can address all peoples. On the other hand, no matter what each person says, all of them bear witness to the power of God at work in Jesus, and all who hear them hear their own language. The story depicts the launching of the mission and also its universal scope and relevance. Let the rule of God that Jesus citing Isaiah announced at the beginning of his ministry at Nazareth go forward: the lame walk, the blind see, and the poor have the good news of God's reign preached to them. As the story of Jesus shows, this comes about only when agents make it happen. Not all accept a transcendent power behind these ideals. Even fresh Pentecostal enthusiasm did not convince everyone. But the project exhibits a transcendent character and purpose.

Luke's symbolism dramatizes another essential characteristic of the mission. To the message of repentance and forgiveness seen in the previous contemplation this story adds reconciliation. This appears in the contrast with the story in Genesis of how God tamed corporate ambition by differentiating peoples' languages. "Therefore it was called Babel, because there the LORD confused the language of all the earth; and from there the LORD scattered them abroad over the face of all the earth" (Gen 11:9; Reflection 7). Nothing divides people more than different languages, and this becomes a source for enmity. In this story, the Spirit turns the disciples' language into a communicating and unifying medium. The Spirit in the disciples and in their hearers erases the boundaries and cools the hostilities built up by differences of language and culture. The supernatural quality of the story can be rephrased in terms of what is communicated: whereas languages may divide, the subject matter may unite. This story symbolizes how Jesus carries a reconciling message. The mission that Luke has in mind does not resemble a crusade. It does not subject or dominate; it simply cannot be communicated by force. Such means negate the content. The mission of the rule of God aims at spreading reconciliation under one transcendent creator who loves all people equally. Jesus' message always interrupts ordinary patterns of behavior, but here one sees that it interrupts division and hatred. The mission empowered by the Spirit reverses the effects of Babel with a social message of reconciliation that follows repentance and forgiveness.

Luke does not mention the church in this story, but it is on his mind. Some regard this story as an embryonic beginning of the church. The picture painted by Luke has the disciples waiting for the Spirit promised by Jesus and, with its arrival, the church movement begins. Historians who study Christian origins question this master narrative. For example, Luke's theology required the church to begin in Jerusalem, even though it is far more likely that the Jesus movement would have taken off in Galilee. Because it is so difficult to recreate exactly how the Jesus movement got started, the imagination is given full play. But however this development is envisioned, the key insight lies in the fact of historical development itself. One should not imagine a comprehensive plan being methodically executed, but an incipient historical movement groping its way forward in different places at different paces. This genuinely historical intuition acknowledges human freedom sensitive to the Spirit of God continually encountering contingent situations and making practical decisions. Luke's theology of the Spirit becomes even stronger when it is released from some of the structure with which he encumbered it. At bottom, Luke's story of Jesus tells of the Spirit of God at work in Jesus from beginning to end. And the end is not an end, but precisely the continuation of the work of the Spirit in the nascent Jewish movement that would eventually come to be the Christian church without necessarily ceasing to be Jewish at its core. The vision of Luke has become a massive historical vision encompassing all of history. In the Exercises it becomes an invitation to internalize the values of what Jesus called the rule of God.

38. Christian Mission

[14]But Peter, standing with the eleven, raised his voice and addressed them: "Men of Judea and all who live in Jerusalem, let this be known to you, and listen to what I say. [15]Indeed, these are not drunk, as you suppose, for it is only nine o'clock in the morning. [16]No, this is what was spoken through the prophet Joel: [17]'In the last days it will be, God declares, that I will pour out my Spirit upon all flesh, and your sons and your daughters shall prophesy, and your young men shall see visions, and your old men shall dream dreams. [8]Even upon my slaves, both men and women, in those days I will pour out my Spirit; and they shall prophesy. [19]And I will show portents in the heaven above and signs on the earth below, blood, and fire, and smoky mist. [20]The sun shall be turned to darkness and the moon to blood, before the coming of the Lord's great and glorious day. [21]Then everyone who calls on the name of the Lord shall be saved.' [22]You that are Israelites, listen to what I have to say: Jesus of Nazareth, a man attested to you by God with deeds of power, wonders, and signs that God did through him among you, as you yourselves know— [23]this man, handed over to you according to the definite plan and foreknowledge of God, you crucified and killed by the hands of those outside the law. [24]But God raised him up, having freed him from death, because it was impossible for him to be held in its power. [25]For David says concerning him, 'I saw the Lord always before me, for he is at my right hand so that I will not be shaken; [26]therefore my heart was glad, and my tongue rejoiced; moreover, my flesh will live in hope. [27]For you will not abandon my soul to Hades, or let your Holy One experience corruption. [28]You have made known to me the ways of life; you will make me full of gladness with your presence.' [29]Fellow Israelites, I may say to you confidently of our ancestor David that he both died and was buried, and his tomb is with us to this day.

[30]Since he was a prophet, he knew that God had sworn with an oath to him that he would put one of his descendants on his throne. [31]Foreseeing this, David spoke of the resurrection of the Messiah, saying, 'He was not abandoned to Hades, nor did his flesh experience corruption.' [32]This Jesus God raised up, and of that all of us are witnesses. [33]Being therefore exalted at the right hand of God, and having received from the Father the promise of the Holy Spirit, he has poured out this that you both see and hear. [34]For David did not ascend into the heavens, but he himself says, 'The Lord said to my Lord, "Sit at my right hand, [35]until I make your enemies your footstool."' [36]Therefore let the entire house of Israel know with certainty that God has made him both Lord and Messiah, this Jesus whom you crucified."

—Acts 2:14-36

Pentecost dramatizes the empowerment of the disciples by the Spirit of God in the Easter experience. The Spirit ignites the expansive character of this faith and the mission to communicate it. This passage shows this mission spirit passing into action in an address of Peter to the assembled crowd. The content of Peter's sermon provides a compact version of the fundamental Christian story. Luke composed it in Greek and placed it on Peter's lips. Although he does not mention the church here, for it would be anachronistic to do so, the story represents the first step toward the gradual formation of a church over decades.

This story opens up many lines of contemplation. The disjunction between the careful and precise Christian story that Luke has crafted and the confused situation of searching disciples after Jesus' death and resurrection lures the imagination down different paths that give rise to particularly useful considerations at this place in the Spiritual Exercises. The impulse to mission passing into action suggests reasons why this mission developed into "church," or at least into some institutionalized form. And this in turn raises the question of why and how such an institutional form relates to a spirituality of following Jesus. In short, why does the mission spirituality of following Jesus draw a person toward an ecclesial spirituality?

Peter's sermon sums up years of theological reflection on what happened in the Jesus event. In an imaginative leap one can place oneself in the period of a group of followers of Jesus, still reeling from his death, then becoming convinced that he was alive and glorified, and now trying to figure how all this fits together. From his own vantage point Luke offers a view of the interpretation that gradually developed over time. Jesus' followers used the Jewish scriptures to inform them on what was going on. The Spirit assumes a new importance as God's agency: God witnesses to Jesus in his ministry by acts in the power of the Spirit. A firm belief grew up that everything that happened was planned and orchestrated by God and in fact foretold: David spoke in the Psalms about the resurrection of the Messiah. Jesus, now at God's right hand, was God's delegate to send the same Spirit that was at work in him to his followers. Everything fits: "this Jesus whom you crucified is the Messiah."

In considering how the community's reflection developed one might notice how the message of the disciples compares with the message of Jesus. Jesus preached the rule of God, and he remained so decisively theocentric that it is hard to think of him preaching himself. This has changed. The new disciples speak from the other side of Jesus' execution and the experience of his glorification. The message in this situation almost automatically becomes the rule of God as presented in Jesus' ministry and ratified by God's ratification of him. This is still a theocentric message in the sense that God, creator of heaven and earth, remains Yahweh. But in this message to their fellow Jews Jesus is Messiah. God has authorized him on high, making his ministry God's revelation of what God's rule looks like. The Easter experience has folded the person of Jesus into the formulation of Jesus' own message of the kingdom of God.

From the perspective of the followers of Jesus who have had an Easter experience and encountered anew the Spirit of God in their group, this story points the way forward. It shows a movement that was open to people. The experience of Jesus risen and the impulse for mission were religious experiences, but they were not private esoteric experiences. They would generate a public movement and not a cult. The Jesus story had to be placed in full view, made known, and broadcast. The public story of Jesus mediating the rule of God had to be shared with others, so that each one could participate in it alongside others in community. In other words, the public character of Jesus' message necessarily generates a public movement. The disciples did not pass it along in secret. Such a public move necessarily and by definition tends to invite involvement and to generate a community. Jesus preached his message to crowds, and now the gradual formation of a Jesus movement will keep that message in the public sphere. This is a message for all that should be heard and considered by all. As in the Easter experience itself, it is far from clear where and how all this took shape in a concrete historical sense. But just as Luke portrays it imaginatively, so too his story encourages people to imagine how this actually happened.

In the case of Jesus' preaching and ministry, the community he addressed was already in place in Galilee and finally in Jerusalem.

He preached the public message of the rule of God within Judaism in order to stimulate reform according to God's word and values. In the same way, the mission of the disciples of Jesus under the power of the newly-poured-out Spirit of God was addressed to Israel. Luke was faithful to history in this respect; even though he knew the church would be opened up to Gentiles, he restricted the ken of the first post-Easter disciples to Judaism. He was content to represent a certain universalism with the Jews and Jewish proselytes from many nations.

Although one cannot easily conceive how this could be an actual early sermon of the post-Easter troop of followers, it allows one to see how the movement will develop its kerygma. The adaptation of the passages from Joel and the Psalms, and more generally the interpretive discovery of Jesus' story in the Jewish scriptures, shows a pattern of Christian theology that remains. The methods used by these first followers of Jesus to interpret the scriptures are not the same as those of twenty-first-century exegesis and critical interpretation theory. But the pattern of interpretation bears a close analogy. These disciples knew that Jesus was risen, for all of them were the "witnesses," and they also knew that the scriptures contained the revelation of God. Scriptural revelation had to bear some correlation with the new world that had been opened up to them. That pattern of finding the connections of mutual ratification between the sources of God's communication and the present situation reflects the logic of Christian theology and in some respects that of all religious traditions.

This sermon of Peter, within the context offered by Luke, invites reflective participation in the Jesus movement getting under way. Initiating the Jesus movement required a seriously new appreciation of Judaism on the part of his audience and set a high standard for the movement to go forward. The sermon called its hearers to a deeper challenge than the one Jesus had held out to his audience, because it is unlikely that he put himself forward as Messiah in such an explicit way. It also asked people to join a distinct movement within Judaism, precisely a Jesus movement, that would not be a secret or private group but an open and participatory one. It asked for conversion. Ironically, after centuries of Christendom, being a Christian in the West today more and more resembles the minority position of the Jesus movement in the earliest time.

The symbolism of Pentecost has Jesus sending the Spirit to animate the disciples to take up his own ministry, and Peter turning immediately to the crowd and addressing them with the messiahship of Jesus as a model for a new way of life. This dynamism carries a message that has been neglected wherever Christianity has become so established as a religion that it loses its sense of mission. This insight finds sharp expression in the aphorism that states the priority of "mission" to "church": the mission of the rule of God generates a church, rather than the established church has a mission. This insight emerges from the story of the gradual formation of the church out of the recognition tied to resurrection faith that God through Jesus had launched a movement in history. It includes the idea that being a disciple of Jesus entails more than benefiting personally from his revealing God; it contains an appeal to take up his cause in history. The message of the rule and values of God in history as Jesus represented them forms an object that is relevant to all human beings, because it is about the flourishing and ultimate salvation of human existence itself. The formation of a movement requiring some structure that later became a distinctive group is not an end in itself, but precisely the necessary historical means by which the mission could continue. Jesus did not found a church, but his ministry became a mission that did. This gives Christian spirituality a distinctive activist character that does not exclude other characteristics but embraces them all. This view turns the commonsense perception of the church having a mission on its head: the mission forms a church, and membership invites participation.

39. The Jesus Movement

³⁷Now when they heard this, they were cut to the heart and said to Peter and to the other apostles, "Brothers, what should we do?" ³⁸Peter said to them, "Repent, and be baptized every one of you in the name of Jesus Christ so that your sins may be forgiven; and you will receive the gift of the Holy Spirit. ³⁹For the promise is for you, for your children, and for all who are far away, everyone whom the Lord our God calls to him." ⁴⁰And he testified with many other arguments and exhorted them, saying, "Save yourselves from this corrupt generation." ⁴¹So those who welcomed his message were baptized, and that day about three thousand persons were added. ⁴²They devoted themselves to the apostles' teaching and fellowship, to the breaking of bread and the prayers. ⁴³Awe came upon everyone, because many wonders and signs were being done by the apostles. ⁴⁴All who believed were together and had all things in common; ⁴⁵they would sell their possessions and goods and distribute the proceeds to all, as any had need. ⁴⁶Day by day, as they spent much time together in the temple, they broke bread at home and ate their food with glad and generous hearts, ⁴⁷praising God and having the goodwill of all the people. And day by day the Lord added to their number those who were being saved.

—Acts 2:37-47

This scene occurs right after the sermon of Peter that illustrated the passing of the idea of mission into action, the beginnings of Christian theology, and how mission is prior to church. This passage describes the formation of the Jesus movement as a result of the disciples' preaching and sketches a picture of the earliest Christian communities. It is an idealistic account, and exegetes question its historical accuracy: it reflects as much Luke's church as the early Jesus movement. But this should stimulate rather than dampen the imagination because, even though the organizational features of a church developed gradually, something got started somewhere and, like Luke, one can imagine beginnings on the basis of their outcome. This contemplation invites a person into this developing history that is blurred but dynamic.

Peter preached to a receptive audience. It would not be so later on in Jerusalem, if Luke's narrative is at all correct. Here they ask "What shall we then do?" And Peter responds: "Repent, and be baptized every one of you in the name of Jesus Christ so that your sins may be forgiven; and you will receive the gift of the Holy Spirit" (Acts 2:38). This describes Christian faith in a formula that includes the rite of initiation. Then Luke typifies a community of the followers of Jesus as it had just been formed: "They devoted themselves to the apostles' teaching and fellowship, to the breaking of bread and the prayers" (Acts 2:42). The leaders of the disciples continued to preach and even perform signs and wonders, and the community developed a kind of common life together in which they shared all their possessions. This seems too settled and serene for a movement that is just getting under way. But because these institutional features in fact fell into place over the course of the next two generations, represent a certain continuity with the historical ministry of Jesus, and remain essential structures to the present time, they help define Christian ecclesial spirituality.

What are we to do? Be baptized. Baptism has been the rite of initiation into the Jesus movement from beginnings that stretch back into Jesus' own ministry. Does "in the name of Jesus the Messiah" differentiate this baptism from followers of John the Baptist, or does it reflect the spontaneous post-resurrection reaction that the rule of God that Jesus preached has been ratified by God? In both cases the language reflects a fundamental understanding of baptism. It requires repentance, for this is adult baptism that seals a change of heart, and it promises God's fidelity. This baptism testifies to God's forgiveness of sin, not the later idea of an "original sin," but moral failures that mark every human life. A person baptized into this sphere of God's acceptance finds forgiveness always at hand. This baptism also empowers people to live a renewed life by communicating God's Spirit. The theology of baptism has developed over the millennia, but Jesus' first followers and those today live within the same context of transcendent acceptance.

Luke moves rapidly from a scene in which the first Israelites accept Jesus and are baptized to a community enjoying fellowship and even a common life together in Jesus' name. Even though he has telescoped events and presents a very orderly community too rapidly, in fact communities with some organization did develop in some places at some time. The pristine form Luke gives it can be considered an expression of early ideals to be striven for. He describes a kind of common life of mutual support, which some think reflects a sense of expectation of an imminent parousia or a radical intervention of God to reestablish Israel in the mode of the rule of God. But the idea of fellowship and community around the person, message, and mission of Jesus practically speaking defines Christianity.

In a community whose bond is the person of Jesus, it is not surprising that his followers recalled and considered his teachings. Those who were charged to recall and transmit them are referred to as apostles by Luke, that is, those sent on mission. But the title "apostle" has a complicated usage that can be misleading, unlike the more inclusive term "disciples." The word "apostle" shows that the Jesus movement carefully attended to preserving the teachings of Jesus and communicating them to those who joined the movement and were baptized in his name. The teaching of the apostles also represents the message of Jesus that was taught publicly. Peter's sermon consists in the interpretation of Jesus as the Messiah, but the teachings of Jesus the Messiah on the rule of God make up the object and substance of the movement.

The phrase "the breaking of bread" is a Lukan term for a meal in the tradition of the meals of Jesus with his disciples. All four gospels epitomize these meals in the Last Supper, and Paul refers to the Last Supper as well (1 Cor 11:23-26). By the time of Paul's writing, it had become an important feature of the Jesus movement that was then gradually evolving toward becoming a church in which it became a fixed and central structure of assembly. How did this practice gradually assume the place it later occupied? What functions did it play in the period between Jesus' death and resurrection and the 50s? This phrase in Luke, when it is appropriated in a later period, releases the imagination to construct various ways in which the meal of disciples might have enabled the movement to begin to take on a substantial form.

In the light of Jesus' death and resurrection the meal came to be interpreted as a Passover meal celebrating a new passage of liberation from sin and death to renewed life. It incorporated prayers of blessing

God and giving thanks. A Eucharistic meal is one of thanksgiving. The meal gathered the new disciples and helped give the movement an explicit continuity with Jesus. It may have fostered the beginnings of organization with persons providing space and hosting the meal.

The meal also fit the prevalent custom of the Roman banquet, which was a structured way of gathering a group for sharing a meal and doing together what the particular group and occasion called for. Here an assembly would involve remembering, celebrating, giving thanks, reading scripture, commenting on it, discussing, praying: in short, being a movement of disciples assembled in community. The common meal promoted unity and mutual care. The poor members of the community could be fed. The meal came to play these many functions in slightly different ways in different places. How these functions actually developed is not clear, but Luke's phrase promotes an Ignatian use of the imagination.

Luke says that the earliest movement spent much time together in the temple and that they devoted themselves to prayer. The first of the two observations seals the continuity of this movement with Judaism. One cannot think of the disciples beginning a separatist movement within Israel or of being over against Judaism in any respect during this earliest developmental period. The deepest ancestry and roots of this movement are completely Jewish. At the same time, the suggestion of their being devoted to prayer suggests a common gathering for prayer and a gradual formation of an identity of this subgroup as the movement of Jesus' disciples.

These activities took on slightly different embryonic forms in distinct or culturally different small groups of new followers of Jesus being attracted by the witness of the disciples. In some such fashion a movement among the constituents of the synagogues and temple began to take shape. At the same time the ministry of the disciples and leaders of the group continued to preach and bear witness to God's rule in Jesus' name. The scene suggests that the signs and wonders that were evident in Jesus' ministry continued in the ministry of the disciples. The Spirit was the empowering agent for this and helped provide a deep continuity of presence to the whole movement.

This scenario that posits a Jesus movement between Jesus and the church speaks directly to an active spirituality. Christian spirituality is essentially ecclesial, the spirituality or spiritualities of a community. But there is no evidence, only counterevidence, that Jesus set up or intended a community distinct from Judaism as the result of his ministry. Development creates the bridge between the community of disciples in Jesus' time and thereafter. This is a bridge of human freedom responding by faith and action to the obstacles and opportunities it encountered. The formation of a church in history cannot mean creating a finished product, but only another stage in a continuing historical project. The church will always be a movement based on and inspired by Jesus. To be a Christian then is to participate in this Jesus movement in history and to be a part of the various elements that hold the church together existentially.

40. Mission to All

¹Then certain individuals came down from Judea and were teaching the brothers, "Unless you are circumcised according to the custom of Moses, you cannot be saved." ²And after Paul and Barnabas had no small dissension and debate with them, Paul and Barnabas and some of the others were appointed to go up to Jerusalem to discuss this question with the apostles and the elders. ³So they were sent on their way by the church, and as they passed through both Phoenicia and Samaria, they reported the conversion of the Gentiles, and brought great joy to all the believers. ⁴When they came to Jerusalem, they were welcomed by the church and the apostles and the elders, and they reported all that God had done with them. ⁵But some believers who belonged to the sect of the Pharisees stood up and said, "It is necessary for them to be circumcised and ordered to keep the law of Moses."

⁶The apostles and the elders met together to consider this matter. ⁷After there had been much debate, Peter stood up and said to them, "My brothers, you know that in the early days God made a choice among you, that I should be the one through whom the Gentiles would hear the message of the good news and become believers. ⁸And God, who knows the human heart, testified to them by giving them the Holy Spirit, just as he did to us; ⁹and in cleansing their hearts by faith he has made no distinction between them and us. ¹⁰Now therefore why are you putting God to the test by placing on the neck of the disciples a yoke that neither our ancestors nor we have been able to bear? ¹¹On the contrary, we believe that we will be saved through the grace of the Lord Jesus, just as they will."

¹²The whole assembly kept silence, and listened to Barnabas and Paul as they told of all the signs and wonders that God had done through them among the Gentiles. ¹³After they finished speaking, James replied, "My brothers, listen to me. ¹⁴Simeon has related how God first looked favorably on the Gentiles, to take from among them a people for his name. ¹⁵This agrees with the words of the prophets, as it is written, ¹⁶'After this I will return, and I will rebuild the dwelling of

David, which has fallen; from its ruins I will rebuild it, and I will set it up, [17]so that all other peoples may seek the Lord—even all the Gentiles over whom my name has been called. Thus says the Lord, who has been making these things [18]known from long ago.' [19]Therefore I have reached the decision that we should not trouble those Gentiles who are turning to God, [20]but we should write to them to abstain only from things polluted by idols and from fornication and from whatever has been strangled and from blood. [21]For in every city, for generations past, Moses has had those who proclaim him, for he has been read aloud every Sabbath in the synagogues."

[22]Then the apostles and the elders, with the consent of the whole church, decided to choose men from among their members and to send them to Antioch with Paul and Barnabas. They sent Judas called Barsabbas, and Silas, leaders among the brothers, [23]with the following letter: "The brothers, both the apostles and the elders, to the believers of Gentile origin in Antioch and Syria and Cilicia, greetings. [24]Since we have heard that certain persons who have gone out from us, though with no instructions from us, have said things to disturb you and have unsettled your minds, [25]we have decided unanimously to choose representatives and send them to you, along with our beloved Barnabas and Paul, [26]who have risked their lives for the sake of our Lord Jesus Christ. [27]We have therefore sent Judas and Silas, who themselves will tell you the same things by word of mouth. [28]For it has seemed good to the Holy Spirit and to us to impose on you no further burden than these essentials: [29]that you abstain from what has been sacrificed to idols and from blood and from what is strangled and from fornication. If you keep yourselves from these, you will do well. Farewell."

[30]So they were sent off and went down to Antioch. When they gathered the congregation together, they delivered the letter. [31]When its members read it, they rejoiced at the exhortation. [32]Judas and Silas, who were themselves prophets, said much to encourage and strengthen the believers. [33]After they had been there for some time, they were sent off in peace by the believers to those who had sent them. [35]But Paul and Barnabas remained in Antioch, and there, with many others, they taught and proclaimed the word of the Lord.

—Acts 15:1-35

Luke tells the story of how, around the year 49, the leaders of the Jesus movement confirmed the mission to the Gentiles. This narrative refers to historical events that Paul, who participated in them, mentions in his Letter to the Galatians. This decision proved to be a major turning point in the history of the Christian mission and church. It sanctioned the spread of the message of Jesus beyond the borders of

Judaism. As a result, the decision became an important factor in the process by which the Jesus movement began to distinguish itself from Judaism and become a distinctively Christian church. The question is how this development affects Christian spirituality.

The story is focused in Antioch, a major city in the Mediterranean basin, the largest after Rome, and the center of activity in the eastern part of the Roman Empire. The Jesus movement had taken hold there early, and its status provides fertile ground for an active imagination. The situation reflects a tension within an essentially Jewish community. There would have been no problem if the Jesus movement were not securely under the umbrella of the synagogue. The tensions must have been diverse and sensitive. This particular conflict arose around Gentiles who were attracted to the Jesus movement within Judaism: did they have to become Jews in order to be Christians, as followers of Jesus were beginning to be called, or could one be accepted into the people of God through Jesus without becoming Jewish? Should the Jesus movement retain adherence to Jewish law, or could Gentiles become Christians without subscribing to it? If they could, how should Jews relate to them? Could they share the same table and foods? The rite of circumcision was a major factor in an issue that transcended Antioch. Representatives were sent to Jerusalem, the problem was debated there, and a ruling came back to Antioch. Although some provisions of Jewish law were to be maintained, as a concession that might enable table fellowship, the way was opened for Gentiles to become Christian without becoming circumcised Jews. Luke's telling of the story aligns with Paul's but is more expansive. It should be noted that the rules were not aimed at division but at holding the factions together in one community.

This decision on the part of the leadership of the Christian movement at that time had enormous historical significance. The ruling in a sense created a fork in the road that opened another path to the Jesus movement. The communities that developed in a more Hellenistic environment, without negating their Jewish roots, would begin to distance themselves from the synagogue. The reflection that follows dwells less on the historical outcome of this decision and more on the spiritual dimensions of the events themselves. What do they say about a relationship to God or self-understanding before God? What is the significance of this story for Christian spirituality?

The history of the relationship between Christianity and Judaism provides a reason to be careful about how one interprets the spiritual significance of this decision. It became part of a long and complex historical development that finally ended in Christianity becoming a religion distinct and separate from Judaism. And this separation supported hostile relations with Jews throughout the centuries. But this shadow side of history is not intrinsic to the decision taken relative to the community at Antioch and the beginnings of the church. Judaism then supported many different subtraditions and factions, and no essential reason prohibited the Jesus movement from continuing its corporate life within the boundaries of Judaism. In many respects Christianity can be understood as a form of Judaism mediated by Jesus for Gentiles. The spiritual value of this event then can be distinguished from its historical aftermath in the break between Judaism and Christianity and apart from any assessment of the merits of that separation.

The narrative of this incident in the still preliterary phase of the Christian movement bears so many facets that focusing on particular aspects of it seems to diminish it. But precisely as a spiritual exercise, one has to ask how it has a bearing on the life of an individual person engaging the Jesus movement that at this point is clearly headed toward becoming a distinctive and autonomous church. Three points in the story have bearing on spiritual life: one lies in the universal relevance of Jesus, another focuses on how this universality sets up a wide horizon for the life of each Christian, and a third lives in the impulse toward reconciliation that occupies an essential place in the Jesus movement.

This story dramatizes a gradual corporate coming to an awareness of the universal significance of Jesus of Nazareth. The Christian story as it has been told up to the point of the Pentecost experience and the formation of a Jesus movement transpired within Judaism. This story looks beyond Jewish boundaries. The Lukan narrative sets this up with an earlier story about the Roman centurion, Cornelius, who seeks entry into the Jesus movement with his family (Acts 10:1-11:18). Peter resolved this crisis by recognizing that the Spirit of God stimulated the desire of the Roman to become a follower of Jesus. The earlier story serves as a premise to which Peter explicitly appeals. The case of Cornelius shows that God gives the Holy Spirit to Gentiles "just as he did to us" and that God "has made no distinction between them and us." That experience of Peter served as the premise for a resolution of this controversy. The bestowal of the Spirit on non-Jews and their seeking baptism in Jesus' name also point outward toward all people and Jesus' relevance for them. Part of the whole Antioch affair, then, consists in an official recognition that Jesus communicates to all. This entails a significant deepening of Jewish-Christian consciousness. Local boundaries expand and reach out to encompass the world.

A second mark of Christian spirituality that this story promotes can be called its universal horizon. A universal or comprehensive horizon need not become totalizing. "Totalizing" suggests an exclusive point of view that eliminates all others or absorbs them into itself without remainder. An appeal to the metaphor of a horizon of consciousness helps to distinguish the expanded universal horizon of the Christian from a totalizing or imperial imagination: it recognizes the limitations of its standpoint.

A horizon consists in the broad sweep of the terrain that lies under the line separating it from the sky; it lies before each person's gaze and measures the range of perception. But each and every horizon is always entertained from a particular place and point of view, from a person's distinctive perspective. Christianity is not in fact everyone's point of view. But the universal relevance of Jesus can be described as giving each Christian a point of view on the whole of the world. Moreover, because Jesus is a human being, he represents a human point of view that can be appreciated by any human being that approaches him. Assuming the point of view of Jesus allows his horizon to make its way into a person's spirituality. It sets out the expansive rule of God as a context for all human life. Like a horizon, the set of God's values that Jesus represents gives a person perspective on the people, places, and events that he or she encounters along the way. It provides the relative proportions of things, the size of their worth in relation to each other, the distance or nearness of their importance, a context to appreciate the strength or weakness of their attraction, and the fullness or relative emptiness of their being. Everyone lives within some horizon; Jesus' representation of God's rule provides one that is comprehensive.

The universality of Jesus and the horizon on life that he provides render him transcultural. In literary terms, Jesus is a classic figure who can be appropriated not apart from culture but within different cultures. Precisely because of his universal appeal, he may in the same measure be appropriated as a reconciling figure. Jesus, as revealer of God, creator and lover of heaven and earth and all things, is universally relevant. But this means that participating in his movement requires an open reconciling spirit. At this point the universality of Jesus' relevance interrupts and cuts across the grain of cultural or religious imperialism. Jesus' appeal to all helps to negate the value of boundaries that divide. Jesus promotes the contiguity of boundaries as the place where differences meet. There, at the borders, where different peoples and cultures and religions encounter one another, Jesus provides a language for mutual exchange. The Jesus movement only truly represents the universally relevant Jesus when it presents him not as imposing God but as revealing God, not as dominating power but as an agent whose Spirit will release empowered freedom, not as one who communicates all truth in an objective container but as an invitation from transcendence to seek the truth in a dialogical quest. Jesus becomes universal when he is recognized as preserving and reconciling differences by promoting a higher form of community that transcends merely local interests. In short, the significance of a mission to all consists in breaking open boundaries that divide.

41. Jesus as Revelation of God

[22]Then Paul stood in front of the Areopagus and said, "Athenians, I see how extremely religious you are in every way. [23]For as I went through the city and looked carefully at the objects of your worship, I found among them an altar with the inscription, 'To an unknown god.' What therefore you worship as unknown, this I proclaim to you. [24]The God who made the world and everything in it, he who is Lord of heaven and earth, does not live in shrines made by human hands, [25]nor is he served by human hands, as though he needed anything, since he himself gives to all mortals life and breath and all things. [26]From one ancestor he made all nations to inhabit the whole earth, and he allotted the times of their existence and the boundaries of the places where they would live, [27]so that they would search for God and perhaps grope for him and find him—though indeed he is not far from each one of us. [28]For 'In him we live and move and have our being'; as even some of your own poets have said, 'For we too are his offspring.' [29]Since we are God's offspring, we ought not to think that the deity is like gold, or silver, or stone, an image formed by the art and imagination of mortals. [30]While God has overlooked the times of human ignorance, now he commands all people everywhere to repent, [31]because he has fixed a day on which he will have the world judged in righteousness by a man whom he has appointed, and of this he has given assurance to all by raising him from the dead."

—Acts 17:22-31

The Spiritual Exercises end with the next consideration, Ignatius's Contemplation to Attain Love, which could be described as a mystical consideration grounded in creation faith. By contrast, this contemplation, more a meditation, turns attention to Luke's account of Paul summarizing the Christian story for the Athenians. This meditation provides a way for each one making the Exercises to summarize his or her cumulative experience.

A couple of notations will explain how the idea of "story" is used in the development of this reflection. Some stories tell of everyday observable events. Other stories, like national or religious myths, are larger and refer less to concrete happenings and more to an imagined and projected world of values. These "sacred" stories provide the horizon for and give coherence, meaning, and direction to the mundane stories. Human beings create the first kind of stories by their concrete actions, while the second come from established traditions that are internalized. Once appropriated, traditional stories play a creative role in the lives of those shaped by them.[2] The reflection that follows raises up for consideration the several stories that run together and become intertwined during the course of the Spiritual Exercises. Spirituality can be understood as a fusion of narratives, and reflecting on how various stories interconnect provides a way to move toward closure of this particular presentation of the Spiritual Exercises.

Luke's this-worldly story or history begins in Nazareth, passes through Jerusalem, and ends in Rome. He begins with the birth of John the Baptist and Jesus and, with a special accent on the role of the Spirit of God, tells of Jesus' public ministry, his journey to Jerusalem where he suffers, dies, is buried, and then is raised to new being in God's own creative life. Then, after Jesus is said to have sent the Spirit, his disciples take up his mission and extend it into the Gentile world even to Rome, symbolically representing through empire the ends of the earth. But Luke's larger theological story encompasses these events on a transcendent level. Luke presents this theological story in the speech or sermon attributed to Paul at Athens.

Luke's story of Paul's sermon in the Areopagus in Athens is another example of a dramatic event that contains a large message. Athens represents the intellectual center of the empire and the capitol of Reason. Luke tells of Paul first preaching here and there in the city before being invited to give a fuller account of his message in a public forum. The speech or sermon composed by Luke lays out the different thought worlds of Greek philosophers and Jewish faith in a God accompanying history. He ostensibly tries to enter into their world with an appeal to a shrine to an unknown god. He then goes on to present a concise version of the transcendent theological story of God revealed in Jesus that ends with resurrection and final judgment of all.

Luke's theological story, addressed to seekers, fits this stage in the Exercises. It recapitulates the Christian story. You Athenians, Paul says, are deeply spiritual but you are still searching. The transcendent story of God and human existence that I present to you responds to the very questions that you and everyone must ask. This narrative tells

---

2. This distinction is drawn from Stephen Crites, "The Narrative Quality of Experience," *Journal of the American Academy of Religions* 39 (1971), 294-97.

of one God, transcendent creator of heaven and earth, whom no finite image can represent, certainly not figures of metal or stone. Yet this God is not distant, because all persons live and move and have their very being within the embrace of this creator God. This God has been announced by Jesus Christ, and God has actually attested to his message by drawing his life, in the face of death, into God's own creative being. This man will be the measure of human righteousness when a final reckoning is accomplished. In this light you should turn your lives around, accept forgiveness and your own acceptance by God, and live in hope, for this same resurrection is yours. This is not the only possible short narrative of Christian faith; Luke himself composed others. It does not substitute for the concrete story of Jesus, but is extrapolated from it to form a remarkably incisive précis.

What may be called a fusion of narratives occurs when one enters into a tradition, a large story or a particularly charged mundane story, to discover and identify with its logic, its beginning, middle, and end. The Spiritual Exercises are the result of Ignatius deliberately entering into the Christian story. In his autobiography he describes for the instruction of others how this occurred. Ignatius, who at thirty had given his entire life to service of the Spanish crown, had a spiritual crisis. In the course of it he internalized the stories of the saints and especially the gospel narrative of Jesus, and in the end he shifted his allegiance and gave his life completely to a higher cause. He placed his life at the disposition of God. The simplicity of this decision is directly proportional to its depth. Ignatius fused his own story with the story of Jesus Christ. At first the dedication of his freedom to this new ideal terrified him; in the end he found it utterly liberating.

Besides an appropriation of a classic story, the fusion of narratives has a second dimension. That dimension consists of re-expressing the narrative in a distinctive way that fits the context of a person's own situation. Stories generally and the story of Jesus in particular cannot be repeated in the same way in linear time, in different periods, places, cultures and contexts. So Ignatius had to do the best he could to create the trajectory of Jesus in his own time and in relation to his own abilities. The story of Jesus inspired his imagination with new vistas that had to be converted into practical possibilities in the world of everyday affairs. One finds these in Ignatius's biography; the Spiritual Exercises represent the dynamics of this transition and a how-to for people to do it themselves in the contexts and communities in which they live.

The Spiritual Exercises can be understood as three stories being fused together in a seminal process that should extend far beyond the intense period of entering into them. They are the story of Jesus with both its mundane and transcendent meanings, the story of Ignatius, who has written his own experience into the way the story of Jesus is presented, and the story of the person who engages in this course of meditations and contemplations. The whole extended series of considerations involves a constant comparing of experiences, insights, and value judgments, and a resolve that blends stories and distinguishes them, appropriates them, and creates new expressions of shared ideas and values.

Bringing the Spiritual Exercises to a successful conclusion might recapitulate the two sides of a fusion of narratives. One side involves assessing the measure in which one has been able to enter into the story of Jesus of Nazareth. The Jesus story contains the foundations of the Christian story. This means allowing it to be what it is and giving it a voice to address one from outside the self. Appropriation has to allow a story to speak for itself. Truly engaging the story of Jesus must allow God to interrupt things as usual. Recapitulation, then, considers how a person has appreciated Jesus of Nazareth and has been drawn into the world that he proposes.

The other side should include prospectively taking stock of the degree to which an internalization of the story of Jesus will impact one's own life. Will the Jesus story result in some distinctive expression in the way a person lives? Such a consideration offers a whole range of degrees of specificity. Recapitulation signifies drawing together decisions made earlier in the Exercises and envisioning how commitments will play out and where they will lead.

This representation of the story of Jesus in the Exercises might fittingly conclude with a word about the end of the story. The difference between a narrative that goes on and on and one that comes to a conclusion is vast: the one makes no more sense than the telling; the other has defined meaning. The story of Jesus comes to an end and it bears salvific meaning: it rescues human freedom, in its personal agent and in the products of freedom's creativity, from oblivion. The God of Jesus is a God of life, and a promise of eternal life is no more implausible than life itself, especially human life. Resurrection makes Jesus' story memorable and salvific. Its significance lies exactly in the continuity between his self-transcending giving and the preservation of its good effects in the eternity of God. But resurrection remains promise and the object of basic trust or hope, and one has to exhibit the courage that such a hope instills in order to appreciate it.

42. Contemplation to Attain Love

Note. Two preliminary observations should be made.

First. Love ought to manifest itself more by deeds than by words.

Second. Love consists in a mutual communication between the two persons. That is, the one who loves gives and communicates to the beloved what he or she has, or a part of what one has or can have; and the beloved in return does the same to the lover. Thus, if the one has knowledge, one gives it to the other who does not; and similarly in regard to honors or riches. Each shares with the other.

The usual Preparatory Prayer.

The First Prelude. A composition. Here it is to see myself as standing before God our Lord, and also before the angels and saints, who are interceding for me.

The Second Prelude is to ask for what I desire. Here it will be to ask for interior knowledge of all the great good I have received, in order that, stirred to profound gratitude, I may become able to love and serve the Divine Majesty in all things.

The First Point. I will call back into my memory the gifts I have received—my creation, redemption, and other gifts particular to myself. I will ponder with deep affection how much God our Lord has done for me, and how much he has given me of what he possesses, and consequently how he, the same Lord, desires to give me even his very self, in accordance with this divine design.

Then I will reflect on myself, and consider what I on my part ought in all reason and justice to offer and give to the Divine Majesty, namely, all my possessions, and myself along with them. I will speak as one making an offering with deep affection, and say:

"Take, Lord, and receive all my liberty, my memory, my understanding, and all my will—all that I have and possess. You, Lord, have given all that to me. I now give it back to you, O Lord. All of it is yours. Dispose of it according to your will. Give me your love and your grace, for that is enough for me."

The Second Point. I will consider how God dwells in creatures; in the elements, giving them existence; in the plants, giving them life; in the animals, giving them sensation; in human beings, giving them intelligence; and finally, how in this way he dwells also in myself, giving me existence, life, sensation, and intelligence; and even further, making me his temple, since I am created as a likeness and image of the Divine Majesty. Then once again I will reflect on myself, in the manner described in the first point, or in any other way I feel to be better. This same procedure will be used in each of the following points.

The Third Point. I will consider how God labors and works for me in all the creatures on the face of the earth; that is, he acts in the manner of one who is laboring. For example, he is working in the heavens, elements, plants, fruits, cattle, and all the rest—giving them their existence, conserving them, concurring with their vegetative and sensitive activities, and so forth. Then I will reflect on myself.

The Fourth Point. I will consider how all good things and gifts descend from above; for example, my limited power from the Supreme and Infinite Power above; and so of justice, goodness, piety, mercy, and so forth—just as the rays come down from the sun, or the rains from their source. Then I will finish by reflecting on myself, as has been explained. I will conclude with a colloquy and an Our Father.

—Ignatius Loyola, *Spiritual Exercises*, 230-237

The Contemplation to Attain Love can be described as creation mysticism. It stands on its own, needs little commentary, and with adjustments easily fits into the framework of the new scientific picture of the universe and the planet. It also contains some fundamental ideas that come together in a way that uniquely summarizes Ignatian spirituality. Although Ignatius intended this to be the concluding contemplation, it should not become an end in itself. It opens out to ordinary life in society and overcomes any disjunction between spiritual experience and ordinary secular life. The Contemplation intends to provide a stimulus to a spirituality of everyday life.

The Spiritual Exercises began with the Principle and Foundation that considered the purpose of creation. It proposes a creation spirituality in the sense that, based on a theology of an intentional creator, it envisages human existence as oriented to an end and what follows from that. A reading of the Contemplation, however, shows that considerable distance has been traveled from that beginning to the end of the Exercises. The change has been negotiated through the sustained programmatic contemplation of Jesus as Leader (The Call of the King). On that premise, this reflection summarizes the spirituality of the Exercises by showing how the Contemplation returns to the premise of creation filled with new spiritual insight and motivation gained from the story of Jesus.

The story of Jesus provides a new context for the doctrine of creation as it appeared in the Principle and Foundation. Taking something out of one context and inserting it into a distinctively new setting can strikingly alter its meaning. For example, a dark painting in an old wooden frame in an obscure space becomes transformed by a new frame hung on a plain bright wall. The original picture remains unchanged. Its being perceived and understood in a radically new light does not change its reality but transforms its effects. It communicates in new ways. This provides a clue for understanding how the metaphysical logic of creation becomes recharged by being inserted into the new space of the story of Jesus.

This scenario of the Contemplation subtracts nothing from Ignatius's original view of creation; and, relative to our time, the scientific picture of creation remains what it is. But in it Ignatius operates out of an expanded framework for looking at the purpose of life. A new relationship of interpersonal dialogue between God and each retreatant fills the space. Following the story of Jesus, his being raised into God's life, what he launched in history, and entering into conversation with God about this over some period of time has transformed the situation. In the Principle and Foundation one responds to God because of the fundamental goal or purpose of human existence. After the Jesus story one responds to God out of love motivated by gratitude for God's initiative of love. A new interpersonal dialogical relationship of love with God transforms the teleological, or means/end, relationship. What follows shows how creation theology, reappropriated through the Jesus story, elicits a spirituality for everyday life in the world.

The first principle of creation in the light of the story of Jesus declares that the creator is personal. God, the infinite sustaining ground of being, should not be conceived as *a* distinct limited person, but as personal nonetheless. Because God is personal, the first principle of spirituality takes the form of a response to love and gift. The personalism transforms the mechanisms of creation into a foundation for Christian spirituality: creation elicits gratitude. The Contemplation proposes an interpersonal context for understanding creation. The new existential context does not deny or oppose a metaphysical view but draws cosmic teleology into an interpersonal and dialogical relationship. In our day, the scientific story of creation provides the concrete data that, after the Jesus story, has to be appropriated in a spiritually personalist way.

Ignatius's formulation of the logic of gratitude, one of the keys to the Contemplation, is found in the second prelude in the three things one is seeking: (1) "interior knowledge of all the great good I have received"; so that (2) I will be "stirred to profound gratitude"; so that this in turn will enable me (3) "to love and serve God's Divine Majesty in all things" (SE, 233). The three dimensions of what is sought together form one positive experience of gratitude for God's love that embraces each person in particular, so that all spontaneously respond out of personal gratitude in a mutual love. The whole exercise rides on the personal experience of being accepted and affirmed by God, leading to what Luther called the freedom of the Christian: God's love *pro me* supports freedom and enables a response of gratitude that overflows in love of neighbor. The first of the three components launches the experience. Ignatius underlines it in the first line of the first point: "I will call back into my memory the gifts I have received—my creation, redemption, and other gifts particular to myself" (SE, 234). The gifts are particular to each one. They define the identity of each unique person. This Contemplation is cosmic in its scope, but absolutely particular and personal in its application to me.

Ignatius suggests specific ways in which this gratitude can be awakened in four aspects of God's presence as ground of being. In the first, God is giving or gifting; in the second, God is present to all creation as a personal presence; in the third, God is active as Spirit; and in the fourth, God appears as the source of all the good found in creation. Contemplating these four points constitutes the "mysticism." It become "mystical" not when one applies a doctrine of creation to the external world but when one encounters God while considering the created world. The vivid recognition of the finite and contingent character of the world can actually mediate a resonant impression of the infinite character of God and the dependence of everything on God. The doctrine surely guides the exercise, but contemplation cannot be reduced to a manipulation of concepts as in an objective deductive inference. The doctrine itself depends on the "mystical" experience.

Two observations of Ignatius concerning love are clichés. But when they are taken seriously, the consequences can be radical. The New Testament pragmatism of the first says that real love manifests itself more by deeds than by words, and it pinpoints the spirituality generated by this Contemplation. Union with God in mutual love elicits action beyond affective feeling. Doing provides a reality check that renders mere affective response suspect. Actions carry a sturdier commitment than psychological consciousness: we are what we do.

The second is perhaps less a commonplace but readily apparent: real love between two persons involves mutual sharing of what one has with the other. This is another essential ingredient in the logic of the Contemplation. The gratitude awakened by the consideration of the gifts of God leads one to want to share or contribute one's talents to God's project, to the rule of God.

Two aphorisms of Ignatian spirituality are drawn from the Contemplation. The first says that one should find God in all things. The second says that, in doing so, a person engages in a form of "contemplation in action." These ideas were expressly developed after the composition of the Exercises, but their roots lie in the personalism of creation mysticism. For example, one asks to be enabled "to love and serve God's Divine Majesty in all things" (SE, 233). The Contemplation should not lead to a peak experience that will be followed by the let-down of ordinary life. It provides a path by which one finds God in the world, in ordinary life, "in all things." This goal is more than inci-dental in Ignatius of Loyola; this signature idea led to his being called a "contemplative in action," and he holds that out to all.

What Ignatius is aiming for here might be called a fundamental disposition of the self, or a durable inclusive value response, or a com-prehensive mindset, or a habitual and pervasive outlook that gov-erns one's activity even when it is not formally elicited or explicitly invoked. One can think of various examples of human relationships or commitments to an ideal, a person, or a group that commands such basic loyalty. The depth and inclusiveness of the commitment allows it to govern all of a person's activities and implicitly to function as the critic or norm of individual actions. When a foundational attitude of gratitude to God has been nourished and built up, it will tend spon-taneously to be actualized in a person's everyday activity. This can be explicitly formulated from time to time, as in the prayer that all one's actions may spring from God, be carried forward by the help of God as Spirit, and be brought to an effective conclusion that represents God's values.

To conclude: this searching interpretation of Ignatius's Spiritual Exercises roots spirituality within the story of creation, but places that story within the context of a cosmic personalism mediated by the story of Jesus. This spirituality consists in radical commitment to this world and the people in it, on the conviction that the very actions that carry out that commitment are responses of love to the God of love that is within it all.

Index